Social Policy

Social Policy

A Critical and Intersectional Analysis

FIONA WILLIAMS

polity

First published in 2021 by Polity Press

Polity Press
65 Bridge Street
Cambridge CB2 1UR, UK

Polity Press
101 Station Landing
Suite 300
Medford, MA 02155, USA

ISBN-13: 978-1-5095-4038-9
ISBN-13: 978-1-5095-4039-6 (pb)

A catalogue record for this book is available from the British Library.

Library of Congress Cataloging-in-Publication Data

Names: Williams, Fiona, Professor, author.
Title: Social policy : a critical and intersectional analysis / Fiona
  Williams.
Description: Cambridge, UK ; Medford, MA : Polity Press, 2021. | Includes
  bibliographical references and index. | Summary: "A leading figure in
  the field offers her view on key questions for social policy and its
  future"-- Provided by publisher.
Identifiers: LCCN 2020053296 (print) | LCCN 2020053297 (ebook) | ISBN
  9781509540389 (hardback) | ISBN 9781509540396 (paperback) | ISBN
  9781509540402 (epub)
Subjects: LCSH: Social policy--21st century. | Social
  problems--History--21st century.
Classification: LCC HN18.3 .W538 2021 (print) | LCC HN18.3 (ebook) | DDC
  306.09/05--dc23
LC record available at https://lccn.loc.gov/2020053296
LC ebook record available at https://lccn.loc.gov/2020053297

Typeset in 11.25/13 Dante by
Servis Filmsetting Limited, Stockport, Cheshire
Printed and bound in Great Britain by TJ Books Ltd, Padstow, Cornwall

The publisher has used its best endeavours to ensure that the URLs for external websites referred to in this book are correct and active at the time of going to press. However, the publisher has no responsibility for the websites and can make no guarantee that a site will remain live or that the content is or will remain appropriate.

Every effort has been made to trace all copyright holders, but if any have been overlooked the publisher will be pleased to include any necessary credits in any subsequent reprint or edition.

For further information on Polity, visit our website: politybooks.com

Contents

Acknowledgements

I am extremely indebted to John Clarke, Wendy Hollway and Janet Newman for their invaluable encouragement, discussions and comments on drafts of the book. My thanks go to Ruth Lister for talks and walks over the Yorkshire Dales and, for their interest, ideas and conversations, to Rianne Mahon, Greg Marston, Ann Orloff, Coretta Phillips, Jane Pillinger, Sasha Roseneil, Tom Shakespeare, Paul Stubbs and the late Bob Deacon. I am very grateful to Mike Farren for taming the bibliography. For care, love and support I thank Rowena Beaty, Jean Carabine, Emilyn Claid, Rowan Deacon, Joe Deacon, Brian and Maureen Lawrence, Gillean Paterson, and the Wharfedale Poets. Special thanks go to Yvette Huddleston and Mandy Sutter for Friday night drinks throughout the pandemic in gardens and parkland, come rain or shine, in person or in spirit.

A source of intellectual stimulation was my association as advisor with Ito Peng's international project Gender, Migration and the World of Care and Jenny Phillimore's cross-national Welfare Bricolage project. I thank the Compass zoom discussion groups for rich debate on political strategies and activism.

An earlier version of chapter 3 was published in *The Struggle for Social Sustainability*, edited by Chris Deeming (Policy Press, 2021).

Finally my grateful thanks go to Jonathan Skerrett and Karina Jákupsdóttir at Polity Press for their patience and encouragement.

I dedicate this book to my grandchildren Zephyr, Bodhi, Nova, Delaney and Victor in the hope that the earth they inherit and change will be more flourishing, just and humane.

A Note on Terminology

Terminology changes. This is especially the case where those social categories constituted through social relations of power and inequality are the focus of contestation. An important first principle is to respect the terms that members of social categories prefer to use to describe how they identify while recognizing that these terms will vary. For example, in the UK, disability studies uses the term 'disabled people' whereas many international organizations such as the United Nations refer to 'persons with disabilities'. Another example is the acronym LGBTQI+, which refers to sexual orientation (lesbian, gay and bisexual) as well as gender identity (queer, transgender, and intersex), while '+' allows for differences within, across and outside those categories. A second guideline is to avoid terms that deprive groups of their personhood, such as *the* poor' or '*the* elderly'. It is more humanizing to talk of 'older people' or 'people living in (or with) poverty'. A third consideration is how to employ those general terms – race, disability, gender – which register the political significance of relations of power without homogenizing the experiences of racism, sexism, disability, and so on. This is particularly an issue for race, where, to begin with, it is important to be clear that the concept is a social construct and not based upon any biological or essentialist difference. For that reason it is often placed within quotation marks as 'race'. Accepting its social construction enables analysis of how race is given meaning over time and place. This book is particularly concerned with processes of racialization in social politics – that is to say, how groups come to be defined as racial subjects and the unequal power relations and inequalities that contribute to and flow from these processes. The concept of racialization allows an understanding that racism operates in various ways, constructing difference through culture, religion, ethnicity, nationality, citizenship status or language, as well as intersecting with class, gender, sexuality, disability, etc.

The adjective Black (capitalized) is often used as a political attribute rather than a description (Black Lives Matter). However, in analysis of race, racism and racialization it is important to recognize multiple identities and heritages which are constituted through experience, geographical and cultural heritage, faith and national citizenship (such as African Caribbean, Black British or British Asian). As well as people from the countries of Asia, Africa, the Caribbean, Central and Latin America, the Middle East and Oceania, historically and today in the UK racism is directed at Gypsies and Travellers, Jewish, Turkish and Irish people, and recent migrants from Central and Eastern Europe.

Recently the use of the term BAME (Black, Asian and Minority Ethnic), or BME (Black and Minority Ethnic), has become standard by public bodies and services and in statistical data. It has replaced 'ethnic minorities' as an administrative category. Its advantage is that it recognizes a degree of multiplicity, and, in the use of the phrase 'minority ethnic' (rather than 'ethnic minority'), it acknowledges that all people, not just minorities, have an ethnicity. The downside is that, in becoming an administrative category, it tends to a static and homogenizing implication devoid of political meaning. Avoiding this means using the term in a context which refers to its multiplicity and political meaning. The term 'people of colour', which derives from the US, is preferred by some to acknowledge their social and political collectivity. In this book, I have used different terms in different contexts and, when referencing studies or statistics, I have followed the terms used in the source material. I have employed the adjective 'white' except in those places where the source material has referred to 'White' as a group. Notes on equality and diversity in use of language can be found on the British Sociological Association website: www.britsoc.co.uk/Equality-Diversity/.

1

Introduction

Welfare states face profound challenges. Widening economic and social inequalities and insecurities have been intensified by the post-financial crisis austerity politics, sharpened by the rise in ethno-nationalism, and cruelly exposed by the Covid-19 pandemic. At the same time, recent decades have seen a resurgence of social justice activism at the local and transnational levels. Major global movements such as Occupy, Extinction Rebellion, Black Lives Matter, #MeToo and Global Women's Strike have been as compelling in their necessity as in their massive mobilizations. Yet the transformative power of feminist, anti-racist and post-/decolonial, and ecological thinking is still relatively marginal to core social policy theory, while other critical approaches – around disability, sexuality, migration, childhood and old age – have found recognition only selectively.

This book offers an analysis that attempts to bring many of these issues together. Combining critical and intersectional approaches with ideas to have emerged out of contemporary struggles for social justice, it examines key issues and themes in social policy today. These range from questions of agency; the constitution of welfare subjects through austerity; the social, ethical and contested relations of welfare; global crises; and the transnational social and political economy of care. The approach informs and connects critical and intersectional analyses of multiple social inequalities and social justice with questions of political practice: not only how to 'do' social politics but also how our lives together might be better lived.

The analysis has three integral elements. First, I argue that we need to contextualize the development of neoliberal and austerity welfare not only in terms of the crisis of financialized capitalism but also in terms of the interconnected global crises of care and social reproduction, the environment and climate change, and the external and internal racializing of national borders. Together these threaten human and planetary sustainability while also generating multiple and intersecting inequalities. The second element translates this global context into national social policy through an analysis of the dynamics of intersecting social relations of power; these are articulated through the meanings, materialities and policies attached to family, nation, work and nature. Third, I explore how the contestations for social justice that these crises provoke provide new political ethics and prefigurative politics, especially in the understanding of new formations of interdependence, relationality and democracy, solidarity, and humanity. These provide a guide to consider the transformative possibilities for a future eco-welfare commons.

There is for me a sense of déjà vu about the marginality of radical and transformative thinking in mainstream social policy. In 1987 I published an article entitled 'Racism and the discipline of social policy: a critique of welfare theory' (Williams 1987). This outlined a new analysis of how imperialism, colonialism and nationhood had framed early social policy and the post-war welfare state; how this analysis should be informed by the struggles of racialized groups; and how these were intersected by class and gender relations. *Social Policy: A Critical Introduction: Issues of 'Race', Gender and Class*, followed, in which I argued that these three social relations needed to be interconnected and central to an analysis of social policy. I offered an analytical framework of family, nation and work through which these social relations were articulated (Williams 1989). I was one of many scholars in the UK at the time pursuing such analyses shaped, as we were, by the strength and limitations of Marxism reflected in the new social movements of the time, especially around feminism, black feminism, anti-racism, and gay and lesbian liberation (Weeks 1977; Wilson 1977; Hall et al. 1978; Lewis and Parmar 1983; Amos et al. 1984; Bhavnani and Coulson 1986; Phoenix 1987; Anthias and Yuval-Davis 1992; Brah 1996).

Fast forward thirty years. In July 2019 the UK's Social Policy Association published a commissioned report: *The Missing Dimension: Where Is 'Race' in Social Policy Teaching and Learning?* (Craig et al. 2019; see also Cole et al. 2020). The report examined curricula of social policy courses, journal and conference content over the previous five years, and BAME (black, Asian and minority ethnic) representation among students and staff. In terms of the curriculum and literature, the report found the lack of focus on race and racism to be 'dismal'. In terms of staff and student representation, this was overwhelmingly white. BAME students did not find the curriculum relevant to their concerns. This repeated the point made earlier by Craig: 'It is still not uncommon for mainstream social policy texts to treat debates on "race" and racism as marginal' (Craig 2007: 610). This is in spite of the fact that, as I argue in this book, since that time policies around the racialization of national borders, bordering practices within the UK, and a 'hostile environment' have all had detrimental outcomes on the citizenship rights and social and economic inequalities of minority ethnic and migrant groups. These have had specific gendered effects but have also provided a policy template for the abjection of other welfare subjects (Tyler 2013; Mayblin et al. 2019; Humphris 2019). Alongside this, there has been a rise across many regions of nationalist, anti-immigration movements and parties in which welfare chauvinism – blaming immigration for declining social provision – has been a central theme. Social policy as a discipline is not alone in its neglect. A Royal Historical Society report (Atkinson et al. 2018) arrived at similar conclusions. British criminology has also been held to account (Phillips et al. 2020), as has sociology (Hesse 2014). It is in these contexts that academics and students in the social and political sciences and humanities have recently put forward demands to 'Decolonise the Curriculum' (Bhambra et al. 2018; Rhodes Must Fall 2018).

While this marginalization is specific to both race and racism, where it is most marked, there are corresponding trends with other critiques. Far-reaching as they were, the earlier feminist analyses lost their 'bite' in mainstream social policy over subsequent decades (Williams 2016). No surprise, then, that in a review of the discipline Ann Orloff comments that, while the debates between feminists and mainstream scholars in comparative social policy have been productive, 'yet the mainstream *still resists the deeper implications* of feminist work, and has difficulties assimilating concepts of care, gendered power, dependency and interdependency' (Orloff 2009: 317; emphasis added). More recently and more specifically, Mary Daly and Emanuele Ferragina (2018) note the lack of integration of comparative family policies research into comparative studies of the welfare state and of austerity. Without this, they argue, not only are particular struggles around equality lost from analysis, but so are the connections of the shifts in social and cultural values and the ways family policies reinforce measures such as targeting, fiscalization or workfare. Set this against a broader political context, in which the gender pay gap, gender violence, everyday sexism, reproductive justice, and (more recently) inadequate recognition of paid and unpaid care work are high on the agenda of feminist organizations such as the Fawcett Society, Southall Black Sisters and Sisters Uncut (and see Campbell 2013; Olufemi 2020).

Other new perspectives emerging from struggles and research around disability, sexuality, migration, childhood and age also find themselves in specialist silos, obscuring their radical implications for social policy. The issue of the environment and climate change has been pushing hard to get on to the social policy agenda over the past two decades (Fitzpatrick and Cahill 2002; Fitzpatrick 2011, 2014; Snell and Haq 2014; Gough 2017;

O'Neill et al. 2018). It has recently been given momentum by the arguments of Fitzpatrick (2014) and Gough (2017): that there is interdependence between social policies to improve the social infrastructure and the need to achieve sustainability. Social policy solutions are needed to ensure just adaption and mitigation policies, and social policy provision has itself to be delivered in a sustainable manner.

Continuities and changes

This complexity of continuity and change is reflected in the world outside of academic social policy. The context of neoliberalism and austerity politics, racialization and dehumanization of border practices, care crises and ecological disasters – including the 2020 pandemic – feels overwhelming. Yet recent decades have seen not only the impact of global social movements that I mentioned earlier but also a resurgence of local feminist and anti-racist activism, eco-activism and anti-austerity campaigns – the last often spearheaded by disability organizations. Alongside these, innovative democratically run decentralized initiatives have been established in communities 'discarded by the market and disregarded by the state', where people 'are already doing economics differently' (Chakrabortty 2018). These include new cooperative schemes, new unions, new forms of municipalism and community development, healthy cities, social enterprises, new models of co-production and service delivery, and new democratic modes such as citizens' assemblies (Featherstone et al. 2020; Miller 2020). New global networks of 'Fearless Cities' are transforming cities through street-level democracy and feminist and anti-racist, pro-migrant solidarities (Barcelona en comú et al. 2019). Many experiments exist in generating zero growth and ecologically sustainable local economies in transition towns (Red Pepper 2020). Transnational movements have developed for indigenous peoples' and migrants' rights, against militarism, and for territorial justice, along with the remarkable international mobilization of school students' strikes against climate change started in 2018. International campaigns for LGBTQI+ rights have achieved significant cultural recognition, albeit uneven and contested, that would not have seemed possible at the turn of the century (Weeks 2007; Abrahams 2019). In addition, in many areas, the Covid-19 pandemic revealed street-level actions of generosity, kindness, mutual aid and care (Solnit 2020).

While this resurgence signifies challenge and change, there is also a sense of intensified continuities – the 'unfinished business' of everyday and institutional racism, sexism, ableism and ageism finding consequential logics in different forms of inequalities, insecurities and child poverty, all of which were magnified by the pandemic crisis. The increased precarity of working conditions, combined with austerity cutbacks in services and benefits, disproportionately affects the wellbeing of black and minority ethnic women (WBG and Runnymede Trust 2017). A systematic account of ethnicity, race, discrimination and racism published in 2020 found that these were entrenched for all minority groups in all areas of society – education, employment, housing, health, criminal justice and policing, as well as politics, the arts, media and sport (Byrne et al. 2020). Even the Conservative government's Racial Disparity Unit worried in 2018 that 'there is still a way to go before we have a country that works for everyone regardless of their ethnicity' (Cabinet Office 2018: 1).

These forms of inequality were reproduced in the disproportionate effects of the Covid-19 pandemic: in the UK, BAME men and women were over four times more likely to die than their white counterparts (ONS 2020a). The high numbers of deaths of care-home residents (ONS 2020b) underlined the low value given to both residents and workers in care homes and the creaking health and social care infrastructure. Disability organizations have been at the forefront of campaigns around welfare benefit cuts; at the same time they have also been the target of a big increase in hate crimes (Burch 2018). Transgender activists have made headway in challenging transphobia, yet trans and gender-diverse as well as LGBTQ people face significantly greater risk of unemployment, hate crime and homelessness, risks which are heightened for BAME trans groups (Bachmann and Gooch 2017; Hines 2013; Abrahams 2019).

New critical thinking that has been inspired by and inspires such activism also involves a double movement of continuity and change: introducing new ideas as well as interrogating and resituating 'old' concepts. In addressing the continuing forms of marginalization both on the ground and in social policy's mainstream, I develop an analysis that is informed by contemporary thinking and activisms within and outside social policy and also connects to critical thinking in social policy that came out of social movements from the 1970s and 1980s. Thus, intersectionality emerged in the 1970s to make visible the struggles of women of colour whose experiences were reconstituted through the intersections race, gender, and class relations of power (Combahee River Collective [1977] 1995; Hull et al. 1982; Moraga and Anzaldúa 1983; Lewis and Parmar 1983; Crenshaw 1989). This re-emerged in the twenty-first century both as a reassertion and a reflection of the power of black feminist thinking and as 'the most important theoretical contribution that women's studies, in conjunction with related fields, has made so far' (McCall 2005: 1771). It serves as a methodological and political concept to reflect the multiplicity of identities and forms of domination and subordination as well as the need to recognize the connections that link theory and method to political practice (McCall 2005; Cho et al. 2013; May 2015; Hill Collins and Bilge 2016; Carastathis 2016; Hancock 2016; Romero 2018; Nash 2019).

That connection between the struggles of then and the possibilities of now has been likened to two bookends holding between them half a century of neoliberalism (Barnett 2020). At one end are the struggles for civil rights, solidarity with the Vietnamese against American imperialism, the Prague Spring, the 1968 student uprisings and the new social movements that followed. Within these were fundamental critiques of exclusions of those marginalized from the so-called universal progress of modernity since the Enlightenment in social, civil and human rights. At the other end, the global struggle for a new humanism is again asserting itself in different forms – the surfacing of a seam of activism that has continued in parallel to neoliberalism. Its impact was marked by the fact that, when Covid-19 struck, most governments felt obliged to prioritize, however incompetently and short-run, people's lives and health over the financial interests of capitalism. This feeling of the value of human life, structured in people's consciousness across the world, was given expression by the support for the Black Lives Matter protests in May 2020.

The 'bookends' metaphor is relevant to social policy. The development of a critical approach to social policy emerged from those sharpened understandings of welfare states in the 1970s and 1980s which provided feminist and anti-racist critiques of social policy and revised the class-centric perspectives of Marxist political economy. In particular, along with critiques based on disability, sexuality and age, they elaborated the social and organizational relations of power within welfare states and looked to participatory democratic and alternative 'prefigurative'[1] ways of meeting people's needs. The uptake in activisms in the wake of the 2008 global financial crisis combined with the changing political context has shaped critical reflections on these earlier concepts. For example, the social concepts of 'race' and 'Black' once served to politicize and unify experiences of racialized oppression, yet, on their own, they do not convey the specificities of experiences of those constituted as minority ethnic groups (Modood [2007] 2013; Murji 2017) or the reconfigurations of diverse migrations (Vertovec 2007; Phillimore et al. 2021). Ethnicity, religion, nationality, language and migrant status (not to mention class, gender, sexuality, disability and generation) shape those experiences in different ways at different times. However, those categories are given shape and meaning through social policies and public (and popular) discourses. Such developments challenged the fixed binaries (male/female, Black/White, gay/straight, etc.) attached to gender, sexuality, race, ethnicity, disability and generation and introduced more fluid and dynamic interpretations of diverse subjectivities, identities and social positionings.

From the 1990s critical efforts were concentrated in reinstating the area of 'the social' into both welfare regime analysis and analyses of the cultural, ideational, organizational and material challenges to the Keynesian welfare settlement (Clarke and Newman 1997; Williams 1995; Lewis 2000; Lister 2003; Béland 2009). These developments influenced new thinking in social policy around both the agency of providers and users of welfare and their psychosocial dimensions and around welfare governance and its fluid and contingent reach to multiple publics (Clarke and Newman 1997; Williams et al. 1999; Lewis 2000; Hoggett 2001; Newman and Clarke 2009; Newman 2012a; Barnes and Prior 2009; Hunter 2015; Lister 2021). In addition, the issue of care has been transformed from being about family policy to a domain of intersecting and intersubjective power relations, a labour as well as a commodity, a relational ethics, and a dynamic central to the postcolonial transnational political economy, to democracy and to intersectional global justice (Sevenhuijsen 1998; Tronto 1993, 2013; Daly 2002; Robinson 1999; Williams 2001, 2018). Earlier anti-essentialist refusals to see 'nature as destiny' shifted to exploring the dynamics of power relations between human life, nature, technology and science in the 'new materialisms', in ecofeminism, and in ideas of the posthuman and critical disability studies (Coole and Frost 2010; Braidotti 2013; Goodley et al. 2014). These new forms of interdependence between the human, non-human and living world have created new challenges of developing eco-social policy analysis (Gough 2017; Jackson 2016) and new models for a wellbeing economy (Raworth 2017; Care Collective 2020) and for the possibility of a social commons (Ostrom 1990; Mestrum 2015; Newman and Clarke 2014; Coote 2017; Gough 2017). Prefigurative activism is now understood as part of the methodology of Utopian thinking (Levitas 2013; Cooper et al. 2020). Postcolonial critiques interrupt the dominant readings of globalization and of welfare regimes that ignore its history in a colonial world order whose logics of racial, gender, sexual and bodily subordination and dehumanization have been carried into contemporary geo-social politics (Mignolo 2011; Bhambra and Holmwood 2018; Shilliam 2018). Within social policy, Mbembe's (2019) powerful concept of necropolitics, which refers to the state's capacity to decide who is and who is not disposable, illuminates an understanding of the relationship between welfare policies and the situation of migrants, asylum seekers and BAME groups more generally (Mayblin et al. 2019).

Piecemeal and marginal to mainstream welfare theory as they may be, these new developments have influenced critical thinking in social policy. I have suggested elsewhere (Williams 2016) that these constitute 'five turns',[2] to: (i) agency, understood in relational rather than individual-ist terms; (ii) political ethics of care, of ecology, and of decoloniality; (iii) the global, post-/decolonial and geo-political relations of welfare states; (iv) prefigurative politics; and (v) the (re)turn to intersectionality. What they have in common is their attention to the complexity and multiplicity of power and inequality and to the connections between cultural, social, economic and political marginalization. They are informed by local and transnational activism. They provide new lenses on an understanding of possibilities of humanness and society's ethical obligations, and, in doing so, they point to possibilities for future social policy. What each of these 'turns' means will become clear in the description of the book's structure that follows.

Structure of the book

The book is divided into three parts: *Orientation* discusses the theories that influence this book and my main frames of analysis. *Analysis* applies these theories and frameworks to three different areas: the welfare austerity decade in the UK, the question of agency, and the transnational political and social economy of care. *Praxis* discusses the implications of political ethics (of care, ecology and decoloniality) and contemporary prefigurative politics for a future eco-welfare commons.

Chapters 2 and 3 contribute to explaining the book's orientation. In chapter 2 I first elaborate and provide an explanation for the point I have made in this chapter: why it was that the theoretical and political insights of feminist, anti-racist and other critical-thinking analyses remained on the edges of the core theories of the discipline. I argue that there were a number of contradictory dynamics involved in this (re)marginalization which came not only from within the discipline but also from social, eco-nomic, political and intellectual developments over that time. The second part of the chapter considers possibilities for enhancing the explanatory power of new critical developments in social policy in order to bring these marginalized issues into the centre of social policy analysis. This involves combining an intersectional analysis with critical approaches to social policy. While acknowledging the limitations of some applications of inter-sectionality, I argue that its strength for social policy lies in its potential to unearth – through lived experiences and struggles – the multiple com-plexities of social power and inequalities (around gender, race, ethnicity, class, etc.) as well as participatory and transformative possibilities for social justice. It challenges fixed and essentialist approaches in which social posi-tions or economic systems are seen as given, natural or overdetermining. It emphasizes relationality, the contingencies of time and place, and the contested, contradictory and unsettled nature of phenomena, and it pri-oritizes ideas that emerge from the margins and inform resistance. At the same time, I argue that it is important to recognize the times and places when the salience of one particular form of inequality is greater, in social justice terms, than the others. It is also important to place an intersectional reading in an understanding of welfare states' relationship to a capitalism that is patriarchal, extractivist and racially structured. It is here and in cri-tiques of the social relations between providers and users of welfare that critical approaches to social policy can strengthen intersectionality.

Chapter 3 synthesizes this combination of intersectionality and critical social policy approaches into a framework for analysing contemporary welfare states. I argue that those analyses of recent developments in neo-liberal and austerity welfare as emerging from the 2008 financial crisis of capitalism are not able to explain the particular forms of gender, race, class and disability-related inequalities that are its consequence. Building on but critiquing Fraser's feminist reinterpretation of Polanyi's analysis of the history of capitalist crisis, I propose that we should contextualize austerity welfare in terms of four intersecting crises, all of which threaten human and planetary sustainability: the financialized crisis of capitalism; the crisis of care and social reproduction; the crisis of the environment and climate change; and the crisis of the external and internal racializing of national borders. Within this frame I develop a second framing for analysis of social policies at the national level. This articulates the key organizing princi-ples of contemporary welfare states as family, nation, work and nature. It is the social relations, changes and contestations in these four domains that unsettle welfare governance, but at the same time these domains are among the principal vectors through which governments seek to legiti-mize their attempts to resettle and restructure welfare.

The second part of the book, on Analysis, contains three chapters. In chapter 4 I apply the family–nation–work–nature analysis to the decade which starts in 2010 with austerity and ends in 2020 with the Covid-19 pandemic. (The pandemic struck as I was over half-way through the book, so references to it are largely time limited to the late summer of 2020.) The analysis focuses on three clusters of social policies during the era, each of which mutually connects one of the four domains of family, nation, work and nature to one of the others. Thus, the first section draws out the intersecting inequalities that are linked by 'hard work' and aspects of family, care and intimacy – the depletion and devaluation of care, the responsibilization of parenting with the attribution of blame, the intersectional effects of austerity on BAME women, and, in contrast, the recognition of relationship diversity. The second focus is on bordering practices in a post-racial context. 'Post-racial' refers to the perspective which regards the issue of race, anti-racism and multiculturalism as a thing of the past, something that is settled. As Goldberg (2015: 34) defines it: 'The post-racial is the racial condition in denial of the structural.' I show how this perspective reinforced assimilation and integration in ways which were Islamophobic while, at the same time, instituting bordering practices that increasingly set minority groups in the population apart and subject to surveillance and to restrictions in their social and civil rights. This includes the well-known case of the Windrush betrayal. The term 'bordering' refers back to external bordering practices against migrants and asylum seekers (discussed in chapter 3) which became the template for the governance of other social groups. This attempt to settle a 'post-racial' common sense signals the creep of necropolitics through 'nation' and 'nature', which is discussed in the third section through three different events: the Grenfell Tower fire; the politics of welfare ethno-nationalism in the Brexit debate; and, last, the Covid-19 pandemic. I show how all three clusters of policy were constituted through a style of governance that was incompetent and indifferent. Its method of gaining public consent for policies was depriving and dehumanizing in two ways: first, a shape-shifting of liberal values of fairness, equality and tolerance which gave rise to quite the opposite outcomes; and, second, the exercise of the classic underserving/deserving divide. As the decade wore on, this binary became more dependent on ethno-nationalist populism. The pandemic was to expose many of the inequalities and incompetencies that marked the decade.

Where chapter 4 explores the constitution of people as welfare subjects, chapter 5 turns to agency, activism and the nuances of contestation. It looks at how the 'turn to agency' from the 1990s in the discipline of social policy was one of its most important critical developments. This chapter explains what prompted the turn and its key shift into understanding agency as relational. It offers an intersectional approach to agency that works in two ways – in understanding the interconnected, shifting and multifaceted nature of power in the exercise of agency and in making visible those spaces of resistance that often remain out of sight. It also focuses on the 'double helix' of agency – that is, where one spiral relates to multiple social relations of gender, class, race, etc., and an interconnecting spiral signifies the relationship between welfare providers and users. This chapter is the book's pivot: it provides an understanding of how resistance and contestation is carried through everyday actions and quiet solidarities of mutual care and support; it explains how this happened during the decade of austerity in spite of earlier ideas that feminism and anti-racism had had their day; and it links to the prefigurative politics explored in chapter 7.

In chapter 6 I turn back to one of the four crises in chapter 3 – care and social reproduction and its links to transnational mobility – to examine the phenomenon of migrant care workers who move to care for the families and households in richer countries, often leaving their own children behind to be looked after by others. The chapter develops an analysis of the imbricating scales of global, national and interpersonal that migrant care workers inhabit. At the global level are both the care market and the possibilities for reform and advocacy through international organizations and transnational migrant support groups. At the national scale migrant care work is shaped by the ways care practices and policies intersect with employment policies which devalue care work and rules and regulations around migration which deem care work unskilled. At the interpersonal scale are a complex of social relations between the migrant care worker and the person for whom she cares or works. At all scales, this is about the intersections of inequalities of gender, race, class, migration status and nationality, underpinned by geo-political inequalities between richer and poorer nations, historically constituted in colonial relations of racialized servitude. This raises challenging questions for the meaning of global social justice. I argue that there are a number of immediate strategies that would improve the position of migrant care workers, but, in the long term, the complex relations of inequality it embodies require, for a start, that the everyday relations of paid and unpaid work are not subsumed under the goals of economic growth but become central to global social justice and strategies for sustainability.

The third and final part of the book explores praxis. Chapter 7 brings many of the themes of the book together. Recalling the point made earlier that some of the most significant struggles today are around the provision of care and support, around climate change and around the dehumanization of racialized groups and migrants, I explore three sets of political ethics – by political, I mean ethics that are not abstracted but grounded in struggles for emancipation. I examine the ethics of care, environmental ethics and decolonial ethics. While there are differences across and within these ethical positions, they share a critique of Western-centric liberal notions of rational white male, able-bodied, heterosexual autonomy. They also challenge neoliberal values of individualism, autonomy and competition and the dependence of capitalism upon economic growth. Instead they promote interdependence, reciprocity, human flourishing and sustainability. Together they expand the notion of interdependence to include moral obligations not only to distant strangers across the world but also to the planet and its non-human and living organisms, to future generations' right to inherit a sustainable planet, and to those past generations who suffered slavery and other forms of dehumanization from colonialism and imperialism. They point to new models for the economy, for deliberative democracy and for the recognition of different forms of knowledge that incorporate a new pluriversal humanism. I combine these guiding principles with the resurgence of prefigurative politics of civil society actors and their attempts to develop in new ways the principles of multiple interdependencies, relationality, democratic deliberation and interpersonal, local and translocal solidarities. With these in mind, I explore commonalities and tensions in different proposals for a social commons and a changed relationship between people and the state, emphasizing the urgency of the need to reimagine the welfare state.

The implications of these and other analyses in the book for teachers, researchers, students and scholar activists are taken up in chapter 8 as a conclusion. I summarize the theoretical approaches in the book and then look at social policy as a field of study in terms of, first, reconstituting its knowledge base with an emphasis on decolonizing the discipline; second, developing relational knowledge and practices; and, third, applying collective reimagination and dedication to the reconstruction of social policy in the aftermath of the Covid-19 crisis.

Appendix I provides an elaboration of the analytical frame of family–nation–work–nature and its relation to welfare. Appendix II links future to past by situating the author in a history of social policy over the past fifty-five years.

PART I

ORIENTATION

2

A Critical and Intersectional Approach to Social Policy

Introduction

In the previous chapter I introduced two ideas. First, that, while there have been major analytical insights on welfare states from many of the feminist, anti-racist, political economy, disability, age, sexuality, and ecology-related critiques of social policy, the core of social policy has been slow or differentially selective in acknowledging them. Second, that, while many of these critiques offer profound analyses, they remain relatively disparate; what is important is to draw together their commonalities, strengths and insights in a way that respects their specificities and argues for their central significance in the discipline of social policy. This chapter elaborates both these ideas, setting out the places different critiques have occupied in relation to mainstream social policy and looking at the combination of political and intellectual forces that have shaped their continuing marginality. In the second half I examine the origins and re-emergence of intersectionality as theory, method and praxis, looking at its potential and pitfalls. I argue that, if combined with some of the key concepts from critical approaches to social policy, it has much to offer in pulling together the disparateness of different critical approaches and in thinking through issues of a transformative perspective on social policy. In sum, I offer an intersectionally informed and multi-focal critical approach. The subsequent chapters apply this in different ways.

Remarginalization of the social

There are a several reasons as to why many of the issues raised by the earlier and subsequent critiques around gender, race, disability, sexuality and age were sidelined or only partly accommodated in mainstream social policy. First, it is important to understand the breadth of these critiques' new frames of analysis of the post-war welfare state. Feminist critiques were to highlight the relationship between the public sphere of work and politics and the private sphere of family and personal relationships. Within that was an examination of the gendered assumptions attached to care, dependency and patriarchal power, as well as the exclusions attached to non-heteronormative identities, subjectivities and relationships. Care and dependency were also critically re-examined from the viewpoints of disabled people, children and older people, challenging bureaucratic and expert dominance over service-users and attempting to prefigure new democratic and participatory ways of doing welfare. In addition, the links between anti-colonial struggles and anti-racism brought the colonial and postcolonial global context of an international division of labour and geo-political inequalities to the fore. This went well beyond the limitations of the hermetically sealed single-nation view of the welfare state. It uncovered a critical understanding of the role of welfare states in nation-building and especially in the rubric of social imperialism in forms of early collectivism of the twentieth century. This sought to subordinate class and gender interests to those of nation and empire and did so by representing social reforms as the fruits of imperialism, which in their turn required national efficiency and healthy workers, mothers and children. This critique made connections between the increasingly significant political economy of migrant labour and the welfare state, especially the role of migrant labour in reducing social expenditure costs and the use of welfare institutions to police immigration. It found connections between the management of the colonies and the pathologization of the cultures and practices of people, especially mothers and their families, who migrated from those previous colonies. Together these critiques called for a more systematic approach to the study of social policy as the dynamic outcome not only of political and economic forces but of multiple social and cultural forces too.[1]

The first set of barriers to their accommodation came from within the study of social policy itself. In a paradoxical twist by the 1990s, at the very point when many of the earlier feminist and anti-racist critiques began to gain greater foothold in the discipline of social policy, not only did the rise of neoliberalism in many countries attempt to dismantle the foundations which made the quest for greater social justice possible, but also the core of the discipline of social policy moved into cross-national comparative study. As it did so, it shed some of these new insights garnered through the previous two decades. The new studies in comparative social policy were influenced particularly by the work of Esping-Andersen's *The Three Worlds of Welfare Capitalism* (1990). This was a major step forward in framing subsequent studies of the variations across different welfare regimes through their impact upon systems of social stratification, employment, and labour markets. It established important theoretical advances in providing a grounded quantitative analysis of welfare regime variations; it centred contestation; and it gave welfare states a significant role in shaping social formations. However, these contestations, histories and social formations focused centrally upon class and ignored gender, race or any other form of significant social division in the origins and development of nation welfare states.

Nevertheless, welfare regime analysis provoked feminist critiques of its marginalization of gender and led to new and inventive analyses of the gendered nature of welfare states. So, for example, Jane Lewis showed how the historical separation of the public and private (domestic) spheres was embedded in a male breadwinner model of welfare in different ways and to different extents in different countries, resulting in different 'gendered welfare regimes'. This focused on the central issue that welfare regime analysis ignored: how far the unpaid labour of women in the family is recognized and valued (Lewis 1992). Other studies sought new concepts to measure that which was missing in mainstream analysis. For example, 'the capacity to form an autonomous household' indicates the extent to which the state frees women from the necessity to enter marriage, or equivalent partnership, in order to secure financial support for them or their children (Orloff 1993; and see Sainsbury 1994 for a redefinition of the gendered logics of welfare). They illustrated how significant contestations around the body and reproductive rights had in many countries wrought important reforms (O'Connor et al. 1999). Shaver's critique noted the need to make room for the institutional complexity of welfare states – that there are no necessary patterns of coherence, unity or linearity in gender policy logics across and within welfare institutions (Shaver 1990). Together, this work provided much richer explanatory power for post-war welfare and overlapped with new feminist critiques of Marshall's concept of citizenship which was central to welfare regime analysis (Pateman 1989; Lister [1997] 2003). It provided a sound basis to analyse the shift, starting at that time in many developed welfare states, from a 'male-breadwinner' model to a more 'dual-earner' or 'adult-worker' model in which women and men were expected to be earners (Daly 2011). A greater convergence was emerging from different models to reconcile work and care, while, at the same time, different policy goals, policy instruments and historical conditions were beginning to shape variations across countries (Platenga and Remery 2005; Lister et al. 2007; Lewis et al. 2008; Williams 2010; Williams and Brennan 2012; and see chapters 3 and 6).

Other critiques – particularly around racism, ethnicity and migration but also around disability, sexuality and gender diversity – were less amenable to the conceptual parameters and quantitative measures of this new cross-national development. Because of this, cross-national comparative studies in these areas were late to the table, mainly emerging some two decades later – immigration regimes (Sainsbury 2012); intimacy (Roseneil et al. 2020); disability (Halvorsen et al. 2017); old age (Walker 2005); transgender (Hines et al. 2018). Lack of quantitative data was a real problem, as many European countries had not by this time instituted the collection of data on ethnicity or sexuality. It was also the case that welfare regime analysis was at first slow to acknowledge those countries that didn't fit with US or European modern welfare state development, such as the paradoxes of post-communist societies (Deacon and Castle-Kanerova 1992) and the rapid changes in Latin America (Gough et al. 2004; Franzoni 2008) and parts of South-east Asia (Peng and Wong 2008). It was also in relation to some of these studies that the geo-politics and colonialism between North and South began to be recognized as a factor in welfare state develop-ment (Midgley and Piachaud 2011), but this had less impact on the rolling forward of welfare regime analysis.

In relation to racism, in the mid-1990s many European countries saw a rise in migration and multiculturalism as well as an emerging political and popular backlash to these, often expressed as claims for new nationalist conditions of eligibility to welfare ('welfare chauvinism' – Keskinen et al. 2016). Cross-national analyses of migration and citizenship regimes were being developed by migration and racism scholars (Bovenkerk et al. 1990; Brubaker 1990; Hammar 1990). With some exceptions (Castles and Miller 1993; Faist 1995; Sainsbury 2012), these were largely outside the discipline of social policy and, even so, did not always relate migration to race and racism. Criminal justice, too, in which much critical work around racism had been developed, such as *Policing the Crisis* (Hall et al. 1978), often stood outside the discipline. Other exceptions at that time also included more intersectional approaches to the gendering, racializing and classing of welfare states (Mink 1990; Ginsburg 1992; Boris 1995; Williams 1995) and the beginning of research on the significance of female migration into care work (Heyzer et al. 1994; Anderson 2000). None of these touched the body of comparative social policy at that time. In fact they were largely ignored. A vacuum opened up in the core of the discipline, one often excused through lack of data, but it was as much that there was no theoretical space for the new-old hierarchies of postcolonial and geo-political realities. The increased pace and differentiation of migration and asylum seeking was beginning to challenge myths of cultural homogeneity and the realities of national boundaries upon which nation-states and their social policies were built. In addition, when the inadequacy of existing immigration policies and social rights was becoming apparent, and when welfare chauvinism was becoming more assertive, few mainstream welfare state / regime analyses were elaborating theoretically or normatively how to counteract racism and racial inequalities or to deconstruct universalism's failure to recognize difference (but see Phillimore et al. 2021 for a cross-national study that does just this, discussed in chapter 5).

These omissions were carried in different ways into the next waves of mainstream social policy, which focused upon the restructuring of welfare states in the context of the rise of neoliberalism. Three examples offer an understanding of the narrow ways in which gender and race (by now well established in wider scholarship) began to be acknowledged. First, the historical institutionalist approach was a particularly important contribution to understanding how the contingency of history and the architecture of political institutions matter in the way they shape political claims and political change (Hall 1993; Pierson 1996; Pierson and Skocpol 2002). This was more open to referencing different inequalities, but what was missing was any systematic engagement with the multiple social relations of gender, race or any salient relations other than class. Second, this openness but eventual narrowness can also be seen in other work on the restructuring of welfare states which uses the conceptual device of 'new social risks' (Bonoli 2007). This refers to the changes that challenged the post-war welfare state: greater female labour-force participation, an ageing society and an increase in single parents, as well as new vulnerable 'risk groups' which included migrants and disabled people. While this formulation acknowledged these groups and the challenges they pose, it tended to focus on the relationship they have to the labour market, as human capital, and to strip them of any claims they might make in their own right, as well as the more profound implications of those claims. Third, and similarly, in subsequent research on the impact of post-industrialism on welfare states, Esping-Andersen (1999) employed 'family', in addition to state and market, as an analytical concept and recommended moving domestic care work from the household to the state or market as the strategy to enable women to enter paid employment. Such investment would increase fertility, secure a tax base and productivity for the future, and protect and provide opportunities for the low-paid and unemployed (see also Esping-Andersen 2009). While the acknowledgement of social provision to enable women to work was welcome, this utilitarian and heteronormative approach ignores the wider aspects of gender equality such as the unequal gendering of household and care work, not to mention the shaping of these by class, migration and race, disability, age, and sexuality.

A second factor that inhibited the influence of the critiques was in the response to the intellectual shift across the social sciences and humanities to post-structuralist thinking. This was challenging to a discipline rooted in the analysis and measurement of structural inequalities and material poverty. The unfolding analyses of governmentalities, following Foucault, spawned a literature on how the restructuring of the (welfare) state marked a shift in how the behaviour of welfare subjects was to be managed (Rose 1999; O'Brien and Penna 1998). In addition, following Butler (1990), the connections between culture, subjectivity, identity, agency and difference began to be explored. These developments furthered an understanding of the complexity of power, but, for some in and out of social policy, questions of difference and the 'politics of identity' were (and still are) characterized as a culturalist shift away from the 'real' material struggle around the growing impoverishment and disempowerment of deindustrialized communities (Gitlin 1995). The separation of economic from other forms of injustice is a reflection of an ongoing current in 'left' politics of assuming that solidarity based on (working-)class interests constitutes the central force for change (Dean and Maiguashca 2018). In their study of minority ethnic women's struggles against austerity in France, England and Scotland, Leah Bassel and Akwugu Emejulu (2018) found that the entreaties to solidarity from socialist and social democratic organizations were often implicitly made in economic terms to a white male constituency and thus provided little engagement with issues of racism or sexism. The idea of race as exogenous to class was to come back to bite during the Brexit campaign (see chapter 4). Back in the critical quarters of social policy, far from ignoring economic polarization, this shift offered opportunities to grapple with the way cultural and economic inequalities were complexly intertwined, as, for example, in John Clarke's examination of what the 'cultural turn' means for the study of welfare states (Clarke 2004; see also O'Brien and Penna 1998; and Lister 2004). It was (and is) still the case, however, that many contemporary and influential studies focus exclusively on material inequalities, a tendency reinforced by the clear polarizing of inequalities emerging from the 2000s. Thus, in Thomas Piketty's analysis of the inequalities of capitalism, powerful and influential as it is, there are no references in the index to gender, ethnic, minority, migrant or disabled inequalities (Piketty 2014).[2]

Third, and more widely still, by the end of the 1990s and into the new century, neoliberal marketized, managerialized and modernized social policies had taken hold, trade unions were weakened in many countries, and there was a decline in local new social movement activism. Although the profiles of social movements dimmed, they did not go away. Activism around disability, sexual citizenship and rights for migrants, for carers, older people and children and environmental policy, influenced pressure-group activity over this period and was reflected in social policy research. There were important struggles against racism with the first recognition of institutionalized racism in the police force, although these were very hard fought and often on the back foot (Macpherson 1999). There was the declaration of women's rights at the Beijing Conference in 1995 and the beginning of important moves for gender equality and anti-racist policy in the EU (Hoskyns 1996; Williams 2003). By 2004 in the UK, civil partnerships for same-gender relationships and gender recognition for transgender people became legal, as did same-gender marriage in 2013 (except for Northern Ireland). The Kyoto Protocol of 1997 led to a raft of climate change and energy legislation from, in the UK, 2004 onwards, while environmentalist critiques and some of the arguments for a citizens'/basic income began to identify the limits of assuming a future based on continuing economic growth and productivism (Fitzpatrick and Cahill 2002). Preparation went on for the UN Convention on the Rights for Persons with Disabilities, which was passed eventually in 2006. In some ways, these developments indicate how feminist, anti-racist and other activists were moving higher up the political hierarchy from their bases in the grass roots into EU and international NGO politics as well as horizontally into more transnational coalitions (Watkins 2018).

Fourth, at the national level, both culturally and politically, particularly in the emerging 'Third Way' politics and New Labour, there was a different shift – away from what were considered 'out-dated' conflicts of both the social democratic politics of class and redistribution and the politics of the new social movements, especially feminism and anti-racism: 'post-feminist' and 'post-racial' became new political catchwords (see chapter 4). John Denham, a former secretary of state in the New Labour government, said in 2010 that it was 'time to move on from "race"', and Theresa May, as Conservative home secretary and later prime minister, went further, to say that 'equality is a dirty word' (both cited by Craig et al. 2019: 1). For others, it was political correctness that had gone 'too far', or cultural diversity that had undermined class solidarity and (mythical) national homogeneity (Alesina and Glaeser 2004; Goodhart 2004). Gail Lewis's study of local government policies in the 1990s termed this as a 'blind-eye' of successive governments to the issue of racism (Lewis 2000), and a study done almost two decades later on the struggles of minority ethnic women identified this as 'political racelessness' (Bassel and Emejulu 2018; and see chapter 5).

Fifth, back within the study of social policy, several further dynamics were significant. One was that paid work became the central social policy referent to welfare reforms in much of Europe and the US, providing the financial and moral imperative to get everyone – men, women, disabled, minority ethnic groups – 'off welfare and into work'. This shifted the axis in what was important in 'the social' (Williams 2001). In so far as there is a longstanding predisposition of social policy research, as well as independent policy research organizations, to investigate the agenda framed by governments (Taylor-Gooby and Dale 1981), then from the turn of the century much of this focused upon the priorities of government and EU reforms – a social investment approach which saw opportunities for paid work for women and disabled people and minority ethnic groups as a way to minimize social exclusion and promote multi-ethnic integration. The combined effect was that much useful empirical work was produced, but the focus of inequalities became narrowed into issues of discrimination, social inclusion, community cohesion and integration.

At the same time, another rather different factor in the social sciences more generally was that the academic studies of gender, race, ethnicity, migration, disability, age, sexuality, childhood, youth, age and eco-social policy themselves became disparate, specialist and siloed. And this too was reproduced in social policy studies. The effect of these two dynamics was that single categories of gender, race, etc., came to signify specific descriptors, stand-alone critiques or measures of diversity rather than as challenges to the theoretical underpinnings of what stands for universalism in welfare. Of course, it is also the case that these critiques have themselves *needed* to stand alone in order to pursue more deeply the specificities of their intellectual journeys, but this separation was influenced by other developments. It was not simply that the fragmentation of social movements was mirrored in the social sciences, or, as some have argued, that feminism's critique of the state dovetailed with neoliberal policies to wither the state, or that feminism was lured into individualist empowerment strategies (Fraser 2009). It was that critical diversities became siloed because the demands of managerialized universities required more intensive academic specialization (defining and leading a new area of study, setting up a specific journal, etc.) for both research assessment purposes and individual career advancement. On the other hand, this separate but parallel existence has not been a one-way movement. Marginalization happens when barriers exist, intellectual or otherwise. It is this that the demands decolonizing the universities challenge (Bhambra et al. 2018; Andrews 2015).

This marginalizing tendency is no worse in social policy than in other social, economic and political sciences. Indeed, as a disciplinary space it can be more propitious: its very eclecticism gives it greater openness to new ideas. Paradoxically, however, its general commitment to social justice can also render it complacent (Phillips and Williams 2021). Feminist scholarship in particular has a high profile in social policy. Yet, at the same time, its frames of analysis still stand at a conceptual distance from core theories. It should be said that, even here, it is the intersection of gender with class that dominates, with only sporadic forays into critical disability, race and queer theories.

Having explained the continuing marginalization of these critical developments, I want to turn this argument around now to make the case for how they need to be central to social policy. One way of doing this is by providing a strategy to bring together their common analytical and transformative strengths in a manner that can also recognize their specific arguments but avoid the siloing effects mentioned here. I assess first the relevance of an intersectional approach in enabling this.

An intersectional approach for social policy

Intersectionality provides an understanding of social inequalities and power as complex, interlinked, shifting and multifaceted, constituting both penalties and privileges. In other words, our experiences of power and inequality are constituted not simply by, say, our gender identity or our racialized and class positionings but also by the multiple places we occupy on the many salient and changing axes of power that exist at any given time. Importantly, it is an approach in which analysis and political practice are closely linked. The concept has a long history emerging from black feminist struggle and critical race studies.

> No other group in America has so had their identity socialized out of existence as have black women. We are rarely recognized as a group separate and distinct from black men, or as a present part of the larger group 'women' in this culture. (hooks 1981: 7)

So wrote bell hooks in her introduction to *Ain't I a Woman? Black Women and Feminism*. The phrase 'Ain't I a Woman?' was a quotation from a speech delivered in 1851 by the African American campaigner Sojourner Truth for both the abolition of slavery and women's rights. hooks's intervention was important in the history of second-wave feminism, as were other activist writings which spoke to an experience in which the race and gender of women of colour decentred them within both feminist and anti-racist/black movements (Combahee River Collective [1977] 1995; Hull et al. 1982; Moraga and Anzaldúa 1983; Lewis and Parmar 1983; Hill Collins 1990). The crucial analytical point to emerge was that race, gender and class could not be understood as single or even incremental axes of oppression but, rather, as interconnected modalities of power that reconstitute identity, experience and practice in specific ways. Intersectionality emerged as the analytic concept in the 1980s to encapsulate this political and institutional problem of invisibility, elaborated by the socio-legal black feminist scholar Kimberlé Crenshaw (Crenshaw 1989). The term became more widespread after the turn of the twenty-first century in a different political and intellectual context, particularly with respect to continuing and widening inequalities, increasing migration and gender diversity. It was to develop critical methodological, empirical and political insights which could be applied to a range of interconnected and contingent social relations and exercises of power (McCall 2005; Lutz et al. 2011; Cho et al. 2013; May 2015; Wilson 2013; Hill Collins and Bilge 2016; Carastathis 2016; Hancock 2016; Bone 2017; Romero 2018; Irvine et al. 2019; Hankivsky and Jordan-Zachery 2019; and, especially, Nash 2019).

For social policy, the importance of an intersectional approach speaks to its potential to critically analyse the complexities of social power and inequalities as well as guiding transformative possibilities for social justice. It operates as theory, method and praxis. It concentrates on excavating the lived experience. It works not as a grand and totalizing theory but as an 'orientation' (May 2015: 3), a way of thinking about complexity, contingency and connectedness in social and political phenomena, and a refusal to reduce phenomena to single causes or solutions. These days, intersectionality denotes as much a political position as a conceptual approach, although, to be honest, the word is too long for a placard and too clumsy as a rallying cry. Nevertheless, what it marks is the importance of alliances across difference as a path to transformative change. This has clear relevance to social policy's concerns with understanding social inequalities and social justice, how to research and make visible those that are hidden, and how to think about the solidarities that can reinscribe universalism with difference.

In recent years intersectionality has begun to be applied to social movements and practice, to politics, and to social and public policy intervention (Wilson 2013; Hill Collins and Bilge 2016; Hankivsky and Jordan-Zachery

2019; Bassel and Emejulu 2018; WBG and Runnymede Trust 2017; Williams 2018; Irvine et al. 2019). The key characteristics of these applications of intersectionality are their attention to the complexity of social inequalities and power and their focus on change and fluidity, challenging fixed and essentialist approaches in which social positions or economic systems are seen as given, natural or overdetermining. Relationality, the contingencies of time and place, the contested, contradictory and unsettled nature of phenomena (including welfare states, their policies and practices) also characterize intersectional policy analysis, as do ideas that emerge from the margins and inform resistance. As Hankivsky and Jordan-Zachery note, it thus enables an understanding of

> the differential impacts of policy on diverse populations . . . it draws attention to aspects of policy that are largely uninvestigated or ignored altogether: the complex ways in which multiple and interlocking inequities are organized and resisted in the process, content and outcomes of policy. In so doing, the exclusionary nature of traditional methods of policy, including the ways in which problems and populations are constituted, given shape and meaning, is revealed. (Hankivsky and Jordan-Zachery 2019: 2)

Intersectionality is not without its criticisms.[3] It is important to note that, as a theoretical orientation, intersectionality has different versions and applications (McCall 2005). It has been criticized for becoming an abstract academic theory – a new (or not so new) 'buzzword' – which depoliticizes the very forces that brought it into being (Davis 2008). Another 'depoliticizing' criticism suggests that, while purporting to be about the multiple and intersecting relations of inequality, the focus on subjective identities and on local, lived experiences in intersectional analysis obfuscates the explanatory power that connects inequality and oppression to global capitalism. Avoiding these pitfalls requires, first, the recollection that the origins of intersectionality in black feminism lie firmly in the struggle against social, cultural, political and economic injustices. Thus, it is important to keep the concept and practice of such contestation central to any contemporary analysis. It is this that protects against reification and depoliticization; and it is this that differentiates it from a mapping of multicultural diversity disconnected from the challenges such diversity makes or is subjected to. Second, one of the promises of intersectional analysis lies in the capacity to link everyday intersubjective experiences to the wider systemic patterns of power and privilege. This means making clear the connections between social, cultural, political and economic injustices so that the nature of the political economy – a form of global financialized capitalism which is patriarchal and racializing – becomes an essential part of the frame of analysis in a way that is neither reductionist nor singly causal, nor monolithic, but allows for its contradictory nature. In synthesizing a critical and an intersectional social policy analysis in this book, the intention is to enhance each in a way that is attentive to the criticisms of both, to build an analysis which can follow through to its political implications.

In the previous chapter I drew attention to the UK Social Policy Association's report on the continuing marginalization of race and racism in social policy teaching. I have explained in this chapter how this marginalizing effect can be seen in other inequalities research but is most marked for race and racism scholarship. In that context, does using an analysis that focuses on the intersections of different social relations of inequality obscure the racialized differences that really matter? A similar argument from a different perspective might be: by focusing on the intersections between different power relations, I am bound to dilute the entrenched and systematic patterns of gender subordination (or disability, or sexuality, or childhood). Obviously this is possible, but intersectionality is a method that depends on prior understanding of different social relations of power. Applying it requires sensitivity to the contingent nature of political context and to the question of salience. In other words, we have to understand the historical, material and cultural specificities of particular forms of social relations: to be aware of the variability in social, economic, cultural and political *salience* of different social relations at different times and places to the issues we are researching.

One example of this, which is discussed in chapter 4, is the salience of the social relations of race and racism in understanding the disproportionately higher mortality rates in the UK during the Covid-19 pandemic for BAME groups (from around four times higher than white counterparts and similarly reflected in other Western countries). It was experiential evidence from BAME groups that began to unlock the role of systemic racism in these deaths and eventually, under pressure, to be recognized by Public Health England (2020a). An intersection of racially subordinated social positions in the labour market, especially as key workers and in the least valued areas of social care and geriatric care, in precarious work, in overcrowded housing, along with morbidity rates associated with health inequalities, placed BAME men and women at greater risk (Qureshi et al. 2020b; Lawrence 2020; Patel et al. 2020). Digging deeper reveals the specific ways in which different forms of racism contribute to these disparities and intersections. For example, all those poverty-related conditions

– work, insecurity, housing and neighbourhood – carry greater risks to ill health, and ill health predisposes to severe illness and death from the virus. However, it is the intersection of these with racisms that intensifies health inequalities for BAME groups (IHE 2020). This includes institutional racism that prevents minority groups from accessing, for example, job opportunities or promotions and structural racism in which negative discourses (a 'hostile environment') shape interpersonal encounters. The greater the exposure to everyday racial micro-aggressions and the emotional labour involved in managing them – what Claudia Rankine (2014: 11) calls 'trying to dodge the build-up of erasure' – itself also generates ill health.[4] As I explain in chapter 4, the generalities attached to the virus and its mitigation strategies worked in specific and intersecting ways both within and across inequalities of class, race, gender, age and disability. It is this dynamic between the general, specific and intersecting which marks the capacity of an intersectional analysis to understand the complexity of social phenomena.

For the analysis in this book, the contemporary context of welfare states and political struggle demands an analysis that can capture not only these intersections of inequality but also those interconnections between different areas of crisis which help shape them. The crises of financialized capital, of care and social reproduction, of climate change and of the racializing of borders are further made salient by the struggles they have provoked (see chapters 3, 5 and 7). This highlights, for example, the salience of bordering practices within the UK's austerity welfare state in which the processes of restricting the rights of asylum seekers have been extended to different categories of benefit claimant. Such connection requires a frame of analysis that allows for the interconnections without reneging on the specificities of gender or race or class (see chapter 4). That said, it is a tricky exercise where I am aware of the limitations in the scope of my knowledge (see appendix II).

A final note on the pitfalls of intersectionality involves not assuming parallels between different forms of difference in the eagerness to seal solidarities. In her critique of crip theory, Kirstin Marie Bone (2017) argues that, while crip theory, like queer theory, seeks to break down the binary of disabled/able-bodied, some versions do so at the expense of obscuring the voices of diversity in disability identities. 'Crip', an ironical reclaiming of 'cripple', she argues, privileges visible disabilities and shifts too quickly into assuming that crip theories of disability are parallel or a subset of queer theory (she cites McRuer 2006). Such claims fail to understand the place of 'rhetorical adjacency' in which solidarity is expressed by being *alongside* disabled people in their struggles, not speaking *for* them or *as* them by claiming 'crip' identity as an able-bodied person (Bone 2017: 1308). By contrast, 'transversal politics' has been one way of describing the communication of 'rooting and shifting' that is required between activist groups to develop coalitional solidarities (Massey 1999; Yuval-Davis 1999), which is discussed in chapter 7. The main point here is that, both in theory and in action, attention is required on how to avoid 'universalistic politics (that overemphasizes commonalities to the neglect of differences) . . . and particularistic politics (that overemphasize differences to the neglect of commonalities)' (Irvine et al. 2019: 8).

An important contribution to refining the methodology of intersectionality is Leslie McCall's work (McCall 2005). She distinguishes between three approaches. Representing these on a continuum, the first, and probably least used, is *anticategorical complexity*, which focuses on deconstructing analytical categories and rendering them fluid and constantly unstable. The second, *intracategorical complexity*, retains a critical eye to the boundaries by which categories are defined and constructed but is interested in the points of intersection *between* multiple categories and their shifting social relations. This approach reveals the erasure of those experiences forged through such intersections (as in the original meaning of intersectionality in black feminist struggle and the point made by Hankivsky and Jordan-Zachery in the quotation above). The third approach, *intercategorical complexity*, while acknowledging the fluidity of social categories, nevertheless employs them as 'anchor points' (Glenn 2002, cited in McCall 2005: 1785) in order to investigate, indeed to measure, the extent and shifting of social relations of inequality *between* and *across* multiple groups. This follows a *strategic* categorizing in order to generate a more complex and comparative picture of power and inequality. It focuses not on the ways single groups transect different forms of subordination and domination but on the overall patterns across multiple groups. This, McCall argues, is the least practised of the three approaches but is the one which she unfolds when drawing upon her quantitative analysis of patterns of class and racial inequalities among women in the United States (McCall 2001). The emerging picture is one of complexity in which no single dimension of inequality predominates and in which the context of *place* in particular shapes the patterns of class, race and gender inequalities. Such an approach is important in that it goes beyond the use in quantitative methods of social categories as static variables and it is particularly useful to social policy in which the measurement of poverty and inequality is integral to its subject matter.

I return in the conclusion to the ways intersectionality is used in this book. For now, I draw out the main points of a critical approach to social policy.

A critical approach to social policy

As well as an intersectional approach, this book employs a critical approach. This may seem oxymoronic; after all, intersectionality is itself a critical approach. But what I intend by emphasizing this is the importance of keeping in play theoretical insights developed in and subsequent to earlier social policy critiques. Through this I define a critical approach as one that places struggles and contestations over social justice at the heart of its theories, analyses and practices of welfare provision and uses this position to question that which is taken for granted in the concepts, methods and discourses used in the field of study of social policy and welfare states (Lister 2010: 57–94). Contestation and contradiction were central to the early Marxist political economy of welfare analyses (Gough 1979; Ginsburg 1979), in which the welfare state was understood as the outcome of an uneasy truce between the interests of capitalism for a healthy, disciplined workforce and the interests and struggles of the working class for protection from poverty, unemployment and ill health. In this was its crucial contradiction: that capitalism couldn't live with a welfare state but neither could it live without it (Offe 1984).

However, it was out of new social movement activism that these concepts were refined and broadened. Their contestations were often about welfare provision in terms both of its logics of redistribution – who got what from benefits and services – and of the interconnected issues of the recognition of people's or groups' moral worth – their dignity and personhood. Crucially, they were about democratic representation and participation in the formation and implementation of policy (Williams 1999; Beresford 2016). Second, they extended the notion of contradiction to people's own experiences of the welfare state: while it provided individuals with the resources and services they needed, it did so in ways that reinforced some inequalities and hierarchies in which they already found themselves. This aspect was later refined in Foucauldian approaches to focus on the way welfare subjects are constituted through discourses and practices of social policies. Third, much of the activism highlighted a new form of struggle around the so-called *social relations of welfare* – that is, the relationship between providers and users of welfare provision. These developments gave rise to new self-help practices, but, more than this, they involved attempts to *prefigure new social relations*. Whether in women's health centres, black people's Saturday schools, co-operatives, forms of early independent living, support services for victims of rape and domestic violence, or the ACT UP support provided by lesbians and gay men for people with AIDS – these projects strove for a new kind of non-hierarchical, caring, respectful and empowering relationship between provider and user. The subsequent development of this aspect of critical thinking is pursued in chapter 5.

Political economy approaches which are relevant to social policy have themselves been refined over time. For example a 'cultural political economy' approach (Jessop 2013, 2015; Jensen and Tyler 2015) takes neoliberal austerity as a governmental project and looks at the changing realities and imaginaries of the ways the political and economic intersect in both capitalist social relations and capitalist accumulation processes. In other words, analysis of political economy is informed by an understanding of social and cultural relations. This is not just about social expenditure cuts but also about the means by which governments extend the very meaning of capital accumulation into the commodification and financialization of everyday life (Jessop 2015: 98). Similarly, John Clarke and Janet Newman's (Clarke and Newman 2012, 2017; Clarke 2019a) understanding of austerity is informed by a 'conjunctural' approach developed from the analysis by Stuart Hall and the Centre for Contemporary Cultural Studies of Margaret Thatcher's 'authoritarian populism' in the 1980s (Hall et al. 1978). Importantly, too, Ian Gough develops a political economy of climate change and welfare which situates the environment centrally in the future of social policy (Gough 2017).

A critical approach questions the taken for granted in mainstream thinking – in this case, mainstream social policy. By 'mainstream' I refer to those bodies of work that establish theoretical or methodological 'cores' for the discipline and shape its subsequent research. Like disciplines, cores vary over time and place, but social policy literature reviews (e.g. Starke 2006), journal content analysis (e.g. Powell 2006) and disciplinary texts demonstrate the development of 'cores'. While I use the heuristic device of distinguishing between 'critical' and 'mainstream' social policy, it will also be clear that the boundaries between the two have shifted over time and have been quite porous. In some countries, social policy exists not as a discipline but as a subsection of sociology, political science, political economy or economics which studies state and non-state welfare policies. Historically, at least in the UK, social policy has been associated with its social reforming origins and the development of European modernity. This means that, as the first section of the chapter showed, the hierarchies, exclusions and otherness associated with European modernity underpin the discipline's theoretical development, even though, by its very subject matter, issues of equality and social justice run through its veins. Here, the crucial and central question becomes what and who is included in the 'social' of social policy and social justice, and this is one of the questions that the book explores.

There are also important aspects of critical thinking which are not just about 'unmasking' power, domination and unquestioned constructions in disciplines. They go beyond this and look to resistance against domination as a way of understanding how things may be transformed. This is similar to the concept of praxis described in the previous section. This is sometimes referred to as 'criticality' (Roseneil 2011). In this way, there are two sides to critical theory: that which, forensically and remorselessly, unpicks power and injustice, past and present; and that which creatively looks to the future. In other words, criticality seeks to transcend that which is sometimes called the 'hermeneutics of suspicion' (Sedgwick 2003). These two elements have been described as 'negative' and 'affirmative' critique (Rebughini 2017). Eve Kosofsky Sedgwick (2003) similarly distinguishes between 'paranoid reading', which remains within the confines of criticism and critique, and 'reparative reading', where the future can be imagined as different from the present. This book adopts the 'reparative' approach that seeks to understand the contradictions, ambiguities and instabilities in global capitalism, neoliberalism and neoliberal welfare states, as well as in everyday discourse about welfare and in political mobilizations. Political mobilization for social justice does not necessarily promote or represent social justice for all. At the same time, as Leonard Cohen sang, 'There's a crack in everything. That's where the light gets in.'

There are some clear similarities between these ideas and those of intersectionality. More than that, each improves the other. The one can help deal with the problems and pitfalls of the other. What intersectionality offers social policy is a more rigorous framing of how the social relations of power and inequality are experienced and operate within and across social groups; it permits a more open-ended view of populations and social policy fields and analyses the contingent ways in which their borders and boundaries are socially, economically, politically, culturally and administratively constructed. It also provides a coherence between its analysis and methods to thinking through the possibilities for coalitional forms of solidarity and political change. This enhances a critical perspective which in its turn secures the analysis in an understanding of the political economy of welfare, but in a way that can simultaneously address the intersections across its cultural, social, moral and organizational dimensions and their contestations, ambiguities and contradictions.

With these considerations in mind, I use intersectionality in this book to look at a number of key contemporary analytical and empirical developments in social policy. In doing so, I focus on those multi-scalar dynamics not usually associated with intersectionality's subject matter – understanding austerity through intersecting global crises of finance, care, racialized borders and climate change. This is pursued at national scale through the intersecting, changing and contested domains of family, nation, work, and nature in the social relations of welfare governance. In other words, this approach analyses the intersecting social relations and social forces within and across different scales, from the intersubjective to the transnational. It focuses on the ways in which different social, cultural, economic and political forces, conflicts and crises come together and unsettle that which is taken as given. I also extend intersectionality's methodological power to focus on the intersections of ethics of care, environment and decoloniality and the possibilities for alternative welfare futures which incorporate intersectional social justice. This does not rely only on intersectionality, or only on the theories mostly closely associated with it, but seeks to align and synthesize other perspectives and concepts in social policy analysis which share and enhance some of its key concepts and concerns. Those writing on intersectionality have stressed the 'provisional' nature of its theorizing (Carastathis 2016: chap. 3). It is not the last word on multiple processes of subordination but looks to both political and intellectual possibilities for change. In this way I draw on work which also carries the characteristics I have described above, which can be found, for example, in some political economy perspectives, critical geography, conjunctural analysis, critical race theory, theories of postcoloniality and decoloniality, critical disability and queer theories, eco-social policy analysis and psychosocial analysis. These, and others, inform my synthesis, while at its core is an insistence on applying to social policy analysis a critical and relational understanding of contingency, contestation, connectedness, contradiction, and a firm resistance to overdeterminism, essentialism and reductionism.

Conclusion

The aim of this chapter has been to set out my broad analytical approach and influences. This may be summed up as an intersectionally informed critical approach. In the journey to this point, the chapter looked first at the ebbs and flows in the influence of critical thinking that originally emerged from new social movements on the core theories of social policy since the 1990s. This offered an interpretation of multiple contradictory dynamics involved in its (re)marginalization, which came not only from within the discipline but also from social, economic, political and intellectual developments over that time. These included the shift within neoliberalism to minimize advances in equality by focusing on delivering social justice through labour market activation and on a political era that saw itself as post-feminist and post-racial. This was also accompanied by the relative fragmentation not simply of those activisms but in their greater specialization and partition within the academy. The upsurge in social movement activism since 2008 in the face of the rise of popular nationalist right-wing politics provides one impelling reason for thinking through how to give these critical analyses greater consolidation in reflecting on the present and the future for welfare states.

In these terms, the chapter considered the relevance of intersectionality as an approach that, on the one hand, combines theory, method and political practice and, on the other, is highly attuned to inequalities and power around race, gender, disability, sexuality and class. I argued that intersectionality's focus on lived experience, on understanding the complex and multiple nature of contestations, social inequalities and social justice, is crucial. It enables hidden injustices to be unfolded and provides an understanding of the relationship between commonalities and specificities and their link to political practices – all extremely relevant to critical social policy approaches. At the same time, as a relatively loose approach, it is necessary to be aware of problems in its application as well as its potential for social policy analysis. In order to mitigate these I turned to key analytical insights from critical thinking in social policy which in some ways are shared with an intersectional approach. These include the importance of contestation, in particular, but also of context, contingency, contradiction and criticality. Together the two approaches can clarify the connections between social, cultural, political and economic injustices to examine the nature of neoliberal welfare states within a political economy of global financialized capitalism which is extractivist, patriarchal and racializing. This requires a frame of analysis that avoids reductionism to single causes or monolithic conspiracy and allows for its contradictory nature. Chapter 3 takes this up.

3

Intersecting Global Crises and Dynamics of Family, Nation, Work and Nature: A Framework for Analysis

Introduction

This chapter translates the discussion in chapter 2 on intersectionality and critical approaches to social policy into a framework for analysing contemporary neoliberal welfare states. It seeks to take account of and go beyond those accounts that locate the forces behind austerity welfare solely within the contradictions of capitalism and neoliberal ideologies. The aim is to provide a way of analysing a more complex picture of the social formations and relations of power and inequality constituted through social policies in the twenty-first century. There are two dimensions to this framing: the first encapsulates the contradictions of global financial, patriarchal, racial and ecological capitalism and their associated crises. These include not only the North Atlantic Financial Crisis of 2008 but also the related and intersecting current global crises of the environment and climate change, of care and social reproduction, and of the racializing of transnational borders. The chapter spells out the different ways in which each of these crises threatens human and planetary wellbeing and sustainability. Also significant are the impacts they have, singly and together, in reproducing existing gender, class, racial and geo-political inequalities in even more stark ways. The second dimension of framing elicits an understanding of how welfare states at national scale attempt to 'settle' the changes and challenges around the intersections of family, nation, work and nature. While these two dimensions of the framework are spatially different – the first at global scale, the second at national scale – these spaces are not separate but interconnected.[1] For example, the racialization of transnational borders is a global phenomenon but operationalized by national and supranational laws and practices. The framework presents a (national) frame within a (global) frame (see figure 3.1, p. 54). This framing is relevant to developed welfare states; here my detailed points of reference are to the UK. Before explaining these two dimensions I summarize some of the main shifts in welfare settlements in recent history.

Neoliberalism, welfare and austerity

Since the 1990s, most governments in developed countries have, to a greater or lesser extent, implemented neoliberal market principles in their welfare states. In general terms this has involved privatization, marketization, consumerism, labour market activation and individual responsibility, especially of self-support through paid work. It has generated the creation of markets and quasi-markets within public services, contracting out services to the private and voluntary (third) sector, and establishing partnerships with these sectors to deliver services. Welfare infrastructure, institutions and governance were reorganized according to new public management principles based on corporate business practice and the normalization of economy and competitiveness as serving efficiency and innovation. In its turn, this development has sought to construct service-users as consumers shopping wisely in the marketplace of health, personalized social care, welfare and education, while aligning services and benefits to the needs and requirements of the labour market and, more broadly, to competitiveness in a globalized economy.

The implementation and success of these principles and practices have varied across welfare states, as has the extent to which they replaced the post-war Keynesian welfare state model (Hall and Soskice 2001; Mandel and Shalev 2009). The earlier post-war model invested in mass state welfare in the broadest sense – health, education, income support, housing and social services – as a way of stimulating the economy, providing employment and enhancing profits and productivity, supported by a three-way consensus from organized labour, capital and the state. This was challenged from different quarters – socially, fiscally, organizationally and politically (O'Connor 1973; Gough 1979, Williams 1989). In the UK, Margaret Thatcher's New Right monetarist policies of 'markets, managers and a mixed economy' was an early attempt from 1979 at implementing neoliberal and neoconservative welfare policies, in common with the US under Ronald Reagan. Similar changes happened later in Australia, Canada, New Zealand, Ireland, Iceland and Latin America, not only from right-wing but also from centre-left governments. However, neoliberalism has not been all of a piece. For example, neoliberal welfare, while changing its internal organization, has also encompassed key elements of the post-war welfare state into its practices (such as the NHS in the UK) in recognition of some of its popular support (Newman and Clarke 2009). It also demonstrates variety over time and place. Bob Jessop distinguishes the above-mentioned countries' forms of economic neoliberalism from at least three other types: those that developed in post-communist countries after 1989; those imposed on developing countries through structural adjustment policies; and those implemented by some Northern European and Nordic countries with strong social democratic welfare histories (Jessop 2015). Although they are not included in Jessop's categories, the East Asian countries of South Korea, Taiwan and Japan might fit more closely to the last category, though with a more nationalist emphasis (Peng and Wong 2008).

In terms of variety over time, in the UK there were two further waves after the New Right. From 1997 to 2010, a New Labour centre-left version of neoliberal welfare combined social investment and anti-poverty programmes with continuing forms of privatization, deregulation and marketization in public services and with labour market activation and self-responsibilization of welfare citizen-consumers. The third wave came after the North Atlantic Financial Crisis, with a long period of neoliberal austerity welfare embedded by the Conservative–Liberal Democrat Coalition and Conservative governments from 2010, punctuated by the Brexit referendum in 2016 and the re-election of a Conservative majority government in 2019. This imposed fiscal austerity, leading to cuts in public expenditure focused on welfare benefits, housing support and social services (especially social care) and hit the poorest 20 per cent hardest. The undermining of the welfare state was profound (Taylor-Gooby 2013; Hills 2017; Farnsworth and Irving 2015; Bennett 2019). Local authority spending was severely cut, as were spending programmes for schools and prisons, with public-sector pay rises held back. While health care was relatively protected, 'efficiencies' in the system meant that services were not able to keep up with demand. The proportionate tax burden was moved towards lower income groups, away from the wealthy and corporations (Ruane and Byrne 2014). By 2017, child and pensioner poverty started to go up for the first time for twenty years (JRF 2017). It remains to be seen at the time of writing how far the Covid-19 pandemic will produce a new wave that either breaks the mould or reinforces it (see chapter 4).

Again, the UK has not been the only country to introduce some form of austerity welfare in response to the financial crisis, although these too differ across the varieties of neoliberalism mentioned above (Jessop 2015; Olafsson et al. 2019). The global financial crisis was uneven in its impact, starting in the US and the UK as a 'North Atlantic Financial Crisis' before affecting Western Europe, but having less effect elsewhere such as Australia. It is also the case that, within Europe, austerity policies have not always emerged as a national response: in the case of Southern

Europe – Spain, Portugal, Italy and Greece – they were imposed by the EU, European Central Bank and IMF, with deleterious consequences to poverty and inequality in those countries (Béland and Mahon 2016: 88–9).

In explaining this third shift to austerity welfare, many social policy analysts of the UK have noted its force as an economic tool in restoring capital's power after the financial crisis and as an ideological tool in seeking to transform not only the relationship between the economy, the state and the individual but the very social relations of everyday life (Tyler 2013; Jensen 2018). John Hills's careful assessment of the first four years of austerity was that its realization in the face of its human damage depended on a 'welfare myth' of 'them and us' – hard-working taxpayers versus welfare-dependent scroungers (Hills 2017; see also Blythe 2013; and the UN's special report on *Extreme Poverty and Human Rights* in the UK, UN 2019).

Richard Seymour's study analyses austerity measures in the UK and the US as articulating an economic, political and ideological response to the financial crisis involving the following processes:

- drastic and long-term 'rebalancing' of economies away from wages and toward profits;
- growth in the power of financial capital with the accompanying spread of precarity in all areas of life as a disciplinary strategy;
- the recomposition of social classes, with more inequality and more intra-class stratification;
- the takeover of state institutions by corporations;
- the shift from welfare benefits as collective provision to coercive workfare, sanction and penalties;
- a cultural economy that values hierarchy, competitiveness and contempt for the vulnerable. (Seymour 2014: 3–4, paraphrased)

My framing of these issues seeks to explore the social and cultural dynamics further in their relation to the economic, ideological and political and how legitimacy for such impoverishing political strategies was sought. Austerity welfare in the UK has reproduced differential disadvantages and advantages while constituting multiple intersections of social exclusion, discrimination and hierarchy, marked by class, gender, disability, race, ethnicity, religion, migrant status, nationality, place and generation. The pro-Brexit campaign in 2016 attempted to coalesce these into a series of cross-cutting binaries (Remain/Leave; us/them; native/migrant; 'white' working class/cosmopolitan elite). As well as, and among, families and youth in deindustrialized regions, it is women, especially lone parents and women of colour, disabled women and men, racialized minorities, and migrant women and men who have been particularly affected by austerity (WBG and Runnymede Trust 2017; Bassel and Emejulu 2018; Scullion 2018; WelCond 2018; Ryan 2019; Morris 2019; Shutes 2017; Edmiston forthcoming). These developments require an analysis at both the global and the national scale that can deal with 'the social' – the complex interconnections, contradictions and contested social relations in social welfare (whether this is austerity welfare or other more moderate neoliberal social policies such as those in the Nordic countries). But this needs to be contextualized, and, while most social policy analyses locate the global in terms of the financial crisis, I argue that we can better understand what is happening to nation welfare states if we have a more complex appreciation of the intersecting crises of a contemporary financial capitalism that were born into and out of different forms of imperial, colonial, postcolonial, patriarchal and planetary exploitation, expropriation and expulsion. I start with these – the four interconnected global crises of capitalism: financial, social reproductive, ecological, and the racialized bordering of transnational mobility.

Frame 1: Intersecting global crises

'Crisis' – a note

Crisis carries several meanings. It can refer to an existing tension that threatens the status quo. Central to a Marxist understanding is that capitalism sows the seeds of its own destruction in that its profits depend upon intensifying exploitation of its labour force, leaving it vulnerable to their inability or refusal to be further exploited (Marx and Engels 1886). More commonly, crisis can refer to a short-lived acute predicament that leads to a turning point; or it may be an enduring chronic critical condition that awaits action. In this sense, Gramsci referred to a crisis being an interregnum when 'the old is dying and the new cannot be born', in which 'a great variety of morbid symptoms appear' (Gramsci 1971: 276). In other words, there is a recognition that the existing order does not work, yet there are not sufficient oppositional ideologies and forces (a counter-hegemony) to reconstruct it, and it gets worse. As important is the need to ensure that the claim to a *global* crisis needs to clarify for whom there is a crisis, and whether all regions of the world experience the crisis similarly.

These meanings and questions cover all four crises I discuss – of financial capitalism, of care and social reproduction, of environment, and of racialized transnational mobilities – in different ways. What they share is that they have emerged from an enduring tension inherent in their relationship with capitalism as an economic system of production and consumption into the specifics of a racial, extractivist and patriarchal neoliberalism. This has reached a critical point where, singly and together, they endanger future eco-social, human and non-human wellbeing and future sustainability. They are also areas of significant international mobilization and struggle which potentially challenge the hegemony of neoliberalism (discussed in chapter 7). For now, my main point is that it is in this conjuncture of intersecting crises that we better understand the shaping of national and supranational social policies.

Much of the relevant political literature on crisis refers to the contemporary crisis of democracy, seen especially in the distrust of political elites, the fatigue of and with social democracy, and the rise of ethno-nationalist populist leaders (Crouch 2011; Streeck 2014; Brown 2015). This is an important dimension, discussed in chapter 4 in relation to Brexit and in chapter 7 in relation to participatory democracy. But it is of a different order to, and more consequential of, the economic, social and planetary crises discussed here.

The global financial crisis

Analyses of the shifts to austerity welfare generally locate its origins in the global financialized capitalist economy, a system which, along with its ideological promoter, neoliberalism, had been supported by national and supranational governments and international agencies (IMF, World Bank) but whose internal contradictions created the global financial crisis (Seymour 2014; Farnsworth and Irving 2015; Béland and Mahon 2016; Olafsson et al. 2019). Capitalism of the twenty-first century has been, especially in the US and the UK, dominated by finance capital, in which, in the context of depreciated wages, products were buyable for many only through borrowing via credit or mortgages (thereby generating profit for the lenders). Mass inability to repay debts accumulated and many banks went bust. In this sense, it was an enduring tension that became an acute crisis. In the UK this hit in 2007 when New Labour was in power. As in a number of other states, the government responded with bank and financial-sector bailouts; for example, they underwrote £51 billion of the debts of the mortgage lender Northern Rock. Unlike their successors they maintained public spending in line with their anti-poverty strategy (House of Commons 2009; Bennett 2019). However, locating austerity as a result of policies to resolve the contradictions of finance capitalism, while crucial in its particularity, tells only a part of the story. There are other social and environmental aspects which emerge from the contradictions of contemporary capitalism that are particularly salient to understanding the landscapes of austerity welfare and resistances to it.

I start with Nancy Fraser's feminist critique of the North Atlantic Financial Crisis, which argues that most analyses of the crisis are gender blind, and the obverse, that feminist theory lacks a framework that links social changes affecting gender relations to this crisis (Fraser 2013). She argues that current global crises are multidimensional and that we need an integrated approach to understand how these dimensions relate to each other. This she provides through a critical reinterpretation of Karl Polanyi's *The Great Transformation* (Polanyi [1944] 1957), a tripartite analysis of the history of capitalist crisis over the nineteenth and first half of the twentieth century. In brief, Polanyi's argument is that capitalism's self-destructive impulse lies in its turning land, labour and money into 'fictitious commodities'. The marketization of each of these domains led to despoiling the land, demoralizing the labourer, and destroying the value of money through speculation.

In Fraser's view, it is the integrated nature of this analysis that is important, along with Polanyi's recognition of the significance of political mobilization, in this case through the conflict between capital and labour, as the key to effect social and economic change. Fraser updates this mobilization to include the significance of feminist, anti-racist and environmentalist struggles. Accordingly, she rewrites Polanyi's three crisis-prone constituents of land, labour and money as the interlinked systemic crises of ecology, social reproduction and finance, respectively. She argues that the same impulse of 'fictitious commodification' is seen today in each of these global crises, with a similar result of destroying the value of the planet's resources, of care and of money, respectively. Thus, in relation to the last of these, money, Fraser maintains that it was speculation that fuelled the global financial crisis in which investment was destabilized and devalued. This led not only to austerity policies, whose disproportionate and immiserating penalties have already been described, but also to undermining the capacity of money to store value for the future. The endangering of future societies is at the heart of Fraser's analysis. Before explaining what this means for the crises of social reproduction and ecology, I suggest that there is a dimension missing in her analysis.

While Fraser mentions the three most significant areas of struggle today as feminist, anti-racist and environmentalist, she identifies only crises attached to the first and last of these – social reproduction and ecology. Issues of racism, immigration and postcolonialism tend to be folded into her explication of these two rather than also providing an understanding of the specificity of the relationship between the logics of capitalism and colonialism over time. Since the 1990s there has been a dramatic dovetailing of immigration and domestic racializing policies (de Genova 2018). First, contradictions between the demands of global capitalism for mobile labour and state tightening of border controls (supported by ethno-nationalist populist politics), alongside the acceleration (at times) and diversification of transnational migration and asylum seeking, has created growing injustices and inequalities (Faist 2018). Second, global widening of social, economic and geo-political inequalities has disproportionately affected minority ethnic groups and indigenous people in spite of civil rights, the end of Apartheid, anti-racist and postcolonial struggles. Howard Winant describes this as a 'racial crisis' in the Gramscian sense of an interregnum in which emancipation is not yet realized but when 'morbid symptoms' appear (Winant 2006: 988). Similarly, Michael Dawson, in a critique of Fraser, says: 'it is "apparent" when we observe the rise of racial strife in the United States and ethno-religious conflict in Europe that racial and ethnic logics are generating crises as deep and perhaps even more dangerous than those of capital, reproduction, the ecology, or politics' (Dawson 2016: 145). (This is a crisis that found its voice in the Black Lives Matter movement.) Thus the combined logics of white supremacy and capitalism in different forms have given rise over time to both exploitation and expropriation.

I term this missing crisis as one of racialized borders and come back to how to define this later. What is important here is that it points to an understanding of capitalist development from the sixteenth century as inextricably tied into the politics of slavery abolition, imperialism, colonialism, eugenics, postcolonial racism, globalization and post-racial racism. This is not to say that racism is determined by capitalism but that the two have intersected economically and culturally over time ever since colonial enterprises emerged in 'the long sixteenth century' (Wallerstein 2004; Bhattacharyya 2018). Profits from imperialism and from slave plantations were central to industrialization, and the racial structuring of the labour market has contributed to conflicts and tensions within capitalism. It is not just, as Fraser critiques, that Polanyi's theory of the history of capitalism's tendency to self-destruction ignores the difficulties that women have had even to sell their labour power, but also, as Bhambra and Holmwood (2018) argue, that it omits recognition of the significance of racialized labour. This is because it is based on a conception of a worker who sells their labour power only for it to become commodified. But this is a worker who is free to do so in the first place. An enslaved worker's labour power is embodied in their enslavement and carries no such freedom to be sold into commodification. To be fair to Fraser, in a later response to Dawson's critique mentioned above, she begins to delineate this distinction between exploitation (the commodifiable worker) and expropriation (the unfree worker) and how they intersect over time and space in 'four regimes of racialized accumulation' (Fraser 2016a).

Now to return to how the three further crises of social reproduction, ecology and racialized borders threaten sustainability and wellbeing.

The crisis of social reproduction and care

The crisis of social reproduction has been central to much recent feminist analysis and is variously also called the crisis of care or the care deficit (Floro 2012; Fraser 2013; Williams 2014, 2018) or 'depletion through social reproduction' (Rai et al. 2014). There are distinctions between the two concepts 'social reproduction' and 'care'.[2] Social reproduction is more general, signifying those social practices of raising and educating children, looking after frail and older people, and feeding and cleaning households. 'Care' refers more to relational practices associated with providing and receiving care, to the ethics it embodies, and to care policies and care economies which operate interpersonally, locally, nationally, transnationally and globally. In this book I generally employ the term 'care' to cover both sets of meanings.

Care may be paid or unpaid, and as such it captures a range of interconnected social and geo-political inequalities. Women's inequalities, at work and in the household, relate to the (unpaid) care and domestic responsibilities they carry. Globally, women do most paid care and domestic work, which is generally low-paid and devalued (Razavi and Staab 2012; ILO 2016). The basic and enduring contradiction between capitalism and social reproductive work is that, while part of it – keeping the current and future workforce socialized, healthy and replenished – is essential for economic production, at the same time much of this work is constituted as separate, part of women's 'natural' predisposition, and devalued. Unpaid care is largely invisible in national accounts even though that activity is an indispensable investment for the economy, and where care is *paid* work it is often low-paid and devalued as 'unskilled' (Himmelweit 2018; Bunting 2020). In both these settings, care is further constituted through heteronormative and patriarchal power relations in which classed, racialized, sexual-ized, generational and disabled inequalities are clearly writ. Of course this is not the only part played by this activity in people's lives, for it also about love – the profound expressions of mutuality, support and interdependence signified by the ethics of care (see chapters 5, 6 and 7).

However, it is in the imperative for profits extracted from people's labour that capitalism exerts intense pressure on, and endangers, the capacity of people to care for others and of societies to provide quality care. This is both enduring and intensifying. The present era of global financialized capitalism has heightened this contradiction to the point of crisis (Fraser 2016b). In the West, the normative model has become that of the 'two-earner' family.[3] While access to paid work has been a long-fought-for right by women, it is now, in the face of wage depreciation, a financially critical necessity for most households, as well as being part of a policy principle of 'hard-working families' and labour market activation for self-support. If women's employment has increased the needs for care support, then it has been further intensified by demographic shifts in developed countries of declining fertility and increased longevity involving longer periods of frail old age. However, within the context of neoliberal welfare, the provision for children, older people and disabled people has been developed by contracting out to the private for-profit sector and providing investment opportunities for multinational companies. However, logics of the market and of care often run in opposite directions (Hudson 2016). A combination of marketization, privatization and social expenditure cuts in many countries after the global financial crisis has given rise to the lowering of conditions of care work, with low wages and zero-hours contracts and poorer accessibility and quality of care. The Covid-19 pandemic was to reveal both the frailty of care markets and the vulnerability of care users and workers (see chapter 4).

The factors contributing to a care crisis in the Global South are both similar and different. The increase in women's involvement in the labour market and the greater reliance on a woman's wage has been global (OECD 2015; ILO 2009). While people are also living longer in poorer regions, care crises result from unemployment, wars, ethnic conflict, climate change disaster and chronic illnesses. These place enormous responsibilities on women to maintain sick, young and old family members with little infrastructural support for basic amenities. They also precipitate women into seeking work through migration, often into care and domestic work in developed countries. At the same time, professional households in developed countries, in a context of increased work hours and marketized provision, ease their work–care imbalance by employing migrant or minority ethnic women to do their households' cleaning and caring. In many countries this is facilitated by state fiscal benefits to those households (Carbonnier and Morel 2015; see chapter 6). In effect, such employment of working-class women of colour, migrant status or lower caste merely obscures those hidden reproductive processes and displaces the effects of the care crisis on to the care workers, families and countries from which they migrate (Williams 2012). While this takes on a new form of worldwide relationship between poorer and richer countries, it also perpetuates a historical racial division of reproductive labour of care work and domestic service provided by women of colour (Glenn 1992). What the existence of this crisis challenges are the priorities of macroeconomic policies of productivism, market competition and consumerism which require the invisibility and subservience of the very processes of human interdependence that enable human flourishing. It is in those struggles – especially by women carers and care workers, trade unions and disability organizations – against the devalued conditions of care and for the state to grant visibility and voice to its users and properly remunerate its workers that these tensions are revealed most clearly (Williams 2010; Esquivel and Kaufmann 2017).

The crisis of climate change and ecology

The third global crisis is that of climate change and ecology, known as the Anthropocene (Lewis and Maslin 2015): that the extent of human activity upon the planet's resources, especially through the burning of fossil fuels, has accumulated carbon in the atmosphere and oceans to the point that, without significant intervention in the immediate term, human life is endangered through global warming. The world is already experiencing the consequences of accelerating floods, bushfires, drought, heatwaves and storms, while in the future the sustainability of the planet and the whole ecosystem is at risk (World Meteorological Organization 2019). The use of 'anthro' in Anthropocene implies that this is the consequence of the activity of all humanity, but processes of resource extraction and exploitation have been a central part of capitalist production and profit accumulation and, in the case of oil and coal, have literally fuelled industrial expansion. Resource exploitation – cotton, tea, coffee – was part of imperialism and colonial expansion through to global capitalism today. Some suggest that, given capitalism's exploitative relationship with nature, a more accurate label, in terms of who is affected by that exploitation, is 'Capitalocene' (Gill 2019: 5) or 'racial Capitalocene' (Manchanda 2019: 2).

The environment and climate change raise questions of equity, equality and justice across populations and regions and over generations (Cahill 2002; Fitzpatrick 2011, 2014; Snell and Haq 2014; Gough 2017). A degraded environment affects health and wellbeing in unequal measures: while the wealthy may benefit from forms of environmentally harmful consumption, it is disproportionately poor people – nationally, regionally, globally – whose lives are impacted (Snell and Haq 2014). Poorer regions are affected incrementally by anything over a 1.5 per cent reduction target in global warming, in contrast to the 'less than 2 per cent' set by the Paris Agreement on Climate Change in 2016 (King and Harrington 2018). The UN's migration agency, the International Organization for Migration, notes that, in 2018 alone, 17.2 million new displacements from disasters in 148 countries and territories were recorded (Ionesco 2019). Within these populations women suffer significantly. According to UN Women and the World Bank, in 2017 women were disproportionately in poverty in developing countries (UN Women 2017). They constitute the majority farmers and carers and are more dependent upon land and resources such as water and fuel which are threatened by climate change; they are particularly vulnerable to gender-based violence and bonded labour if displaced by disasters; and they have less political voice in decision-making (Action Aid 2019).

Further, measures to prevent global warming can also be disadvantageous to particular groups. For example, biofuel production as a replacement for oil has created greater competition for marginal agricultural land and has deprived women, especially indigenous women, of their livelihoods (Women's Environmental Network 2019). These forms of exploitation, expropriation and expulsion are mirrored in the developed world. Carl Anthony's book *The Earth, the City, and the Hidden Narrative of Race* (2017) documents the ways in the US in which racial and planetary subordination and racial and environmental injustice go hand in hand over time. This moves from the colonization of both peoples and the earth to the ways in which gentrification, expulsion and the deregulation of water and waste hit minority communities (Anthony 2017, cited in Manchanda 2019; see also Pulido 2016).

'Environmental racism' has been used to describe the ways in which, in Europe, marginalized and minority groups are disproportionally subjected to environmental hazards such as living in proximity to toxic waste, or having limited access to clean air, water and other natural resources (Vincze 2013). This has particularly affected the siting of Roma and Traveller people. In the UK, one report found that minority ethnic groups, by virtue of their place of residence near main roads and motorways, are exposed to 17.5 per cent higher concentrations of dangerous particulates (ENDS Report 2009: §53).

In 2019, the global pandemic of the Covid-19 virus brought the deadliest of a series of epidemics and is another form of environmental risk to sustainability. It represents a micro-biological facet of the macro-exploitation of resources affecting human health and capacity for production, and it bears similar challenging features, outcomes and lessons. It is associated with globalization, flourishing in high-density urban areas in which 68 per cent of the world population now lives (WEF 2020a). Some epidemics, such as Zika, travelled on the climate-changing winds of El Niño. Covid-19 respects neither class nor borders, yet is more deadly for older and physically vulnerable people and more devastating for socio-economically disadvantaged groups or racial minorities (see chapter 4). As with the financial crisis, the markets, always focused on the short-term, were unable to stop themselves from falling. Like climate change, the pandemic presents random, unpredictable risks. This challenges the basis of welfare states that are built on a range of relatively predictable risks. Both require robust multi-scalar global, national and local governance for interdependent political, public and expert co-operation to develop social and physical protection.

In so far as the mitigation of climate change challenges the continuation of consumerism, economic growth and exploitation of the earth's resources, it also challenges the assumption, first, that the welfare state is afforded and legitimated only through capitalism's commitment to economic growth; and, second, that mitigation and adaptation policies require multi-scalar forms of co-operation and expenditure (from global to local) which profoundly tax how we think about the relations between 'overdeveloped' and developing worlds and the development, implementation and funding of a future eco-social policy (Fitzpatrick 2014; Gough 2017). Third, climate change has constituted a challenge to anthropocentric relations of power: the assumed right of the human world to dominate and exploit the non-human world, demanding instead not only strategies to mitigate the effects of climate change but a new way of being with the interdependencies of the ecosystem.

The racialized crisis of borders

It is in the identification of the contemporary conditions of transnational borders as a *crisis* that the notion of 'crisis' becomes tricky. To call the flight of populations from wars, fragile states, ethnic conflicts, collapsing economies, environmental disasters, crime, violence, and the poverty of geo-political inequalities a 'migrant *crisis*' or a 'refugee *crisis*' is to risk misrecognition of the dynamics that have contributed to the problems experienced by migrants, particularly those regarded as 'unskilled', asylum seekers and refugees. These were the terms that dominated media and political discourses around the movement of Syrian refugees and asylum seekers in the summer of 2015 and continued to do so long after, weaving in and out of a growing ethno-nationalist populism. The *Daily Mail* warned repeatedly of a migration and / or refugee 'crisis', associating it with illegality, criminality and Islam, a phobia that has become increasingly gendered (Gray and Franck 2019). In so far as 'crisis' implies danger and difficulty, then these discourses signify this phenomenon as a disaster and danger not for those risking their lives but for sovereignty, governments and resident populations of migrants' European destinations or, for the US, by Muslims and those crossing the Mexican border. Where Trump accused Mexican immigrants of being criminals and rapists in 2018 (Jacobs 2018), Viktor Orbán, the Hungarian prime minister, claimed a clear correlation between 'illegal' immigration and terrorism. In both cases the material construction of borders became 'spectacles' of mythical threats to the nation and dehumanization and exclusion from it (Cantat and Rajaram 2019).

Such representation detracts, first, from the experiences and suffering experienced by those who are migrants, refugees or asylum seekers, including death at sea or suffocation in the backs of lorries. By 2016 over 3,000 refugees attempting to enter Europe by sea had drowned; worldwide it was over 4,000 (IOM 2016). Second, the idea of 'crisis' as portending mass migration exaggerates both the impact and the long history of migration into Europe. Between 2011 and 2016, 884,462 asylum applications were made across Europe. In fact, general international migration started to slow down a little after 2007 (OECD and UNDESA 2013) at the same time that refugee migration started to accelerate. There were 11.7 million refugees under the UNHCR's mandate in 2013 – 1.2 million more than the previous year (UNHCR 2013). While some countries (Germany, Sweden) took proportionately more and some less (Britain took 0.06 per cent of its total population), the average amounted to only 0.25 per cent of the total European population, an easily absorbable number (figures cited in Bhambra 2017: 396–7). Indeed, immigration and asylum seeking have historically been relatively steady phenomena in Europe. Third, the crisis panic of today correlates migrants with danger, illegality, conflict, violence and terrorism. In doing so it has legitimated the ratcheting up of coercive border controls, detention and deportation policies, which now characterize immigration controls across the world: the precaritization of work and citizenship together (Geiger and Pécoud 2010). As Yuval-Davis and her colleagues argue, bordering has re-emerged as 'a principal organizing mechanism in constructing, maintaining and controlling social and political order' (Yuval-Davis et al. 2019: 5). As such, it affects all social groups and not simply migrants and minority groups. At the same time, it is the restrictive legal and social policies of immigration that lead to the desperate conditions in refugee camps, such as Sangatte on the French coast, and, as Alex Sager argues, that *create* the illegalization of immigrants and the so-called crisis:

> Illegalization is closely connected to securitization in which migration is treated as primarily a security issue. The language of crisis contributes to securitization so that restrictive, coercive border controls become the norm. Measures such as offshore detention of people seeking asylum or the repatriation of refugees to more dangerous regions become more palatable when they are seen as responding to a crisis. (Sager 2020: 15)

Subscribing to a 'migrant' or 'refugee' crisis is thus to compress the biases of methodological nationalism – privileging the perspective of the nation-state – with sedentarism – seeing mobility as an unnatural state.

Yet there *is* a crisis in both the experiences of refugees and migrants and the abdication of responsibility by global, supranational and national governance to address this dehumanization and the wave of xenophobia that reproduces it. Global governance is about the 'management' of migration and is at some distance from the demands of migrants' rights' movements: it is presumed that it can be managed in a technocratic, top-down manner. '"Management", however, leaves little room for participation, and migrants and their movements are thus seen as policy objects with hardly any agency of their own' (Rother 2018: 858, citing Piper and Rother 2012: 1737).

In relation to Europe, Nicholas de Genova calls this 'an unresolved *racial crisis* that derives fundamentally from the postcolonial condition of "Europe" as a whole' (de Genova 2018: 1765; original emphasis). I term this 'the racialized crisis of borders' in order to combine how the shaping of hierarchies of exclusion and inclusion at national borders is (i) both part of the postcolonial condition and (ii) also represents a set of dehumanizing technologies and racist practices extended *within* national borders through restrictions to social welfare entitlements. For example, formal barriers and legal restrictions to accessing health care by asylum seekers and undocumented migrants have legitimated formal *and* informal practices of exclusion to minorities within welfare states (Phillimore et al. 2021). The term intends to capture the conjuncture of three processes of othering at work (whose articulation in the UK I explore in chapter 4):

- the dehumanization of migrants, asylum seekers and refugees at national, supranational and global scales, described above;
- its contagion with heightened national racist policies and practices and their extension to other groups of welfare claimants (internal bordering practices);
- its justification through both the assumptions of the 'post-racial' and the rise of ethno-nationalist populist politics.

Although migrants seeking asylum are not usually the same migrants who end up in, say, care and domestic work, hospitality and agriculture (although they may be), many in both groups are, one way or another, survival migrants. In other words, the distinction between economic migrants and refugees/asylum seekers holds only to a certain degree. They are linked through, first, the political debates that set state sovereignty against human rights and humanitarianism, often in an appeal to a (mythically) homogeneous and/or imperial history and, second, in an everyday struggle to survive in which support has been minimalized.

The Cameroonian postcolonial scholar Achille Mbembe conceptualizes this particular dynamic as 'necropolitics', in which sovereignty carries the power to expropriate a group's humanity and, at its most extreme, life itself (Mbembe 2019). Necropolitics builds on Foucault's concept of biopolitics (state power as the exercise of control over populations) in order to take account of inheritance of imperial and colonial forms of power in contemporary governance in Western late modernity. This results in populations subjected to the status of the living dead (think the migrant and refugee camps, prisons and detention centres). It applies as much to the reduction of rights of asylum seekers, refugees and migrants as it does to the history of environmental degradation which has been built on genocide and enslavement. At the heart of necropolitics is fragility between the systematic creation of (racialized) enemies and an acute existential dependence upon them (as exemplified in the 'crisis of care' above).

Accepted scholarly convention premises that cosmopolitanism has become embedded in Europe's universalist moral traditions, acting especially through the establishment of the European Union as a corrective to nationalist deviations (Calhoun 2009) and replacing the historical conflict and genocide of the Second World War with peace, prosperity and human rights. Yet, as Sian and her colleagues document, by the twenty-first century across Europe there existed a 'high level of everyday, often casual, racial discrimination and the resulting perception across many groups and communities of systemic hostility' (Sian et al. 2013: 9). In many different ways this reflects and is reflected in restrictive material and cultural policies, especially against Muslim women. Take, as an example of the first, rules introduced in the UK in 2014 to prevent migrant workers from claiming housing benefit or job seekers' allowance (a benefit for people who are out of work) for six months after entry and then only on proof of a habitual residence test. And as an example of the second, by 2016 France, Belgium and the Netherlands banned the full-face veil worn by some Muslim women, with some cities in Switzerland, Spain and Italy following suit.

While the Schengen agreement established freedom of movement within member states, encouraging a European citizen sensibility, it has, especially since 2016, tightened its borders to non-EU citizens, creating the sort of illegalization and dehumanization referred to above. By 2019, far-right anti-immigration nationalist parties existed in most European Union member states, with nine countries gaining over 17 per cent of the vote, and in Hungary's case 49 per cent. In Germany the nationalist Alternative for Germany was the biggest opposition party in the Bundestag (BBC 2019a). What is important to bear in mind here is that Europe is not only a cosmopolitan collectivity of nation-states, it is also a collection of former colonial powers (Gilroy 2005). The European Union was formed as decolonization was taking or had just taken place; nonetheless, the making of subsequent multicultural and postcolonial citizenships was wrought through racial and gendered relations of domination and subordination, not only externally in relation to colonized people but also internally with respect to the Roma or indigenous people (Ponzanesi and Blaagaard 2012). By the 1970s, for example, the UK had established rights to citizenship based on (white) patriality. Gurminder Bhambra argues that Europe was a racialized project from the beginning, and it is 'the politics of selective memory that is currently playing out in Europe. In this way, Europe claims rights that belong to its national citizens but need not be shared with others . . . reflecting earlier forms of domination' (Bhambra 2017: 404).

At the same time, from the 1990s, it is the growing assumption of a 'post-racial Europe' that intensifies this amnesia and dilution of policies and practices within the EU to combat racial/migrant/refugee injustices. 'Post-racial' is where multiculturalism presumes a 'splash of colour that becomes a metaphor for a landscape no longer polluted by the horrors of racism' (Sian et al. 2013: 15). This parallels 'the move to racial neoliberalism, where the deregulation of markets exacerbates and embeds racial inequalities' (ibid.: 4). It has created a political discourse in destination countries in which an economic cost–benefit analysis of migration – migrants as units of skilled and unskilled labour – predominates over the ethics of international solidarity, interdependence, hospitality or human rights. On the one hand, in common with the other three crises, all these developments point to the ways in which the discourses of welfare, sustainability, social protection, solidarity and human rights are being jeopardized. On the other, such rights have always been contingent upon constructions of nationality, and what these bordering practices demonstrate is an intense dehumanization – moving the border from human to 'infrahuman' (Gilroy 2014).

Intersections of colliding crises

The final point is that these four crises are interconnected: they have commonalities in constitution and effect, as well as interlocking dynamics. The commonalities include not only endangering sustainability and solidarity for future generations but also that they challenge the patriarchal, racial and eco-social dimensions of neoliberal capitalism and its modes of production, reproduction, consumption, accumulation, commodification and growth of which they are the outcome. A similar observation is made by Gargi Bhattacharyya in her eloquent elaboration of the term 'racial capitalism'. This she defines as constituting three interlocking regimes – exploitation, expropriation, expulsion – which bring together the racial, social reproductive and ecological crises: '[I]n a time of ecological crisis, populations already depleted by exploitation or expropriation or both become increasingly vulnerable to expulsion' (Bhattacharyya 2018: 37).

I have already begun to point to some of the intersections of the four crises. For example, neoliberalism and the financial crisis have given rise to greater precarity of labour and to austerity cuts in social expenditure. These hit women hardest by removing support for caring responsibilities and by its impact on those who work in care services, as well as those who have care needs. Most developed countries have come to depend upon migrant workers to keep down their labour costs of health and social care services enforced by social expenditure cuts, and, at the same time, those rights of migrant workers have been curtailed (see chapter 6). Declining citizenship rights and the backlash against multiculturalism reduce migrant workers to units of labour or 'surplus populations' (Bhattacharyya 2018). Some policies introduced to restrict the rights of asylum seekers or migrants to housing or income support have subsequently been extended to other groups of benefit claimants as part of austerity policies (see chapter 4). This interweaving of people both exploited *and* expropriated that extends beyond (but mostly includes) racialized groups is part of the 'new logic of political subjectivation' of financialized capitalism (Fraser 2016a: 176). In particular, debt – the very motor of the global financial crisis – not only leads to housing dispossession in the developed world but also creates the means by which agricultural workers in developing countries lose their land to corporations growing or finding new forms of profitable energy. In this way they face expulsion, the third consequence of this logic. Expulsion was also the fate of migrant domestic workers sacked by their employers at the beginning of the Covid-19 pandemic (see chapter 6).

Flood disasters in low-income countries hit women hardest in terms of exacerbating and endangering both their caring and earning responsibilities. Furthermore, climate change is currently leading to greater displacement of people and enforced mobility into a world in which mobilities are increasingly restricted. According to the Asian Development Bank, by 2009, several million people had been displaced by rising seas and typhoons in South Asia (cited in Floro 2012). However, the intersection of these two crises needs to be conceptualized and debated carefully. Highlighting the urgency of attention to climate change often resorts to discourses of securitization and the apocalyptic threat of the clamour of displaced refugees and conflicts as resources become scarce. Yet these feed into the very ethno-nationalist 'othering' discourses that have degraded the lives of migrants and refugees. Sager (2020: 15) counsels: 'While climate change will no doubt contribute to migration, this ignores a potentially even more perturbing scenario: a crisis of stasis in which people who do not have access to basic resources are unable to migrate.' In this sense, the pandemic crisis was a dress rehearsal.

Within the present neoliberal paradigm, the market is seen as the dynamic and flexible solution to the financial, environmental, mobility and care crises through green technologies or access to care markets. However, these not only tend to deal with the short-term rather than the long-term, and therefore to postpone the basic tensions they precipitate, but they do not attend to the existing inequalities and distributional imbalances of which they are part (Floro 2012: 22; Pettifor 2020). As Ian Gough has argued, the more that climate change and its policies fall on degraded welfare states, the more the poorest groups will suffer. More globally, this creates a 'tragic contradiction between growth, climatic instability and egregious inequality. All strategies to eliminate global poverty are untenable unless the shares of the poor are raised: in other words unless a more equitable model of the global economy is introduced' (Gough 2017: 83). It is also the case, as I have been arguing in this section, that 'the poor' are created by a postcolonial geo-politics which is regionalized, gendered and racialized and whose capabilities for sustainability are being depleted. Furthermore, the material conditions in which the capacity to provide or receive quality care is depleted is mirrored in the 'carelessness' which underpins the treatment of migrants and refugees.

Both singly and together, the implications of these crises profoundly challenge the principles and practices of capitalism and particularly of neoliberal patriarchal and racial global financialized capitalism. Importantly, they are contested by global and local activists and social movements. Most dramatic have been Extinction Rebellion in 2019 and the second wave of Black Lives Matter in the middle of the global pandemic (see chapter 4). The translation of the Chinese word for crisis is 'danger at the point of juncture', popularly understood as positing both danger and opportunity. In this sense, in these contestations new ethical and political bases for future strategies, alliances and alternatives are being articulated. This is a story I pick up in chapter 7.

Frame 2: The intersections of family, nation, work and nature

This account of intersecting global crises provides a frame for understanding the development of and challenges to neoliberal and austerity welfare states. But it does not indicate the position played by institutional social policies (national, regional or global) in mediating or mitigating these crises, or how some of the logics described in this chapter enter the political or social (b)ordering of society through nation-state welfare. Nor do we get a view of some of the equally salient but hidden aspects, such as the shifts in heteronormativity, or the impact on disabled groups, or what relevance environmental policies have to social policies. It is also the case that none of these crises or their intersections is manifested in national welfare states in the same ways but, rather, depends on their legacies, social formations and forces, and path dependencies. To look at these issues requires a different but related framing that can translate these global crises into an analysis of the specific institutional, discursive and contested social policies and intersecting social relations at the national scale. (See figure 3.1 on p. 54.)

The framework of the intersecting social relations of family, nation, work and nature derives from one that has helped guide my critical

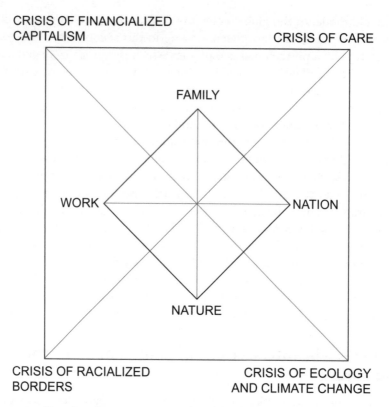

CRISIS OF FINANCIALIZED
CAPITALISM

CRISIS OF CARE

FAMILY

WORK

NATION

NATURE

CRISIS OF RACIALIZED
BORDERS

CRISIS OF ECOLOGY
AND CLIMATE CHANGE

Figure 3.1 Framing the intersections of neoliberal welfare

understanding of both welfare states and the discipline of social policy (for example, Williams 1989, 1992, 1995, 2001, 2012, 2018). The proposition I originally applied is that *family, nation* and *work* constitute central organizing principles that shape and are shaped by welfare states. They are shaped differently in different countries according to particular institutional and cultural legacies, path dependencies and power relations. I explain these before looking at the fourth domain of 'nature'. The three domains signify what stands for family life, care and intimacy (*family*); nation, nationhood, nationality, population and citizenship (*nation*); and paid and unpaid labour (*work*); and the social relations of power and inequality through which they are constituted. It is important to emphasize that the terms are signifiers for domains of difference and complexity; they are not prescriptive. Indeed, in relation to 'family', in chapter 7 I argue, for example, that 'care' represents a more inclusive organizing principle for society than 'family'. As signifiers they recognize that the meanings attached to the three domains are socially constructed and that they change in form and meaning over time and place. They are constituted not only through institutional policies and governmental techniques and practices promoted by political actors (through welfare, education, law, etc.) but also through their material conditions, power relations, (competing) discourses, and different social and cultural norms, beliefs and practices, as well as by claims made by civil society through social movements or campaigns or other social forces. (Appendix I provides a fuller description of the constituents of all four domains and their intersections with welfare states.)

Importantly, the three domains, like the social relations through which they are organized, are not fixed but constantly intersecting – making and remaking each other. For example, the implementation of child-care policies can change the gender composition of the workforce, which in its turn may shift women's and men's understanding of what they want from relationships. The conception of national identity as 'tolerant' because a country is multi-ethnic and has race discrimination policies and same-gender marriage legislation may denote progressive attitudes which nevertheless are rooted in a binary position where the heteronormative and/or ethnically dominant have the power to allow 'others' to be 'tolerated'. In this way, the framework points to the significance of salient and intersecting social relations (class, gender, race, disability, sexuality, age, and so on) within the economic, political, social and governmental aspects of welfare states. They can be understood as the domains that help constitute and challenge the social, material and moral hierarchies of welfare subjects.

At the same time, these are often contradictory, uneven and contested domains, as are the social policies that shape and are shaped by them. Welfare governance in this way can be understood as an ongoing attempt to 'settle' the changing and challenging conditions of family, nation and work. Welfare settlements often reinscribe lines of inclusion, exclusion and marginalization, and these can create fault lines which surface later. For example, as described earlier, the post-war welfare state represented an important set of social policies that served to protect people's welfare and wellbeing from cradle to grave. However, it did so within a context of colonialism and a conception of citizenship in which women in general and men and women migrants from the former colonies were constructed as second-class citizens and excluded from access, directly or indirectly, to many benefits and services. By the 1960s and 1970s, social movements began to challenge these exclusions. The New Right under Margaret Thatcher serves as a second example. The New Right's settlement attempt combined welfare neoliberalism with a social conservatism which linked traditional ideas of the male breadwinner family and a nation of empire to the need for a strong state, less state intervention, and a concerted attack on those who threatened family, nation or work. These threats were embodied in lone mothers, those who defended or practised same-gender relationships, BAME youth, the trade unions and striking miners. This was an intense struggle by the New Right to settle the dislocations and contradictions of deindustrializing post-Fordist conditions of work and the post-traditionalist and postcolonial hierarchies of family and nation. In the end it was not only their economic policies but the mismatch of their attempt to resettle the social by moving backwards in time, compared with the reality of, in particular, new family forms, a multicultural society and working mothers, that contributed to their defeat in 1997 by New Labour, who promised 'modernization' of the economic, the social and the organizational.

The application of the family–nation–work framework has changed over time. At a simple level, it's an aide-mémoire of aspects and dynamics to keep in mind in any social policy analysis that seeks a more complex understanding of contemporary social relations. In this way it also provides the conceptual means to critique social policy ideas and approaches using an intersectional analysis. More broadly it offers a way of capturing the multifaceted and intersecting social dimensions of change and contestation in welfare states at the national or sub-/supranational scale, which are also understood as articulating with global social and economic conditions. These conditions in the twenty-first century, I have suggested, are represented by four intersecting crises. Thus family–nation–work loosely reiterates the crises of care, racialized borders and financialized capitalism. However, it is also necessary to register the crisis of climate change and the environment within the family–nation–work framework in order to take up the serious critiques that have developed within the discipline of social policy in this century. These argue for a radical rethinking of future social policy in terms of the urgent priorities of ecological degradation and climate change. In addition, they introduce a new set of interdependencies and relations of power between human and the non-human and living world. Two of the most developed attempts to rethink this from the perspective of social policy come from Tony Fitzpatrick and Ian Gough, who develop proposals for eco-social policy (or eco-welfare) that bring measures to reduce the risks of climate change and enhance sustainability into alignment with social policy (Fitzpatrick 2011, 2014; Gough 2017; see also Fitzpatrick and Cahill 2002; Snell and Haq 2014, O'Neill et al. 2018). Here I summarize the main arguments for such an alignment.

First is a need to recognize the interdependence between social policies aiming to meet basic needs and reduce inequalities and the achievement of sustainability. The forms of globalized capital accumulation, the constant goal of economic growth, the rise in inequalities and the decline in social welfare infrastructure need to be tackled together. This means understanding the way in which environmental justice is linked to social and economic justice, including intergenerational justice. As the previous section outlined, it is those in the most disadvantaged socio-economic groups and regions of the world, especially women, who are at greatest risk from the effects of climate change (Robinson 2018). Within developed nations, climatic events, air pollution, toxic emissions, fuel poverty, food insecurity, transport costs and an insecure, deregulated housing market affect the welfare of the poorest communities, particularly where degradation of the planet meets racial injustice (Anthony 2017). Each of these encompasses issues to do with environmental policies.

Second is the question as to how sustainability, adaptation and mitigation policies can be developed and implemented in ways that are socially just and equitable. For example, a carbon tax would be regressive on poorer individuals, especially those who have less access to resources to decarbonize their cars or houses. A food or fuel policy that depended on individual household responsibility for reorganization could fall disproportionately on poorer women.

Third, this means addressing how social protection, employment, health, education, social care and wellbeing can be developed in a sustainable manner. For example, at a practical level, how far do employment policies generate sustainable jobs, and how far are houses, schools and hospital buildings run on eco-friendly technology? More broadly, the economic model of developed welfare states has been dependent in part on tax revenues that in turn depend on a growth economy and, with it, the prioritization of productivism, the ethic of paid work and a consumption-based society. Social insurance is a system of dealing with individual and calculable risk, but the effects of climate change (and pandemics) are both unpredictable and can affect large populations and countries. This requires a different approach to security and protection that is geared towards long-term collective solutions and international governance and solidarity. It presupposes the importance of global governance, but also, since many policies to deal with the sources of planetary instability imply changes in everyday practices, forms of participatory democracy at local community level (see chapter 7).

In this short description it becomes clear that the dynamics of family–nation–work and welfare are integral to environmental inequalities and to the determination of future eco-social policy. The framework is therefore extended to family, nation, work and nature (see appendix I). In this way nature signifies the conditions, social relations, changes and challenges of the human and non-human eco-system. The meanings and discourses, policies and practices attached to this domain, as with family, nation and work, shift over time and place.[4] This part of the framework is relatively formative at this stage, reflecting the early integration of social and environmental policies in practice. It seeks to inform the book's orientation, analysis and praxis in order to recognize the argument for integrating social with environmental policy. It does this (i) by developing the intersections of the ecological crisis with other global crises; (ii) by illustrating, where salient, the ways in which environmental injustice intersects with the complexities of welfare-related social inequalities, most notably in an analysis of the Covid-19 pandemic; (iii) by applying an intersectional approach to understanding collective action by environmentalists and others with a view to possibilities for alliances; and (iv) by examining synergies and tensions in the political ethics of care, environmentalism and decoloniality and in their and others' prefigurative programmes for transforming the welfare state into an eco-welfare commons.

Conclusion

This chapter has set out a framework for analysing social policy in the twenty-first century that, first of all, centralizes four key global crises which endanger future sustainability, solidarity and wellbeing and serve to reinforce historical and contemporary gender, racial, class and geo-political inequalities, precarities and dehumanizations. The framing extends from the economic exploitation generated before and after the global financial crisis into the expropriation, expulsions and depletions of human and non-human life associated with the crises of care, ecology and the racializing of transnational borders. These are all part and parcel of the contradictions and contestations in patriarchal, racial and extractivist dimensions of contemporary financialized capitalism. As such, they need to be central to the way we think about the intersecting challenges to both the hegemony of neoliberalism and the shapes of future welfare states.

The second stage of framing involved translating these crises that operate transnationally and globally into a way of capturing the specific and intersecting institutional, discursive and contested social relations that shape and are shaped in national welfare states. Here I have built on my framework of family, nation and work as the key organizing principles of welfare states to include, formatively at this point, nature as a fourth and emerging principle. I argue that the social relations, changes and contestations in these four domains act both to unsettle and to provide the means to settle and restructure welfare states. The importance of this framework is that it allows an understanding of how the four global crises (and their contestations) shape welfare at the national level; it permits a much fuller appreciation of the multiple and intersecting nature and forms of socio-economic inequality, domination, division and subordination, as well as how legitimacy for such impoverishment has been sought, deployed, mitigated and contested.

This and the previous chapter have outlined my theoretical orientations. The following three chapters demonstrate their use in three sets of analysis: the decade of neoliberal austerity in the UK; an understanding of agency and resistance within the social relations of welfare; and the transnational political and social economy of care.

PART II

ANALYSIS

Unsettling/Settling Family–Nation–Work–Nature: From Austerity to Pandemic

Introduction

In 2019, the United Nations special rapporteur on extreme poverty and human rights concluded that austerity in the UK was both an ideological and an economic strategy:

> Although the United Kingdom is the world's fifth largest economy, one fifth of its population (14 million people) live in poverty, and 1.5 million of them experienced destitution in 2017. Policies of austerity introduced in 2010 continue largely unabated, despite the tragic social consequences. Close to 40 per cent of children are predicted to be living in poverty by 2021. Food banks have proliferated; homelessness and rough sleeping have increased greatly; tens of thousands of poor families must live in accommodation far from their schools, jobs and community networks; life expectancy is falling for certain groups; and the legal aid system has been decimated. (UN 2019: 3)

In the same year, the United Nations Human Rights Office's special rapporteur on contemporary forms of racism, racial discrimination, xenophobia and related intolerance said of the UK:

> Reliable reports have shown that the austerity measures have been disproportionately detrimental to members of racial and ethnic minority communities, who are also the hardest hit by unemployment . . . At the same time, racial and ethnic minorities are overrepresented in criminal justice enforcement and underrepresented within the institutions that adjudicate crime and punishment. (UN Human Rights Office 2019: 1)

In 2017 the concluding observations of the Committee on the Rights of Persons with Disabilities on the UK (CRPD 2017) highlighted insufficient legislation and support to promote independent living; lack of accessible services and community facilities; lack of funding to local authorities; and, in particular, lack of support for parents of disabled children.

The decade of austerity saw three administrations: a Conservative–Liberal Democrat Coalition, led by David Cameron, Theresa May's Conservative government, and, at the end of 2019, three years after the Brexit referendum, a Conservative majority led by Boris Johnson. In many ways these governments continued New Labour's deregulated economy and policies of privatization, public–private partnerships, marketization, 'welfare to work', a pushback on multiculturalism and asylum seekers' and migrants' rights, the responsibilization of individuals and families for their wellbeing and opportunities, and a growing technological awareness of climate change.

However, it also differed in a number of significant respects. Major cuts to public services and benefit levels were rationalized as a fiscal response to the financial crisis. These hit the capacity of local authorities to provide local services. Council spending between 2010 and 2018 fell by over one-fifth on average – more in the North and in urban areas – hitting especially housing and social care (IFS 2019). In addition, an intensification of financialization saw services such as pensions, housing, education, child care and health care funded through access to finance capital, which in turn used these services as a source of profit accumulation, moving from New Labour's quasi-social investment state to a social investment market (Dowling 2017). One example, whose outcomes the pandemic exposed, is the NHS reform enacted by the 2012 Health and Social Care Act, which replaced primary care trusts with clinical commissioning groups. The aim was that these would promote efficiency through market competition and would expand the role of private companies. This re-created the NHS as a fragmented collection of public and private enterprises in which the public share of the health service dwindled (for the full story, see Leys 2016).

Between 2012 and 2019 the number of NHS beds fell by 5 per cent against increased demand, as well as the pressure created by insufficient facilities in social care to deal with the discharge of older and frail patients (King's Fund 2020a). An acknowledged crisis in the NHS by the middle of the decade led to two emergency injections of funding, amounting to £4.5 billion by 2019. However, much of this money went to pay the continuing costs of private finance initiative companies' contracts to build the hospitals required by the NHS. Between 2010 and 2015 these companies made pre-tax profits of £831 million (CHPI 2017).

Cuts to income support had devastating social and economic consequences for poverty, homelessness and food insecurity, as described in the UN references above. By the second half of the decade, it became clear that certain social groups were particularly affected by austerity, among them women and children, especially low-income and lone parents and women of colour, disabled people, migrant workers and asylum seekers. In 2020 a review of health equity in England since 2010 showed that life expectancy had stalled for the first time in a hundred years. For women on low incomes living in deprived communities, it had gone into reverse, and intersections between socio-economic status, ethnicity and racism had intensified inequalities in health for BAME groups (IHE 2020). Women with families, especially lone mothers on a single income, found it more difficult to access affordable accommodation and became at greater risk of homelessness. This was particularly significant for migrant women and women experiencing domestic abuse and violence (WBG 2020a). Reports of and convictions for domestic abuse have both increased in recent years (ONS 2018a). Together, these developments marked an increase in multiple forms of insecurity (Edmiston 2018; Lister 2021), all of which were revealed and expanded by the pandemic.

This chapter provides an analysis of the period that starts with the consequences of the global financial crisis for government social policy from 2010 and ends with the global pandemic crisis of 2020, which was to amplify the impact of austerity welfare and associated inequalities. The analysis uses the framework of family–nation–work–nature intersections, as outlined in chapter 3, as a way of understanding how the four global crises around finance, care, the racialization of borders, and environmental neglect became constituted through national social policy, and the effects that these have had on specific groups of welfare subjects. It shows how these domains have been, at different times and in different configurations and with varying salience, central vectors in the social governing projects of austerity welfare.

The chapter examines the decade in four parts, which I summarize here to provide an overall map of the arguments. The first part focuses on policies around family life, care and intimacy and their intersections with work, class, race and nation. I show how parenting policies became a way of reproducing neoliberal values of self-responsibility and choice while also creating binaries of blame between respectable and risky families. The discourses surrounding these gave legitimacy to cuts and caps in welfare reform that were to affect women and children in particular. These served to change the relations between citizens and state through harsh forms of sanctions-backed welfare conditionality in which eligibility to benefits became dependent upon claimants behaving in prescribed ways and penalized by removal of rights if they failed. This marked a much stricter workfare policy of getting people 'off welfare and into (any) work', as well as a retreat from the safety-net concept of welfare provision as support, such as for the wellbeing and care of children or as mitigation against hardship. I show how this was just one of the ways in which women's responsibilities to care became subordinated to the requirements of paid work in an attempt to settle an accommodation to the growth in precarious work. The devaluation and depletion of care was intensified in other ways too: the neglect of social care and its paid workers; the diminishing of children's rights to wellbeing; and the financialization of the care sector. While women suffered in the austerity decade, new qualitative and quantitative intersectional research showed clearly how a combination of new financial cuts and old processes of sexism and racism hit BAME women particularly hard.

As a link between family, intimacy and nation, I also look at how the LGBT Action Plan introduced in 2018 allowed for a representation of the UK as a tolerant and diverse nation. This is far from the divisive, racist and disablist understanding of the nation that emerges in the second part of the chapter, which focuses on how 'bordering practices' became institutionalized within a range of policies, procedures and practices in health and welfare services and how this was made possible by the ideological context of the UK as a 'post-racial' society. While such policies build specifically on colonial ideologies of subordination and ethno-nationalist ideas of belonging, as in the case of the Windrush betrayal, they applied their technology to other groups such as Roma and disabled people.

Running through these practices is the creep of necropolitics, on the one side, and the growing dependence of government on ethno-nationalist rhetoric and morally authoritarian governance, on the other. Both emerge in the third part of the chapter, which uses three cases to illustrate the intersections between necropolitics, the 'nation', the effects of neoliberal and austerity welfare and, in the last case, 'nature'. They are Grenfell Tower, the welfare politics of Brexit and the Covid-19 pandemic. These were moments of unsettling/settling where the politics of whose lives matter and whose do not became public, none more than in the Black Lives Matter protests of the summer of 2020.

In all the cases I examine in the chapter other aspects of governance emerge. The attempts to seek consent for these developments have involved not only demonization but also a 'shape-shifting' of apparently liberal values such as 'fairness', 'living within our means' and 'levelling up' which sought public legitimacy for policies that did the opposite: 'hostile environment' 'securitization' or 'troubled families'. In addition, the implementation of these austerity policies has been as messy, incompetent and opportunistic as much as they have been politically focused, and born out of 'institutional indifference' (Lister 2018), 'carelessness' (House of Commons 2020) and a combination of 'displacement, layering, and drift' (McEnhill and Taylor-Gooby 2018). They represent the political splicing and reassembling of different policy ideas, often untested, with appeals to different social forces and, until the 2020 pandemic, a cavalier refutation of experts and expertise (Clarke and Newman 2012, 2017). However, if the pandemic shifted this, it also revealed chaos, limited leadership, blame avoidance, studied indifference and even greater incompetence by virtue of the hollowed-out capacities of the state.[1]

At the same time, none of this should imply settlement, acquiescence or stability, for internal contradictions and external challenges have continued. In the concluding part I look at examples of areas that responded to different pressures and also, in recognition of the multinational UK, at Scottish policy on social security. Overall, I seek to demonstrate how successive governments have used a variety of policies, techniques, practices, moral rhetorics and narrative structures that have, directly and indirectly, attempted to consolidate and settle the conditions, crises and challenges attached to family, nation, work and, latterly, nature within its neoliberal austerity project.

1: Work, family and nation: the depletion and devaluation of care

Throughout this century, 'hard-working families' has been a political and moral rallying cry summoning female and male parents together with any adult children (of whom two-thirds aged between twenty and twenty-nine still live with their parents; Hill and Hirsch 2019). Many of the core areas of family policy – child benefits, parental leave, early childhood education and care services (ECEC) – have been based on or directed towards engagement in the labour market. While some reflect concerns with equal sharing between partners (shared parental leave and pay introduced in 2015), they also register a move away from universal support for families and children towards greater targeting of low-income families. In this respect they mirror similar shifts in other developed welfare societies (Daly and Ferragina 2018). In the UK, however, family policies have also shoehorned into place many aspects of neoliberal and austerity welfare and, in doing so, have reinscribed unequal social relations within and between families.

The term 'hard-working families' mobilizes paid work as a central moral principle in opposition to the 'welfare dependency' of economic inactivity.

At the same time it positions other unpaid activities, such as care, as subservient to paid work but also subject to discipline and judgement. This hierarchy is reflected within paid work, where care workers and cleaners are among the lowest paid and, until the 2020 pandemic, the least recognized. This section looks at these seemingly contradictory developments: the direct and indirect responsibilization of parents for the flourishing or failure of their family members; the depletion and devaluation of care as support, practice, commitment and employment; the intersecting gendered and racialized inequalities of austerity welfare; and policy responses to LGBTQI claims for equal civil rights.

Parenting: responsibilization and blame

Policy and debate around parenting affords a good example of the cultural and political formation of an anti-welfare common sense and the ways in which media and political discourses have worked to harness public support for restrictive welfare policies. These dynamics build on political traditions of identifying an 'underclass' set apart culturally and morally from the rest of society (Welshman 2013) and the construction of a 'parenting crisis' whose gender neutrality often cloaks the specific targeting of mothers and runs 'like a golden thread through a much longer history of neoliberal politics' (Jensen 2018: 12). More widely, they illustrate the attempts to reproduce neoliberal values of individualism, competition and self-responsibility within and across families, paradoxically in the goal of all pulling together for austerity.

Austerity was announced in 2010 by the prime minister of the Coalition government, David Cameron, in these terms:

> Freedom, fairness, responsibility: those are the values that drive this government, and they are the values that will drive our efforts to deal with our debts and turn this economy around.
> So yes, it will be tough.
> But we will get through this together – and Britain will come out stronger on the other side. (Cameron 2010: 5, cited in Clarke and Newman 2012: 304)

Binaries of blame

Here the value of 'fairness', generally associated with social democratic or social justice politics, is thrown together with 'freedom' and 'responsibility', two traditional Conservative values, to defend the 'tough' measures that were about to be taken in an attempt to restore the indebted post-crisis economy. The statement, and others like it, recalls the solidarity and sacrifice of post-war austerity of 'all pulling together'. The discourse went on to locate 'unfairness' as the shared experience of hard-working families perceiving others (their neighbours, families without work, migrants) milking the benefits system, getting 'something for nothing', exploiting the very freedoms that taxpayers granted them. Responsibilities were matched with implicit and sometimes explicit blame – for poverty, worklessness, ill health/disability, or one's children's conduct/failure. The result was to establish a set of binaries between families.

If one set of binaries was to position the families that paid their state taxes against those who needed state support, then another was to represent the former as 'resourceful' as against the latter as 'risky' (Jensen and Tyler 2015; Jupp 2017b; Jensen 2018). This was echoed in the employment binary of 'strivers' and 'shirkers' coined by the then chancellor, George Osborne, and amplified by the notion of 'troubled families'. The important point is that these were not mere words; they became the rationale for a series of policies with social, material and emotional effects.

The 'tough' measures taken included, as mentioned earlier, a series of cuts, caps and freezes in benefits established in 2013 in the Welfare Reform Act. In 2017 there was a further cap to means-tested support, limiting it to the first two children. Analysing the political and media discourse leading to these cuts, Tracey Jensen and Imogen Tyler (2015) show how this attack on larger families and children's rights resulted from the pincer-like power of media and politicians. A media campaign which focused initially on the shocking case of a man who committed a revenge arson attack that unintentionally killed six of his children became an emblematic story about abuse by benefit claimants. Newspapers ratcheted up the (factually incorrect) amount of benefits that had been coming into the man's household. 'Benefit broods' was the term used to generalize from this exceptional and horrific case to all large families receiving benefits. The theme was picked up by government ministers to defend their forthcoming cuts. In April 2013 the chancellor said, in a statement to be echoed and reinforced later by the prime minister, 'I think there is a question for government and for society about the welfare state – and the taxpayers who pay for the welfare state – *subsidising lifestyles like that*' (cited by Jensen and Tyler 2015: 477; their emphasis). Being on benefits was aligned with a 'lifestyle choice' and was intended to incite the moral disgust of 'responsible' families, especially those who were themselves struggling. Such stigmatization became the vector though which cuts and caps, the means by which a generation of welfare claimants were made to pay for the financial crisis, were legitimated.

Troubling families

The 'Troubled Families' initiative had already laid some of this thematic groundwork. In August 2011, following the shooting dead in Tottenham of Mark Duggan, a father of four children, by police who believed (wrongly) that he was armed, rioting then spread to other parts of London and the country, with burning and looting, over 3,000 arrests, five deaths, and damage to the value of some £200 million (Jensen 2018). Subsequent research found that the participants were significantly more likely to be in poverty and to live in deprived neighbourhoods and that the police shooting had sparked longstanding grievances about distrust in the police and racist stop and search procedures (Lewis et al. 2011, cited in Jensen 2018: 2–7). The government responded to the events through the discourse of bad parenting – in Cameron's words: 'a complete lack of responsibility, a lack of proper parenting, a lack of proper upbringing, a lack of proper ethics, a lack of proper morals' (Cameron 2011, cited in Jensen 2018: 3).

This unsettling moment of early austerity was met through the Department of Communities and Local Government's 'Troubled Families' programme (2012–15). The identification of those families who bear the material and psychic bruising of community deprivation as the cause of that deprivation has a long history in concepts of an 'underclass' (Welshman 2013). In this case, 'worklessness' became viewed as a key behavioural characteristic rather than as a condition of structural unemployment. What was different was that the 'tough' approach was wrapped up in notions of holistic support, opportunities and fiscal realism. Local authorities, strapped for cash, were offered a payments-by-results approach in keeping with a rational economic market model. Accordingly, Eric Pickles, minister for communities and local government, managed to fold all these together in reporting that the programme gave 'new opportunities for families to turn their lives around . . .; more economic security for local communities blighted by worklessness; and more economic stability for taxpayers as we reduce the bills for social failure and get this country living within its means' (DCLG 2014, cited in Jupp 2017b: 269). In fact, the programme's evaluation found that, 'across a wide range of outcomes, covering the key objectives of the programme – employment, benefit receipt, school attendance, safeguarding and child welfare – we were unable to find consistent evidence that the Troubled Families Programme had any significant or systematic impact' (DCLG 2016: 49).

This should not underestimate the commitments at local level to support families. According to another study, local interpretations and actions were some way removed from political claims and rhetoric (Hayden and Jenkins

2014; see also Crossley 2016). At the same time, social workers have also found themselves under pressure from different forces to ensure child protection. Progressive moves to recognize children's rights marked by the UN Convention on the Rights of the Child, ratified by the UK in 1992, and the creation of a commissioner for children in 2004, along with high-profile cases of failure to provide protection (e.g. the tragic death of Victoria Climbié in 2001) have heightened this pressure. However, as Brid Featherstone and her colleagues argue, under the move to a 'Troubled Families' philosophy, the principle of children's rights took on a neoliberal twist which decoupled the child from their close relationships and reduced the emotional meaning of those relationships to parenting skills. Here, a construction of children as individuals 'unanchored in networks and communities . . . with superficial understandings of the importance of histories, attachments and legacies' created conditional and punitive encounters for families – that unless they (particularly mothers) shaped up their children would be shipped out (Featherstone et al. 2014: 29). As I describe later, this existence of an underlying threat within services that offer essential support became even more intense for migrant mothers (Humphris 2019).

Responsible choices

It is not the case either that austerity governance let 'resourceful' families off the hook of individualized parenting responsibilization, although pressures have been more covert. Families found they had choices. In popular culture, the structural constraints upon women ('interrupted' careers, lower pay, greater care responsibilities) were represented as individual choices to manage their lives: health, home and motherhood became sites for exercising the moral choices of self-management (Rottenburg 2018). Policies for reconciling work and care continued through austerity. Maternity leave was extended and shared parental leave and statutory shared parental pay introduced in 2015. This appeared to mark a recognition for more gender-equal parenting, except that, under the rubric of offering parents choice, no quota for fathers was set (as in other countries) and the effect was minimal; 2 per cent of those taking leave in 2016 were men (Windebank 2017). Children's success (or failure) was also subject to responsible choices – of schools, of parenting patterns. Even social mobility, a term so parsed in structuralism, became reinterpreted in part as parental responsibility to pursue opportunities for their children. In 2011 the Child Poverty Commission became the Social Mobility and Child Poverty Commission. In 2015 'Child Poverty' was dropped. By 2017 four of its commissioners had resigned, citing lack of government commitment to its work. A proposal to change its name and focus to 'social justice' was rejected by Theresa May's government. In contrast, in 2019 Scotland managed to bridge the two approaches by launching the Social Justice and Fairness Commission.

The depletion and devaluation of care

The global crisis of care manifests itself in particular ways in national contexts. In an important essay, Shirin Rai and her colleagues conceptualize 'depletion through social reproduction' (DSR) as a way of unpacking the care crisis – its different contexts; its different sites, individual, household and communities; and its effects on human wellbeing (Rai et al. 2014). Crucial to this are (in the main) women – their bodies, and their time, support and energy to fulfil care responsibilities to ensure human flourishing. Women also constitute the majority of paid workers providing services (cooking, cleaning, social and health care) that ensure repair, renewal and flourishing. By devaluation of care, I refer, as noted above, to the place that the practice, ethics of, and commitment to care occupy in social policies and the particular effect on the welfare of children and those who, through older age or disability, require care and/or support.

One illustration of both depletion and devaluation of care is the 2012 Welfare Reform Act. Some background: the Act streamlined existing financial support benefits for working-age people into a single Universal Credit paid monthly in arrears. This was in part a response to a fragmented system, which nevertheless enabled the introduction of new harsh forms of sanctions-backed welfare conditionality. In this, eligibility to benefits is dependent upon out-of-work claimants agreeing to a contract to seek paid work and in which they are punished by restrictions in benefits if they fail. Such policy is based on an assumption of economic rationality that behaviour will change under financial incentive, explaining worklessness, low pay or homelessness in terms of individual behaviour rather than the intimate, social and environmental context of people's lives. Combined with a series of cuts and caps on benefits since 2010 and a freeze from 2016 (meaning a fall of 6.7 per cent for an out-of-work lone parent between 2010 and 2019; House of Commons 2019), this has been more effective in *creating* poverty and even destitution, including homelessness, fuel poverty and food hunger, than in getting people into sustained paid work. The effects have been particularly harsh for lone mothers, disabled people, migrants and homeless people (Dwyer 2016, 2018). However, the punitive and disciplining measures which impel welfare subjects to be 'off welfare and into paid work' have been institutionalized and contractualized such that they outweigh rights (Lister 2011). This is about 'redrawing the boundaries of desert whilst supplying compliant labour for a "flexible" labour market' (Morris 2020: 276). (Some of these measures are mitigated in Scotland – see pp. 116–17).

The gendered effects of this policy in relation to the intersection of family, care and work are significant (Bennett 2012; Fawcett Society 2015; Andersen 2019). The policy requires parent couples to identify one 'responsible carer', an identity automatically attributed to a lone parent. When the youngest child of the 'responsible carer' (usually the mother) is aged one, the carer is then *required* to start to discuss transition back to work, and by the time the child is aged three or four to have started a maximum of sixteen hours a week, rising to full-time when the child is thirteen. Research on mothers on Universal Credit found, first, far from reconciling tensions between work and care, the requirements and threat of sanctions put enormous pressure on mothers of young children because the availability and costs of child care did not necessarily cover the time and energy needed to meet either their responsibility to job-search or the resources available to them to access child care (Andersen 2019). Second, the terms of the contract they entered into and the nature of the scrutiny they experienced overwhelmingly positioned the responsibility for their unpaid child care as subordinate to the requirement to enter paid work. Far from a choice or a right to enter paid work, the contract turned willingness into compulsion under duress, and mothers felt their child-care responsibilities were devalued as a 'barrier' to employment. In other words, their care was devalued and their capacities were depleted. Furthermore, in aiming to relieve women of their 'dependency' on the state, it subjected them to unprecedented scrutiny and control (Millar and Bennett 2017).

Subordinating care to paid work
Taking into account the precarious nature of much of the work available, this adds another layer of insecurity to mothers' lives as well as those of their children. While many unemployed people would prefer the dignity of a wage to benefits, this articulation of welfare with work has also been about 'settling' an accommodation to the nature of paid work under financialized capitalism. In this century, forms of non-standard employment have increased in labour markets across the world (ILO 2016) and have intersected in particular ways with migrant, age, racial and gender inequalities. In the UK, women and younger workers are more likely to be in non-standard employment (ONS 2018b). This positions young workers

as dependent on their families and without a secure stable labour market future. Non-standard employment includes work on temporary and fixed contracts, as well as part-time, on-call, sometimes involving zero hours, subcontracted and agency work and self-employment, where the gender pay gap is 32 per cent (O'Reilly et al. 2015). Women constituted 69 per cent of low-paid earners in 2020; they are less likely than men to be in full-time work and increasingly more likely to be in self-employment (WBG 2020a). This is also shaped by racial inequalities. In general the pay gap between BAME and White workers has hardly moved over the past thirty years. It is at 9 per cent for Black male non-graduates and 17 per cent for Black male graduates; for BAME women, graduate and non-graduate, there is a 10 per cent gap (Clark and Shankley 2020). Poorer working conditions have been generated through both greater deregulation of the labour market and weaker employment rights and also shaped in some sectors by new digital technologies (as in the 'gig economy') and automation. While some of this work offers flexibility for those with higher educational qualifications, it poses problems of lack of security or chances for skill acquisition and progression and lower wages for others. Ninety per cent of workers in the gig economy earn less than £10,000 per annum (DBEIS 2018), involving uncertainty and lack of control over hours, less safe working environments and less representation (Moore et al. 2017). Self-employment is less a choice than a factor of discrimination in fixed paid employment for many BAME earners (Clark and Shankley 2020). Unsurprisingly, by 2019, more than half of those households in poverty were in paid work (JRF 2020).

The Welfare Reform Act moves away from the male breadwinner model, yet these practices reproduce women's disadvantaged labour market position by requiring them to enter paid work on male terms, unencumbered by other responsibilities (Andersen 2019). However, the eligibility to allowances of second earners (usually women) is set higher, reducing the incentive to enter paid work. There are also aspects of policy which reinforce the vulnerability of women living with domestic abuse, such as paying benefits into a single bank account (see WBG 2019, which also contains important recommendations). Simultaneously, by drawing partners of welfare recipients into the mandatory work regime for the first time, it reaggregates couple parents as a single unit, where a mother's access to welfare benefits can be jeopardized not only by her own behaviour but by her partner's as well, affecting the whole family's security.

Diminishing children's rights to wellbeing

The devaluation of care and its subservience to paid work and the market is illustrated by policies affecting those most in need of care and support. First is the decreasing commitment to *children's* rights to welfare. New Labour had a social investment approach to children which saw them as requiring support as workers and citizens of the future (Lister 2003; Williams and Roseneil 2004). A commitment to end child poverty by 2020 included the Sure Start programme, which provided child-care support for families in the most deprived areas (Anning and Ball 2008). After 2010 the budget was merged with other programmes, and funding was reduced by almost a half – and even more for youth services, which was cut by 65 per cent. By 2018 up to 1,000 Sure Start centres had closed or scaled down their services, predominantly in the more deprived areas (Smith et al. 2018). Further to this, the aim of early years education and care became focused on making young children 'school ready' rather than on encouraging creativity and imagination (Burgess-Macy et al. 2021). In 2016 the commitment to end child poverty was dropped. In addition, child tax credits were capped, so that only the first two children of those born after 2017 are eligible. By 2019, 600,000 children had been affected by this policy, 59 per cent of them in working households (HM Revenue & Customs and DWP 2019).

The intersection of migration with childhood affords a further example of a hardening against children's rights to welfare in favour of the objective of restricting migration. Those undocumented or unaccompanied children and young people whose claims (or parents' claims) to asylum or settlement have been refused or held in abeyance can be denied access to aspects of health care, accommodation, post-16 education, and legal help (Coram Children's Legal Centre 2013). Many find themselves at the discretion of local providers, where access to support is often premised on a 'culture of disbelief' of the child's experiences, and a legal system that is complex (Children's Society 2012). This is in contravention of their rights under the UN Convention on the Rights of the Child. Even for those who have rights to register as British citizens, the costs (in 2019) were £1,012 per person. Without that, they can be denied work, education or social security as they transition to adulthood (Refugee and Migrant Children's Consortium 2018).[2]

In different ways, indifference about the impact of policies on vulnerable groups is reflected in the provision for children with special educational needs. In spite of the introduction of Educational Health and Care Plans, budgetary and testing pressures on schools have contributed to over 8,500 children with special educational needs not being allocated a school place and being schooled or looked after at home (Ward 2019). Similarly, in 2017/18 there were 75,420 looked-after children, the biggest annual rise in eight years, while local authority funding and provision was reduced. The biggest increase was in those aged sixteen+ who require residential accommodation. The independent sector now provides 75 per cent of children's homes, and these have merged to constitute three main companies who make profits of around £251 million per annum, while smaller providers find it hard to survive. However, such growth has been dependent on major loans. The Local Government Association (2019) warned that many homes were financially unstable, threatening the sort of collapse that happened in old people's private care provision when Four Seasons and Southern Cross providers went bankrupt (Rowland 2019). The consequences of the necessity to make a profit here has been at odds with the principles of continuity and variety and proximity of care required by these vulnerable groups and their families. Reports of abuse and the death of disabled residents in Winterbourne View and Whorlton Hall have heightened concern about the way care of learning disabled groups is devalued (BBC 2019b).

Markets and the depletion and devaluation of care

What also shifted was the more intense development of private markets and financialization in care provision with a lowering of quality and affordability. In 2013–14 the child-care market was worth £4.9 billion (Gyimah 2015, cited in Lewis and West 2016). By 2018, 84 per cent of child care for under threes was in the private sector, with a growth of international chains increasing their share of the market (Penn 2018). Private-market child care is costly for parents: between 2008 and 2017 child-care costs had risen four times more than wages (TUC 2018). In part response to this, in 2017 the Conservative government extended 15 hours' free child care to two-year-olds from low-income families in addition to the existing 30 hours for three- and four-year-olds. However, in aiming to expand the child-care market, governments deregulated registration and inspection procedures, took away local authorities' quality-assurance procedures, relaxed carer–child ratios, and dropped earlier plans to raise the skills of child-care workers, all of which has undermined quality (Lewis and West 2016; Burgess-Macey et al. 2021). This particularly affects children in deprived areas, whose access to child care is usually limited to private, voluntary and independent provision. This is less well subsidized (by those parents who can pay) than in wealthier areas, has higher ratios and lower-skilled staff than in state nurseries, and is less competent in catering for language, literacy and diversity needs (Mathers and Smees 2014).

Social care for older people has consistently been recognized to be in crisis (King's Fund 2019). In 2011, the Dilnot Commission Report on Social Care laid out proposals for the funding of social care to be discussed and acted upon as a matter of urgency. A decade later, a promised Green Paper on social care had not appeared, and promises in 2019 to 'get social care done' were not fulfilled in the first pre-Corona crisis budget in March 2020. Principles relating to empowerment in the 2014 Care Act and new personalization plans intended to tailor old people's care support to their needs were restricted to what the local market can provide and limited by reductions in local authority funding and the number of care workers, the closure of day centres and other collective forms of care. A report from Age UK (2019) described this as a 'dysfunctional care market', which led to some areas of the country having seriously insufficient care services to meet local needs whether people could pay or not. This involved hospital beds not being available owing to a shortage of specialist staff, an acute lack of care home beds, and a crisis in domiciliary care where hours of care had been reduced by 3 million between 2016 and 2019. This depletion of care in local communities has fallen to family members to provide support. The support by 5.4 million carers (mainly but by no means exclusively women) saves the state more than £132 billion per year (Toynbee and Walker 2020: 188).

Also important in this picture of the devaluation and depletion of care are how the conditions of the social care workforce, of whom 83 per cent are women, 17 per cent are non-nationals and 21 per cent are BAME workers, contribute to this crisis. They are among the lowest 10 per cent of all workers – the median pay in March 2019 was £8.10 per hour, and a quarter of all social care workers were on zero hours contracts, rising to over half for those in domiciliary care. Over 90 per cent of work is in the independent sector. The workforce shortage was estimated at 7.8 per cent in 2019 (or 122,000 jobs) (Skills for Care 2020). All these aspects were to become critical both in the pandemic and in changes to immigration rules (see below). These experiences also highlight how women in general and BAME women in particular have been hit by austerity measures.

Women and austerity: intersecting inequalities of 'race', gender and poverty

As early as 2012 the Fawcett Society calculated the toll of austerity on women's lives, as they are particularly affected by the combination of cuts to public-sector jobs, wages and pensions; cuts to services, especially those provided by local authorities such as gender-based violence services and voluntary groups; and cuts in legal aid and support for reproductive health (Fawcett Society 2012; Women's Resource Centre 2016). In contrast, assessments of the Treasury and the Department of Work and Pensions of the effect of spending reviews and reforms were considered limited, poor in quality, lacking direction in their understanding of consultation and inequalities (WBG and Runnymede Trust 2017: 7). This was despite concerns from parliamentary committees and earlier reports – another case of institutional indifference and incompetence.

As a response, in 2017 the Women's Budget Group, a network of leading feminist economists, researchers, policy experts and campaigners, in combination with the Runnymede Trust, the UK's leading independent race equality think tank, produced a report entitled *Intersecting Inequalities: The Impact of Austerity on Black and Minority Ethnic Women in the UK*. The report is important not only for its results but also for pioneering a methodology of quantitative measurement of the cumulative intersectional effects (here, race, poverty and gender) of austerity policies (welfare benefits, taxation changes and public spending cuts). It stands as an example of how marginalized inequalities can be revealed through such methods. The quantitative analysis was combined with a qualitative study in Coventry and Manchester which was carried out in co-production with trained peer researchers from those communities (WBG and Runnymede Trust 2017: appendices 1–3).

BAME women are a heterogeneous group, but there are certain characteristics they share which are aggravated by the principles and measures of austerity, especially the work-related conditionality and cuts and caps of the Welfare Reform Act. They are more likely to be living in poverty: in 2015/16, 50 per cent of Bangladeshi, 46 per cent of Pakistani and 40 per cent of Black/African/Caribbean households lived in poverty compared with 19 per cent of White British households (JRF 2017, cited in WBG and Runnymede Trust 2017). They face a combination of sexism and racism in the labour market and face higher rates of unemployment, even accounting for qualifications. In 2014 Black households were more likely to be headed by a lone parent: 91 per cent compared with the England and Wales average of 11 per cent (ibid.). They were more likely than White households to be in social or privately rented housing and concentrated in urban centres and therefore particularly affected by local housing allowances no longer being linked to actual rents, rendering those in urban areas worse off. This is also an issue that intersects with the effects of climate change on health: 'Heat stress, air pollution or carbon emission, are higher in urban than in rural settings. Hence, humans living in urban areas are at particular risk for higher morbidity and mortality and reduced well-being' (Krefis et al. 2018).

None of the tax cuts (increasing the personal allowance, corporation and fuel duty cuts) has improved the situation of poor people in general or BAME women in particular. Indeed, by 2020 these changes had cost poor people £37 billion, whereas the £41 billion of tax cuts benefited mainly the better off. Asian women lost on average over £2,200 of their net income (19 per cent) by 2020; for Black women, this was £2,000 and 14 per cent respectively; and for Black and Asian lone mothers it was £4,000 (15 per cent) and £4,200 (17 per cent) respectively (WBG and Runnymede Trust 2017: 3).

However, these losses are compounded by cuts in public services. Cuts to local government (between 30 and 50 per cent between 2010 and 2017) represented cuts of about £222 per head in the most deprived areas. This has been particularly harsh in social care. In addition, the freezing of schools spending together with efficiency savings on the NHS have passed on financial and health costs that affect the poorest most. Lack of funding has seen a decline in specialist BME voluntary organizations (Craig et al. 2019). These and other local cuts, in transport, Sure Start centres and specialist refuges, hit women and poor families harder. Cuts to social and health services impacted those women who work in them, and, here too, BAME women are a significant part of the labour force. BAME women have particular health needs compared with both BAME men and White women (WBG and Runnymede Trust 2017: 32). Cuts in social care have disproportionately affected BAME populations (CarersUK 2011). In education, two of the provisions that have been supportive to BAME women are the Education Maintenance Allowance, which provided support for post-16 education, and English for Speakers of Other Languages, both of which have been cut and/or restricted in access (WBG and Runnymede Trust 2017: 34–6; see also summary by Pearson 2019). Overall, the decline in average living standards of these cuts has been 7.5 per cent and 6.8 per cent for Black and Asian families respectively and 5 per cent for White families (WBG and Runnymede Trust 2017: 4). Together with the benefit and tax cuts, the poorest families' living standards will have dropped by 17 per cent, those of lone mothers by 18 per cent, and those of Black and Asian households by 19.2 per cent and, by 2020, 20.1 per cent.

The qualitative data in this report reveals the human immiseration of these statistics, where women face constant existential precarity and anxiety. This is augmented in a different study which includes migrant women (Bassel and Emejulu 2018). These authors' starting point is that, while it has sharpened the precarity of minority women, austerity represents continuity as well as a change. Continuity refers not only to the material injustices outlined above but also to the ongoing problem of invisibility ('normative absence and pathological presence' – Phoenix 1987). This applies both to their experience of austerity *and* to their resistance against it. Thus, they argue that 'Centring minority women's articulations of both crisis and resistance is a way to subvert the dominant narrative of both "crisis" and "activism"' (Bassel and Emejulu 2018: 10). The articulation between these two dynamics of invisibility shows why such work on intersecting inequalities is important to challenge prevailing ideas. Bassel and Emejulu argue that the hegemonic representation of the consequences of austerity is of a squeezed middle class and a deprived and disadvantaged white working class, especially in the deindustrialized regions of the North. It was such representations of austerity that enabled the Brexit campaign, which I discuss later, to lend legitimacy to hostility towards immigration.

Diversity, inequalities and nation
Both in keeping but also at odds with the compound effects of difference discussed so far in this section is this statement from the minister for women and equalities, Penny Mordaunt, in 2018 in the introduction to the *LGBT Action Plan*: 'This Government is committed to making the UK a country that works for everyone. We want to strip away the barriers that hold people back so that everyone can go as far as their hard work and talent can take them. The UK today is a diverse and tolerant society' (GEO 2018).

The millennium marked significant recognition for many identifying with LGBTQI+ struggles for civil rights and seemed a long way from Section 28/2A of the 1988 Local Government Act, which prohibited the 'promotion of homosexuality' in schools and libraries. This was repealed in 2000 in Scotland and in 2003 in England and Wales. Civil partnerships were introduced for same-gender couples in 2004 and marriage in 2013 (2019 in Northern Ireland). Also in 2004, the Gender Recognition Act permitted trans people, upon approval through a Gender Recognition Certificate, to change their birth certificates and marry in their acquired gender. In 2010 the Equality Act extended and consolidated anti-discrimination legislation around gender, race relations and disability to include religion, sexual orientation, gender reassignment and age.

These developments and the reference to a 'diverse and tolerant society' may seem at odds with the punitive contribution of austerity to widening and intersecting inequalities described in previous sections and the simultaneous policies, described later – securitization, assimilation, the creation of a 'hostile environment' for minority ethnic groups and migrants,

Grenfell Tower, and Brexit politics – all of which have served to illustrate or intensify structural, institutionalized and everyday racism. However, what they all hold in common is a construction of 'the nation' in differing and contradictory ways that seek to find social and cultural legitimacy with different publics.

New Labour's administration sought to 'modernize' policies around family life and intimacy in line with changing social attitudes and practices, claiming, quite erroneously, that this relegated struggles for gender, sexual and racial equality to past history (Williams 2004; McRobbie 2004; Jensen 2018). Before the 2010 election the Conservative Party was eager to shake off its image as a traditionalist, homophobic, family-values party and, in coming to power with the Coalition, undertook to continue New Labour's reforms. The reforms noted above are very important in providing recognition, visibility and legal rights to many LGBTQI+ people. In addition, they provide footholds to pressure for further improvements. However, the fact they are framed in particular neoliberal and heteronormative ways serves also to circumscribe such potential. In the above quotation taken from the *LGBT Action Plan*, equality is presented as something for which individuals strive in order to reach their potential (through hard work and talent), an individualist strategy that became part of the anti-discrimination approach of the newly formed Equalities and Human Rights Commission (EHRC – see below). Again, on the one hand, in its legal transition from civil partnership to marriage, same-gender marriage could be seen to have influenced heterosexual practices in the demand for it to be extended to opposite-gender couples, a right granted in 2019 in England. Yet this is also framed within a 'natural' heteronormative temporality in which love leads to long-lasting relationships (GEO 2018: 1). It appeals to a desire to be seen as 'ordinary' rather than the challenging of heteronormative convention (Hellesund et al. 2019).

In an analysis of this policy document and the speeches around it, Matson Lawrence and Yvette Taylor argue that these characterize the UK as a modern, progressive nation, a 'global leader', and, in a neo-colonial twist, one that acknowledges its 'special responsibility' to the countries of the Commonwealth in showing the way forward (GEO 2018: 27). Yet the *Action Plan* has little to say about LGBT asylum seekers (who are often forced to 'prove' their sexuality or trans status), refugees or the position of EU LGBTQI+ citizens after Brexit. The conception of modern progress is seen as linear and inevitable (Lawrence and Taylor 2019: 11–14), in spite of a wealth of evidence in the *Action Plan* itself of experiences of systemic and even increased violence and discrimination, and also in spite of the decline in members of the Conservative cabinet supporting same-gender marriage. In 2013, only two cabinet ministers opposed same-gender marriage; in October 2019, more than half the cabinet (eleven) had opposed it (Duffy 2019).

While the plan is self-congratulatory, it is also cautious. For example, in spite of over a decade of evidence of criticism of the 2004 Gender Recognition Act for its requirement that people are medically certificated (Hines 2013), it recommends only further consultation and review. In addition, while attending to the categories of LGBT, which conflate gender with sexual identity, it minimizes Q (queer) and I (intersex) claims, both of which look to non-binary conceptions of gender identity which are positioned outside the frame of tolerance.

In turning in the next section to look at policies affecting different minority groups, it becomes clear that, while British society may well be culturally diverse, not only does the assertion of tolerance need to be questioned but the meanings of 'diversity' and 'tolerance' require critical contextual understanding.

2: Bordering practices in the post-racial

This section brings together two concepts: the *post-racial* and *bordering practices*. The first refers to the political and cultural context; the second to governmental policies and practices that represent one of the features of that context.

Post-racial settling

Since the 1960s, British social policy has demonstrated a consistent inconsistency between, on the one hand, representing immigration as problematic and requiring increasing control and restriction and, on the other, developing race relations legislation to combat disadvantage and discrimination. The latter has often been a response to intense campaigning such as that following the murder of a black teenager, Stephen Lawrence, and the failure of the police to pursue the four white men who murdered him. While this forced an acknowledgement of institutionalized racism in the Metropolitan police force (Macpherson 1999), at the same time the 1999 Asylum Act began the erosion of economic and social rights of asylum seekers. This formalized the use of detention centres as a routine rather than an exceptional measure and replaced cash benefits for asylum seekers with vouchers to deter the new racialized welfare subject: the 'bogus asylum seeker'. Disorder from minority ethnic youth in 2001 in northern towns was represented as a threat to social cohesion, the failure of minorities to integrate and the charge that minority groups were leading 'parallel lives' (Cantle 2001). The 2002 Nationality, Immigration and Asylum Act introduced a test of citizenship for migrants. By 2013 Theresa May had tightened the Act to enable the state to deprive a British citizen with a criminal record of their citizenship, even when they have no other citizenship. She argued that citizenship was no longer a right but a privilege (Ross 2013; Shamsie 2018).

This erosion of rights was facilitated by a view that responsibility for integration and assimilation for both settled minorities and new migrants lay with those groups rather than with the white British community. This began the displacement of multiculturalism both in the UK and in Europe (Modood [2007] 2013; Murji 2017) and was part of the shift into a post-racial context in which existing cultural diversity was seen to have made anti-racist and even multicultural strategies redundant (see Hesse 2011; Sian et al. 2013; Murji 2017). In fact, as a policy principle of the 1970s and 1980s, multiculturalism was relatively progressive in accepting and not resisting the reality of cultural pluralism, but it still tended to obscure the ways in which postcolonial hierarchies of 'race' give rise to institutionalized racism in welfare (Williams 1989) and criminal justice (Hall et al. 1978). By the end of the 1990s, multiculturalism had taken on a more dialogic and anti-racist meaning, especially with the publication of the Parekh report, *The Future of Multi-Ethnic Britain*, which opened a debate on what it meant to be 'British' (Parekh et al. 2000). Political opposition turned this around to make 'culture' central to an understanding of difference, and this assisted the erasure of racism. The notion of 'diversity', while useful in signalling heterogeneity, similarly took the sting out of the reality of everyday, institutional and historical racism. It became something to be managed rather than critically examined within education, health, welfare and policing, and socio-economic inequality (Lewis 2000).

In 2007 the Commission for Racial Equality was abolished, as its functions were taken over by the Equality and Human Rights Commission (EHRC), followed by the creation of the Commission on Integration and Cohesion. Together their remits served to subordinate anti-racist and anti-discrimination policies to individualist and assimilationist strategies (Goodfellow 2018; Flynn and Craig 2019). The requirement for the public sector to monitor discrimination was challenged as unnecessary 'red tape' (although such duties were continued in Scotland) (Meer 2017: 671). The EHRC brought together multiple areas for protection against discrimination and for their human rights. At first sight, this would seem to progress two forms of recognition: the intersectionality, first, of inequalities and, second, of human dignity and respect as a common bond. However, in many ways it also represented a dilution of single forms of equality strategies, a move reflected in the reduced budget of the EHRC to less than one of the single equality bodies that preceded it. Also, in practice, a complainant can claim against direct discrimination on only two grounds (Meer 2017: 669). The emphasis on human rights reflects the EU approach to social justice. However, Sian and her colleagues demonstrate in a study of racism in Europe that this approach was also part of a shift to post-racial governance in which the adoption of a 'remedial individual justice model of human rights' moved the struggle against racism on to an individual plane. It represented a move away from structural and systemic racism in that it 'de-historicises racism and fundamentally disempowers anti-racist struggles' (Sian et al. 2013: 40).

The Race Disparity Audit set up in 2016 also reflected this double movement. It signalled a commitment to make public the increasingly evident disparities experienced by racialized and minority ethnic groups in their use of public services. For example, the Lammy Review in 2017 found that, in spite of constituting 14 per cent of the population, BAME people represented 25 per cent of prisoners and 40 per cent of those in custody (Ministry of Justice 2017: 3). It highlighted lack of trust between BAME people and police and made thirty-five recommendations relating to better co-ordination between the criminal justice system and other local services. The government agreed to review action on these recommendations. At the same time, the dropping of restrictions on stop and search procedures – which was a critical element in the racializing processes of policing – was justified on the basis of tackling knife crime, but by 2018/19 black people in particular were ten times more likely to be stopped and searched by police (Brown 2020), even though the majority of young people convicted for knife possession – 62 per cent across England and Wales – were white (Ministry of Justice 2017). After the Black Lives Matter protests which highlighted this, a review was promised. In similar vein, the Race Disparity Audit had failed to identify a unified and comprehensive strategy either to *combat* the disparities that were emerging or to attend to the disparities associated with the pursuit of immigration and counter-extremism laws and policies (UN 2019: 6; Meer 2017).

The last point is important. The turn against multiculturalism and towards the promotion of 'British values' came with the 'war on terror'. David Cameron, the prime minister at the time, articulated this connection in 2011, when he said that terrorism showed the failure of multiculturalist and human rights approaches and that Britain needed a stronger national identity (BBC 2011). The Prevent Strategy, initially developed by New Labour, seeks to target individuals and groups who advocate extremism and at the same time engage in this with civil society. However, evidence suggests that this twin approach has served to heighten anti-Muslim racism and Islamophobia, to subject Muslims to extensive surveillance, and, with the help of the media, to extend suspicion to the general Muslim population as 'a threat to the nation'. At the same time, it was contested and reshaped by local governance actors and Muslim communities on the ground (O'Toole et al. 2016). Without this, as a report published by the Runnymede Trust concluded: '[Prevent] alienates the very people it claims it wants to engage with; contrary to the "British values" it extols, in its implementation Prevent involves denial of basic human rights' (Cohen and Tufail 2017: 41). The main criticism of the strategy is that it assumes rather than defines both an understanding of key terms such as 'terrorism', 'extremism' and 'British values' and how to assess who is vulnerable to 'radicalization'. In attempting to deal with its failures, government widened the use of discretionary powers to monitor extremism by public-sector workers such as teachers, academics, nurses and doctors, which did not go uncontested (Yuval-Davis et al. 2019; UN 2019: 13; see also Docs Not Cops, www.docsnotcops.co.uk).

In addition, the gendered effects of the strategy played into existing ways in which Muslim *women* are positioned as threatening both to British values and to women's emancipation: both in danger (of forced marriage and female genital mutilation) and dangerous (to British values). Part of the strategy involved engaging with Muslim women as mothers, sisters and wives to prevent the radicalization of young men. In doing so, it framed Muslim women as passive victims and conflated patriarchal practices with terrorism (Rashid 2017). Such framing undervalues Muslim women's own voice, agency, campaigns and support groups that exist against patriarchal practices (whose funding has also been hit by austerity measures – Rashid 2017; WBG and Runnymede Trust 2017). Representations of the veil, and particularly the niqab (full veil), in media and political discourse as a hindrance to integration and a marker of Muslim female submission abounded, even in some feminist discourse (Diana 2018). The New Labour home secretary Jack Straw (2006) expressed this opinion in asking Muslim women constituents to remove their niqabs when speaking to him. A cruder version was repeated in 2019 by the prime minister, Boris Johnson, who demeaned veiled Muslim women as 'bank robbers' and 'letterboxes', after which there was a 375 per cent spike in hate crimes against Muslims, two-thirds aimed at women (Parveen 2019). Belatedly, in 2017 the policy was extended to include far-right extremism following the murder of Jo Cox, a Labour MP, by a member of far-right groups (Home Office 2019).

Together these moves registered a fixed binary of 'tolerance' that focuses particularly on religion as 'culture' and distinguishes between those who have integrated against those who have not. It reinforced anti-Muslim sentiments and precluded any sort of debate on the meanings of Britishness or the positioning of a minority religion in a secular society (Modood 2020). At the same time, it was the extension of existing bordering practices on asylum seekers, refugees and migrants to different resident marginalized groups that began to subject more social groups to the material and emotional punishment of exploitation, expropriation and expulsion, or what Tyler (2013) calls 'social abjection'.

Bordering practices

Broadly, bordering practices refer to those processes and practices employed in institutions of welfare that serve to create hierarchies through boundaries of inclusion and exclusion from social rights (Guentner et al. 2016; Humphris 2019; Yuval-Davis et al. 2019). More specifically, the term refers to those processes, practices and rhetorics through which the citizenship status of particular groups of both nationals *and* non-nationals has been degraded. In addition, it is argued that the template for this erosion has been that used on asylum seekers and migrants, described in the previous section and in the analysis of 'racialized borders' in chapter 3. In this section I illustrate the practices that contributed to this process. These have involved:

- the bureaucratic construction of complex and often changing categories of migrant and welfare subject statuses which then serve as rationale and/or condition for removing a right or access to another service such as housing or health care;
- the use of health and welfare workers to police conditions of eligibility; the use of discretion to make decisions for which front-line staff are not trained and/or are constrained by their own conditions of work;
- the legitimation of removal of rights by mobilization of popular sentiments of nationalist/racist/classist/sexist/disablist protectionism around welfare ('welfare chauvinism') that reduce subordinated differences of body, language, religion, origin and culture into categories

of 'below human', combined with rhetorical forms of seeking consent ('fairness');

- indifferent and incompetent governance whose dehumanizing effects can be understood as a form of necropolitics (Mbembe 2019) and the institution of conditions of exploitation, expropriation and expulsion at the national level.

Two sides of the same coin

The first example comes from the overlap of immigration policy with welfare conditionality. In 2011 David Cameron, as prime minister, argued that the need to reduce 'welfare dependency' and increase immigration control were two sides of the same coin. 'The real issue', he argued, 'is this: migrants are filling gaps in the labour market left wide open by a welfare system that for years has paid British people not to work' (BBC 2011). This unevidenced association threaded its way through policies throughout the decade. Migration system reforms increasingly made explicit the central principle that migrants are units of labour who are required to meet their needs through their wages, with forms of conditionality and penalty attached to the labour market and rights to residence, to health care, and to earnings-related benefits. The right to permanent residence after five years for EU migrants was granted only where there has been evidence of continuity of employment. The differentiated levels of conditionality and reductions in social rights to citizens *and* migrants create both similarities between the two groups and increased inequalities among and between them (Shutes 2016: 702; see also Morris 2019). In addition, as Bruzelius and Shutes argue, the dynamic between social policies and *internal* mobility represents another way in which the welfare conditionality attached to migrants' transnational mobility is mirrored in inequalities of access to non-nationals and nationals alike. For example, where place, postcode or residence restrict or permit access to housing, education, social assistance or health care, it affects the service-users' capacity to be mobile (Bruzelius and Shutes 2019).

Until 2020 the complex categorizing of rights operated through EU and non-EU distinctions as well as in skill levels, but, with the commitment to Brexit in 2019, this focused much more on skills. The rule that applied to non-EU migrants to have to be sufficiently skilled and earning enough to gain entry, and to show even higher income to be able to bring in family members, was in February 2020 proposed for *all* migrants as part of a post-Brexit plan. (Note that citizenship *is* granted to a migrant with £2 million to invest in the UK.) The level of earnings, originally £30,000, was scaled down after protests from unions. The NHS and organizations such as the UK Homecare Association pointed out that this was higher than the level of income of many migrant workers, especially those in health, social care and domestic labour, that it would rapidly exacerbate the already 120,000 vacancy level, and that the labelling of such work as 'unskilled' was demeaning (UKHA 2020). This was two months after the Covid-19 pandemic had started. It was to have repercussions (see below), as did other rights-reducing rules made to extend 'No Recourse to Public Funds' to more asylum and migrant groups and to introduce a surcharge for using health care. The latter placed health workers in an invidious position of policing patients as to their migration status. This echoed the irony of the post-war welfare state that migrant workers were essential to the provision of public services but had fewer rights to access them (Williams 1989).

In addition, the right to permanent residence after five years is only granted upon evidence that there has been continuity of employment. This and restrictions based upon skill and earning power penalize migrant women because, first, they are more likely to be in care and other work designated as unskilled; second, their earning power is lower because of gender disparities in wages; and, third, their attachment to the labour market may not be continuous (Shutes 2017). All or any of these may threaten a woman's status as 'worker' and therefore her eligibility to benefits and residence. While a year is allowed for pregnancy and child care, when the child is one, the mother must show readiness for work or lose her support. (For citizen mothers, the age of the child is three, although she may be required to show evidence of work-seeking before then.)

Social abjection and necropolitics
The second set of examples highlights the dehumanizing effects of these and other restrictions and how they coalesce into what Imogen Tyler (2013) calls *social abjection*. This refers to the ways in which particular groups who experience poverty – asylum seekers, refugees, unemployed young people, disabled people, Gypsies and Travellers – are 'transformed into symbolic and material scapegoats for the social decomposition that has a negative, degrading impact on us all' (ibid.: 211). Thus refugees are transformed into bogus asylum seekers, disabled people into welfare scroungers, young people into feckless 'chavs', evicted Gypsies and Travellers into 'scum'. These processes build on historical, patriarchal and colonial roots of subordination but are reconstituted by the effects of neoliberal austerity, the erosion and erasure of citizenship rights, and the discourses and technologies of everyday media and politics. In this way, Tyler argues, general-

ized social and economic insecurities of the population are harnessed and hardened into a form of public consent for punishing and disenfranchising particular groups in poverty. I return to Tyler's analysis and her focus on agency and resistance in chapter 5. Here I look at how these dynamics dehumanize asylum seekers.

The UK's asylum regime is one of the toughest in Europe. It has the largest number of people held in detention centres, half of whom have sought asylum and have experienced trauma in their countries of origin; there is no limit on detention (AVID 2020; Refugee Council 2020; Migration Observatory 2019). These are effectively prisons for those waiting for documents, or those who have overstayed their visa, or because of intentional or unintentional law breaking. Only 48 per cent of applications for asylum were granted in 2019 (Refugee Council 2020). Access to accommodation is complex, with local authorities and voluntary and faith organizations playing a vital role under diminishing resources (Hutton and Lukes 2015). In 2020 asylum seekers in the community received £37.50 per week to cover food and all personal needs, an amount at half the weekly income of the poorest citizens, and many are not allowed to seek work. Lucy Mayblin calls this a policy of 'purposeful impoverishment' in which even the small rewards of everyday living – shopping, cooking – are saturated with intense anxiety. The attrition attached to this is a form of 'slow violence' (Mayblin et al. 2019). This dehumanizing subjection, with its expropriation of dignity and expulsion from a society to mere existence combined with the possibility of being sent back into a country of former expulsion, amounts to sovereignty as necropolitics (Mbembe 2019 – see chapter 3). This amounts to 'the capacity to define who matters and who does not, who is *disposable* and who is not' (Mbembe 2003: 40, cited in Mayblin et al. 2019: 111; original emphasis).

While it is important to hold on to the specificity of postcolonial hierarchy in this abjectification of migrants and asylum seekers, the impact of welfare reform on disabled people amounts to a further dynamic of displacement and disposability. 'Fairness' was the rhetorical means to develop popular consent for austerity, both in terms of 'all being in it together' and by targeting those who were acting 'unfairly'. Among these were disabled people or, as they began to be characterized, those who fake illness to shirk their work responsibilities (Clarke and Newman 2012).

Television comedy programmes mocked working-class disabled people; newspapers asked readers to report disabled shirkers (Ryan 2019). What is interesting is how the representation of disabled people changed over time and how, as a social group, they shift in and out of the boundaries of inclusion in family, nation and work. The post-war welfare state legacy saw disabled people as care-dependent objects of pity and compassion, a position which disability movements successfully challenged from the 1970s, claiming independent living and the right to work and to have a family life. The 1990s saw the Disability Discrimination Act, the launch of the Disability Living Allowance and the promotion of independent living. The 2012 Olympics in London represented the Paralympic athletes as national heroes. Yet, as austerity bit, they were turned into potential scroungers, fraudsters and a threat to the national economy and national recovery. After implementation of more stringent work-capability tests on disabled people in 2011, the incidence of disability hate crimes went up. Official figures show a 30 per cent increase in reported hate crimes between 2011/12 and 2017/18 (Home Office 2018; see also Burch 2018).

There is a longstanding correlation between disability and poverty (and also to disabled people as a threat to the nation – Williams 1996). By 2018 it was estimated that 4 million disabled adults were living below the breadline (Ryan 2019: 14). Ironically, the new reforms reconstructed the claim by disability organizations for the right to employment into a moral responsibility to be self-sufficient through paid work, unless severely restricted by disability from doing so. Such pressure to be economically self-sufficient failed to account for discrimination at work – a half of disabled workers experience bullying or harassment at work (Scope 2017) and a disability pay gap of 13.6 per cent (15.6 per cent for disabled men of Bangladeshi origins – Chandola and Zhang 2018).

The reforms reduced disabled people's financial support by up to one-third, with half a million disabled people who were unable to work losing up to £1,500 a year and the possibility by 2023 of disabled people losing up to £4,000 a year (Ryan 2019: 23–4, pre-pandemic calculation). However, two measures in particular institutionalized the discourse of disabled people as scroungers: the assessment work-seeking capability assessment (WCA) and the 'bedroom tax'. Both methodology and application of the WCA (which was subcontracted to the private companies Atos and Maximus) have been discredited because of the lack of knowledge of and empathy towards the limiting nature of applicants' medical conditions on the part of those charged to implement it. More than half of appeals made by claimants against decisions were upheld (Morris 2020: 277). In addition, it was claimed that the companies were under pressure from the Department of Work and Pensions to get results, although this is denied by the department (Pring 2020). The majority of those assessed (62 per cent) had mental health problems, and allegations were made that a rising number of deaths and suicides were the result of disabled people having their benefits cut following a 'fit-for-work' assessment (Lockley 2019).

The bedroom tax penalized tenants claiming housing benefit if they had a spare room and encouraged them to downsize. However, disabled people need extra space to store equipment such as wheelchairs or for a carer to stay over if they need help, and moving home entails far greater costs and inconvenience because of the need for adaptations. Cuts and the rising costs of services to achieve independence, such as specialist advisors or transport, have added to financial insecurity. Where disability intersects with lone parenting or with race, then these effects are compounded (Ryan 2019; see also WBG 2018a). Disabled lone parents are twice as likely to be unemployed as non-disabled lone mothers, and their overall loss from disability services and benefits by 2021 is estimated to be £7,000 a year (Ryan 2019: 156). In 2017 the UN rapporteur monitoring the application of the UN Convention on the Rights of Persons with Disabilities in the UK called the situation a 'human catastrophe' (Lockley 2019).

A further aspect of bordering practices is examined by Rachel Humphris (2019) in her in-depth study of Romanian Roma families seeking leave to remain. Here, bordering practices moved out of the assessment centre, benefits office or court and into the private space of the migrants' own homes. Those charged with assessing their deservingness were support and social services staff. So mothers found themselves in ambiguous and fragile encounters with welfare officers and volunteers where they were under scrutiny and surveillance, being judged as to their deservingness for citizenship as mothers and home keepers, but also dependant on these visits for information and support. The particularly marginalized existence of Roma families and the cultural stereotyping about Roma family life enacted by local authorities and staff gave rise to a visceral fear that their children would be taken away (expropriation, if not expulsion). At the same time, the staff visitors, schooled in home visiting as a support and assessment practice, were experiencing cuts to their services, the stress of an audit culture, and little training to apply increasingly more complex and hostile rules to migration claims. In this way, the process of determining a category of (un)deservingness was performed through a brittle two-handed play of degrading-dependent bordering practices. Important in this study is the recognition of the complexity of the social relations of welfare and the minimal room for manoeuvre for both practitioner and user, an issue to which I return in chapter 5.

The Windrush betrayal

The final example – the Windrush betrayal of 2018 (Gentleman 2019) – illustrates practically every element that constitutes bordering practices: the intersections between migration policies and the conditions of citizens; institutional indifference and ignorance; the necropolitics of 'the hostile environment'; the use of health and welfare professionals to police that environment; and the frame of 'post-racial' governance. In 2010, members of the BNP (British National Party) and UKIP (United Kingdom Independence Party) found (some) local, national and EU electoral success. In an appeasing response to more vocal anti-immigration sentiment and mobilization in 2013, Theresa May, as home secretary, instituted what she called a 'very hostile environment policy' against 'illegal' immigrants. (The popular term 'illegal' is a misnomer: it means those who are undocumented – have not – or not yet – been permitted to remain). This policy included sending vans with placards round areas of high migrant residence in London with the slogan 'GO HOME OR FACE ARREST' and detailing the number of arrests made that week (they were withdrawn after a public outcry).

At the same time the Home Office subcontracted the private firm Capita to contact people suspected of not having applied for leave to remain in the country; they were given targets for the number of deportations. These included, wrongly, many of the Windrush generation (so-called after the name of the ship that brought the first immigrants from the Caribbean), who had arrived and settled as Commonwealth citizens in the 1950s and 1960s with, formally speaking, the rights of British citizenship, and therefore had had no cause to seek leave to remain. Now in their sixties, seventies and eighties, these citizens received letters threatening them with deportation. At the same time, landlords, employers, the NHS, the banks and others were required (or else face a fine) to make ID checks and to refuse access to services unless proof of legal residence in the UK was produced (see figure 4.1). This resulted in people losing their jobs, their homes, their benefits, medical care and the right to re-enter the country after visiting abroad. One hundred and sixty four people were sent to detention centres, and some were returned to countries they had left as children; eleven died (Younge 2018a; Gentleman 2019). The home secretary in post when the scandal broke, Amber Rudd, denied the existence of targets and later resigned when evidence was produced. After public protests the deportations stopped for a while, although they continued a year later. An independent review set up by the Home Office and led by Wendy Williams found that the department had a defensive culture and demonstrated 'an institutional ignorance and thoughtlessness towards the issue of race and

15th April 2018

Dear Homerton University NHS Trust

cc. Diane Abbot MP

I am writing this in sorrow and mounting shame and indignation. Last week my husband [...] received an appointment to see a kidney specialist at Homerton hospital. He also received with the appointment letter a long form asking him all kinds of questions in order to prove his reasons for being in this country and requesting he bring passport and other proofs of entitlement to his hospital appointment. He is a 79 year old British citizen who came here from Trinidad in 1962 and has lived here since then, married, settled, brought up 3 children and worked continuously till his retirement. He was puzzled about being sent this form and showed it to me, but his puzzlement has turned to outrage as he has realised that he has only been sent this form because he is a citizen from a racial minority from a Commonwealth country.

Who is doing the racial profiling that resulted in this form being sent? How has it happened, when his entitlement to treatment is not in question (he has a British passport, is permanently domiciled in the UK, has NI and tax records all easily accessible and in public records), that he can be asked to "prove" he can be treated. Why was I not sent such a form when I attended hospital?? Because I was born here? Because I am white? I am ashamed of how my country is now treating its ethnic minority citizens and want my husband to receive an apology for this insulting letter.

We want to know who in the Trust authorised these forms to be sent out to patients and what the Trust is going to do about this insulting and upsetting and possibly illegal behaviour.

Needless to say he will not be completing the form and I dare anyone of your staff to refuse to treat him.

Yours sincerely

Celia Burgess-Macey

Figure 4.1 Letter to an NHS trust[3]

the history of the Windrush generation within the department, which are consistent with some elements of the definition of institutional racism' (House of Commons 2020: 7). The government changed the term 'hostile environment' to 'compliance environment', although, as the UN special rapporteur on racism noted, this rhetorical shift would need to be matched by practice (UN 2019: 15).[4] Indeed, such 'ignorance and thoughtlessness' was highlighted by Parliament's Public Accounts Committee in September 2020 in reviewing the Home Office's immigration enforcement:

> We are concerned that if the Department [Home Office] does not make decisions based on evidence, it instead risks making them on

anecdote, assumption and prejudice. Worryingly, it has no idea of what impact it has achieved for the £400 million spent each year by its Immigration Enforcement directorate. There are major holes in the Department's understanding of the size and scale of illegal immigration and the extent and nature of any resulting harm. (Public Accounts Committee 2020: 1)

3: Necropolitics, nation and nature

One theme of this chapter marks the creep of necropolitics, the power of the state to determine who matters and who doesn't matter, who is or isn't disposable. In the following three case-study illustrations, the focus is on moments rather than policies in order to illustrate many of the policy developments discussed so far. These are moments of unsettling/settling, of revelation of the politics of who matters and who does not, and how the three 'Es' – exploitation, expropriation and expulsion – operate in tandem through family, nation, work and nature.

Grenfell Tower

In the morning of 14 June 2017, people woke up to horrific pictures of Grenfell Tower, a 24-storey high-rise block of 129 flats in North Kensington, London. After midnight, a fire had broken out from a flat on the fourth floor. Within 15 minutes the building was ablaze. At least seventy-two people died and 208 families were traumatized and made homeless.

Soon afterwards it became clear that there were material causes of the fire. Many of the materials used in the refurbishment of the building, which was completed in 2016, were combustible and allowed a fire in one flat to spread up the building through external flammable cladding. The fire brigade initially told residents to stay put. Those who survived ignored this advice, although some people died falling down the blackened-out stairwells. A public inquiry was set up under Michael Moore-Bick, and its first part was published in 2019 (Moore-Bick 2019). The event speaks to wider social policy processes. These concern the history of housing provision; the governance and quality of social housing; and the deregulation of the building industry. In particular, it is the way these intersect with the race, gender and class dynamics of urban gentrification, the representation of social housing of high-rise estates, and both the 'hostile environment' and environmental racism against minority ethnic groups and migrants, who made up the majority of Grenfell tenants.

Privatization, commercialization, contracting out and public–private partnerships in social housing have been part of welfare state changes since the 1980s. From the 1950s until the 1980s, 126,000 council houses were built a year; since then around 2 million have been sold according to 'the right to buy' introduced in 1980. By 2018 fewer than 6,500 were built. Meanwhile austerity welfare and the rising costs of renting exacerbated housing need for low-income families and young people, and some 277,000 people were homeless in 2019 (Shelter 2019). The financialization of housing led to local authorities boosting their budgets by selling off municipal housing for regeneration and gentrification, especially in London, where land values and foreign investor speculation are high (Hodkinson 2018). However, also significant were the ways in which the contracting out of housing services and the development of public–private forms of housing management were to surface in particular ways in the Grenfell tragedy.

First, the effect of the Coalition and Conservative governments' commitment to 'cutting red tape' – the 'enemy of enterprise' – combined anti-EU rhetoric with encouraging unrestrained private business development. One consequence was to make building regulations subject to compliance through self-certification. This included fire regulations. As local authorities contracted out to increasing numbers of private companies, then inspection became more complex to carry out. In addition, winning contracts could depend upon speed of 'sign off', an advantage held by local authority building teams (Hodkinson 2018: 15). Value for money became a central organizing principle. Ironically, an account by Hagan (2018) also points to the Department of Energy and Climate Change being keen to meet its environmental targets through better insulation of properties and, in that process, being influenced by the plastics industry in shaping the approval of what were to become lethal forms of insulation. An independent study found that, far from being environmentally friendly, the toxins that penetrated the soil around Grenfell seventeen months after the fire posed a serious health risk to the local community and those who had survived (Hopkins 2019).

Second, the management of tenants and buildings moved from local authorities to public–private partnerships, in this case to a quasi-private company – the Kensington and Chelsea Tenant Management Organisation, which was effectively the (remote and inaccessible) landlord. Between 2014 and 2016 the 'regeneration' of Grenfell Tower took place, and one outcome that became clear was the shift from direct accountability between tenants and the local authority as landlord to a more complex relationship between private contractors, inspectors and the Kensington and Chelsea Tenant Management Organisation (KCTMO) working with the local authority, the Royal Borough of Kensington and Chelsea (RBKC). In this set-up, the voices of residents had little resonance. When residents and the Grenfell Action Group repeatedly raised concerns about existing fire risks and guarantees of the safety of refurbishment, they were overlooked. They had good reason to be concerned: in 2009 six people had died in a smaller fire developed through the cladding at Lakanal House social housing in Southwark. Here a review had been called for but not set up. However, at the subsequent Grenfell Inquiry, the inadequacy and abuse of safety regulations of building materials became clear. Kingspan, the company that made insulation products for high-rise buildings, marketed these as 'safe' to local authorities when they had submitted only the foil facer on the material for safety testing (Malik 2020).

Residents felt that the management organization was not run on behalf of the tenants, or by the tenants, but just to manage the tenants. People who complained were seen as troublemakers. One tenant said after the fire: 'KCTMO just think these people are nothing – they don't matter' (quoted in Platt 2017). They felt that power was stacked against them: had they wanted to take legal action, they would have found that their access to legal aid no longer existed because, like local community groups' funding, it had been cut. In the context of lack of respect and accountability from the KCTMO, the building companies and the local authority, there developed a lack of trust from the residents (ibid.).

This relationship needs to be placed in a wider context. The residents – most of whom were tenants – were among the poorest in the borough. The RBKC represents dramatically the widening of inequalities that has taken place over the past thirty years, since it contained in 2015 both those falling into England's multiply deprived 10 per cent and those in the least 30 per cent deprived (DCLG 2015). But these are not simple economic inequalities: many of the residents were from minority ethnic groups, or were recent migrants or refugees: the 2011 census registers just over half in the Grenfell postcode area as born outside Britain (Shilliam 2018: 170). The first dead person to be identified, Mohammed Alhajali, was a Syrian refugee. Some residents were single parents, some were disabled people living on benefits, a minority were unemployed – they were, in the rhetoric, 'hard-working families'. While being low-income workers, they still carried education, skills and training experience at a level overqualifying them for the jobs they occupied, a characteristic of many BAME and migrant workers (ibid.). They were the workers who serviced the city.

The regeneration of the tower needs finally to be understood as part of contestation between local authorities' plans for gentrification versus residents' claims for improved services. In these terms, the cladding was claimed to be for aesthetic purposes rather than thermal efficiency (Hodkinson 2018: 16). In addition, as council housing has deteriorated, tower blocks have acquired a degraded image: problematized as centres of antisocial and criminal behaviour – and for this reason low in the choice of social housing tenants. After protests by youth in both 2001 and 2011, social housing residents were targeted for blame, with negative narratives about single mothers and racially segregated inner-city estates (Tyler 2013, 2015; Shankley and Finney 2020). According to Danny Dorling (2011), most children who live above the fourth floor of tower blocks in England are black or Asian. Housing tenure is complex across ethnicity, yet black and minority ethnic groups and migrants occupy disproportionately the least desired housing sectors because of economic disadvantage, immigration rules, and a long history of direct and indirect racism in allocation procedures (Shilliam 2018; Shankley and Finney 2020). Stir into this mix the fact that, as described earlier, there has been a hardening of media, state and public hostility towards people in poverty, social housing tenants, single mothers and racialized groups, it becomes clear why the residents of Grenfell Tower felt they were 'people who don't matter'. Nonetheless, determined organization and voice was heard after the fire through local community, faith and action groups in fighting for rehousing, providing emotional support and demanding a public inquiry. Some took the campaign against inflammable cladding to other housing estates across the country (see chapter 5).

Exactly a year before the Grenfell Tower fire, the Brexit referendum took place.

Brexit nation

The chapter has shown how austerity welfare in the UK has reproduced multiple intersections of social exclusion, discrimination, poverty and hierarchy, marked by class, gender, race, ethnicity, disability, sexuality, age, nationality, migrant status, place and generation. The Brexit campaign and the after-effects of the referendum in 2016, in which 52 per cent voted to leave the EU, were to throw these up a dramatic and dualistic path of Remain or Leave. It was and will be a significant moment for an understanding of social policy because of the ways in which welfare chauvinism in its different forms – but mainly ethno-nationalist – were employed by the Vote Leave campaign as a mobilizing axis to conjoin different disaffections of different parts of just over half the electorate. I look at how this condensation of difference happened and how it has been understood.

The appeal of the Vote Leave campaign was to a sense of disaffection and loss (Andreouli et al. 2019; Clarke and Newman 2019). For some, that centred upon the impoverishment of their communities and the services within them, especially health care, housing and policing, but also the loss of security of long-lasting employment and family life. A second area focused upon lack of political or collective voice, a distrust of centralized political parties in a context of powerlessness when hospitals closed, or industries moved abroad, or bus services disappeared. The campaign linked these feelings to three main targets (Clarke and Newman 2019: 72): first, it argued that the EU, in taking away national sovereignty and control of political decision-making, had made Britain not only dominated by EU bureaucracy but also subject to high financial contributions to the EU budget (Andreouli et al. 2019). Vote Leave pledged £350 million would be available to the NHS after Brexit (it was not: for an explanation of the EU budget, see ONS 2019). The second target was the so-called metropolitan-cosmopolitan elite, who, it was argued, were out of touch with ordinary lives, protected from austerity, and had fostered and benefited from multiculturalism and equal opportunities. Third were migrants, who, by virtue of free movement within the EU, it was argued were taking jobs away from 'British' workers and accessing free education, health care and housing. More than half the social media adverts for the campaign focused upon fears of immigration, in particular on the implications of Turkey joining the EU. Despite the fact that this has not been part of present or future EU policy, one advert read: 'The EU is expanding and plans on granting Turkey visa-free travel. This will put enormous pressure on the NHS, our border security and economy' (Griffin 2018).

Together these groups were said to have contributed to the decline of Britain. Rolled into the first two groups was also a distrust of 'experts' – particularly economists and the judiciary, whose judgements and authority were presented as expressions of self-interested privilege. What the Vote Leave campaign offered, according to Boris Johnson at the time, was a chance to 'take back control of this great country's destiny' (Hope 2016). Putting the 'Great' back into Britain became, as it did for Trump's 'make America great again' campaign in the US, a key articulating trope, speaking to an imperial past which it connects to a natural destiny of Britain in the future as a leader of nations. It invokes a sense of pride and belonging to overcome the sense of loss and of what Paul Gilroy calls 'postcolonial melancholia' (Gilroy 2005).

In the invocation to feelings of loss, disaffection and anger, Vote Leave shifted the mode of political engagement which elevated rhetoric over reason and feelings over facts (Andreouli et al. 2019): 'telling it how it is'. While for some voters this felt like a new popular engagement, it also legitimated a release of racist and misogynist discourse and action. There followed a spike of almost 20 per cent in religious and racially motivated hate crimes (CSI 2019). Just before the vote, a member of a far-right group murdered Jo Cox, a young female Labour MP, in public in South Leeds. This brought to attention the extent of online bullying and offline harassment of women in positions of power, especially politicians (Inter-Parliamentary Union 2016).

The appeal to ethno-nationalist welfare chauvinism was drawn at one and the same time from a longer unsettled postcolonial racism in the UK, from the logic of immigration policy-making since the 1960s but especially since the 1999 Asylum Act, and, more recently, from the punitive approaches to documented and undocumented migrants combined with the retreat from stronger anti-discrimination laws, as described in previous sections. While this assemblage of influences was clearly a central ingredient in the Vote Leave mix, some of subsequent media and political commentary focused not on this but on the 'left behind' white members of the working-class electorate.

A strong narrative in the aftermath of the referendum from political scientists and commentators was that the Leave vote represented the revenge of a working class left behind by globalization, deindustrialization, and the out-of-touch cosmopolitan and political elites (Hobolt 2016; Calhoun 2016; Streeck 2017; Goodhart 2017). This pointed to the impoverished working-class regions of the North of England, the Midlands and South Wales, where the Leave vote was relatively high, in the same way that the Trump victory in the US was ascribed to the Rust Belt and the white working class (Hochschild 2016; Inglehart and Norris 2016). It is also a view expressed by some on the left. In November 2019, in the run-up to the election, Len McCluskey, general secretary of Unite, the UK's biggest trade union, said that, while migrants should not be blamed, the Labour Party needed to 'take a tough line' on the freedom of movement for EU migrants in order to face the concerns of the white working class in 'forgotten towns and cities' – positioning these 'ordinary people' against 'many of those who live in metropolitan political and media circles' (Elliott et al. 2019). While experiences of impoverishment, decay and the harsh implementation of Universal Credit unquestionably precipitated a contribution to disaffection (Mckenzie 2017), there are problems with these interpretations.

To begin with, the binary of white working class against metropolitan elites is challenged empirically by the demographics of the Leave vote, which displayed an unusual alliance: 52 per cent of Leave voters lived in the South of England, mainly in the Home Counties, 59 per cent were middle class, and only 24 per cent from the bottom two socio-economic categories, and they tended to be older (Dorling 2016; Ellison 2017; Cochrane 2019). In other words, the narrative does not tell the whole story as to why people voted Leave; it detracts from the racialized nature of the campaign (Bhambra 2017) and the different and uneven regional expressions of national identity caught up in the vote. Taking the four countries of the UK into account, it was only England that voted to leave, at odds with Scotland, Wales and Northern Ireland. However, within England, London and the larger (more cosmopolitan) English cities voted to remain (Cochrane 2019). In addition, in representing the actions of certain (white) sections of the working class as *the* working class, or *the* 'left behind', it refuses the complexity of the way class is constituted through different social relations and the different forms of resistance by those who *have* been hit hardest, such as disabled organizations who have been at the forefront of anti-austerity campaigns (see earlier) and black and minority ethnic women's struggles against far-right racism and the cuts and for migrants' rights (Bassel and Emejulu 2018; and see chapters 5 and 7). It renders invisible the political agency of these groups, who have not been left behind so much as '*left out*' (Bhambra 2017: 228). Also, in some interpretations, the loss to the Leave working class is defended as 'racial self-interest' rather than articulated through racism and imperial nationalism (Kaufmann 2017; Goodhart 2017). As Bhambra points out, defending the perception that some white members of the working class are facing working and housing conditions that have long been the experience of many Black and minority ethnic workers is to pose the right to relative white advantage in terms of a threat posed by the presence of EU migrants (Bhambra 2017: 221). Similarly, this is not borne out empirically. Research shows that EU migrants work in areas of labour shortage, are better educated than the native population, make contributions in taxes that outweigh any receipt of social benefits or services, and that, even after EU enlargement, migration was around a quarter more than emigration (Flynn and Craig 2019).

The argument here is about the misrepresentation of a section of the white working class as constituting either 'ordinary people' or the working class in general. It is not to say that working-class Leave voters were simply racist 'dupes' to right-wing ethno-nationalist propaganda. Deindustrialization has hit areas in the North, the Midlands and Wales hard. But political agency is neither simple nor fixed; people hold different and contradictory views at one and the same time. However, the political narrative of the Leave campaign offered a way of attaching the disaffections of different groups in a way that bound them together in a 'common sense' of English nationalism which represented itself as British (Clarke 2019a). In other contexts, in other narratives, such alignments can shift.

Nature and nation: the pandemic crisis

At the end of 2019 unprecedented bushfires in Australia came to a peak. Around the same time, severe floods affected the North of England, Wales and the North Midlands. Heavy rains precipitated swarms of locusts that destroyed crops in many countries of the Global South, most severely in East Africa. Fires swept California. This was not the end of what felt like nature's wrath. In December 2019 the first reported case of a new virus, subsequently named Covid-19, emerged in Wuhan in China. A month later the World Health Organization declared a Public Health Emergency of International Concern. By mid-May 2020 the virus had spread to 188 countries, with 4.3 million reported infections and 300,000 recorded deaths (Johns Hopkins University 2020). One-tenth of these deaths were reported in the UK, and almost one-third in the US, although mortality rankings were to fluctuate. By October 2020 the death rate in England and Wales had reached 54,325 (ONS 2020c) and was set to rise even further, as a new more contagious variants of the virus emerged before the vaccines had begun to be rolled out.

Before these events, the UK's commitment to the 2016 UN's Framework Convention on Climate Change (the Paris Agreement) seemed promising. In 2019, Parliament passed legislation requiring the government to reduce the UK's net emissions of greenhouse gases by 100 per cent relative to 1990 levels by 2050 in order to make the UK a 'net zero' emitter. However, by 2020 the Institute for Government warned that government had not begun to consider the huge scale of the work to meet this (Institute for Government 2020). The Environment Bill promised to create a watchdog to protect the natural environment (its discussion was delayed late in 2020), and in November 2020 Boris Johnson announced a ten point net-zero plan as part of a move towards a Green Industrial Revolution (DBEIS 2020). This contained important commitments which could act as a benchmark for the 2021 COP26 global climate summit. What it lacked was detail on co-ordination, funding or planning (Newsom 2020).

The global pandemic crisis demanded immediate co-ordination, funding, planning and collective responsibility and sacrifice not known in the UK since the Second World War. Lockdown meant that all but essential services, shops, schools, universities and businesses were closed and people had to stay at home. With the exception of the most vulnerable, they were only allowed to buy food or to take exercise locally. Some sectors of employment shut down completely and the care responsibilities of households increased massively. No inter-household visiting was permitted for almost four months. Many families went through the trauma and grief of not being able to be with their sick and dying kin in hospital or even, for some, to attend their funeral.

The virus was unequal and complex in its three-way impact: on health, on the emotional, social and economic consequences of mitigation policies, and on the impact as recession bit. It cruelly amplified existing inequalities and insecurities and exposed the underfunding of social infrastructure after a decade of cuts and austerity. In turn these hugely challenged the leadership capacities and competence of governance. By the end of May 2020 the UK was a 'global leader' in all the wrong ways: it had one of the highest death rates per 100,000 population (Johns Hopkins University 2020). At the same time, in spite or perhaps because of the trauma, the crisis generated new forms of mutuality and solidarity between neighbours, local communities, new and old networks, and civil society organizations (Solnit 2020). Most striking was the public recognition of the value of 'key workers' – health and care workers especially – and, as the country went into lockdown, an appreciation of clean air and green spaces liberated from the daily toll of traffic and factory pollution. As states in many countries, including the UK, upturned neoliberal principles and increased public borrowing to subsidize the loss of wages by workers and businesses in lockdown, there was a growing recognition that life could not go back to 'normal'. Not only did this invoke from some much stronger commitments to global co-operation and leadership, it also elicited a sense from others that there could be no return to austerity, nationalism and inequality, that the social and economic impacts of the crisis had to be borne equitably, and that possibilities existed for setting out and enacting a new vision of post-pandemic green reconstruction. In all of these turning points, the issues of gender, race, ethnicity, migration, age, disability and their intersections with socioeconomic inequalities of class, region, exposure and occupation, were prominent.

Not all risks are equal

The impact of the virus worked disproportionally on existing inequalities in multiple ways. Somatically, death from the virus is disproportionate by age: those over seventy are at greater risk, and this increases with the frailty of old age. Risk is also greater for those with underlying health problems at all ages. Men are more likely to die from Covid-19 than women: they constituted two-thirds of those who died in the working-age population (aged twenty to sixty-four) in the first two months that the virus spread in England and Wales (ONS 2020a). Deaths were seven times higher than average for men in lower-paid occupations, particularly for security guards, chefs, bus and taxi drivers, and machine operatives. Men and women working in social care where they were particularly exposed to the virus were twice as likely to die (ONS 2020b), and deprived areas bore the brunt of fatalities (ONS 2020c). These figures represent the first wave of the virus. As it continued, first declining and then by autumn beginning to increase, the geography of infection and hospitalization rates remained stubbornly associated with regionalized inequalities (Dorling 2020). In addition, Black men and Black women were respectively 4.3 and 4.2 times more likely to die from the virus than people of White ethnicity (ONS 2020a). Similar figures were found for people of Asian and mixed ethnicities, and, even if they were slightly lower, they were much higher than those for the White population. Factors contributing to death, illness and deprivation were multiple, as the following examples illustrate.

BAME populations are younger on average than people of White ethnicities and therefore should have lower rates. This disproportionate impact was also recorded in the US and Sweden and has yet (in 2020) to be properly investigated, but initial analyses demonstrate a complex intersection of multiple factors in which BAME groups experience the effects of racism and specific racial inequalities in employment, housing and health care (see Qureshi et al. 2020a, 2020b; Lawrence 2020). The intersection of health inequalities mentioned earlier for BAME groups (IHE 2020) points to pre-existing chronic health conditions and co-morbidities – themselves related to poverty – that create greater vulnerability to poor outcomes from COVID-19 infection.[5] BAME groups are more likely to live and work in conditions that engender chronic ill health and also greater exposure to Covid-19, such as in areas of urban density, which were particularly affected by the virus, and in overcrowded households in the more insecure private rented sector. BAME workers are over-represented in the lower-paid and more precarious segments of the labour market and as key workers have been more exposed to the virus. A clear example is the NHS, where BAME groups comprise 21 per cent of the staff, yet by April they comprised 63 per cent of all Covid deaths among NHS staff (Cook et al. 2020). This includes BAME doctors and consultants, for whom these socio-economic inequalities would not have seemed to apply, except for the fact that BAME doctors tend to be concentrated in the less prestigious areas of geriatric health care, which meant they were more exposed to the virus (Qureshi et al. 2020b). The evidence presented to Public Health England from BAME groups provided repeated experiences of workplace discrimination and harassment that meant, for example, that demanding better PPE measures at work was difficult (Public Health England 2020a; see also King's Fund 2020b). The report from this consultation contained key recommendations about the importance, for example, of collecting ethnicity data on health care and doing research *with* and not just *on* minority ethnic communities. But the overall issue of racism was passed to the setting up of a new commission on racial disparities. This will join six existing commissions whose recommendations have yet to be acted upon.

All these conditions were intensified for migrant workers and asylum seekers, many of whom have 'No Recourse to Public Funds' or a £650 surcharge (in 2020) to use the NHS. Under public pressure, this was subsequently temporarily withdrawn for migrant NHS and care workers. While important, this creates a principle that access to public services is by reward rather than right. During the critical stage of the pandemic many migrants continued to work, as they had no access to the pandemic unemployment benefit and were fearful of eviction or deportation. Charities also reported food hunger among asylum seekers (Qureshi et al. 2020b). Many among the Filipino migrant workforce are long-resident undocumented domestic and care workers. During the pandemic more than half lost their work and all source of income (Kanlungan 2020).

Some groups were affected by the deleterious social and economic consequences of mitigation policies rather than the physical impact of the virus, particularly women and young workers. Women workers are more likely to be in health, care and food retail work, which involved greater exposure to the virus. With younger workers, they occupy the lowest-paid jobs on part-time, temporary or zero-hours contracts. Where these were terminated, they were often not eligible for the pandemic income support measures. Women have jobs that are less amenable to working from home, which meant that, when schools were closed, coping with child care posed an intense problem (Dorling 2020). This affected parents of children with disabilities, who depend on specialist care services even more intensely. Some of these conditions also hold for younger and older earners who disproportionately lost employment or were furloughed and, without significant public training and reskilling programmes, face major difficulties in finding future work (Gustafsson 2020). Women, especially lone parents and BAME and migrant women, face particular challenges of poverty and homelessness which, without gender-sensitive support, are likely to increase in the future.

By the beginning of May, 20 per cent of households with children were unable to access enough food because of loss of income and disorganiza- tion with the substitute food vouchers for children on free school meals. This was even greater for larger families, lone parents and parents with a disabled child (Food Foundation 2020). With the closure of schools and nurseries, and also because of job loss, women found that they were taking on more home schooling and domestic work, setting in train for the future a reversal of any moves towards gender parity at home and at work (IFS 2020). An estimated 10,000 private nurseries will close permanently through non-viability (WBG 2020b). Disability also took its toll during the pandemic because of the combined impact of loss of income *and* local ser- vices. Disabled women in particular faced extreme isolation and poverty (WBG 2020c).

School closures also reinforced unequal educational impacts on those children for whom online access to schooling is difficult because of lack of technology. As well as the danger of food insecurity, many children have suffered generalized anxiety in the loss of support from friends, especially where home conditions are stressful (UNICEF 2020). Self-isolation put women and children at greater risk where they live with abusive partners: the National Domestic Abuse Helpline reported a 25 per cent increase in requests for help, a situation made more critical by the cutting back on funding for domestic abuse support centres. In all of these respects, migrant women with no recourse to public funds found themselves increasingly vulnerable (WBG 2020d; Grierson 2020).

However, it was deaths from Covid-19 among residents and staff in care homes which amplified the low value given to frail older people and care workers. Similar concerns were raised by disabled people's organizations and their eligibility for hospital intensive care treatment (WBG 2020c). People with learning disabilities were six times more likely to die from the virus than the able-bodied population, and at a younger age (Public Health England 2020b). By the beginning of May 2020 there had been over 8,000 deaths in care homes in England and Wales and a further 4,200 deaths of care-home residents in hospitals, which amounted to almost a third of all Covid-19 deaths at that point (ONS 2020b). (In Scotland this was 45 per cent.) Figures at this stage were subject to possible underestimates, but the total death rate among care-home residents was significantly higher than during the same period in 2019.

While older people were the most vulnerable to the virus – and this was the case across all countries – a number of political and systemic aspects are also implicated. The government failed to prioritize care homes either for testing, tracking and tracing for those carrying the virus or for the distribution of personal protective equipment until after the peak of deaths. A quarter of care staff work on zero-hours contracts across different residential homes and domiciliary services, making them highly susceptible to transmission. In addition, older patients discharged from hospital into care homes were not routinely tested. Sometimes, sick residents were not admitted to hospital. Once the virus was introduced into a home it was difficult to stop its spread without the existence of separate isolation homes. Private care homes were expected to procure new protective equipment in a market that had gone globally competitive. In the first month 131 care workers died of the virus (Samuel 2020).

Health and social care infrastructure
Front-line health-care staff and social care workers everywhere made heroic efforts to deal with the crisis, risking their own lives. It should be said that the pandemic presented unprecedented financial, organizational and public health challenges for *every* affected country; some managed much better than others, notably Taiwan, New Zealand, Germany, Norway and Denmark (all with female prime ministers). In the UK, not only was the damage of austerity and structural problems from cuts and health and care reforms exposed, but also revealed was an over-centralized state dependent on subcontracting, along with a hollowed-out capacity for central governmental leadership, transparency and consultation.

As noted earlier in the chapter, before the pandemic hit, the NHS had been struggling to cope with increasing demand on accident and emergency departments, a lack of acute beds, and staff shortages. The social care system had become increasingly organizationally separate from the NHS as a largely private-for-profit provision and had been described as 'dysfunctional'. The winter of 2018/19 had seen hospitals working at maximum capacity, and critical warnings were given for the winter of 2019/20. However, much earlier, in 2011, 400 public health experts in an open letter to the House of Lords warned that the 2012 Health and Social Care reforms would 'undermine the ability of the health system to respond effectively to communicable disease outbreaks and other public health emergencies' (quoted in McCoy 2020). One reason was that the removal of independence from the newly created Public Health England rendered it less effective as a change agent by being brought closer to Whitehall and away from the NHS. This became obvious during the first two months of the pandemic, when it was left to independent public health experts to warn of the failure to go into lockdown earlier (six weeks after the death toll in Italy was being headlined) or to continue with a test, track and trace strategy, or the dangers of coming out of lockdown without those measures in place (Monbiot 2020). Other criticisms focused on the failure to prepare properly for the pandemic. These pointed to the grim contradiction that, in 2019, both the US and the UK topped the international Global Health Security Index for preparedness for a pandemic (GHSI 2019), yet within a year both countries were topping the mortality rate index (Pegg 2020). As early as 2006 the UK started its pandemic flu planning, which included setting aside funding, essential stocks and vital equipment. But after 2013 the amount of money dedicated to this was lowered by almost a half, so that equipment was not available when the crisis came. By January 2020 the reality of Covid-19 showed that it was more deadly than flu. In spite of this the government followed the procedures for flu, and even in early March the prime minister played down the effect of the virus with advice to 'Wash your hands and business as usual' (The Guardian 2020).

Challenges to the style and substance of governance
In the probability of a future inquiry into the management of the pandemic more criticisms will ensue. In the meantime I suggest that the public health and economic measures required to mitigate the impact fundamentally challenged the government's economic doctrines, neoliberal individualism, disdain for the public sector and for experts, nationalist complacency, ethno-nationalist contempt for migrants, and shape-shifting and centralized style of governance. What it assembled, as it struggled to articulate public advice to put community safety before individual self-interest, was a set of measures that swung erratically between major concessions to these challenges and reversion to type.

To begin with, the management of the pandemic required on-the-ball strategic public planning and clear public communication and consultation, both with scientific experts and with those charged with action in health and social care, together with municipal and regional authorities and the third sector. In so far as people were expected to sacrifice their own needs for the good of community safety, trust in leadership was essential. One of the main criticisms, mentioned earlier, was that the government was late to introduce lockdown and that instituting it even a week earlier could have saved a significant number of lives (BBC 2020a). This dithering registered a suspicion of expert advice and a tendency to downplay environmental 'crises'. In January, the prime minister took a week to arrive at the scene of the floods that had left many families homeless and destitute, echoing the way in which Theresa May failed to make an immediate visit to the site of the Grenfell Tower fire. The position of most cabinet members had been outright opposition to 'experts', and this reached its apotheosis during the Brexit campaign, when 'experts' had been one of its main targets. Michael Gove had said that 'the country had had enough of experts' (Clarke and Newman 2017). Yet the development of a pandemic strategy depended on consultation with scientists and public health experts. The government pandemic team of ministers was keen to insist that their decisions were informed by 'the science', but they did not communicate clearly what that science was or how it fitted the context. As a leading scientist, Sir Paul Nurse, director of the Francis Crick Institute, commented, the government failed to acknowledge what could only be tentative knowledge from scientists dealing with a new virus, and that they needed to communicate clearly in the public domain an explanation for decision-making backed up by evidence (Cowburn 2020). Such a communication strategy would have required honesty and humility and an engagement with people's own concerns and sacrifices. But this was a government whose campaigns and governance had relied upon shape-shifting rhetoric, ethno-nationalist supremacy, slogans, parsimony with facts, and avoidance of blame. Sometimes the slogans worked ('stay at home'); sometimes they did not ('stay alert').

The situation also demanded a strategy based on a thorough understanding of how different parts of public services fitted together, whereas government policy had been to treat public services as a suitable case for privatization with a trajectory of increasing fragmentation and dwindling co-ordination. This also required consultation with local and regional authorities, who had better on-the-ground knowledge. The mayor of Manchester, Andy Burnham, complained that decisions had been centrally driven and were sometimes out of kilter with local circumstances (Halliday 2020). While only future analysis will show which strategies worked and which did not, the easing of lockdown in the summer was based on the decline of infections in London, but this was at the same time as infections were on the increase in Yorkshire, the North East and the North West. Indeed, the Scottish and Welsh governments did not follow England's example in this respect. Paul Nurse again criticized the failure to utilize smaller laboratories in the country, whose offers to develop testing were shelved, rather than large commercial ones. Similarly, when track, trace and test measures were finally initiated in June, they were organized centrally, subcontracted to SERCO, rather than based in the regions where organizers could use their local knowledge.[6]

As the infection rate increased and revealed the deadly nature of the virus, not least to the prime minister himself, who ended up in intensive care, the reality of the crucial dedication of public-sector workers in health, social care and municipal services became obvious. Every Thursday evening the population came out of their homes to 'clap for carers'. These were groups of workers whose demands for better pay, conditions and capacity had been repeatedly ignored or rebuffed. Furthermore, many were BAME and migrant workers who had for the past six years been presented with a 'hostile environment'. In entering solidarity with health and care workers, the prime minister reinscribed the NHS as an emblem of 'Britishness' in the war against the virus which British sacrifice and spirit would win, to the backdrop of the commemoration of VE Day in 1945. (Later in the year the remarkable achievement of a vaccine by Oxford University scientists in collaboration with the company AstraZeneca was similarly signalled as a symbol of British greatness.) This nationalist rousing was doused by the acknowledgement that many in the NHS were migrant workers who, because of government immigration policy, did not even have free access to health care. This was a point where the government backed down, by cancelling the hospital surcharge for migrant NHS and care workers, but at the same time as it ushered in an Immigration Bill that would deny entry to many of those who were currently working in the low-paid areas of health and social care.

The greatest breach in public trust was news that the prime minister's chief special adviser, Dominic Cummings, had broken the law and guidelines of the lockdown (the Coronavirus Act 2020) by driving his wife and son 250 miles to stay in a house on his father's estate when they had symptoms of the virus. He further drove his family to a local beauty spot in order to 'test his eyesight' that had deteriorated during his illness. In defending him, the prime minister asserted that Cummings had 'followed the instincts of every father' to protect his child. It was 'common sense'. In this way he subverted any notion of collective responsibility for either 'stay safe' or 'stay alert' to one of the primacy of individualist family self-interest (Syal et al. 2020). In his own defence, Cummings said his four-year-old child would have been vulnerable had he and his wife fallen ill together. However, the guidelines allowed for travel only for people under extreme duress, such as a woman experiencing domestic abuse. This rendered the actions of the many who had made sacrifices of not being with family members when they died, or making do with cox-and-box child care while ill, to individual miscalculations of risk and regulation rather than efforts to place collective safety above their own needs.

More paradoxical was that a government committed to holding back public expenditure was forced by circumstance and public pressure to reverse the parameters of public finance. Hotels were taken over temporarily to enable those sleeping on the streets to be housed. By March the chancellor had introduced a furlough salary retention scheme that recognized widespread loss of earnings and employment by paying 80 per cent of wages (up to £2,500 per month) to those not needed by their employers. It included migrant workers affected by the 'No Recourse to Public Funds' ruling and employees unable to work because of child-care responsibilities as a result of the closure of nurseries and schools. Access to furlough had to be agreed with the employer and benefited mainly workers in secure full-time employment. An 80 per cent taxable grant of average annual earnings was made payable to the self-employed earning less than £50,000 a year. The income support system was also expanded: Universal Credit standard rate increased by £20 per week, as was the local housing allowance, but not the Employment Support Allowance for disabled people, or statutory sick pay. Over £300 billion was set aside for loan guarantees and grant funds for businesses, and cuts were made to business rates. The total package increased envisaged public borrowing for 2020/21 to £175 billion, and the total costs were much higher than after the financial crisis (IFS 2020). In addition, the pandemic contingency fund was increased from £10.6 billion to £266 billion. These amounts were higher than in other European countries largely because the UK was starting from a lower base of public expenditure. Overall the crisis threatened a major recession, with an increase to over 3 million unemployed and a 35 per cent drop in GDP (OBR 2020).

These were vital moves, but they left major gaps which reproduced and intensified the very insecurities and inequalities created by austerity. Furthermore, they introduced many for the first time to the rigours of Universal Credit. The New Economics Foundation's calculations found that there were 1.6 million people at risk of both losing their employment and falling through the government's net. In order of greatest risk, these were young people, older workers, BAME workers, and women workers – those most likely to be in fixed-term and zero-hours contracts, the under-employed, the self-employed and social renters (NEF 2020; see also WBG

2020a). More fundamentally, these were temporary measures which, when withdrawn, would reveal mass unemployment, personal debt, homelessness and businesses closures. For many, the call to 'build back better' was for a long-term financial reconstruction similar to the post-war Marshall Plan (WEF 2020b); for others, it was a plan that was coupled with tackling climate change (Pettifor 2020) and more (see chapter 7).

As all this unfolded, on 25 May 2020 bystanders' videos of the killing in public of George Floyd, an African American, by a white Minneapolis policeman went viral and sparked the biggest series of protests since the 1960s, under the banner of Black Lives Matter, not only in the US but across the world. They brought to a head the long-time violently racist practices of the police as well as systemic institutional and everyday street racisms. The slogan 'I can't breathe' – the last words that George Floyd uttered – embodied both the dehumanization experienced by people of colour and the pandemic itself, where not being able to breathe was the symptom of illness and death which had ravaged Black communities. Some mobilizations led to the removal of statues celebrating men who had supported slavery and other acts of white supremacy. In Bristol, England, young people of multiple ethnicities pulled down the statue of Edward Colston, whose money from the slave trade had helped build the city, and threw it in the river. The worldwide anti-racist protests pointed to fundamental questions for the twenty-first century. In what ways could these movements generate a profound and democratic reckoning of the historical and structural forces of racism? Could the recognition of dehumanization of people of colour help unlock the dehumanizations experienced by other marginalized groups? How far is humanity capable of inhabiting a planet (which also cannot breathe) and sharing it equitably? Nation challenged; nature gasping; families weeping; work transfiguring.

4: Not all of a piece

Together these final events of the decade demanded a no going back to austerity along with the multiple inequalities it had reproduced. This raises two issues to which this chapter has only referred in passing – how contestation provides an important impetus to change, and how crises and contestations outside of formal politics create spaces for new thinking on transforming society. These are issues discussed in chapters 5 and 7. There is also a third issue, which is that policy-making is contradictory and diverse – an assemblage of responses to different social forces (Clarke et al. 2015).

The analysis I have given so far is not the whole picture. Policies were not only more contested by different forces, but they were also more contradictory and more regionally and nationally diversified by processes of both uneven deindustrialization and national devolution. Contradictions surfaced from emerging cracks in the social geology: over the decade there were anxious recognitions by governments that inequalities and social immobilities needed to be tackled. For example, a surfacing seam through the decade was where the binaries between the 'deserving' and 'undeserving', responsible and risky families, skilled and unskilled workers, British and Other, began to break down, when the lives of resourceful 'hardworking families' began to look like those of 'the undeserving' – trapped in low-paid work, dispossessed, indebted, and with restricted mobility. There was recognition of this in a post-referendum speech by Theresa May in 2016 when she made a reference to 'the just about managing' ('JAMS'):

> If you're from an ordinary working-class family, life is much harder than many people in Westminster realise. You have a job but you don't always have job security. You have your own home, but you worry about paying a mortgage. You can just about manage but you worry about the cost of living and getting your kids into a good school. If you're one of those families, if you're just managing, I want to address you directly. (May 2016)

If this rhetoric refracted the danger of solidarity across dissolving binaries, then the years of Brexit discussion regenerated new/old divisions. As part of her neo-protectionist 'One Nation' speech, May promised to deliver more reforms than any government since the 1980s had even dared to suggest (Streeck 2017). They hardly happened, or if they did they were quite circumscribed, as I show below. But these were also about responding to mounting evidence or claims about social injustices from civil society. Such responses are important in providing toeholds of recognition around which groups can mobilize. One example of this is the UK National Living Wage, introduced in 2015. The policy built on and went further than New Labour's Minimum Wage by increasing it for workers aged twenty-five and more. It also introduced greater penalties against employers who did not comply. Sixteen- to 24-year-olds are eligible for a minimum wage at a rate lower than the Living Wage but graduated according to age cohort. This then set the terms for a campaign for a 'Real Living Wage' which keeps a watch on levels as well as arguing for a different measurement of adequacy based on people's needs (see Living Wage Foundation, www.livingwage.org.uk).

However, it is also the case that the technologies of recognition used by governments can become a further obstacle to social justice: two (or fewer) steps forward, one step back. An example of this, mentioned earlier, is same-gender marriage recognition. Another is the Racial Disparity Act of 2016, a commitment to review data on racial disparities, also discussed earlier. This recognition of obstinate forms of racial disadvantage in the use of public services has become an important reference point for campaigns, but at the same time it has not provided adequate strategies to deal with racial injustice. This came to a head after the Black Lives Matter protests in 2020: first, because the report by Public Health England (2020c) entitled *Disparities in the Risks and Outcomes of Covid-19* included neither the significant amount of evidence reported on structural and personal racism, nor the spatial impact of air pollution which affect BAME groups, nor any recommendations for action (Qureshi et al. 2020b); and, second, as noted earlier, the government response was to set up a Commission on Inequalities, which would further delay any concrete action.

A further example which responds to racial and gender injustices is the Modern Slavery Act, passed in 2015. This prohibits slavery, servitude and forced or compulsory labour; sexual exploitation; organ removal; and services obtained by force, threats or deception, and/or from children and vulnerable people. It links together human rights, social and economic rights, and children's rights and attempts to deal with a social problem whose practices cross international borders, especially trafficking into sex work or labour-intensive manual work or services. It also highlights the need for ethical business practices by corporations. While the Act was ground-breaking, the tools to prosecute presuppose corporate compliance; in the nature of large business organizations, this is not only difficult to enforce but in many cases is at odds with accepted systems of profit-making in competitive businesses, which depend on the power to cut the costs of labour in supply chains (Simic and Blitz 2019). At the same time, it is often poverty and the lack of alternative wage-earning opportunities that render people vulnerable to the processes of modern slavery. In their study of trafficking and coercion in sex work in Jamaica, Katie Cruz and her colleagues show how sex workers' vulnerability would be better tackled by starting with the decriminalization of sex work and homosexuality (Cruz et al. 2019). There is also little in the Modern Slavery Act that aims to empower those workers found to be in conditions of slavery, for example by having access to legal aid. What obscures the structural context is the way the Act frames modern slavery in terms of its victims on the one side and malevolent traffickers and criminal employers on the other, as if both were exceptions to the globalization of capital and labour rather than part of an exploitative postcolonial logic of globalized production processes and increasingly restrictive migration regimes. Furthermore, the presentation of the state as protector conceals the ways in which it is state immigration policy that renders many groups of migrants vulnerable to exploitation. In fact, because of the way trafficking is seen as synonymous with illegality, the greater restrictions on immigration controls are presented as being in the interests of migrants (Anderson 2013). Nevertheless, in spite of these limitations, the Act does legitimize ethical business practices. Further, as Coretta Phillips argues, this revival of the term 'slavery' allows for the articulation of experiences of those who have found themselves controlled and exploited in this extreme way and shows how 'the intersecting harms of exploitation, vulnerabilities and dependency operate over time and space' (Phillips 2019: 47).

Along different lines were the responses to significant pressure from women's organizations over violence against women and girls. 'Revenge pornography' was made a criminal offence in 2015. 'Coercive and control-ling behaviour' that includes not only physical domestic violence but also forms of emotional and economic controlling and intimidating behaviour became a punishable offence by prison sentence also in 2015. Legal aid was allowed for victims, and a Domestic Abuse Bill in 2019 set out a number of important procedures which would strengthen the co-ordination and pri-oritization of support for victims and their children. This includes making it a statutory duty of local authorities to provide refuge. However, the capacity of local authorities to carry out new responsibilities is severely constrained by a decline of 24 per cent in funding allocated to domestic violence since 2010 (Cooper and Lacey 2019). During the pandemic, extra ring-fenced funding was provided to enable local authorities to commis-sion support for women and children. While this was welcomed as a first step, there was concern that it did not make up for the losses to local authorities (House of Lords Library 2020). These losses have hit poorer areas and specialist services for disabled people and BAME women (WBG 2018b). Further, the Bill does not offer protection to migrant women who have no recourse to public funds, because that status would disallow their use of a refuge (Step Up Migrant Women 2020).

Much of the analysis in this chapter has focused on the political legiti-macy for austerity policies which have had a significantly negative impact on the lives of particular groups in the population. In this, as the quota-tions at the beginning of the chapter illustrated, the economic and the ideological are seen to go hand in hand. The financial crisis may thus be assumed to have exacerbated a widening of inequalities between the top 10 per cent and the rest of us. My concern has been on a mix of social, political and economic relations of power, but is this borne out by a focus solely on economic inequalities? In terms of overall wealth inequalities, a report from the Resolution Foundation showed that, by the end of 2020, neither the financial crisis in 2008 nor the pandemic had dented the assets of the wealthiest 1 per cent, who own 23 per cent of the total wealth in the UK. This difference is twice that of income inequalities (Leslie 2021). More detailed research of economic inequalities, measured in terms of trends in hourly wages, household income and non-pension wealth, shows a complex picture (Obolenskaya and Hills 2019). In the two decades from 1995/6 to 2015/16, for the bulk of the population there was relative stability in economic inequality, especially compared with the period when the New Right came to power, when income and earnings really began to diverge. The share for the top 1 per cent was higher in 2015, but other measures of income inequality were similar to where they were twenty years earlier, apart from a brief rise just after 2008. This does not imply any significant moves towards equality – far from it – but that there was a growth in wages and living conditions in the decade from 1995/6 which then flattened out to keep high levels of inequality intact. Yet, within this overall latter stagnation of inequality, there are significant changes across and within different groups. Of the most marked is the difference between 2005 and 2015 in the wages, income and wealth of younger people and those over fifty-five. This has particular significance for future generations, given the likely impact that the post-pandemic recession will have on younger workers and for the support needed for younger adults with families. The economic prospects for men and women aged thirty to thirty-four declined sharply during this decade, whereas pay grew more than a third for men and women aged fifty-five plus (ibid.: 11–12), although poorer and single pensioners did not fare so well. Indeed the poorer sections of all groups in terms of age, gender, disability, ethnicity/nationality/migrant status, socio-economic group and area were consistently worse off. The research identified those who fared very badly during the slow-growth second decade as including the poorest lone parents, the poorest Londoners, the poorest social tenants, disabled households in general, and especially the pay of disabled women. In addition, households in the East Midlands and the North East and Black African households all showed losses in their resources (ibid.: 22). In many ways this bears out the intersectional analysis earlier in the chapter on BAME women (which also took services into account) and disabled people. It also confirms the questioning of the identification of 'Northern white working class' as representing *the* 'left behind', as discussed earlier in the consideration of Brexit.

Finally, the last bit of this more diverse picture of the decade is devolutionary social policy, a further aspect of the relationship of welfare to 'nation'. The UK is, internationally, one of the most centralized policy-making polities, but in this century its conception of the alignment of nation and social policy has been challenged by both the devolution of power to Scotland, Wales and Northern Ireland from 1999 and the creation of city regional devolution, especially with the election of mayors since 2017. Both provide an experimental basis for a divergence from Westminster. Indeed, the pandemic opened up fissures between the devolved nations as each followed different virus-security strategies, and as the regions challenged central government's financial mitigation support. As an example of divergence, I look briefly here at Scotland's recent social security policy. Although Scotland has historically pursued a number of public policy differences, such as in education and the legal system, it has also diverged in not having tuition fees and having free care support for older people, greater security for tenants, and more generous maternity and neonatal support.

Following the Scottish referendum a number of new areas were devolved, including aspects of social security and tax. The reforms in the 2018 Social Security (Scotland) Bill (delayed because of the pandemic) mark three key divergences from the Welfare Reform Act. First, among the guiding principles is social security as a human right, which assumes at the outset a person's eligibility, unlike the UK system in which the claimant has to demonstrate their eligibility. A central principle is respect for the dignity of individuals and that engagement with employment support will be voluntary and not mandatory. Second, the approach is one of redistributive social investment – targeting poverty (increasing a range of support for children, increasing support for carers, improved support for disabled people) and providing public services while maintaining efficiency and economy. Third, it sets out 'a framework for a new way of doing things' (Patrick 2018: 2) in developing the policy. This includes not only consultation with the third sector and social security experts but also 'experience panels' – those with direct experiences of poverty and use of the benefit system. However, while Scotland has the power to make its own priorities, it has little control over its financial resources (Stephens and Fitzpatrick 2018). It will have to set up its own system alongside aspects of the UK system that could be difficult to implement and even more difficult for claimants to navigate. And although the policy is progressive compared with the UK social security, the Scottish government has exercised caution in its fiscal policy. Nevertheless, the Scottish Bill will iterate support as a progressive alternative to the punitive and demeaning UK system.

The issue of Scottish independence also raises the question of how the Scottish nation is defined. On the one hand, it appears to present its nationalism as different from England's in being relatively progressive and expressing openness to multiculturalism. Scottish identity is rooted not in patriality but in a commitment to the progressive project of Scotland. However, as Bassel and Emejulu comment in their study of minority women, austerity and politics, this leads to a certain complacency that anti-racism does not need discussion and can be put to one side to get on with the more urgent issue of Scottish self-determination (Bassel and Emejulu 2018). Racism is an issue that is seen to belong to England. In this way the authors found that, for minority women, there were few spaces for debate and action on racism and anti-racism. It is not surprising then that Nasar Meer's analysis of Scotland's approach to race equality does not find the same progress as that in social security: 'while there may be burgeoning broader "Scottish approach" underway, it is not yet necessarily discernible in the area of race equality policy' (Meer 2020: 248).

Part of the problem is that the usual consultation processes with advocates on the ground have not produced a consensus about the priorities for action, as for gender and LGBTQI+ equality. This raises interesting questions about how far the Scottish political approach, which has been dominated by the SNP, broadly centre-left and resting on the strengthening of a Scottish national identity, will be required to rethink that identity in order to sustain dialogue with its BAME communities and produce a consensual ethos for race equality in the run-up to a new referendum on independence. Reporting on views from young activist Scottish people of colour after the 2020 Black Lives Matter protests, Eilidh Akilade found that these protests had given activists more of a public space for anti-racist politics, even though few of them thought independence on its own would guarantee greater discussion (Akilade 2020).

Conclusion

The chapter has shown how the British government's social policy has been shaped by the four intersecting global crises – of financialized capitalism, of care, of ecology, and of racialized borders. In this shaping I argued that it attempted to use austerity measures to settle the unsettling relations of family, nation, work and nature, although this settling remains to be seen for nature in the form of the pandemic. 'Hard-working families' continued to hyphenate the domains of family and work in a situation where financial compulsion to submit to the precarities of work was privileged over care needs and responsibilities for children and older people, a combination which affected particularly women on benefits and those experiencing current and enduring racial inequalities in their intersections with poverty. This depletion and devaluation of the capacities for care was reinforced by other processes – privatization and financialization of care provision, the low pay of care workers, and governmental indifference. Aspects of family policy were also weaponized to differentiate between those acting responsibly and resiliently in the face of austerity and those whose 'lifestyles' posed a risk to national economic efforts. In this, as in many other techniques used by government, a velvet glove of liberal rhetoric – fairness, equality, disparity – clothed an iron hand of division and dehumanization. This was especially the case around parenting and was reproduced in different ways in the bordering practices involving particular groups of claimants – BAME and migrant groups, lone mothers, social renters and disabled people – and served as justification for penalizing measures in the Welfare Reform Act. But it did not stop with claimants, as shown by the denial of access to benefits, health care, employment and financial services to some members of a generation of British citizens who had arrived from the former colonies in the 1950s and 1960s. The technology of policing and surveillance through public-sector workers as well as by landlords, employers and banks was further deployed in securitization measures against Muslim people, compounding multiple and intersecting inequalities and exclusions.

If this showed the spread of the necropolitical divisions between those whose lives matter and those whose don't, then this intensified in the second half of the decade. In spite of the tragedy and shame of the Grenfell Tower fire, which shone a dreadful light on every facet of the lives of BAME and migrant people and neoliberal housing policies in austerity London, by 2019, under the influence of the far-right UKIP/Brexit party, generalized insecurity became more securely tied to an ethno-nationalist notion of the 'left behind'. This was represented as a working class whose optics were white, largely male and northern. The Brexit campaign attempted to reposition these groups as the *unjustly dispossessed*, as against those (migrants, minority ethnic groups, disabled, asylum seekers) for whom exploitation and expropriation, and even expulsion, were to be expected. Central to this claim was the idea that ending immigration and cutting ties with the EU would restore the welfare state and job security to the 'native' population. On a landslide election, the new prime minister, Boris Johnson, promised not only to break with the EU and control immigration but, like May before him, to 'level up' in order to 'heal' national divisions. Restrictions on migration in the new Immigration and Social Security Co-ordination (EU Withdrawal) Bill 2020 were promised as part of the same logic – to deliver jobs for 'native' workers. Yet, no sooner had the new migration restrictions been announced – which sealed the routes through which lower-paid health and care staff from other countries would be able to enter the country – than the global pandemic of Covid-19 struck.

The effects of this traumatic public health emergency were not only to amplify multiple socio-economic inequalities and the incompetence of a hollowed-out, over-centralized state but also to turn upside down neo-liberal logic, as policy was forced to place the health of the population above the needs of the market. Capitalism, for a short while, went into suspended animation. The government's policies were to undermine its own reliance on its class, race and gender binaries. First was the 'levelling down' in many parts of the population, particularly as businesses closed, of those forced to apply for Universal Credit. In spite of the £20 per week increase and the withdrawal of some of its more dehumanizing features, new parts of the population began to experience the insecurities of claimants and the vicissitudes of the system. Second, the virus exposed the dependence of the population on a National Health Service and acts of care by others, whether in paid health and social care or in local mutual aid organizations. Third, the disproportionately high numbers of deaths of those in the BAME population, many of whom *were* those (low-paid) health and social care workers, reinforced the contradiction between the value and selflessness of their work and their political, social and economic devaluation. This was reinforced by the world witnessing on social media the death of an African American, George Floyd, by a white Minneapolis police officer kneeling on his neck until he expired. The Black Lives Matter protests that swept around the world faster than the virus itself seemed like a turning point. 'I can't breathe' became the protest slogan, symbolic of both state and street racism and the mode of attack by the virus.

The final section picked up a thread running through the chapter: that pressure and contestation from different forces around aspects of family, nation, work and nature forced governments over the decade to concede to reform: an LGBT Action Plan, the Domestic Violence Bill, the Racial Disparity Unit, the Modern Slavery Act, the Living Wage and the ten point net-zero plan. There were significant limitations to these reforms, but, in common with the challenges to the power and ideology of Westminster to come from the devolved nations and the regional powers, they demonstrate that nothing is ever settled. This provides the link to the next chapter, which focuses upon the enactment of agency and resistance in the social relations of welfare governance.

The Social Relations of Welfare: Subjects, Agents, Activists

Introduction

The previous chapter focused on the ways in which people are constituted – both materially and discursively – as *subjects of welfare*. The framework of family, nation, work and nature enabled an understanding of how the social relations attached to multiple forms of inequality, power and privilege shape the terms on which people, as welfare subjects, access and/ or provide welfare goods and services. However, people are not simply welfare subjects, for they bring to their encounters with welfare services their own experiences, meanings, identities and actions. These can have the effect of reconstituting, for good or ill, or both, the ways in which welfare services are delivered to or by them. In other words, agency is central to an understanding of welfare states as dynamic and often ambivalent sets of relational spaces that are open to tacit or explicit acceptance, resistance and contestation.

The chapter explores these ideas in the following way. While in the introduction to the book I referred to the 'turn to agency' as being one of the important changes that reset social policy research and thinking from the 1990s, here I seek to explain four aspects of this: (i) what prompted this turn; (ii) important developments in understanding the concept of agency in social policy research; (iii) its application to the social relations of welfare – that is, the relationship between providers and users of welfare; and (iv) how agency relates to different logics and spaces of resistance and contestation over social welfare. The chapter offers an intersectional approach to agency which works in two ways – in understanding how interlinked, shifting and multifaceted social relations of power are manifest in the capacity and exercise of agency; and in making visible the forms and spaces of contestation and resistance that often remain out of sight. It also connects to the four themes in chapters 3 and 4 around resistance to capitalism, individualism and consumerism, the depletion of care, climate change and racialized borders through understanding the relationality and interdependence of agency. In the move from welfare subject to agent, it is also informed by Foucault's analysis of the different forms taken by agency and resistance to subjectivation.[1]

The turn to agency

The 1990s generated a call in the discipline of social policy to give greater thought to the concept of agency (Titterton 1992; Le Grand 1997; Deacon and Mann 1999; Williams et al. 1999; Lister 2004). Michael Titterton's was an early attempt to mark out a 'new paradigm' for social policy research, arguing that the 'old paradigm' had worked with 'a somewhat mono-lithic, indeed uni-dimensional, view of human agency: uniform needs and uniform responses are often simply ascribed to individuals within the vul-nerable groupings with which the study of welfare typically concerns itself' (Titterton 1992: 2). He had a point. Within the traditions of mainstream social policy in the UK, the dominant research frame had been heavily structuralist and quantitative. It provided analyses of measurable outcomes for social groups – access to benefits and services to alleviate certain identi-fiable risks and ends (poverty, unemployment, housing, health, care of 'the vulnerable', education). These social groups were categorized objectively in terms of classifications by the registrar-general, by researchers or by policy-makers. That is, they were defined as socio-economic/occupational groups or groups in administratively defined need – single parents, frail elderly, poor, chronically ill, etc. The people who inhabited these fixed categories tended to be represented as passive beneficiaries (or not, as the case might be) of different policies, whose content might vary according to dominant political ideologies. Even in the political economy approach, where agency is central to the analysis, this was represented *collectively* through the actions of the organized working class, a perspective that was to be challenged by other forms of collective action, as explained in chapter 2, and by a more fluid approach to both individual and collective action.

This is not to say that personal experience or the actions of groups or individuals were never referenced, but that they carried illustrative rather than explanatory value. There were exceptions: Titmuss's analysis of vol-untary blood donation was based upon an understanding of people acting out of altruism. It showed how this system both depended upon individual altruism yet also reinforced social altruism, and, as such, it provides an example of how policies could work with the grain of human agency (Titmuss 1970). It was more the case that, particularly in poverty studies, the structuralist emphasis upon the inadequacies of employment, housing, education or income support policies (Townsend 1979) represented an important counter to highly individualist right-wing approaches or those that looked beyond the individual to blaming poor people's collective actions or behaviour or 'underclass culture' for their poverty (Boyson 1971; Murray 1990). Without an alternative understanding of human action, it seemed as if right-wing thinkers of the time had all the best tunes.

To set this in political context, it's possible to see three alternative approaches to agency that developed through neoliberal welfare governance. When the New Right came to power in 1979, they articulated a more elaborate notion of the welfare subject's agency as a 'consumer' exercising 'choice' to meet a 'diversity of individual needs' in the market of welfare provision (see chapter 3). This contrasted the self-reliant employed taxpayer straining to exercise their agency through individual choice with the freeloading welfare dependant. This approach also argued that introducing market mechanisms into welfare state 'monopolies' would make management, procurement and delivery more economic, entrepreneurial and efficient, thus placing welfare managers, professionals and providers into a market efficiency frame. This understanding was supported by public choice theory in which the agency of welfare users and providers is assumed to be driven by rational and well-informed choices that maximize interests in cost-beneficial ways (Osborne and Gaebler 1992).

This perspective was modified by New Labour, who, while embracing the managerialism of their predecessors, attempted to balance responsibilities with rights and identified a wider range of agency which mixed the 'old' with the 'new'. There were 'citizen-consumers' acting in the pursuit of enlightened self-interest; the 'vulnerable' who needed support; and 'welfare dependants' who needed to exercise their responsibilities to be off welfare and in paid work (Williams 2001; Newman and Clarke 2009).

Both of these can be contrasted with a third approach that had emerged from new social welfare movements, community-based groups and organizations, especially those focused on service-users such as the disability, feminist health, mental health and anti-racist education movements. These, too, had moved away from the 'old paradigm' to emphasize the importance of voice, empowerment and control in access to welfare provision ('Nothing about us without us', as the disability slogan goes). This approach signified both personal testimony and representation of welfare subjects as active, empowered citizens, exercising their agency through user control and participation in democratically run public services (Beresford and Croft 1986; Campbell and Oliver 1996; Williams 1992, 1999; Lister 2004; Beresford 2016). This approach, which seeks to transform the social relations of welfare, also became influential in voluntary organizations, NGOs and self-help groups (Williams and Roseneil 2004). Indeed, some social movements transformed the administrative categories imposed upon them, such as lone mother, carer or disabled person, into political identities to stimulate collective organization and action (e.g. CarersUK, Disabled Peoples' International; Gingerbread; single parents; equal families). In addition, many education, health and welfare professionals did not shift wholesale from the paternalist altruism of the old paradigm into the managerialism of the new even when the norms and values of their institutions did. Many carried with them the 'old' values of public service, as well as alternative values of participation and democracy (Barnes and Prior 2009; Newman 2012a).

The existence of these different approaches showed that the binary between old and new paradigms was too simple. At the same time, it confirmed that what these three approaches had in common was an emphasis on welfare subjects as potential *agents of their welfare destiny*; where they differed was, first, in their conceptions of that agency and how it was empowered – as a rational economic consumer (New Right), an enlightened, responsible and self-interested citizen-consumer (New Labour), or an active, empowered citizen (community and other welfare groups) which combined the individual and collective in new ways. The second difference was in the organizational approach to realize this agency: respectively, as market-managerialism, public–private managerial partnership and local democratic participation. It should be said that, on the ground, these differences developed in less distinct and more overlapping ways.

The dynamics of agency

Back in social policy research, the turn to agency produced diverse inquiries. One argument was that the new focus on welfare subjects as creative human agents negotiating their strategies of welfare management was important but should not lose sight of the old emphasis on structure (Williams et al. 1999). However, both agency and structure needed to be much more sensitive to the multiple and intersecting social relations of gender, race, ethnicity, disability, sexuality and age, as well as the discursive, relational and expressive dimensions of both agency and structure. Accordingly, their work made the following points.

• Welfare users and the welfare providers both inhabit multiple and intersecting social relations of power to which they assign greater or lesser power over time and place; there is no fixed binary between users and providers, as people can move in and out of both positions.

- This encounter is subject, to a greater or lesser degree, to dominant social relations of welfare, and these change over time and place (e.g. professional, managerial, bureaucratic, consumerist, egalitarian).
- Users and providers bring their personal histories and experiences (subjectivities), their identities (how they see themselves and their relationship to society) and beliefs, which all affect their agency.
- Agency is both constrained and enabled by a distribution of structural, social and relational resources, and these can constitute both risks and opportunities (Williams et al. 1999: chap. 8).

This approach began to elaborate agency and provide a way of bridging agency to structure. Since then, these aspects have been developed further by different writers, which I now explore.

Agency as relational

To start with, the idea of agency as relational provides an important alternative account to the concept of *homo economicus* so central to public choice theory and to the welfare subject as consumer – the assumption that people's actions are driven by economic rationality in weighing up the costs of action. Research by Simon Duncan, Ros Edwards and their colleagues unpicked what they described as the 'rationality mistake' in the introduction of welfare-to-work policies by New Labour in the late 1990s (Duncan and Edwards 1999; Duncan and Smith 2002; Duncan et al. 2003). This was the assumption that parents, and especially lone mothers, will, in the right conditions (better training, more child care, and a benefits system to make work pay), adopt a rational and instrumental cost–benefit calculation to take up paid work. Their research showed forms of moral reasoning which are more complex and more diverse than this. People's decisions are shaped by their moral and socially negotiated views of what is the right thing to do, as well as by the contexts in which they find themselves. They are worked out in relation to others rather than individually. They also vary across different social groups – in relation to child care, they are deeply gendered but vary with class, place and ethnicity, as do the meanings of what it is to be a 'good mother', 'good father' or 'good partner'. Furthermore, commitments to care for children are often 'non-negotiable' and take priority over other considerations. The researchers found that the values of some mothers were shaped by different beliefs: what might be seen to be 'traditional' gendered views of the needs of a young child to be cared for by its mother; others took the view that it was a mother's responsibility to provide for her child through her wage, while still adhering to a strict gendered division of labour. Yet other mothers who were partnered saw stay-at-home mothering as a form of creative rejection of capitalist values and expectations.

A philosophical perspective that supports this view of agency as relational comes from care ethics (Tronto 1993; Kittay 1999; Sevenhuijsen 1998; Robinson 1999; Williams 2011). It offers a feminist critique of liberal notions of justice for their hyper-individualist take in which autonomy and rationality are seen as the basis of moral reasoning. In this, the individual is viewed in abstract terms and rooted in a Western idealized notion of (masculine) behaviour, which is also assumed to be universal. By contrast, a care-ethical approach starts from the premise of the interdependency of human beings as the basis to reasoning and action. It understands relationships and responsibilities to concrete others as the grounding for justice, for human flourishing and for sustainability. This critique, which bears similarities to the ethics of environmentalism (Jackson 2016), to social transformative principles of Buen Vivir to emerge in Bolivia and Ecuador (Solón 2018) and the African philosophy of Ubuntu (Ramose 2003), represents an important conceptual underpinning to practical prefigurative politics. I return to this at the end of this chapter and in chapter 7.

The psychosocial dynamics of agency

A further important observation in relation to the turn to agency is that agency is more complex than the conscious cognition of a 'deliberative subject' (Newman 2012b). The agency of welfare subjects needs to be seen beyond their constitution through policy discourses (Lewis 2000; Froggett 2002; Hunter 2003, 2015; Hollway 2006). Paul Hoggett (2000, 2001) in particular argues that the embrace of agency has tended to see agency as a 'good thing' – as generative and positive. Instead, he proposes not only that we should view agency as relational rather than autonomous, but also that we should question the conception of agency as belonging to a *unitary and rational* subject. He offers an account which acknowledges the fragmented status of the self that manifests contradictory and ambivalent motivations and actions. Without such a conception we are likely to provide an 'over-socialised' interpretation of human behaviour (2000: 10) – that is, one that explains actions in terms of external social context and ignores the complex and contradictory ways in which these are internalized and given expression through individual experience. This refers to the way emotions – love, fear, hate, despair – play out in action. Looking to these enables us to grasp better the emotional injuries that emanate from, for example, being ignored, shamed, belittled or ridiculed – experiences that work in different ways through sexism, racism, classism, ageism, ableism and homophobia and the privileges attached to whiteness, financial security, masculinity, heterosexuality and able-bodiedness. Or, to put it differently, to understand better the forms of fear and defensiveness and unconscious privilege that give rise to racism, sexism or disgust of those in poverty. It enables us to capture the ways in which ethno-nationalist populism, misogyny or hate of those with disability can be mobilized (Andreouli et al. 2019). Similarly, a psychosocial understanding of the failure to attend to the gravity of climate change locates collective and individual indifference, disavowal and denial in the complex emotional responses to potential disaster that emerge from managing the fear and anxiety it creates (Hoggett 2019).

Drawing on the object-relations school of psychoanalysis, and Klein, Bion and Winnicott in particular, Hoggett argues that our agency needs to be understood in terms of our intersubjectivity: how our fears and self-alienation are fed back to us through our intimate and social worlds in ways that make us less or more able to contain them. The less contained they are, then the more likely they are turned in on ourselves or out onto others. An inability (or, more properly, the extent of an inability, as we are all caught up by ambivalence) to accept in oneself particular conditions – say, of vulnerability, dependency, cultural, bodily or intellectual difference – can lead to splitting these off into distaste or disgust, which is then projected onto others. The attack on 'a dependency culture' can result from disgust of the very idea of dependency (Hoggett 2001: 44). Important in Hoggett's work is his prefigurative consideration of what would be the 'good enough' conditions for the containment of fear. He looks to the emotional foundations of understanding, dialogue, generosity and care as a basis of a 'society as an interdependent community of friends and strangers' (2000: 209) in which, for example, the capacity of communities to hold their differences, while neither essentializing nor inferiorizing them, establishes a crucial basis for the development of locally run and locally organized welfare services which are universalist in principle and diverse in practice.

Relating agency to action

Within social policy research, one of the areas over the twenty-first century where this move to investigate agency through 'voice', based on qualitative and participatory research methods, has been particularly marked is in poverty studies (Lister 2004, 2013, 2021; Ridge 2009; Shildrick et al. 2012; Walker 2014; Daly and Kelly 2015; Wright 2016; Patrick 2016; Edmiston forthcoming). Ruth Lister has argued that, in order to understand poverty, we need to move beyond the counting of 'the category of people who do not count' (Lister 2015: 140, citing Rancière 2004) to appreciate what poverty means to those who experience it and how it shapes the possibilities for agency. In recent years, when, as chapter 4 showed, media, popular and political discourses have treated people in poverty as objects of derision, inferiority, disgust, contamination or pity, then rendering people as subjects of their own lives is vital in challenging such dynamics of subordination (Jones 2011; Tyler 2013; Lister 2015).

Lister's analysis (2004, 2015) of the agency of people living in poverty is important in a number of ways.

- It nuances practices of agency from the everyday to the strategic. In other words, it locates agency as both personal and political.
- It is drawn from research and campaigns in which people with experience of poverty participated, in particular the Commission on Poverty, Participation and Power (CoP 2002).
- It draws lessons from the Global South as well as the Global North.
- It conceptualizes agency as relational and shaped by the constraints of both lack of *resources* and lack of *respect*. This may be the effect of stigma, shame, otherness, and so on. In other words, it is not just the material aspects of poverty but also their social and relational encounters which are significant in people's experiences.
- Agency is not just about acting in positive ways. Many people are heroes of their own lives (Gordon 1988), but Lister warns against romanticism in a similar way to Hoggett above. The deprivations of poverty can inflict psychological damage so that actions can be ambivalent and not necessarily constructive, either for the individual, their close family, or their community. Of course, in this respect, people in poverty are no exception; they are just more exposed to these strains.

Taking account of these insights, Lister provides a taxonomy of agency along two axes: vertically, from *everyday* acts to *strategic* action; and, hori-

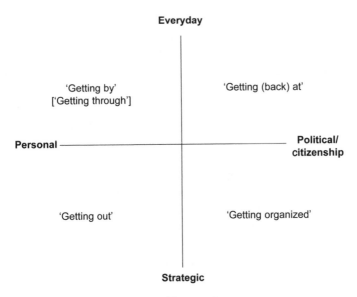

Figure 5.1 Forms of agency exercised by people in poverty
Source: Lister (2021: 129).

zontally, from *personal* to *political* acts. The four quadrants may be summarized as follows:

- *'getting by'*, which involves everyday coping strategies;
- *'getting (back) at'* through day-to-day acts of resistance;
- strategies to *'get out'* of poverty;
- strategies to *'get organized'* and effect change.

'Getting by' – everyday personal coping strategies – entail not simply the energy and endurance to cope on very little money but the stress caused by having to deal with unpredictable events – cars packing up, illness and bereavement, as well as 'techniques for managing shame' (Walker 2014: 122, cited by Lister 2015) – for example, ensuring that children do not 'look poor' (Ridge 2009). The constraints of few resources also make reciprocity difficult – a vicious circle where asking for support becomes less easy. At the more political level of day-to-day individual resistance, *'getting (back) at'* acts are about countering feelings of resentment or exclusion, which may tread a line between legality and illegality. Taking and not declaring cash in hand for small tasks may reflect both material inadequacy and a demand for societal recognition. Angela Rayner, a Labour MP, described this in an interview on BBC radio (BBC 2017). She came from a low-income working-

class family near Manchester and at sixteen became a teenage mother. On the one hand, she said she wanted to prove she wasn't the 'scumbag' she felt that the world thought she was. On the other hand, she also felt, 'if you don't care about me, why should I care about you?'. She was defiant. Not paying her gas bill or the Provident man (debt collector) was not about 'skanking the system'; for her, defiance was about survival and about being a good mother for her son. Rayner was exceptional in many ways in exercising her agency, to become first a shop steward and then an MP and to '*get out*' of poverty, the third dimension of personal agency.

In the context in which popular and political discourses construct people in poverty as lacking ambition or aspiration, qualitative research on people's experiences of trying to get out of poverty shows that, however determined, sometimes the accumulating structural barriers of an ongoing insecurity of low benefits when out of work and then low pay and poor conditions in work overwhelm resilience and, in particular, people's health and self-esteem (Shildrick et al. 2012). In-depth qualitative research in the UK on adults receiving benefits on the effects of policies and practices that are intended to *activate* people into labour market found they had almost the opposite effect (Wright 2016). The lived experience of claiming benefits was damaging to a sense of agency and self-reliance, especially where people's circumstances were considered to be the result of individual 'life choices', where efforts to improve their situation were consistently thwarted, and where inadequate income and punitive policies served to undermine self-esteem. A study by Jane Millar and Tess Ridge, which was both qualitative and longitudinal, followed lone mothers and their children over fourteen to fifteen years and was able to capture the effects over time on both mothers and their children. In the UK, almost three-quarters of lone-parent households live below the specification required for a decent standard of living. In spite of the fact that most of the women were in paid work and devoted themselves to their children, and the children also both helped and went without, the emotional and material difficulties of 'getting out' were persistent: 'It's the grind that gets you down, every single day . . . I think what contributes to my being ill was having so many years of having to cope' (Millar and Ridge 2017: 2; see also Edmiston 2018, forthcoming).

Lastly there are politically strategic actions to '*get organized*' and effect change. This is about collective action. Poverty itself is a modality – that is, a set of specific social relations constituted through people's relations with others and within the structuring of social, cultural, political and economic power relations (Lister 2004; Ridge and Wright 2008). As such, it intersects with both personal biography and other identities and social relations – gender, race, class, disability, age, etc. – to reconstitute the particular experience of poverty. Yet most social movements have been based on collective identities as sources of pride precisely on these intersections – woman, Black, LGBTQI, disabled. As Lister notes, this is more difficult where poverty carries such stigma that makes it less amenable as a mobilizing identity. Nevertheless, initiatives such as the Scottish Poverty Truth Commission and the Leeds Poverty Truth Commission, based upon being 'experts by experience', have organized people in poverty to ensure that their voices are heard in the development of policies. Mobilization around poverty is sometimes driven through another identity. Intersectional feminist groups, Black coalitions and disabled organizations have been at the forefront of protests against austerity and benefit cuts (Black Activists Rising against Cuts; Sisters Uncut; Disabled People against Cuts). Sometimes it is as residents or local communities that people identify and protest – for example, after the Grenfell Tower fire in 2017 the existing residents' association demanded accountability from the local authority and set up campaign organizations to make connections with other residents living in tower blocks across the country who were campaigning for their cladding to be removed because it was flammable (Grenfell Action Group; Justice4Grenfell). Importantly these were also groups that provided mutual care, support and advice for grieving families and those traumatized and made homeless by the fire.

Research that has applied and developed Lister's taxonomy includes a study of how far the Sure Start programme had empowered parents (Williams and Churchill 2006). Sure Start was arguably one of the more progressive anti-poverty policies of New Labour's first term, set up in 1999. Based on the American Head Start programme, it aimed to provide services to engage, support and empower parents of young children, initially in 20 per cent of the poorest districts in the UK's deprived areas. It was a different approach to poverty, more in line with community development programmes of the late 1960s. Although it was criticized for its paternalism (Clark 2006), and this was true of some of it, this research found that in some (not all) neighbourhoods the parenting support it offered, whether focused upon health, employment or child care, made a real difference to mothers' and children's lives and promoted both individual and collective empowerment. In part this depended upon a different mode of interaction, where programme leaders and staff worked inclusively and respectfully to ensure that parents from the beginning articulated what the area needed and how to use the funding. Supportive services offered parents, especially mothers, the chance to move on from 'getting by', especially in times of crisis, to 'getting better' – developing confidence and self-esteem – as well as 'getting together' with other parents and 'getting organized', for example, to pressurize for a safer and more child-friendly environment (see also Jupp 2017a). Local autonomy was withdrawn from 2003 as the programmes transformed into Children's Centres (Lewis 2011). As the services were diluted to focus on enabling and encouraging women into paid work, they lost their radical potential and were more in line with New Labour's social investment approach to parents and children (Gewirtz 2001; Williams 2003; see chapter 4).

Agency in the social relations of welfare

Much research on agency focuses on the welfare subject as a user of services. But welfare subjects are also those who deliver services as paid or as unpaid workers. The relationship between paid professional providers and users is historically constituted in the organizational power of authority and/or knowledge. This intersects with class, gender, race, disability, sexuality, age and other modalities and is shaped by the organizational characteristics of the service. I look here at two examples of how to understand this intersectional complexity.

Gail Lewis's (1996, 2000) study of minority ethnic women's experiences as social workers in the 1990s provides an important exemplar of the intersectional complexity of this relationship in a field which can implicitly normalize white providers' experiences – and where, furthermore, the identities of racialized groups are often presented as belonging to a collectivity rather than to individuals. This downplays the possibility of individual agency within which, as Nell Painter observes, there is an implicit assumption that white people have psyches whereas black people have community (Lewis 2000: 172). In line with a more psychosocial approach, Lewis proposes that, in order to theorize experience, we need to 'concentrate on its historical specificity and excavate its embeddedness in webs of social, political and cultural relations which are themselves organized around axes of power and which act to constitute subjectivities and identities' (Lewis 1996: 27). She shows how identity is a pivotal link between those discourses and practices which position us as social subjects and which generate our subjectivities (Hall 1996: 6).

Lewis's analysis proposes that the female social workers of African-Caribbean, African and South Asian origins in her study mobilize the significance of their experience as racialized women (struggling against and standing up to racism and poverty; collective memories of resistance; responsibilities for care across extended families) to locate themselves within axes of class, race and gender. These experiences serve to affirm the contribution and value they have as social workers vis-à-vis their black and white female service-users over whom they have organizational power. But they also employ these experiences to assert their value vis-à-vis other social workers (largely white, most of whom are women) in an occupational setting where they feel subordinated. In articulating these multiple identities ('multivocality') they draw on both oppositional discourses of race and gender and professional social work discourses of care, support and empowerment. In this way, experiences forged through the intersections of class, race and gender provide both a personal and a categorical resource to claim identities that enable agency in professional contexts which can be simultaneously enabling and subordinating.

What is also important in this study is the way in which Lewis connects experience, identity and agency to the policy-making of the organizational, institutional and national context, both local and central. While some of that context has since changed, much has not, as the discussion in the previous chapter on the Windrush betrayal showed (and see Hunter 2015). The broader historical context to which Lewis refers is one of a postcolonial Britain in which governmentality has focused on the regulation of racialized groups in different ways at different times since the Second World War. First was the arrival of Commonwealth 'coloured immigrants' from 1948, when they were seen primarily as replacement labour. Second, following the 1962 Commonwealth Immigrants Act, 'immigrants' and their communities became problematized in different ways, especially through the pathologization of family life. Third, from the mid-1970s, racialized populations became associated with the crisis and 'the enemy within', requiring control and containment. It was this period that saw the construction of 'ethnic minorities' – subjects who carry 'the status of being a citizen/subject whilst simultaneously being constituted as an essentialised "other" who is now a permanent figure in Britain' (Lewis 2000: 203). Lewis focuses on a particular 'moment in racial time' from the early 1980s, when many local authorities began to respond to anti-racist resistance by introducing equal opportunities policies and 'ethnically sensitive' practices (see also Stubbs 1984). At the same time, while dominant narratives attempted to reproduce white imperialist notions of Britishness, black professional activists were articulating their critiques of education and social services practices. This was a struggle over who belonged to the 'nation', who described it, and who was entitled to its rights. Education and the personal social services, in particular, were to become the welfare institutions through which resolution of this tension emerged. So the recruitment of 'ethnic minority' social workers was one way to meet criticisms of the racial structuring in social service departments which had found black and Asian workers on the lower grades. But, in the context of riotous rebellions of the early 1980s, it was also a way of rendering the new 'ethnic minority' subjects and their families more governable. This was achieved by delegating the responsibility for such governability out of sight to local authorities and, ultimately, to their newly recruited black and Asian social workers. In this way, rather than understanding these social workers as simply 'pawns' in a game of racial governmentality, Lewis brings to the fore their agency in coping with their complex positioning in a web of inclusion, incorporation and exclusion.

Bringing 'racial time' into the post-financial crisis decade of the twenty-first century provides the context for a different study, exploring agency in the contemporary social relations between providers and users of health care in superdiverse city neighbourhoods across four European countries – Germany, Portugal, Sweden and the UK (Phillimore et al. 2015; Phillimore et al. 2021). This study combines two concepts that speak to contemporary social changes in relation to both social and racial / migrant formation and its intersection with changes in health-care provision (Phillimore et al. 2019b, 2019c; Pemberton et al. 2019). The first is *superdiversity*, which describes the acceleration and speed of migration over the past thirty years. This has seen a shift in Europe (particularly with EU enlargement after 2004) from former postcolonial patterns of migration to a more fragmented movement of migrants from a greater variety of countries to places where there is no necessary historical connection (Vertovec 2007). The new migrants are diversified by gender, age, ethnicity, religion, rights, entitlements, immigrant status, labour market experience and places of destination. They may settle or move between countries, or between cities within countries, while holding close to transnational family and friends. This change has also seen the creation of neighbourhoods characterized by a heterogeneous and fluid mix of old and new migrants and longstanding (often older) non-migrant residents. At the same time, what has also changed in these countries is the impact of neoliberalism and austerity to create more or less fragmented health-care systems composed of provision from public, private, alternative, and voluntary and civil society organizations. Along with this has been a rise in anti-migrant political discourse, often focused upon reducing entitlements of migrant workers and their families on health and welfare provision (as described in chapter 4) and the racialization of migration mobility (as described in chapter 3).

The second concept, *welfare bricolage* (derived from, inter alia, Deleuze and Guattari [1972] 1984; see Phillimore et al. 2019c), depicts how, in this context where entitlements and rights may be complicated and services directly or indirectly inaccessible, users negotiate and piece together ways to meet their needs from the array of personal, informal, private, public, voluntary, local and transnational resources. Providers, too, operate in a system in which ethnic, national and other forms of diversity intersect with complex calibrations of citizenship status. These create new layers of challenges over and above the ongoing and unresolved social and racial inequalities in health care attached to earlier generations of migrants (Chouha and Nazroo 2020). Bricolage describes the ways in which providers need to be creative and flexible in order to be responsive in the context of dwindling resources and the presentation of more complex needs (Phillimore et al. 2019a). Both groups are *bricoleurs*, reconstituting health-care provision through their actions and relationships.

The context for users in the study was structured by the intersection of different health-care and migration regimes of the four countries, but migrant users were forced for different reasons to search different resources, especially when the obvious resource of 'universal' publicly available health care failed to deliver (Phillimore et al. 2019b). That failure might be the result of communication problems brought about by different cultural approaches to health, intensified by a pathologizing attitude, or (often wrongful) denial of right to health care, all contributing to a sense of distrust by the user (Bradby et al. 2020). In such conditions, users sought knowledge and advice from family and friends, from local private resources such as Chinese medicine or yoga, from local voluntary advice centres, and from the internet. Relatives in their countries of origin sent medicines and medicinal foodstuffs which were not available where they lived, or users travelled home to seek professional or private advice or surgery which was cheaper, more familiar and respectful. Bricolage entails working with a patchwork of opportunities and constraints conditioned by differential access to knowledge, networks, finances, the capacity to be mobile, and the proximity of alternative resources (Phillimore et al. 2019a, 2019b, 2019c).

The bricolage picture for providers is multidimensional (Phillimore et al. 2019a). On the one hand, in the context of inadequate staffing, managerial and bureaucratic requirements to reduce time allocations for patients, lack of translation services, and services which are already stretched to meet the local population's complex needs, some providers problematized their patients as difficult. Complaints focused on patients' poor diets, housing and employment conditions, cultural habits such as wearing the burka or hijab, or not following unwritten norms of engagement. On the other hand, providers also sought innovative and creative ways of dealing with these issues. This involved creating networks with voluntary services and charities which could help with financial and health problems, employing multilingual staff or local people as translators, doing outreach work, open and active listening, and providing flexible services, including drop-in and group sessions (Phillimore et al. 2021).

The concepts of superdiversity and bricolage have been criticized for being descriptive rather than analytical and of detracting from the power differentials through which they are constituted (respectively, Ndhlovu 2016 and Dagnino 2007). One argument is that superdiversity describes migration from the perspective of the Global North and, like multiculturalism, assumes a level playing field of diverse subjects; it fails to show the intersections operating across and within superdiversity and its positioning within the global politics of migration (Ndhlovu 2016). Bricolage, by contrast, can be criticized for the implication that the agency of providers and users is precisely what neoliberal welfare ordered: on the one hand, self-responsible welfare consumers shopping around and acting on choice to meet their health-care needs and, on the other, proactive providers managing needs and enabling those choices to be made. As such, bricolage practices exist in 'perverse alignment' with neoliberalism (Phillimore et al. 2019b; Newman 2012a, after Dagnino 2007).

These criticisms are relevant to the two concepts as concepts, but, in this study, they are contextualized constructively within the politics of time and place: superdiversity within the politics and history of ethnonationalist welfare; bricolage within the politics of austerity and the mixed neoliberal economy of welfare. While acknowledging the criticisms, the authors of this project argue that the concept helps mark out new ways in which some populations are in flux and that terms such as BAME do not capture the fluid nature of diasporic belonging of these groups, who cannot be reduced to a minority ethnicity and often do not possess the critical mass that enables them to be seen as 'a community' (Phillimore et al. 2019b, 2021). The concept highlights instead the significance of how *place* constructs people's sense of belonging (Pemberton et al. 2019). In this way, its intersection with bricolage creates a more dynamic understanding of health-care practices as fluid and ambivalent, mediating and experimenting, constrained and enabled by relational and material resources, and, for users, iterating across local and transnational scales. It makes visible those processes that are hidden in accounts which silo users into social categories and providers into state actors. As a cross-national study, it provides a methodology that meets many of the criticisms of comparative welfare regime analysis (see chapter 2). It combines quantitative analysis with community-based qualitative research, it emphasises place as much as nation, and it addresses questions of difference and intersectionality as aspects of power within the social relations of health care. In addition, it allows an appreciation of where the spaces are in these processes of assembling and reassembling in which agency might signal, prefiguratively, 'acts and logics of resistance' and how services might change for the better, to be recognized as part of an 'ecosystem' of health care (Phillimore et al. 2019a, 2019b, 2021). They look to combining the ethics of care with a focus on 'cultural safety' towards a 'decolonizing practice' which goes beyond culture and ethnicity as defining individuals' characteristics of need. This involves the practitioner and service-user working together to identify health-care needs which also take account of the social relations of power experienced both socially and within the health-care system.

Together the two examples in this section illustrate ways to frame an analysis of agency within the temporal and spatial dynamics of the social relations of welfare and, beyond that, the politics of neoliberal welfare. Both point implicitly to resistance and to prefigurative practice, which is taken up below.

Logics of contestation and resistance

The critical analysis in this book draws attention to 'contestation' as an important dimension in understanding the instability and ambivalent trajectories of welfare states. This is a big topic (see Clarke and Newman 1997; Todd and Taylor 2004; Newman and Clarke 2009; Barnes and Prior 2009). It points to a broader debate around the politics of redistribution, recognition and representation (Honneth 1995; Fraser 1995, 2013: part II; Hobson 2003) – that is to say, how far collective struggles are about economic justice (redistribution), social justice (recognition) and/or participatory parity (voice). All these are very relevant to welfare politics (Williams 1999, 2010). My focus here, however, is narrower – to point to some of the different logics through which individual or collective agency challenge, implicitly or explicitly, dominant social policy outcomes, practices and strategies. I have selected three – 'spaces of power', 'structures of feeling' and 'subjects of value' – which give a sense of the diverse conditions and effects of agency.

Spaces of power

The phrase is drawn from the title of Janet Newman's study *Working the Spaces of Power* (2012a). This examines how women activists of different generations in public and third-sector employment negotiate the purpose and meaning of their work in the context of neoliberal governance. In this case, it is the last years of New Labour, the financial crisis and the start of the Coalition's austerity programme. Newman shows that in this period of governance, which was frequently described as 'post-feminist' – that is, where feminism was deemed to have outlived its necessity – those politics were continued by women in their places of work, where they found spaces which they were able to influence and shape. For example, some of the new strategies that neoliberal governments introduced were about entrepreneurialism, community mobilization and localism, which were intended to stimulate community action by delegating to localities responsibilities for dealing with declining neighbourhoods, housing, care needs or getting people into work. Activists worked to 'translate' or reframe these projects with different notions of partnerships, community responsibility or entrepreneurialism that involved aims of anti-racist, feminist and disability empowerment with democratic practices of social and economic reciprocity and mutual aid. Those who had lost public-sector jobs through cuts often moved into the voluntary sector, setting up campaign groups, for example, to make women's unpaid care more visible or to do detailed accounting of the effects of cuts on women's lives or new forms of inequality, or to use their status as 'insider-outsiders' to bring their different networks together. What had been termed as being 'In and Against the State' in the 1970s (see chapter 1) became not renewed but reconstituted in the early 2000s as emergent, creative and innovative ways of working across the boundaries of different sites of paid work and extramural activism.

Many of Newman's observations recur in Eleanor Jupp's study of activism conducted later in 2013 and 2014 among two groups of low-income women: a migrant group in London working on school inclusion for a social enterprise and two housing estate residents' groups in Stoke-on-Trent (Jupp 2017a). By that time the effects of austerity had shifted some of the focus of these groups' work as support services were cut, as migration rules became more restrictive, and as struggles for safe green spaces for children were overtaken by the need to ensure people had food and housing security. But what characterized their activism was an iterative border-crossing between coping with their own and others' experiences and traumas of everyday life, the public worlds of social support across public, private and voluntary sectors and networks, and local policy-making. Jupp calls this working 'at the intersections of policy and governance and everyday life' (2017a: 358). They operated as women both inside and outside these borders, able to encourage the self-determination of the women around them. By contrast, a study of minority women[2] activists conducted at the same time by Leah Bassel and Akwugo Emejulu (2018, and see below) found less evidence of this sort of room for manoeuvre in the voluntary sectors of France, Scotland and England. Cuts in funding and organizational restructuring to meet the requirement to be competitive and entrepreneurial had shrunk the spaces in which 'minority women activists could articulate and advance their intersectional social justice claims' (ibid.: 75). This led to activism around self-care and the 'DIY' politics of survival, similar to that found in Jupp's research.

All these studies follow links in the ways feminist and anti-racist activisms may have become less visible as neoliberalism raised its game. Yet they did not go away, in spite of the formal structures of policy-making and politics serving to render them irrelevant. Newman (2012b) challenges the idea that feminism had become incorporated after the second wave by the spread of neoliberalism, seduced by goals of individual empowerment of professional women ('leaning in', as Sheryl Sandberg 2013, described it), or that it surrendered its best ideas to capitalism (Fraser 2009; and see chapter 1). Her study offers alternative ways of understanding the relationship between neoliberal governance and feminist action, not as one of incorporation or selling out but of finding the spaces of power, working across boundaries and through 'perverse alignments'. Interestingly, as a form of postscript to their study, Bassel and Emejulu note that, since their fieldwork, new stronger intersectional organizations of anti-austerity political activists had started to emerge (e.g. Sisters Uncut; Sisters of Frida, Focus E15). From the end of 2017, too, mobilization took on a more global dimension though the movements #MeToo, XR (Extinction Rebellion) and Black Lives Matter.

Campaigning through spaces of power
Campaigns around care afford good examples of working through spaces of power while also challenging dominant policy frames. The social relations of care and support involve multiple and complex relations of power and control, autonomy and interdependence. As a practice it may include unpaid and paid carers, as well as people requiring support and/or care. These positions involve gender, race, disability, class, age, migrant status

and more. Neither is this fixed: older people, disabled people and children may also be unpaid carers.

Historically, campaigns have tended to focus on one constituency or another. Much of the early feminist research and activism in the 1980s around paid and unpaid care focused on the invisibility of women's unpaid care, which was framed as the 'burden of care' (Finch and Groves 1983). This was also partly a response to government policy of moving away from institutionalized care to community care – proposed as a cost-efficient exercise. The costs, it was argued by feminist writers, would be borne by women in the community. While this was important in making this work visible, it also implied that those who receive care – disabled children and adults and older people – represent a dependent obstacle in women's fight for autonomy. The argument marginalized the agency and independence of disabled people – principles at the heart of disability movement struggles – as well as those of older people and children.

Intersectionality works in different ways: disabled feminists have long called out the white male-dominated disability movement (Morris 1991). Yet it is still relatively rare, especially in policy documents and campaigns, for the main constituencies of care – unpaid carers, care recipients and paid carers – to be considered in one frame (but see Shakespeare 2000; Williams 2010; Social Platform 2012; Shakespeare and Williams 2019).

The organization CarersUK was developed out of campaigns from the 1960s and 1970s to make visible the unpaid care carried out by (mainly) women for sick, frail older, and disabled family members. This challenged the assumed naturalization and invisibility of women's caring role and familial responsibility (Barnes 2001, 2006). CarersUK's strategy has been to show the extent of unpaid care (6.5 million carers according to the 2011 Census), its monetary value (in 2019, according to CarersUK, this was estimated at £132 billion a year); and the loss to productivity by people leaving employment in order to provide care for a partner or relative (Yeandle and Starr 2007). By 2008 the organization influenced the New Labour government to produce a National Strategy for Carers, which set out a ten-year vision of principles to be met through a partnership between central and local government, the NHS, the third sector, families and communities (Yeandle and Buckner 2007). Part of their success was that they positioned themselves as working *in partnership* with different sectors, which found favour with the tenor of New Labour's modernization agenda. Their claims also dovetailed with an earlier shift from institutional care to a more cost-effective community care. Second, in mobilizing around the 'business case' of productivity lost by carers leaving employment, this fit with a model of labour market activation in prioritizing economic activity over unpaid work. In some ways, then, people's recognition and rights as carers were granted not necessarily because of the value of care but because of their potential as earners. This was the key space of power they could occupy to forward their claims. The recognition they won and the material and community support that followed generated a very important resource and representation for kin and non-kin carers over the following decade. This was especially important as austerity cuts to benefits, local authorities and voluntary organizations began to bite. Ongoing campaigns include an improvement to the Carer's Allowance; the recognition of carers' leave in the workplace; and, with added vigour since the pandemic, the need to value carers' work and to prioritize social care funding (CarersUK 2020).

The UK's National Centre for Independent Living (1985–2011) was critical in articulating the rights and measures for independent living. It was run by and for disabled people and stressed their rights to autonomy and control in negotiating their needs for support. It argued successfully for direct payments to be paid to disabled people rather than their carers and, later, for personal assistance as a mode of support to be employed and controlled directly by disabled people. 'Disabled people have never demanded or asked for care! We have sought independent living which means being able to achieve maximum independence and control over our own lives. The concept of care seems to many disabled people a tool through which others are able to dominate and manage our lives' (Wood 1991: 199).

These demands challenged quite profoundly the social relations of disability and care and, internationally, have had a global influence in shaping the 2006 UN Convention on the Rights of Persons with Disabilities. They challenged assumptions of dependency and practices of paternalism by unpaid or paid carers and demanded the right to articulate their needs. Second, they confronted the practices of segregation and institutionalization by drawing attention to the disabling barriers of the built environment, medical discourses, and social exclusion and employment discrimination (Shakespeare 2014).

The move to independent living dovetailed with diverse policy perspectives of the time: arguments of community care in terms of cost-efficiency; mental health radicalism for the closure of institutions; and dominant ideas about the autonomous welfare consumer. The claim for direct payments also fitted the personalization agenda of the 1990s, in which services are matched to individual needs. Personalization also ran along with privatization (Yeatman et al. 2009, McNicoll 2016), in which the employment of personal assistants (PAs) would operate with a functional market and an informed disabled consumer experienced in hire and fire procedures. By 2017, 70,000 disabled people were employing 145,000 PAs in the UK (Skills for Care 2017). This has been indispensable for disabled people to maintain work and family commitments, but, in the context of austerity, there have been difficulties – for example, in hiring where the market was sparse, as in rural areas (Porter et al. 2019). After the closure of the UK Independent Living Fund in 2011, people have had to depend on cash-strapped local authorities to fund their support packages.

The austerity policy paradigm reinforced the idea of independence and autonomy as being active in the labour market, effectively turning what had been for disabled people a claim for the right to work into a responsibility and narrowing the meaning of independent living. As chapter 4 shows, in the welfare reforms since 2012, which prioritized welfare to work, disabled people have not fared well because of the lowering of benefits, the removal of some disability-related benefits, and much more stringent work capability tests (Halvorsen et al. 2017; Ryan 2019). Rather than enhancing agency, these moves have been damaging to it.

At the same time, the personal assistants' scheme has been innovative. PAs tend to choose this work for a disabled person rather than as a paid agency carer or a residential carer (Porter et al. 2019). There is greater flexibility, and the work is more relational and less task-oriented, with a sense of purpose in making independence a possibility. There is half as much turnover as in social care (Skills for Care 2017) and the wage is on average higher (despite decreases since 2008). Disabled people have freedom to hire and fire without oversight from statutory services, professional groups or the voluntary sector. But without recourse to advocacy this can put a worker (and an employer) at risk of exploitation (in some places voluntary organizations mitigate difficulties). In Finland, the trade union JHL found it was difficult to unionize PAs because of their employment isolation in homes. In setting up a virtual network on the internet, the union found success in organizing PAs and in providing them with peer support from other PAs. The innovation of the PA system for both parties is that it is liberated from professional or managerial definition and control, but the relationship also demands significant emotional acuity on both sides. How the recognition of the significance of that might be translated into policy is pursued in chapter 7.

Structures of feeling

Through this chapter I have emphasized a way of understanding resistance and contestation in welfare which draws attention to its complex forces and formations – ebbs and flows – which are contingent upon both time and place. Newman (2014) uses Raymond Williams's (1977) concept of 'structures of feeling' to analyse this (see also Hall 2011; Clarke 2019a). Williams drew attention to the more inchoate ways in which resistance is formed – not sometimes even articulated as an idea but as a feeling on its way to emerging as a more collective concept. This is different from 'official' policy discourses and from ongoing 'common sense' (which are two sets of the ideas with which I analysed the austerity decade in chapter 4). Newman makes the point that the practices attached to emergent feelings can become prefigurative, setting the template for a new way of doing things, aligning the means with the ends (Cooper et al. 2020).

Research with New Zealand benefit claimants in 2007–8 and in 2013 illustrates some of these ideas (Edmiston and Humpage 2018). The period saw the incremental withdrawal from claimants of the social rights of citizenship through similar welfare reforms to the UK's austerity measures (and before the election of a new coalition government led by the centre-left). The authors' interviews showed three types of reaction to this new social citizenship: resignation, resistance and reconfiguration. Most of these responses were 'for and against social citizenship' (ibid.: 3), expressed as a critique of government policies, especially as reforms kicked in. Some responses worked within the regime of entitlement, by, for example, going along with the conditions of self-reliance and good behaviour expected of them and identifying other claimants, especially migrants, as undeserving. Others defended themselves against their exclusion, for example by challenging the work ethic as against their own priorities of caring for their children. Some took this further, into 'an alternative political imaginary that could give authentication to the civic contribution, capabilities and practices underpinning the prevailing welfare landscape' (ibid.: 16). It is here, the researchers conclude, that new spaces are possible for rethinking a notion of a democratic and deliberative welfare politics.

Changing patterns of family life and intimate relationships afford another example of how changing 'structures of feeling' can accumulate to create sentiments that counter dominant ideas. Many of the changes in Western societies' family lives have emerged as people began to think differently about their relationships in the context of the material and relational conditions surrounding them, and often these changes have been ahead of policy and also decried by those in power. In the 1960s it became more accepted that marriage was not a prerequisite to a sexual relationship; in the 1980s marriage and parenthood were uncoupled; and by the turn of the century the assumption that committed intimate relationships require co-residence started to be challenged by LAT relationships (living apart together) (Levin 2004; Williams 2004).

The diversity of living arrangements and relationships increased in many ways: cohabitation, separation, divorce, lone parenthood, step-families, single-person households, minority and mixed heritage families, same-gender marriages, and queer, trans and variant gender relationships. By the turn of this century there was an accumulating socially conservative discourse that many of these changes registered a decline in people's morality and their commitment to each other and their children (Murray 1990; Dennis and Erdos 1992; Duncan Smith 2006). However, qualitative research from Leeds University, which asked individuals what mattered to them in close family and personal relationships, especially as they changed, found that there was no absence of moral agency in people's close relationships (Williams 2004). Moral reasoning based on mutual care informed the way they negotiated the 'proper' way to behave. What it means to be a good mother, father, grandparent, partner, ex-partner, lover, son, daughter, friend, and so on, was crucial to this reasoning. In addition, the ethical guidelines that accompanied these feelings included fairness, attentiveness, mutual respect, trust, reparation, being non-judgemental, being open to communication and accommodation, and being adaptable to change. While this 'compassionate realism of good-enough care' (Williams 2004: 74) co-exists with defensive, misogynist attempts to reassert patriarchal, homophobic and racist practices, it offers a structure of emergent feelings that makes possible the acceptance of same-gender marriage, the continued pressure to improve domestic violence and sexual harassment law, and awareness of everyday sexism and institutional racism (Bates 2014; Campbell 2013).

Subjects of value

In chapter 4 I referenced Tyler's concept of social abjection as a way of analysing the processes by which different social groups – asylum seekers, refugees, unemployed young people, disabled people, Gypsies and Travellers – are turned into scapegoats. The popular common sense generated by political and media discourse allows sections of the population to split off from their own experience of social decline and place their fears on to an external 'other'. Where Lewis's (2000) context (see above) was located in the constitution of the 'ethnic minority subject' in the governing of racialized groups, Tyler speaks to a later context. The conditions facing migrants and refugees in the new century mark a turning of the screw in the growing inaccessibility of national citizenship rights since the 1981 British Nationality Act (see chapters 3 and 4) combined with integration as the mode of acceptable minority citizenship. Most poignant in this is the rise in numbers of failed, undocumented and stateless refugees awaiting or refused asylum in detention centres. Not only do the (private for-profit) detention centres mark that historical dehumanization and disenfranchisement of despised populations (people with mental health problems, disabled people, people with learning difficulties), but such people are rendered both *outside* the boundaries of national citizenship yet contained and constrained *within* the national borders of the state in ways that fix them in time and space (Tyler 2013: 73).

But this is not without resistance, as 'revolting subjects' find ways to reconstitute themselves both as citizens with rights *and* as 'subjects of value' – that is, as people whose lives matter. Acts of resistance in these conditions take on a symbolic and embodied form that challenges that very physical containment. Tyler recounts 'parables': of Abas Amini, a Kurdish-Iranian asylum seeker who in 2003 sewed up his mouth, ears and eyes in protest against deportation, an act symbolizing speaking out through the inability to speak, being blinded to make himself visible, and sewing his ears against the failure to be heard. It also reproduced conditions of torture that he would face if deported. His case received publicity, negative and supportive. Tyler argues that such acts open up a political space beyond the invisibility and acceptance of abjection.

Other acts of resistance comprise the naked protests of women at Yarl's Wood Immigration Removal Centre in 2008 against the deportation of a Burundian woman and her British-born baby and the subsequent forcible separation of a protester from her child, as well as the indeterminate incarceration of children and the effects on their health. Again this protest was made public. It linked to the protest of female nakedness (seen as a curse and a threat) used in 2002 by women on the Escravos oil facility in the Niger Delta in Nigeria as part of a struggle for compensation for the environmental destruction of their communities. The chain was carried into the US in 2010, when a group of women peace activists called CodePink carried out a naked protest against an oil spillage in the Gulf of Mexico. Tyler sees these transnational protests as a life-affirming resistance to abjection and the political economy of neoliberalism – a sort of 'maternal commons' (Tyler 2013: 124).

This idea of a 'maternal commons' as a contesting idea is pursued in different terms by the study mentioned earlier, *Minority Women and Austerity: Survival and Resistance in France and Britain* (Bassel and Emejulu 2018; see also Emejulu and Bassel 2018). In the context of Brexit populism, these authors argue that the narratives about Brexit representing the mobilization of the 'white working class' hit by austerity and global neoliberalism refuse not only the multiplicity of class composition but also the different forms of resistance by those who *have* been hit hardest. Minority women are thus invisibilized as political agents: 'Minority women have distinctive patterns to their political behaviour that are often ignored, misrecognised or devalued in the wider political science literature and in the formal practice of politics' (Bassel and Emejulu 2018: 8). The study found that minority women had many different claims, but one aspect that linked their activism against far-right racism, against the cuts, and for migrants' rights was a political ethic of care in building solidarity – a form of praxis and prefigurative politics (Emejulu and Bassel 2018: 114; see also Hall 2020). In other words, in the face of 'political carelessness' (institutional indifference and incompetence, as well as dehumanizing state policies around welfare and migration) and 'political racelessness' (institutional 'blind eye' by both left and right to intersectional race–class–gender claims), the solidarity forged through caring for the self and caring for close others (as a process of self-respect) is extended to caring for Others. This combines the action of validating and valuing those whose voices have not been heard. More than that, it carries the possibility of creating coalitions with those whose emerging political subjectivities have taken them into practising in the present that which heralds a transformative alternative for the future. It is repeated in research where 'emotional proximity' pulls women into material support work (Jupp 2017a, 2017b), a characteristic of activism which Hall calls the 'quiet politics of austerity' (Hall 2020). This microactivism of caring solidarity becomes one way in which activists assert themselves as 'subjects of value'. These research studies activate the point made by Sevenhuijsen in her elaboration of the ethics of care and 'caring solidarity':

> The feminist ethic of care points to forms of solidarity in which there is room for difference, and in which we find out what people in particular situations need in order for them to live with dignity. People must be able to count on solidarity because vulnerability and dependency, as we know, are a part of human existence and we need each other's disinterested support at expected and unexpected moments. (Sevenhuijsen 1998: 147)

One of those (un)expected moments is climate change. How might agency be understood in relation to climate change? On the one hand, relational spaces of families, households and communities are increasingly recognized as key sites of action (Jamieson 2016). On the other, the narrative of action that focuses on moral responsibility can lead too easily to a dismissal of 'irresponsible others', of environmental heroes and villains, which takes no account of structural inequalities and constraints on people's lives (Bulkely et al. 2014; Boddy et al. 2016). Better to situate action for environmental justice in terms of the recognition of the other: 'in an increasingly globalised world we must "confront" our own "otherness" . . . as well as relationality and necessary interdependence in an unequally precarious world' (Boddy et al. 2016: 372). Care for the self, care for others, and care for the world.

Conclusion

This chapter has unfolded an understanding of welfare subjects as agents within the double helix of welfare in which one strand turns upon the intersecting social relations of gender, race, class, disability, age, sexuality, and so on, and the other turns upon the social relations between providers and users. I started by explaining how the dominance of structural explanations for the causes of poverty left progressive arguments without an adequate theory of agency just as New Right neoliberalism asserted its belief in the infallibility of the (welfare) market in which rational economic (welfare) agency would naturally emerge. The development of research on the dynamics of agency located it not in a notion of unconstrained self-sufficiency but in the actions of people relating to others and both constrained and enabled by the unequal distribution of resources available to them. These resources cover the material, the symbolic, the relational and the psychodynamic. Lister's taxonomy of agency running from personal to political and from everyday to strategic was used to illustrate these dynamics.

In turning to discuss the social relations of welfare, I drew on two studies which captured these dynamics within the intersection of 'racial time' with modes of welfare governance. The first was Lewis's classic study of how black and Asian social workers were employed as part of a government strategy to 'reach' ethnic minority populations and how they positioned themselves within this. Racial time in the second study is illustrated through superdiverse neighbourhoods in contemporary European cities in which austerity has hit to a greater or lesser degree. 'Bricolage' is the concept used to refer to the ways in which both users and providers stitch together strategies for meeting health needs from an array of private, public, voluntary, alternative and transnational resources. Implicit in both accounts is how resistance is carried through everyday actions. Contestation is explored further in the last section in its different forms: not only as public campaigning but as the quieter acts of self-determining commitment to others and Others in which cracks in the unstable foundations of welfare provide the spaces to make connections, alliances and networks. Sometimes contestation emerges as 'structures of feeling' not yet articulated as an idea but grounded in the aggregate of people's everyday practices.

Several themes thread through the chapter: the iterating links between subjectivities, identities, subject positions and agency; how different forms of resistance provide glimpses of transformation and prefiguration; the multivalent meanings of resistant action around inclusion, exclusion and incorporation; how an intersectional approach reveals forms of resistance that remain outside theoretical and political normativity; and the subtle shift in temporalities of possibility for working in and against dominant organizational power. Finally, a practical ethics of care emerges as central to the forging of solidarities, small and large. One of the experiences of the Covid-19 pandemic was to bring this lesson home. Shokoufeh Sakhi is an Iranian exile living now in Canada after an eight-year prison sentence in Tehran, two of which were in solitary confinement. During the pandemic lockdown she blogged: 'When was the last time we collectively stayed conscious for this long about the effects of our actions on other people? Can we give that proper recognition? Recognising the presence of an ancient feeling, our care for others? In this are the seeds of our empowerment and a global solidarity' (cited by Taylor 2020).

Intersections in the Transnational, Social and Political Economy of Care

Introduction

During the Covid-19 pandemic in 2020, the World Bank warned of a huge rise in poverty to the extent of famine in poorer regions of the world because migrant workers were unable to send remittances back to their families. Many migrant workers in precarious work without social protection had become unemployed, but also the remittance agencies were closed down (Mora and Rutkowski 2020). Remittances in 2019 amounted to $709 billion – three times the amount of overseas aid. Half of migrant workers are women, and a significant proportion work in domestic and care work (ILO 2015). As the virus spread, many of these women in the Gulf States found themselves expelled from the households who employed them and forced to find a way back to their homes in South East Asia (Amnesty International 2020). In some cases, as Anghel (2020) recounts in relation to some Romanian migrant care workers dismissed from their employment in Italy, in trying to return to home, they found the country did not want them, fearing they were carrying the virus.

This chapter is about such workers who migrate from poorer countries into care and domestic work (here summarized as 'care work')[1] in richer countries, of whom 80 per cent are women (ILO 2015). This phenomenon provides a lens through which to see connections between the most significant social, cultural, political, demographic and economic changes in the twenty-first century. It encapsulates many of the world's historical geo-political inequalities as well as ongoing inequalities of gender, race and class, to name but a few. And it also raises some of the most important challenges to social policy and to global social justice. It is, in short, an illustration of one dynamic of a global patriarchal and imperialist capitalism in its relationship to welfare states.

In chapter 1, I referred to 'the global' as one of the critical turns that has influenced the discipline of social policy (Deacon 2007, 2013; Yeates 2001, 2014; Béland and Mahon 2016). This turn was important in several ways:

identifying the role of international organizations in shaping the policies of national governments; linking social policy with international political economy and development studies; bringing the Global South into the picture in its relation to the Global North; and going beyond the methodological nationalism of cross-national social policy (Kaasch and Stubbs 2014). Bringing feminist and postcolonial perspectives into play has been important, and these underpin the analysis here. This chapter applies the framework developed in chapter 3 by elaborating one of the four global crises – that of care in its intersection with the social expenditure cuts and neoliberal welfare associated with the global financial crisis, together with systems and rules of migration. It uses an intersectional approach to understand the imbricated dynamics of migrant care work at the micro-, meso- and macro-scale (Michel and Peng 2017) – that is to say, the relationship between the individual and collective agency of migrant care workers and the structures that constrain and/or enable them as they traverse through many interconnected scales from interpersonal micro-processes in the care relationship, through the local, national, transnational and global. Acknowledging the criticism that the concept of 'scale' may assume that different scales – local, national, transnational, global, etc. – stand in a 'natural' or hierarchical 'top down' relationship to each other (Isin 2007; Clarke 2019b), the intersectional analysis here presents a more fluid understanding in which different scales 'bleed' into each other and in which the social relations within those scales are constituted through time and place.

The chapter starts by summarizing the significant global changes and continuities represented by migrant care work. It locates the bigger picture in terms, on the one hand, of the histories of racialized, classed and gendered care work and, on the other, of the intersecting dynamics of the transnational political and social economy of care. Though global in its reach, there are significant variations and layerings at the meso-scale across countries and regions. Those are analysed in terms of the institutional intersections of employment, care and migration regimes. The micro-scale focuses on the intersecting relations of inequality and power in close encounters of care. The last section returns to the global in terms of the implications of the contestations around migrant care and domestic work for global social justice.

A story of changes and continuities

The transnational movement of women into care work reflects a more general social change in the global increase of women's involvement in the labour market and the greater reliance in both the Global North and the Global South on a woman's wage. Figures for OECD countries show an average rate of 63 per cent for female labour force participation (OECD 2015). In developing countries, too, female participation in formal work (often as breadwinners) has increased and, by 2008, ranged from 24.7 per cent in the Middle East to 62.9 per cent in sub-Saharan Africa for women over twenty-five, both increases from the previous ten years (ILO 2009: 9). In part this is because of new employment opportunities following the liberalization of international trade in line with neoliberal globalization. This has led to expanding manufacturing industries for export in which female labour is preferred because it is cheaper and more productive (Razavi and Staab 2012). While this also results from their improved access to education and increased aspirations, it reflects the necessity of women to become earners because of the decline in the value of men's wages and their unemployment. Women usually enter a segmented labour market where their pay is less than men's and their social protection absent or limited. These constraints shape decisions to find better opportunities through migration. In developed welfare states, women's increased involvement in paid labour reflects some of these changes (education, decline in male wages, sole parenting, poor conditions of work, lower pay) while also being part of both economic necessity and (as shown in chapters 3 and 4) the move from a male breadwinner to a new normative ideal of the adult worker society in which hard-working men *and* women support themselves and their families through employment.

This influences the second change: the growing need in developed countries for care for older people and young children, intensified by ageing societies and declining fertility and heightened by political imperatives towards social expenditure cuts. Such care needs are no less insistent in poorer regions, where unemployment, wars, ethnic conflict, natural disasters, economic crises and chronic illnesses place enormous responsibilities on women to maintain their families with little infrastructural support. It is this that intensifies the reason for women to migrate in order to provide financial support for their families. The paradox of looking after the care needs in richer countries is that it intensifies the caring responsibilities of those left behind (Withers 2019a), often conceptualized as 'the global care chain' (Ehrenreich and Hochschild 2003).

Third, migration patterns too have changed. Almost half (48 per cent) of the world's 258 million international migrants are now women; they outnumber male migrants in Northern America, Oceania, Latin America and the Caribbean (UN 2017). Many find work in low-paid care and domestic work in private homes or institutions. In some countries, such as Indonesia and the Philippines, the export of qualified nurses is part of national policy and bilateral agreements (Guevarra 2010; Peng 2017).

Fourth, care provision has also changed in many destination countries, where care policies have shifted over the past two decades from providing public services (or, in some places, no services) to giving people cash payments or tax credits to buy in care or domestic help in their private homes. The reliance on voluntary but especially for-profit provision has led to care being treated as a commodity that is bought and sold in the market (Williams and Brennan 2012). The contracting out of provision such as domiciliary care, nurseries or residential homes to the private sector has often been accompanied by worsening of pay, conditions and labour shortages (see chapter 4). It thus attracts those with least negotiating power, and this is often female migrant or minority ethnic labour.

It is in the accumulation of these four changes that migrant women workers, already often disadvantaged by their migrant and racialized status, are susceptible to the poor conditions that beset the low-wage economy of care and domestic work. According to the International Labour Office, domestic and care work across the world carries all the hallmarks of non-standard employment – temporary, part-time, precarious, low waged, insecure, flexible, and without collective organization (ILO 2016). Migrant care workers' precarity has been exacerbated (as shown in chapter 3) by migration policies in many countries of destination, which have become increasingly restrictive towards so-called unskilled workers, a category that often includes care workers (Anderson 2010; Boyd 2017). This has been accompanied in many countries by backtracking on multiculturalist policies and by populist and political xenophobic and anti-immigration sentiment that increases the existential insecurity of foreign workers (Michel and Peng 2012). In a nutshell: these processes of deterrence operate in spite of the dependence that developed countries have on low-paid migrant workers to meet their care needs in ways that contain their social expenditure costs. Further, this 'transfer of caretaking' (Parreñas 2001, 2005) serves to exacerbate care needs in the countries of migrants' origin. It is the point where the post-financial crisis cutbacks intersect with the crises in care and racialized borders.

The changes described here are overlaid upon older continuities. First are gendered inequalities, where women globally carry responsibilities for care and domestic work (UNRISD 2016). Second is the continuing devaluation of care, whether as paid or unpaid work, both hidden from the economy and subordinated to productivism (Tronto 1993; Sevenhuijsen

1998; Federici 2012). Third are the conditions of imperialist and post-colonial hierarchies that have shaped the contemporary racially structured labour market. Significant here is the legacy of the racialization of servitude. In the US, minority ethnic groups have historically carried out the care and domestic labour of dominant classes (Glenn 1992; Romero 1992). In Britain, it was traditionally working-class women, often Irish, who were in the personal service of upper- and upper-middle-class households, a privilege which it was assumed would disappear with the rise of domestic technology. In the 1950s and 1960s in the UK, the recruitment of health and care workers from the colonies provided both cheap labour for the new institutions of the welfare state and met a labour shortage which otherwise would have had to be filled by British married women in a period in which women were assumed to have primary responsibilities for the home and children (Williams 1989). By the 1990s, domestic service for professional dual-earner families increasingly became the norm (Gregson and Lowe 1994). Today, especially where public provision is residual and gendered care responsibilities within the home are relatively unchanged, the employment of migrant domestic and care labour serves to enable female citizens to stay in paid employment. Both then and today, these workers provide cost-effective ways of securing the family norms and care needs in their countries of destination, even while these norms, needs and sources of labour have changed.

As well as change and continuity, the picture of migrant care work spreads across a diverse and wide canvas. To begin with, it is not just a Global North–South phenomenon. Care and domestic workers also migrate within North and South regions. Domestic workers from Indonesia go to Malaysia, Singapore and Saudi Arabia, which also recruits women from the Philippines and Sri Lanka. Following the enlargement of the European Union in 2004, more educated younger women migrants from Central and Eastern Europe worked in care and domestic work in Northern, Western and Southern Europe. Germany receives elder care workers from Poland, while Poland receives domestic workers from Ukraine. These trails transect older tracks from colonial relations, with Indian and African workers going to the UK and South American workers to Spain. Some workers travel to and fro for weeks or months; others find their conditions of work force them to move from one country of destination to another; some settle; others return home. At the same time, the extent of dependence of migrant care workers varies across countries, as do migration status, employment conditions and the characteristics of care provision, a situation of 'converging variations' (Williams 2012).

Table 6.1 Intersecting scales and categories of analysis

Micro: the everyday experiences of care and care work (and the claims to emerge from them) – saturated in the social relations of both inequality and care relations of gender, class, race, disability, age, sexuality and migrant status.

Meso: the institutional, social, political and cultural factors which shape this relationship – the intersection of national care, migration and employment regimes.

Macro: global capitalism, with its geo-political, gendered, imperialist and postcolonial hierarchies and inequalities – the intersecting dynamics of the transnational political economy of care – the transnational movements and practices of care labour, care capital, care commitments and transnational political actors.

Source: Adapted from Williams (2018: 550).

In order to analyse this complex relational space, which moves from the economic, social and political dimensions of globalization to the most intimate practices of care carried out in private homes, I combine the multi-scalar approach outlined above with an intersectional analysis. Table 6.1 summarizes the three contextual scales – the micro-scale of everyday interpersonal care; the meso-scale – which registers the institutional, social, political and cultural factors which shape the relationship at micro-level but also shapes and is shaped by the processes at macro-level. Here the dynamics of the transnational political economy of care are part of a global capitalism and especially its gendered imperialist and postcolonial inequalities. Importantly, the analysis *within* each of these scales focuses on their intersecting dynamics to draw attention to the complex formations of power and inequality, structure and agency that characterize them. As the analysis unfolds each of these scales, it demonstrates more closely some of the key relationships in the framework developed in chapter 3 (which is summarized in figure 3.1). I start with the micro-scale of migration care work.

Micro-intersections layered in close encounters

The practices of care are saturated with complex interpersonal emotional and physical encounters between care-giver and recipient. When this is paid care work, the social relations are made more complex, first, by the social positionings of both parties attached to class, race / ethnicity, religion, gender, age, sexuality and disability, second, by the employment and migrant status of the care worker and, third, by the sometimes intimate and bodily nature of care work. The first two can be extremely variable. The worker may live in the home of the care recipient or in an institution such as a nursing home; she may work a few hours a week, a few hours a day, or long hours; her work may involve caring and/or cleaning for an older, frail or disabled person; or it may involve being their personal assistant. An employee may be self-employed, receive cash-in-hand as part of the grey economy, or may work for a private agency or for a local authority; she may have limited access to collective organization or representation, especially if she is isolated in her recipient's home. As a migrant, she may be working under a special permit or a temporary visa, or she may be undocumented, and these insecurities may be exacerbated where her ethnicity, nationality, religion or migrant status are racialized.

At the same time, these different conditions and positionings are overlaid by the social relations of care – what in chapter 5 I called the 'double helix' of welfare relations – and, on the part of the recipient, these may construct multiple vulnerable dependencies of frailty in old age or assumed dependencies of disabled people and, on the part of the worker, lead to experience of insecure employment and the indignities of racism and sexism or homophobia, especially where care has little social or economic value. These complexities attach not only to care work in employers' homes (such as cleaning, child care or looking after a frail person) but also to work in institutional care.

In a study of migrant and minority ethnic workers in mainly institutional-based care for older people in London, Paris and Madrid, a feeling of a 'hierarchy' of vulnerabilities made them sense their own experiences of racism were ignored (Sahraoui 2019). That is to say, institutional regulations covering older people's vulnerability were placed higher than vulnerability to racist abuse towards the worker by care recipients or managers. In this way, a Senegalese worker in Paris complained that, although equality laws regarded homophobia and racism as offences along with age discrimination, in his experience this was not the case: 'Racism is an offence isn't it? . . . punished by French law. But we say it's an elderly person, it's not . . . When you work 10 or 12 hours, you come, you sweat, you take care of the person, you wash him/her . . . you prepare breakfast . . . you even feed the person, you bend, you sweat, you're called negro, domestic . . .' (Sahraoui 2019: 162).

This study unfolds the ways in which the workers experience their working conditions. While old-age care work carries all the objective indicators of precarious employment and commodification of care in which private care home owners transfer their economic costs on to their workers, the subjective experience is that '[P]recariousness is substantial to life itself, it is thus a condition shared by all, albeit differently. Bodies that are racialised – as are migrant and minority ethnic care workers – are exposed to specific social, economic and political forms of precariousness' (Sahraoui 2019: 115; see also Gutiérrez Rodríguez 2014). The work is hard physically and emotionally and involves the challenges of residents who can be aggressive or even violent; it requires careful communication and it produces forms of reciprocity. Yet being able to meet such relational needs was, for the workers, a source of pride. Sahraoui concludes that a rights framework, while essential, is just not enough to deal with the multiple forms of subordination experienced by these workers. Rather, she says, we need to apply an ethics of care that gives the workers (both men and women) their pride and dignity as part of social justice.

Cranford and Chun (2017) provide a different example of this complexity in a case study in which the care relations do not follow the assumed patterns of social or economic power where the employer is of a wealthier dominant ethnic group and the worker is poor, female, of minority ethnicity and a migrant. Both care workers and care recipients in their study are from the minority ethnic and racialized urban community of Oakland Chinatown in California. By virtue of California's in-home supportive services, the recipients are older and disabled people, and many, like their workers, are poor. Recipients are allowed to employ family, friends or agency staff as care workers, and they share employment responsibilities with the state, which pays the employees directly as well as recognizing the union that represents care workers. The question here is whether these different features shift care away from traditional relations of coercive servitude towards a potentially more reciprocal model in which the dignity and conditions of both worker and recipient are recognized and respected. The researchers find elements of both continuity with the old model and changes to the new (as well as care recipients who can be kind or callous). However, what made for the continuities was underpinned by insufficient state funding that gave rise to precarious, low-paid work as well as difficulties in regulating home-based employment. And what made for a better model of care had to do less with shared ethnic and racialized positioning of workers and recipients and more with workers' capacity for collective agency through both the unions and an advocacy organization for women immigrants. Importantly, too, alliances with disability movements ensured representation of the experiences of recipients. In a sense, these alliances represent a form of 'intersectionality in action'.

Institutional intersections at the meso-scale

Many of the issues raised in the previous section implicate laws and policies made at national scale in which different institutional, political and cultural processes shape such interpersonal care relations. Here, too, it is useful to look at how these processes intersect, for this can provide an understanding of the diverse ways in which the migration–care nexus operates in different countries, even where those countries are faced with similar pressures (see table 6.1). This cross-national diversity has been termed one of 'converging variations' which has been shaped by the way a destination country's *care regime* intersects with its *migration regime* and its *employment regime* (Williams and Gavanas 2008; Simonazzi 2009; Williams 2012, 2018). By 'regime', I refer not only to clusters of state policies around care provision, migration rules and employment policies but, importantly, to cultures, practices and legacies in different countries, as well as major forms of social relations of power and inequality in care, migration and employment. These too are shaped by the forms of mobilization and contestation – for example, the capacity of workers to join a union or of advocacy for people with significant care needs (Williams 2012; see also Shutes and Chiatti 2012). So, for instance, care and employment policies often reflect the balance of gender relations as to whether women are supported in their paid work commitments by care provision. In some countries the care of older people is historically seen as a familial (or women's) responsibility; in others, it is one shared with state provision through domiciliary and institutional care.

As the last section showed, the application of anti-discrimination measures in both care and employment are also significant, and these vary across states. These three regimes are, arguably, the most salient in shaping a country's response to its care crisis.[2] While this analysis focuses on countries of destination, the framework can be applied to countries of migrant workers' origin (see Withers 2019a for a similar analysis for Sri Lanka). These three policy–culture–practice regimes also represent more focused and specific aspects of the first three dimensions of the family–nation–work–nature frame used in chapters 3 and 4 (an example below from Australia offers a connection of these to nature).

The intersection of the three regimes allows an analysis of migrant care work that shows how welfare states' responses to aspects of the crisis of care have converged, but, at the same time, historical legacies, path dependencies, cultural practices and political forces have shaped these responses in different ways. Take for example Europe, where Spain and

Italy are both countries with a strong history of familial (female) care provision. The rise in women's employment and ageing has led to what has been called a move from a family model of care to a 'migrant-in-the-family' model (Bettio et al. 2006). In these countries, state allowances assist families in employing care workers – of whom 63 per cent and 73 per cent, respectively, are migrant workers – to look after frail old family members in their homes (Leon 2010; van Hooren 2008). Furthermore, migration policies in these countries have in the past been relatively open, with domestic worker quotas and amnesties for irregular care worker migrants. In Italy, amid prevailing anti-immigration mobilization, new immigration policies in 2009 criminalized undocumented workers, yet an exception was made for *badanti* – home-based domestic/care workers – allowing them to become regularized (di Martino et al. 2013), thus reflecting the reliance of both the state and families on this low-cost care provision.

This dependence on migrant workers to provide familial care of older people is also evident in Spain. This was one of the European countries hit hardest by the global financial crisis and the demands of the EU/IMF bailout in 2009, after which general unemployment rose to a peak rate of 27 per cent. This has affected migrant care workers in a number of ways. The squeeze on household incomes led to a decrease in their hours, conditions and pay, evident in remittances sent back home, which were halved in Spain between 2006 and 2016 (Hellgren and Serrano 2017: 5). However, for many migrant care workers, return to their home country was not a viable option. Also, they are an essential source of care labour. Indeed, in spite of tightening immigration measures on non-EU migrants and an increase in non-eligibility of migrants to social rights, general immigration since 2009 in Spain levelled off rather than dropping dramatically. In some Spanish cities there has also been significant mobilization in support of migrants' rights (see chapter 7). It remains to be seen what the effects of the Covid-19 pandemic will be, although early reports suggest that migrant workers have been hard hit in Spain (Burgen and Jones 2020).

By contrast, while the care regime in the UK has a tradition of public provision for elder care, this has not, until recently, been the case for child care. The care economy has seen these areas of provision become dominated by the private sector (which has seen worsening conditions – see chapter 4), so that migrant workers, especially in London and the South East, are much more likely to be employed by private-sector residential and home-care services. Migrants constitute around 20 per cent of workers in adult social care (Cangiano et al. 2009; Franklin and Brancati 2015). The migration regime has developed a restrictive points-based system which favours skilled workers, and this shapes the care labour market. After the points system was introduced in 2008, nurses and senior care workers were no longer eligible for the skilled labour work permits allowed to migrants from outside the EU. These individuals still continued to migrate to the UK but ended up in care jobs for which they were overqualified and for which they have constantly to renew their work permits, or else stay undocumented. Brexit preparations combined with the pandemic have led to contradictory moves – on the one hand, a rising demand for more nurses and care workers and, on the other, immigration policy that has restricted entry to workers earning below the average salary of nurses and care workers for the EU and outside the EU (see chapter 4). This has produced an impasse between the care, migration and employment regimes, with the government's Migration Advisory Committee (2020) warning of 'stark consequences' for the country's capacity to supply care, especially in the light of the pandemic.

In those European countries whose care policies have been more socialized and women-friendly, there have also been changes of a different kind which encourage the employment of migrant domestic workers. This is represented by the policy of offering tax credits to households to assist in buying home-based domestic services. Austria, Germany, Belgium, France, Finland, Denmark and Sweden have all actively promoted domestic work in this way (Carbonnier and Morel 2015). This has been justified in two ways: as a form of job creation and social inclusion for marginalized workers (many of whom are migrants and resident minority ethnic women) and as a 'productivity boost' that enables professional women in the labour market to maintain their productivity as highly skilled workers in the knowledge economy. However, it also intensifies divisions in the labour market between the highly qualified and well-paid and those without qualifications in precarious low-paid work, as well as a trend towards the fiscalization of welfare, which tends to favour better-off households. It is a form of social policy that can be presented rhetorically as supporting gender equality in access to paid work and reconciling work and care responsibilities, but in reality it intensifies gendered class and race inequalities.

Australia provides an example of two contrasting sets of employment conditions in care provision. While public provision for older people's care has been marketized, there is a tradition of stronger standards in employment in the child-care sector, which means that this sector has far fewer problems with labour shortages than care work with older people (Brennan et al. 2017). At the same time, Australia's highly regulated migration regime, which traditionally has focused on skilled workers, turns a blind eye to the growing numbers of temporary migrant workers in low-paid work, including those in care homes. In an early warning of the intersection of care and climate change crises, the Australian government in 2018 considered proposals to create migration pathways for young people from the Pacific Islands, a region vulnerable to rising sea levels, to go to Australia and New Zealand as care workers for older people (World Bank 2018). Such instrumental measures neglect a migrant worker's likely concerns as to how far migration rules would allow family members to join her in the event of possible evacuation, as well as fears about the loss of her culture and homeland.

South Korea and Japan deal with common social and demographic problems faced by many OECD countries: increasing shortages of workers in elder care and child care. However, while many other countries have followed a market model, with cash subsidies for home-based and/or live-in care often provided by migrant workers, Japan and South Korea have increased their publicly funded services and subsidies (such as long-term care insurance) to meet their care needs, and also government policy resists the employment of migrant home-based workers (Peng 2017). A highly selective migration regime allows (often only those defined as 'co-ethnic') migrants only into institutional care work. What marks regimes of Japan and Korea is a high degree of institutional regulation combined with a cultural aversion towards 'foreigners' (especially in the private home) and a historical legacy of socialized care. Both these emerged from the development of those countries' welfare states as a form of nation-building constructed through the ideas and practices of an imagined cultural/racial/ethnic homogeneity (ibid.) – a process also present in earlier twentieth-century welfare state foundations of Europe and North America (Kettunen et al. 2015). It is this, embodied in Japan by lack of social citizenship rights to minorities (Hirano 2020), that persists in the face of global empirical trends towards the acceptance of (some) mobile labour.

However, these aspects are not reproduced in other East Asian countries. Taiwan, Hong Kong and China have pursued a market model that depends on low-paid home-based care carried out by migrant workers (Laliberté 2017). Here, Confucian values of filial piety are used to defend quasi-family care by migrants in the home, even though in China religious values have long been repudiated. Furthermore, in China, it is the administrative boundaries between provinces rather than between countries which construct the *rural* migrant as low-paid, insecure and racialized (Hong 2017).

What these different cases show is that, while there is a global phenomenon that, in the following section, I characterize as a transnational political and social economy of care, there is significant variation in how this operates across different countries. These variations represent more than differences in care policies. They are the specific outcomes of the conflicting and contradictory intersections of institutional, cultural and social dimensions of care, employment and migration regimes. This provides an illustration, albeit brief, of the different ways in which the domains of family, nation and work and even nature transect in different ways in different countries. There are three further implications from such analysis. The first is that cross-national studies need not only to account for those areas such as care policy to highlight gender inequalities and mobilizations but also to recognize the range of social relations that care embodies. Second is the significance of migration as an area of policy and regulation that also expresses the social relations of race and ethnicity which are central to the nation-building trajectories of welfare states, and thus central to the ways in which citizenship, equality and universalism become institutionalized. The third is that this phenomenon of migrant care work poses fundamental questions about social justice and the revaluation of care, which I discuss in the conclusion. The following section outlines the broader context of the micro- and meso-dynamics.

The transnational political and social economy of care

The concept of a transnational political and social economy of care (TPSEC) (Williams 2011, 2014; Mahon and Robinson 2011; Razavi and Staab 2012) attempts to grasp the broader context framing the conditions and constraints of migrant care work. I argue that there are four key elements in the TPSEC: (i) the transnational movement of care labour; (ii) transnational care commitments; (iii) transnational expansion of care capital; and (iv) transnational political actors.

The transnational movement of care labour

Central to the study of migrant care work is the movement of care labour (Parreñas 2001, 2005; see also Anderson 2000; Heyzer et al. 1994; Hondagneu-Sotelo 2001). Parreñas's seminal *Servants of Globalization* (2001) is a study of Filipina migrant domestic workers' experiences in Rome and Los Angeles and their families' experiences in the Philippines. It conceptualizes the system in which these workers are caught up as 'the international division of reproductive labour'. This makes a number of important connections. First is the historical relationship of reproductive labour to race, gender and class by building on Glenn's (1992) work on the racial division of reproductive labour mentioned earlier. This identifies the continuing role in care and domestic service that black and minority ethnic women have played in the US. Second, the analysis makes links to the specific yet central incorporation of women from poorer regions into globalized production processes by drawing on Sassen–Koob's (1984) gendered analysis of the new international division of labour and the development of global cities. These cities form the focus for specialized firms employing highly professionalized male and female workers whose catering, cleaning and care needs are serviced at low cost by migrant workers – in other words, by an international reproductive labour force. Third, the study connects to the discursive nature of nationhood and its contribution to the subordination of migrant groups, with reference to the ways in which globalization opens up national economies while encouraging a political closure through nationalist (anti-immigration) sentiment (ibid.). What Parreñas adds further to this is an analysis of the partial citizenship status that these systems construct for migrant women in this work.

Parreñas's analysis focuses mainly on work in private households and private businesses. However, as I have shown in the previous section, there is another important deployment of migrant care labour as part of child and social care provision, which may be in public or private institutions and care homes. This has been a particularly significant development in attempts by developed welfare states to cut down social expenditure costs in order to meet increasing needs. In addition, there is a parallel movement and recruitment of skilled health workers from poorer regions into public and private institutions in richer countries (Yeates 2009; Yeates and Pillinger 2019). It is also the case that this mobility operates the other way round – for example, where service-users move to receive or pay for care in another country, such as Japanese older men who travel to Thailand to receive long-term care (Miyashita et al. 2017).

The transnational dynamics of care commitments

These care commitments refer to the transnational institutions and networks which workers create to connect across the diasporic space they and their families inhabit as they migrate and leave family behind. It refers also to the emotional and care labour women deliver for their families in their home country. Oliveira (2017) calls these 'transnational care constellations'. She describes how Sara, an undocumented mother of two from Mexico, simultaneously cares for the child of her employer, one of her own children, whom she has with her in New York, and her other child, who has remained in Mexico but with whom she keeps in constant touch by phone. A great deal of emotional flexibility is required to hold these complex layers in place. At a wider level, the existence of diasporic relationships carry policy implications that affect all workers involved in transnational movement: opportunities for family reunion, time off for care emergencies, weddings and funerals, and the portability of allowances and benefits across national borders.

Another aspect of these commitments which links to the movement of care capital is that of remittances – 'care abstracted in remittances' (Withers and Piper 2018: 591). A number of states of migrants' origin, such as the Philippines, Nepal, Indonesia, Sri Lanka and some Caribbean and Pacific islands, encourage migration as a way of attracting foreign exchange. The orthodoxy of development economists is to view this as a form of development investment and a 'triple win' situation for both the countries of origin and destination and for the migrant worker and her household (explained in de Haas 2010). A more critical view suggests otherwise. In her study entitled *Children of Global Migration* (2005), Parreñas analyses this export of care labour, which provides the Philippines with its largest source of foreign currency. This is the result of inequities stemming from the effects of structural adjustment policies which increased foreign debt and reduced the capacities of the Philippine state to improve its own health, care and education infrastructure (Guevarra 2010). At the same time, social and economic instability and lack of access to public services provide the economic context in which families make moral decisions about their collective wellbeing – that it is better served through the migration of a family member to increase their economic security.

Matt Withers's study of Sri Lanka shows how its fragile economy, history of ethnic conflict, and loan conditionalities from the IMF have thrown it onto a treadmill in which it is dependent on remittances; however, there is no guarantee that the state will use these to develop the sort of infrastructure that might enable people to find better employment in their own country. It is more likely that funds from foreign currency are used on gentrification projects in urban areas than on the urban or rural poor (Withers 2019b). Yet remittances *are* important to both the migrant workers and their families, for housing, education, and living costs, although some of it also goes in repaying the costs of the migration itself (see below). The biggest 'winners' are the countries of destination. For example, in the

Gulf Cooperation Council States, temporary migrant workers represent between 32.3 per cent (Saudi Arabia) and 95 per cent (Qatar) of the labour force involved in building these countries' infrastructure and caring and cleaning for its families under highly exploitative conditions (Withers 2019b: 431).[3] Nor is there support for the claim that these workers benefit from skill development; they are usually overqualified for the work they do.

The transnational expansion of care capital

Commodification trends in national welfare states have accelerated the intervention of the private market in health, social care and nursery care, making care big international business (see chapter 4 on the financialization of care provision). In long-term care, the British United Provident Association has operations in Spain, Ireland, Thailand, Hong Kong and Saudi Arabia. International corporations now dominate much private care-home provision in the UK, their debts the source of profit for loans from offshore private equity companies and hedge funds and their continuity subject to finance decisions of these companies (White 2016). In 2011, Southern Cross, one of the largest care-home providers in the UK, went bankrupt and was bought by Four Seasons Healthcare, which also went bankrupt, in 2019. It was refinanced several times until its debts were taken into control by a US hedge fund, H-2 Capital (Rowland 2019). A similar rise and fall took place with ABC Learning, the private provider of early education and care in Australia (Brennan and Oloman 2009). In addition to the distress caused to service-users as provision closes, this business model, operating through debt, risk, expansion and profit, undermines the principles of individual needs and continuity and quality of services. Moreover, the labour-intensive nature of care means that profits are made through economies of scale, forcing the smaller specialist providers out of the market.

A further area of profitability comes from those who are involved in brokering migrants' journeys and placing them in their future employment. These too are often exploitative. Migrant domestic workers in Hong Kong and Taiwan who are mainly from Indonesia and the Philippines can pay up to three months' salary for their placement, along with training and relocation costs (Laliberté 2017). This means that for the first few months the worker might work for nothing and be, in effect, indentured labour. Other studies have shown how agencies in Europe reinforce existing forms of racial exploitation in reproducing their employer clients' racialized hierarchies by placing Eastern Europeans and Filipinas in more favourable positions than workers from Muslim or African countries (Williams and Gavanas 2008).

While the exchange value of remittances plays an important role in the supply of care labour, also significant is the demand from states for migrant care workers to keep their care labour costs down. Many states are global employers working alongside private agencies in the recruitment of skilled health-care workers (WHO 2016). According to the OECD (2019), the number of foreign-trained doctors working in OECD countries increased by 50 per cent between 2006 and 2016 (to almost 500,000), and the number of foreign-trained nurses increased by 20 per cent over the five-year period from 2011 to 2016 (to almost 550,000). The main countries of destination are the United States, followed by the United Kingdom and Germany, while there have also been rapid increases of foreign-trained doctors in Ireland, France, Switzerland, Norway and Sweden. While to some extent these increases are part of a South–North 'brain-drain' and a more general increase in skilled worker migration, it also marks increased internationalization of training. For example, a doctor from India working in Ireland may well have trained in Central or Eastern Europe.

Transnational political actors

Transnational and international political actors involved in improving the rights and conditions of migrant care workers constitute the fourth aspect in the TPSEC. On the one side is *transnational governance*, represented not only by the IMF's constraining powers on developing countries but also by the policies, agreements and conventions in which international organizations (IOs) such as the International Labour Organization have played an important recent role, as well as the WHO in health care. On the other side, local and *transnational networks of care and domestic work activists*, along with feminist activists and academics inside and outside the IOs, have been an important source of pressure.

Three main sets of migration discourses operate within and outside the IOs on the global governance of migration (Mahon 2021). The first and dominant one is that of managed migration, which sees the role of global governance as being to set the rules of agreement between global capital's demand for labour and the supply from poorer countries (the World Bank and, to a lesser extent, the International Organization for Migration). A more critical approach is rights-based in line with social protection and supported by trade unions (such as in the ILO). The third has been the development of feminist pressure, which has sought to bring both female migration *and* gender equality to the discussions (INSTRAW, UNIFEM and UN Women). The historic passing of the ILO's Convention no, 189, 'Decent Work for Domestic Workers', in 2011 was an example of transnational women activists working successfully with an IO. This raised many important considerations for challenging the exploitation of migrant care labour, which I pick up in the concluding discussion on care-ethical global justice.

Conclusion: towards care-ethical global justice

This chapter has presented a framework for understanding some of the most important dimensions of the social and political economy of contemporary care relations. It has employed an intersectional analysis to reveal how the practices of care are woven into a range of social relations which attend to care-giving and care-receiving. It has argued that analysis must be able to connect these practices at the local level with institutional, social and cultural regimes of care, migration and employment at the national level. These configure differently in different countries while also being subject in different degrees to the marketization, labour activation and austerity trajectories of neoliberalism. However, care is also a global issue and, in its manifestation through migrant care work, is part of geo-political inequalities between richer and poorer nations, historically constituted in colonial relations of racialized servitude, reconstituted for contemporary times through the transnational political and social economy of care. Each scale reiterates how the alterity produced by these geo-political inequalities subordinates care workers as racialized migrants and how that subordination is compounded by a constant devaluation of the paid and unpaid work of care.

How then to think about change? The ILO's Convention no. 189 ('Decent Work for Domestic Workers') was a significant marker of progress. It set terms for rights to decent working conditions and collective organization to be ratified and implemented by its member states (the UK has not ratified it).[4] In many ways the processes involved in determining this policy were as significant as the policy itself. Grassroots domestic worker organizations across the world were brought together in an International Domestic Workers Network. Jennifer Fish (2017) describes how the inclusion of this network in the negotiation of the convention to give workers greater visibility, recognition and dignity was a new departure for the ILO. It went beyond the usual tripartite social dialogue of states, unions and employers by having 'real' domestic workers who could testify to their own experiences; and it was forced to consider the hitherto 'invisible' informal economy – 'the work that makes all other work possible'. It also set the terms for collective engagement at different scales. In the US, where a Domestic Worker Bill of Rights was passed in New York state and California, the pressure for reform created a circular process of mobilizing. This generated demands from local organizations to national NGOs and policy-makers and on to international protocols, whose ordinance could then become the basis for further pressure for implementation at both national and local level (Boris and Undén 2017).

This convention represents 'a benchmark in the construction of a more egalitarian community' and 'a 'moral compass for the treatment of those most at risk within societies' (Fish 2017: 250). But there is still further to go. For it also reflects limitations in the thinking of international organizations to see through the 'fractured gaze' (Mahon 2018). In other words, the problems that attend contemporary domestic and care work belong not only to the conditions of workers in richer countries but to the conditions arising from the history of colonial and postcolonial development and geopolitical inequalities affecting women in poorer countries (also applicable to Central and Eastern European countries and the conditionalities set by the IMF following the liberalization of their economies in 1989 – Deacon 1992). In addition, Convention 189 focuses on decent paid work more than it does on the intersecting devaluation of paid and unpaid care in both countries of origin and of destination. Matt Withers's analysis of Sri Lanka (2019a) proposes that, as well as a 'decent work' agenda, a 'decent care' agenda is necessary to begin to address the redistribution of unpaid care work which underpins inequities in the labour market.[5]

Strategies for reform operate in three ways: first, they should involve both short-term and longer-term goals; second, they should apply geographically in countries of migrants' origin as well as in the destination countries; and, third, pressure has to be brought to bear at local, national, bi-lateral, international and global levels of policy-making in a way that continually iterates across them. Among these would be, for example, the regularization of care and domestic work, union and community representation for workers, prioritizing migrants' right of citizenship, including family reunion, rights to contracts, social protection, training, language acquisition, and freedom from discrimination.

Cutting across these are links that require co-ordination across different sectors. One conclusion to be drawn from the analysis here is that care, migration and employment policy areas often operate without reference to each other, especially where the care sector depends on 'unskilled' migrant workers while migration policies are restricting migration to 'skilled' workers (Boyd 2017; Brennan et al. 2017). Parallel strategies at the local and national level in countries of migrants' origin could develop further opportunities for representation for potential migrants, for social dialogue and for co-ordinated development of ethical emigration policies, as well as for countering the understaffing and underfunding of public health and care infrastructure (see Pillinger 2011).

At the global level, some of the developments in global health care strategy may be instructive. The World Health Organization's '2010 Global Code of Practice' (WHO 2010) recommended a more extensive application of bilateral ethical recruitment codes in health care, which have been implemented in a number of countries to prevent the 'poaching' of health-care workers from poorer countries, combined with the guarantee to provide free training and support for returning doctors and nurses. This was important in building on a human rights approach as well as prioritizing measures to counter global inequalities in health (Connell and Buchan 2011). Although it represents soft rather than hard law and raises as many new complexities as those it seeks to answer, it nevertheless provides a route towards thinking about material redistribution and reparation in the face of the geo-political inequalities generated by migrant care work. It encompasses some important guidelines in moving towards global social justice, including the right to health, worker autonomy, accountability, transnational reciprocity and mutualism, and fair workplace practices (ibid.: 14–15) which could also be applied to care work.

Within this, the recognition of the different claims of those groups at the centre of care provision is also important: not only workers and the trade unions and migrant advocates that support them, not only carers of children or older people, but also those service-users who access support. While the professionalization of care work might be a strategy to raise the value of care and care workers' opportunities, disability organizations have long challenged the part played by professionalization in enhancing the power of professionals over service-users (Shakespeare 2014). Overcoming this requires the involvement of user groups in monitoring training that is person-centred rather than task-oriented – being attentive to people's needs, being non-judgemental, recognizing human dignity. It also requires an intersectionality in action – alliances and dialogues between the different groups making claims around care policies (Williams 2010).

One part of putting this into a longer-term perspective requires that care is seen as central to global social justice – that is to say, that the everyday relations of care carried out, paid and unpaid, within unequal socio-economic, gendered and racialized relations are embedded conceptually and strategically in global social justice. In the political discourses of national and global social policy actors, paid and unpaid care work is often hidden, subsumed under the requirements and duty of paid work for individuals and economic competitiveness for nation-states. Care is a practice, a responsibility and an ethic in people's everyday lives, and it is part of what it means to be a citizen. People are not only holders of individual rights, but they have care needs and care responsibilities that shape their actions and decisions. In policy terms this necessitates the recognition of care, the representation of its providers and receivers, and the rights and redistribution of care needs and responsibilities as central tenets in global justice. Ethically, politically and practically, care constitutes the social reproduction activities that sustain society as much as labour, local, national and migrant, sustains the economy and ecological justice sustains the planet. It is within this framing of justice, sustainability, interdependence, humanization and hospitality that we might begin to think through the complexities of the politics of migrant care work and the struggles around it. The following chapter picks up these themes.

PART III

PRAXIS

Towards an Eco-Welfare Commons: Intersections of Political Ethics and Prefigurative Practices

Introduction

There can be no going back. This has been one of the strongest collective responses to the 2020 pandemic's magnification of social, economic and political inequalities, vulnerabilities and fragilities. 'The pandemic marks the end of an era and the beginning of another – one whose harshness must be mitigated by a spirit of generosity' – was how Rebecca Solnit summed up her account of the huge engendering of mutual aid, solidarity, kindness and empathy enacted by many ordinary people in many countries. This represented not only a counter feeling to the competitive, consumerist individualism of capitalism but also 'an energy source that can drive a better society, if it is recognised and encouraged . . . It can be the basis for the future, if we can recognise the value of these urges and actions, recognise that things can and must change profoundly, and *if we can tell other stories about who we are, what we want and what is possible*' (Solnit 2020; emphasis added). Many activists and thinkers have emphasized that now is the time to articulate the sort of world we want to inhabit (Lister 2020; Mazzucato 2020; Barnett 2020; Mbembe 2020; Roy 2020; Klein 2020). 'Build Back Better' has become a popular slogan (Knight 2020). This imperative was underlined and its quest fundamentally redefined by the Black Lives Matter protests that started in the US and spread across the world (Bogues 2020; Jones 2020). In fact, even before the pandemic, as I noted at the beginning of the book, emerging and remerging forms of collectivism and activism were characterizing civil society politics in transnational, national, regional and local spaces, both in spite of and because of neoliberal austerity and ongoing racism, sexism, ageism and ablism.

This chapter is about how these twin developments can help rewrite our imaginations to develop a 'welfare commons' to transform the relationship between state and civil society. The concept of the 'commons' summons a way of re-embedding that which has been disembedded, dispossessed, dehumanized, colonized and commodified – public space, public services, land, populations, humanity, finance, time to care, people to care, natural resources, non-humans, technology and creativity (Ostrom 1990; Mestrum 2015; Newman and Clarke 2014; Williams 2015; Coote 2017; Gough 2017). The chapter pulls together many of the themes and threads that run through the book. It elaborates in tandem two of the 'five turns' I identified in chapter 1 that inform new social policy thinking: the 'Utopian' and the 'ethical'. In relation to the first, I argued (chapter 2) that the importance of an intersectional method was that analysis should inform praxis. Utopian thinking, I suggested, should be practical and take its cue from the significance of prefigurative politics in the social movements and radical municipalism of the 1970s and 1980s – that is, practising in the present what might herald change for the future. In other words, transformative thinking should *ground* its inspiration in contemporary prefigurative practices. By the 'ethical turn', I mean those guiding principles which are not based on abstraction but worked through in everyday lives and, through this, serve to challenge the universalization of an ethical subject based on Western modernity's liberal notions of rational male autonomy. Chapters 5 and 6 reference the ethics of care, but here I extend the discussion to focus on commonalities and specificities in the political ethics of care, of environmentalism and of decoloniality. With these in mind, I then look at prefigurative practices or processes that have particular significance for reimagining welfare. I focus on relationality in state and services and in global and local spaces of possibility, on a deeper deliberative democracy, and on intersectional solidarity and alliances for recalibrating the practice of humanity. Finally, I draw together these intersecting ethics and practices to suggest some guidelines for constituting an eco-welfare commons as well as issues requiring further discussion and debate.

Ethics grounded in the struggles of care, the environment and decoloniality

I suggested in the discussion about intersecting crises in chapter 3 that the contestations that have attended the crises of financial capitalism, of care, of the climate and environment, and of internal and external racialized borders profoundly challenge the principles and practices of neoliberal, patriarchal and racial global capitalism. This is because, singly and together, in challenging the economic insecurities and social inequalities attached to these four crises, they articulate political ethics and ethical politics for future strategies, alliances and alternatives. The conjoining of 'political' with 'ethical' is deliberate because, as I argue below, morality and politics are not separate spheres but entwined through an understanding of the social relations of power.

Political ethics of care

In chapter 5 the idea of agency as a relational concept was supported with reference to the feminist ethics of care. Central to care ethicists' critiques of the limits of liberal theories' accounts of the self, autonomy, rights, justice and equality is that they are based on a Western androcentric understanding that it is the individual's inherent rationality and autonomy which enables abstract and impartial moral judgments (Tronto 1993, 2013; Sevenhuijsen 1998; Kittay 1999, 2015). Care ethicists argue that our autonomy is relational, as are the moral practices that flow from this. These exist and operate in relation to others, and it is not autonomy but interdependence that is the basis of human interaction. Central to that interdependence is care: 'Care helps us rethink humans as interdependent beings' (Tronto 1993: 21). In turn, care is central to human life: 'Care is not a parochial concern of women, a type of secondary moral question, or the work of the least well off in society. Care is a central concern of human life' (ibid.: 180). To receive and to give care is a potential we all share: it involves all of us, whether women, men, old, young, able bodied and/or disabled. At the centre of care is an ethic of nurturance and human flourishing. Herein lies its contradiction: it is central to human life yet, as other chapters have shown, deeply devalued across inequalities of gender, race, class, migration, disability, sexuality, age and geo-politics.

Asserting the ethical and political value of care has been central to care ethics. Thus Joan Tronto argues that, as a practice, care involves different principles informing action in different contexts. She identifies these as attentiveness (being open to the needs of others); responsibility (being able to assume responsibility for others' needs); competence (being able to carry out care-giving); and responsiveness (being able to judge the response to the receipt of care and learn from the experience of the other). As an activity that binds us, care provides the potential for social solidarity, as the first paragraph of this chapter showed. Sevenhuijsen (1998) takes this into the political realm of citizenship, adding the values of plurality, communication, trust and respect. She argues that, in receiving and giving care in the right conditions of mutual respect and material support, we learn civic virtues of responsibility, trust, compassion for human limitations and frailties, understanding others on their own terms, and an acceptance of human diversity. In these terms, care contributes to being a citizen.

In this way care ethics move beyond the personal to the political. Tronto (2013) argues for care ethics to be prescribed for a 'caring democracy' – a more pluralistic and egalitarian politics where 'care can serve as a strategic concept to involve the relatively disenfranchised in the political world' (Tronto 1993: 21; see also Engster 2007). Similarly, Barnes (2012) applies the principles to how we 'do' politics in a more 'care-full' way, a view also developed in a notion of 'mindfulness' in politics (Lister 2020). In addition, these ideas have been applied to a critique of international relations and liberal notions of cosmopolitan justice (Robinson 1999, 2013; Held 2006) and to intersections of race, racism, colonialism, slavery and migration (see chapter 6; Mahon and Robinson 2011). Interdependence is not simply about relations between intimate others within neighbourhoods or communities but extends to relations between countries. For example, Clark Miller's (2010) development of 'cosmopolitan care' develops from a critique of theories of moral cosmopolitanism as cosmopolitan justice (Pogge 1992; Nussbaum 2006) in which the 'hyper-individualized' moral subject exercises impartial and rational judgement. This, she argues, ignores the relationality of people in terms of both close others and identities, as well as their finitude and dependency. Understanding this requires cross-cultural sensitivity to particular contexts and geo-inequalities of power. While there *are* basic needs which are universal, the ways people experience these differ (Clark Miller 2010: 155). Care as a cosmopolitan ethic between distant strangers demands solidarity and political action across countries as well as awareness of where countries are situated in global power structures. Articulated by the Care Collective (2020: 21), this engenders a 'radical cosmopolitan conviviality'.

The early developments of care ethics in the 1980s were focused more on the particularity of care ethics to women (Gilligan 1982; Noddings 1984), a position sometimes criticized as essentialist. However, Patricia Hill Collins's contribution, which locates an 'ethic of caring' within African American black feminist practice and thinking, deserves mention (Hill Collins 1990). Rooted in the traditions of African humanism, this ethic is defined by Hill Collins as personal expressiveness, knowledge based in feeling and connection, and empathy. In turn, these come from a belief in individual uniqueness; situated knowledge rooted in feelings in which emotions and intellect are connected and not separate; and empathy is based on an attempt to understand the situation of others.

This idea of individual uniqueness strikes a different trail from the previous discussion. In fact, one of the criticisms of care ethics lies in the shift from the focus on autonomy to one on interdependence and whether this obscures the demands for autonomy by those who have historically been denied it. This was mentioned in chapter 5 with respect to disabled people. In her critique of the ethics of care, Anita Silvers (1995) argues that the historical denial of autonomy and the abusive power inherent in many institutional care experiences means autonomy should not be rejected and replaced by care as an alternative morality or an acceptable moral person-hood. In turning care into a virtue, this places a moral onus upon the cared-for person. Without the structures and conditions for equality, it becomes incumbent upon the cared-for person to ensure that the carer behaves vir-tuously (ibid.: 42). Silvers's argument is reminiscent of similar arguments that people whose ethnicity marks them out as a minority are positioned to feel responsible for putting white people at their ease when issues of race are discussed (Eddo-Lodge 2017; Rankine 2020). In doing this, Silvers argues, the ethics of care deflect from the paradigm of equality, and it is this that can better meet the demands for civil rights for disabled people, as well as connect to the struggles of other marginalized groups.

These are important arguments (see Shakespeare 2000; Williams 2001; Shakespeare and Williams 2019). In their defence, Tronto and Sevenhuijsen do operate within an equality paradigm with an awareness of multiple inequalities in care relationships, and this has been extended to global or cosmopolitan ethics of care, as noted above. But perhaps there are some points of emphasis that can cut through these differences. One is about the concept of autonomy and how it fits with the ethics of care. The ethics of care requires that interdependence be seen as the basis of human interac-tion, that this presupposes that human flourishing is the key to our sustain-ability, and that the conditions for this – care and co-operation – are also central to society. In that case, autonomy and independence do not wither away but become strategically about *the capacity for self-determination* (relational and collective) rather than the expectation of individual self-sufficiency (Clark Miller 2010).[1]

Second, applying an intersectional approach to care can also cut through the binaries around care. This would recognize that, while relationships of care are structured around social relations of power, these relations are not fixed (Hankivsky 2014). Even though there is a symbolic and systematic material inequality between able-bodied and disabled people, we can in practice be carers or cared-for in different situations and do not necessarily occupy one single position in this binary. Able-bodied paid carers may find themselves in an exploitative relationship with the person they care for by virtue of class, race, gender and other social relations. Disabled people may be active carers even though their structural position can render this invisible.

Third, Silvers's insistence is on an understanding of how collective historical experience contributes to contemporary political positioning and a consequent sensitivity of that in writing about care relations. This is important and similar to the notion of transgenerational trauma or haunting (Bhattacharyya 2018) experienced by descendants of indigenous populations, of the Holocaust, and of slavery and colonialism. It resonates with the discussion below in relation to decoloniality and the long historical shadow of dehumanization.

In an interesting point of connection between disability and the need radically to revise the taken-for-granted human in humanism, Goodley and his colleagues (2014) recommend Braidotti's theory of 'the posthuman' to critical analysis of disability. Braidotti's argument is similar to care ethicists' rejection of Enlightenment rationality in favour of relationality, but more extensive (Braidotti 2013). She argues that the conditions of our lives make redundant the assumptions in humanism of a central ethical subject as an able-bodied, white, Western heterosexual man. Not only has this been challenged by the struggles by feminists, anti-racists and others, but the complexity of our times and the enlarged relation of being with the non-human world and technology require an expanded sense of interconnection of what constitutes our community and territoriality. It provides us with multiple attachments of belonging and is capable of universalistic reach based on a strong sense of collectivity and relationality. Goodley and his colleagues argue that the writings of critical disability studies illustrate this thesis well. On the one hand, the struggles of disability movements are about getting on to the human register after centuries of dehumanization. On the other, they present new versions of what human is. For example, disabled people, more than any others, experience the extension of relationality to technologies and non-humans. Cochlear implants, guide dogs, Makaton, the one-to-one classroom assistant, do not make the disability disappear but reconfigure the disabled child/adult in their relationality to non-humans, humans and technologies. Such concerns with the posthuman also surface in subsequent care ethics writing. Maria Puig de la Bellacasa (2017) extends Tronto's definition of the ethics of care to the non-human living and non-living world in order to engage with what interdependence and co-existence with these worlds means for a speculative ethics.

Overall, the implications of care ethicists' arguments point to significant change in the systems for cultural, social, economic and political organization. Whether narrowly human or extendedly posthuman, giving care its value involves challenging neoliberalism's register of self-care as 'a pervasive order of individualized biopolitical morality' (Puig de la Bellacasa 2017: 9). On the one hand, this involves developing a caring, democratically run infrastructure which revalues paid and unpaid care and gives people and communities time and both financial and practical support to be able to care and be cared for. It requires equal access to public space and transport, as well as policies that counter poverty and discrimination. Making *care* an organizing principle for policies affecting intimacy, citizenship, belonging and environmental sustainability begins to turn around how we think about relationships, borders, states and global governance (Care Collective 2020). For example, care as a principle enables a recognition of different forms of kin and non-kin relationships rather than assuming that care is necessarily confluent with heterosexual family life. I return to these ideas in the following sections of the chapter, but I note here that the question of giving care its *economic* value is central to challenging many aspects of the devaluation of care. It also provides a link to the following discussion on environmental ethics. The report *Creating a Caring Economy*, by the Women's Budget Group (WBG 2020e), says this means an economy that prioritizes care of one another and the environment through the measure of wellbeing rather than through maximizing economic growth. Its seven principles include many aspects mentioned here and combine equality principles with investing in all aspects of welfare provision, not only care but also housing and public transport, taxation and benefits, and a strong national and international environmental policy.

Environmental ethics

Unlike the ethics of care, which is represented by a fairly well-defined, if changing, body of research and application, environmental ethics comes out of a much more diverse field influenced by different political understandings. Fitzpatrick identifies liberalism, communitarianism (including republicanism) and eco-feminism as the most prominent (Fitzpatrick 2011: chap. 6). There are also many associated with indigenous and decolonial movements such as Buen Vivir. In addition, ecological strategies differ in terms of whether to work within or against capitalism / patriarchy / racial and colonial capitalism and within or without the state based upon different explanations for environmental damage and the climate crisis. This has been a rapidly growing area of mobilization in recent years, especially of young people through the global social movement of Extinction Rebellion (XR). Its three demands – Tell the Truth, Act Now, and Go Beyond Politics – reflect a strategy to empower citizens to recognize the urgency of convincing those in power about the scientific implications for the future and the necessity of using non-violent disruptive civil disobedience to do so.

At first sight there is much overlap of arguments of care ethics with many of the critical environmental perspectives which I discuss here. They also start from a critique of Western liberal philosophy, but for ecologists the critique is of the separation of 'man' from nature and the acceptance, if not promotion, of his dominion over nature. Eco-feminism, which has a strong emphasis on women in formerly colonized countries and the international division of labour, links this man–nature separation to the subordination of women – man as reason over women as nature. In this they express early versions of neo-humanism in the embrace of a non-human world, an ethic of worldwide connectedness and a rejection of Western rationality and reasoning enacted through its dependence on science and technology (Mies and Shiva 1993; Plumwood 1993). This is a more critical approach to science than most orthodox environmentalist perspectives.

More generally, the principle of interdependence extends beyond human interdependence to infer three sets of ethical obligations: that human interdependence within the planet is *global*, demanding strategies that address all parts of the world; that it involves a holistic *planetary* interdependence and therefore an ethical obligation to consider non-human beings and living organisms; and that it is *intergenerational* and behoves us to think about the needs of future generations.

In common with care ethicists, there is a critique of the economic system and its growth-productivist imperatives measured by GDP. These ethical obligations and critiques are brought together in Kate Raworth's influential book *Doughnut Economics* (2017), whose concepts and principles emerge out of work on international development. Raworth argues that we have to be rid of orthodox economists' figure of *homo economicus* (see chapter 5) and replace him with what it takes to make flourishing societies that express humanity, justice, generosity and human spirit. The eponymous doughnut is a compass-like series of concentric circles which act as a guide to enable us to consider what is required to arrive at a space which is both 'an ecologically safe and socially just space for all humanity'. Three conceptual principles frame her argument. First is the need to consider the social foundation of the basics for life as drawn from the UN's 2015 Sustainable Development Goals (UN 2015). These include sufficient food, clean water and sanitation, access to energy, cooking facilities, decent housing, a minimum income and decent work, education, health care, and information and support networks. Second, these have to be underpinned by the principles of gender equality, social equity, political voice and justice (Raworth 2017: 45). Third, practically, economists (and we could add social scientists and practitioners in general) should *act in service* to human flourishing; *respect the autonomy* of communities by ensuring their engagement and consent and recognizing their differences; exercise *prudential policy-making* which minimizes harm; and *work with humility* by being transparent, accepting one's limitations and being open to alternatives (ibid.: 161).

This argument for a more humanistic approach to the economic system is reflected more generally in Amartya Sen's capabilities approach. This argues against orthodox development economics that puts commodities at the centre of its theories and, instead, for people's needs and an enabling society to provide the conditions to enhance their capabilities to meet those needs. More specifically, in relation to the environment, Tim Jackson argues for a new definition of prosperity (away from GDP) based on a relational understanding of wellbeing as human flourishing. Like many ecological economists, Jackson draws on Martha Nussbaum's 'central capabilities for human flourishing' (Nussbaum 2006), which include life, bodily health, bodily integrity, practical reason, affiliation, play, and control over one's environment. Jackson further maintains that moving away from efficiency and productivity as the objective of paid work creates the possibility to engender value in those areas of paid work such as care and craft work, in which satisfaction based on quality of service makes them less amenable to increasing productivity (Jackson 2009). This would also include attention to time: developing a strategy of shorter paid working hours would contribute to a cleaner environment, to gender equality, mental health, and local empowerment by allowing women and men time to share unpaid care and community-based activities (Coote and Franklin 2013; Raworth 2017; Gough 2017; Harper and Martin 2018; WBG 2020e; Pettifor 2020).

A further area of similarity with the care ethics approach is in applying the notion of environmental ethics to democratic processes, albeit in ways that are more material than affective. Much activism has been rooted in local organizing around, for example, regenerating aspects of land for local use, developing schemes for more economical and environmental access to utilities and food, participatory budgeting, and protests around fracking. These are often networked internationally, as in the global municipalist movement (Barcelona En Comu et al. 2019; and see below). The focus on local organization has a strong connection to the politics of the commons influenced by *Governing the Commons: The Evolution of Institutions for Collective Action*, by the Nobel Prize-winner Elinor Ostrom (1990).[2] Based on her research with indigenous peoples across the world, she drew up principles for self-organizing the governance of common resources based on reciprocity, trust and effective communication. Building on this, Tim Hollo, director of the Green Institute in Australia, argues for 'ecological democracy' (Hollo 2019). The failure of many governments to confront the climate crisis and growing social and economic inequalities reflects a crisis of democracy itself, characterized by disconnection and loss of trust, cultural homogenization, and domination. Ecological democracy, Hollo argues, centres on three principles – interconnection, diversity and impermanence. Interconnection emphasizes the holism of participatory political processes, from the local to the global, where decisions are made for and by people at the most local level. The state's role is to enable this within a commitment to equity and sustainability backed by scientific evidence and democratically decided processes for limiting abuse and harm. In this, diversity co-exists with universalism and decentralization which respect the complexity, intersectionality, uncertainty and ambiguity that can characterize local deliberation. This Hollo suggests is the most difficult tension – that the time-scale for climate change demands urgency while respecting deliberative processes takes time. (I would add that events – such as the pandemic – can also speed up changes in social practices.) But applying the principle of impermanence to strategies requires sensitivity to the changing needs of contexts of time and place.

Ostrom, Hollo and Raworth provide impressive and enriching analyses and proposals from which to think through a welfare commons, a task developed by Ian Gough (2017) and discussed below. Not all eco-policy writers agree with some aspects of their analyses, although they would go along with much of Gough, for example, argues that relational well-being is relevant only at the local level but not for climate justice at the global level, which needs to be based on the conception and quantitative objective measurement of universal human needs (Gough 2017; see next section). While many of the above accounts are underpinned by a commitment to gender equality and geo-political differences in North–South development are mentioned, there is a marked lack of reference to where racial inequalities, decoloniality and environmental racism fit and how this affects ecological ethics and strategies. This is surprising, since many accounts acknowledge the Buen Vivir movement as a source of inspiration. This movement, developed in different ways by indigenous people in Ecuador and Bolivia and shaping their governments' policies, centres on a cosmovision in which people strive to live in harmony with nature (see, for example, Solón 2018). It understands the unity of space and time to be in a constant state of becoming, as is the relationality between individuals and their communities – neither exists without the other. It seeks to be redistributive within a respect for difference and diversity, while recognizing that the struggle for decolonization is constant both personally and politically. This is not just an academic point. In 2019, Wretched of the Earth, a grassroots collective for 'indigenous, black, brown and diaspora groups and individuals demanding climate justice', wrote an open letter in alliance with forty-eight other groups representing, among others, disability, migrant, LGBTQI, feminist and BLM groups, to XR (Wretched of the Earth 2019). While agreeing with the demands of XR (see above), they argue that these are framed by a particular perspective. First, the emphasis on science ignores the generations of knowledge and politics about the earth fostered by indigenous groups. Second, the stress on the future impact of climate change bypasses the reality that many poor communities in the Global North and Global South have been suffering for some time from environmental degradation. Third, the strategy of non-violent civil disobedience ignores the reality of racialized groups' experience of racist policing and puts them in a more dangerous situation.

One exception to the omission of racial politics is Hollo, who writes, in relation to Australia, of the 'gaping wound' at the centre of our politics – 'the ongoing genocide of indigenous people'. He says: 'Instead of seeking ways to "recognize" indigenous Australians in the constitution, we should humbly ask First Nations people to lead us in a conversation about the country we want to be' (2019: 12). Following on from this, what then constitutes decolonial political ethics?

Being human as praxis: political ethics and decoloniality

The intersectional analysis in this book has drawn upon both postcolonial and decolonial perspectives. For example, discussions about the relationship between 'nation' and the constitution of racialized inequalities and policies to mitigate or manage these have generally placed them within an understanding of the post-war welfare state as a postcolonial project. This was shaped in different ways by the formal ending of the British Empire in Africa, Asia and the Caribbean, in which colonial relations in Britain nevertheless continued to be embodied in whiteness and enacted upon minority ethnic welfare subjects, often from former colonies. A decolonial approach points to a much longer history dating back to the conquests by Europeans starting some five hundred years ago in the Americas, in which dispossession, extractivism, dehumanization and slavery were part and parcel of colonialization, capitalism, patriarchy and modernity, a history which informs the analysis in chapter 6. The difference between the two perspectives is both temporal and geographical, but, as Bhambra explains, they have in common an unsettling of the social relations of power upon which modernity's knowledge is built and the creation of a new narration based on submerged knowledge of and by colonized others – 'a new geo-politics of knowledge' (Bhambra 2014: 120, citing Lugones 2011). Decolonial critiques, then, draw attention both to the abstract claims of universalism in mainstream thought and how such claims serve to obscure alternative and marginalized knowledges, to ignore the context of colonialism and its afterlife, and to associate mainstream thinking with originality and global influence. Here I look at decolonial thinking about the notion of 'human' in an understanding of globalism and universalism.

While both the ethics of care and environmentalism locate their critiques in the binary thinking of the Enlightenment, the decolonial critique drives back more deeply into what the Jamaican writer Sylvia Wynter calls 'the colonial construction of being' from the fifteenth century, through which domination was built upon the construction of people as types, modes and genres (Wynter 2003).[3] Central to this, and influenced by Fanon's *Black Skin, White Masks* ([1952] 2008), is a European conception of 'Man' who over-represents himself as though he were 'the human itself' (Wynter 2003). It is this conception – abstracted from everyday life, invested in a white Western view of the world in which generic appeals to equality and universalism are excluding and boundaried in their progressivism – which has become the yardstick of normality in what counts as human in ethical and political discourse (McKittrick 2015). In other words, those marginalized and marked as different throughout the history of modernity are continually excluded from this normativity even, or especially, in discussions involving the idea of the universal, and, in the case of racialized peoples, they are constructed through history as, in Paul Gilroy's (2014) words, 'infrahuman'. While struggles countering the infrahuman challenge the dehumanizing practices of police and of state and employer practices, for Wynter the struggle is more than being against, more than being allowed into present humanness; it is one of consciously and communally creating a *new* 'ecumenical' notion of what it means to be human – that is to say, a humanism which acknowledges and repairs this history and moves towards peaceful co-existence. This represents a move from *homo economicus* to *homo narrans* – narrating a new humanness, a new way of performing human. This is why Wynter calls 'Being Human' a praxis. In the context of the climate crisis, she argues, this is a praxis that becomes more urgent. It requires, as Gilroy argues, a new 'planetary humanism' (2014: 28).

For some writers, this project of creating a new humanness necessarily means that constructing decolonial ethics must be put on hold because it carries the danger of simply returning to or attaching itself to 'the self-same figuration of ethical subjectivity that they genuinely seek to question, or even, annul' (Odysseos 2017: 452). Others, however, have attempted to develop such ethics (Dussel 2013; Grosfoguel 2011; Dunford 2017; Barreto 2018). Dunford, for example, takes the concept of cosmopolitanism, which expresses much liberal progressive thinking as a global ethic in the idea that solidarity and moral obligations extend globally beyond intimacy, community and nation (Pogge 1992; Held 2002). Thomas Pogge (2002) also uses the concept to argue for a human rights-based approach to poverty. The political attraction of these positions is an important stake in current conditions of rising ethno-nationalism and dismissal of human rights and the global bodies that institutionalize them. As an example, the UK's Brexit negotiations in 2020 include withdrawal from the application of the EU's Charter of Fundamental Human Rights. However, Dunford's critique is that Pogge's definition of cosmopolitanism rests on a Western-centric universalism based upon individualism and generalizable to all (Pogge 1992: 48–9), a point similar to that made by care ethicists, above. He asks whether it is possible to develop a decolonial framing of global ethics without adopting the ideas of individualism and universalism inherent in moral cosmopolitanism (Dunford 2017: 381). After all, since decoloniality involves the global challenge to the ongoing 'colonial matrix of power' in which the racialized, gendered and geo-political intersections constitute global poverty and inequalities,[4] then decolonial ethics must be global (ibid.: 386–7). Drawing on a number of decolonial writers, he points to two ways in which it would diverge from mainstream cosmopolitan ethics: *border thinking* and *pluriversality*.

While mainstream cosmopolitan thought is constructed through abstract universalism with no reference to the geo-political positioning of the thinker/speaker, and often without the voices of the implied 'universals', border thinking depends upon those marginalized by coloniality and dehumanization to be 'the producers of moral theory' (Dunford 2017: 388). This is the production of 'subaltern knowledges and practices' (Escobar 2004: 3), also invoked by Wynter and Bhambra above and also echoing aspects of care and environmental ethics. Furthermore, since such thinking refers 'not to where you reside but [to] where you dwell' (Mignolo 2011: xiii), then it is incumbent upon those outside the borders not merely to imagine what those on the borders are thinking but also to engage, listen and respond. In addition, as discussed earlier with reference to care ethics, Buen Vivir and Ubuntu,[5] the individual is understood to be the referent not for moral deliberation but for one's commitment to close others, or, cosmovisionally, to nature as well. Counter-critique contends that such knowledges give rise to cultural relativism and to a local particularity that is unable to proceed to the global (Gough 2017: 40). In my view, this placing of subordinated knowledges as merely particular and cultural as against a universal global knowledge is to create an unnecessary binary. As Dunford argues, the borderlands are at the hard end of globalization, where struggles often involve taking on global corporations and reparations.[6] Theirs is not a retreat into pre-modern forms, far from it – many competing perspectives emerge from the different threats they face and involve thinking beyond modernity. This is 'transmodernity', as opposed to a Euro-modernity in which an uninterrogated universalism is presumed. Dunford cites Escobar's analysis (Escobar 2007) of the Zapatista movement, which combined and transformed indigenous cosmovisions with Marxism and Thirdworldism (Dunford 2017: 389). This reinforces the view, argued strongly elsewhere (Comaroff and Comaroff 2015; Gilroy 2014), that knowledges and practices from the Global South and the borderlands of the North best fulfil this capacity to think beyond modernity. This relates to the second idea of pluriversality.

Pluriversality means making the possibility for deep dialogue across existing groups, cultures and cosmovisions. The aim is less to arrive at consensus than to foster a solidarity and commonality based upon respect and understanding of the position of others. Because multiple groups, cultures and communities are threatened by global coloniality, their central value is for creating a world in which solidarity across many worlds fit, or are made possible (Dunford 2017: 390, citing the Zapatistas). In this sense, it does not promote an 'anything goes' relativism, since a perspective (say, of racism or sexism) would be unacceptable as it would not permit the possibility of solidarity across many different worlds. What it does is see equality and difference as inseparable because an allowance for difference is premised on the acceptance of all as equal in the first place.[7] But does this also imply that decoloniality or Western cosmopolitanism is just another perspective in play? Dunford suggests that this is not the case and that decoloniality represents an imperative rather than an option, but an imperative which still leaves the door open for many worlds to co-exist. Pluriversality offers a process though which global values can be formed and re-formed, applied and reapplied to judge practices, policies and social institutions.

Where does this discussion leave the concept of human rights? After all, like cosmopolitanism, the Universal Declaration of Human Rights

(1948) was an important expression of human freedom, even though it is based in liberal-individualist thought. José-Manuel Barreto (2018) provides a series of suggestions about how to 'decolonize human rights', following a similar argument to Dunford's above. He neither rejects human rights nor embraces them but seeks to reclaim them through the critical process of decolonizing them. This involves a dialogue with Eurocentric thinking and the rewriting of a history of human rights. This rewriting views human rights not as the West's triumph of human rights declarations but in pre-existing historical struggles against slavery, colonial racism and the legacies of modern imperialism, all of which operated with a notion of human or natural rights. Human rights emerge in this century as the political vocabulary of struggle with which to mobilize against violence, dispossession and damage from states, transnational corporations, and financial and commercial institutions. This is about developing a new understanding of the 'human' as well as the 'rights' of human rights.[8]

This turning of abstract individualist concepts into active collective practices runs through decolonial rewritings. For example, Rinaldo Walcott's essay on Sylvia Wynter's collected work discusses the Caribbean as constituted through multiple identities and ethnicities from different parts of the world. This multiplicity is neither resolved nor dissolved but is the crucible for making and remaking new possibilities for being human – the forging of a 'vernacular cosmopolitanism', in which the 'cosmo-political' is a work-in-progress (Walcott 2015: 197–8). This is a grounded political practice and not just a principle of cosmopolitanism. At the centre of such work is, as Anthony Bogues argues, a politics of new ways and forms of human life and living, in which the Black Lives Matter protests in 2020 mark a historic moment in opening a space for a radical imagining of these new forms by insisting on a discussion and an enactment of the historical and contemporary power and privileges of whiteness (Bogues 2010, 2020). In the meantime, attempts to create new global ethics are conditioned by a 'strategic universalism' (Gilroy 2000: 96) – a possibility-in-process of becoming, as Wynter would say, ecumenically human.

Translating ethics into practical eco-social politics

How, then, do the commonalities and tensions in these ethical perspectives translate into a set of practical-political propositions for a new social commons of welfare? The discussion above found that all perspectives emphasize the *relationality* of our being and our *interdependence* as its living enactment. This interdependence is not only between co-existing humans;

in putting all the ethical perspectives together, they add up to *five further sets of moral obligations*.

- First, relationships of interdependence are *planetary* in the sense of an interdependence between humans and the ecosystem of non-human beings and living organisms.
- Second, they are planetary in a geographical sense of *global* interdependence.
- Third, these interdependencies summon up *intergenerational* obligations not simply to children and their rights in the present but also to the future generations who will inherit this planet.
- Fourth, they invoke the dehumanized racial suffering of *past generations*, which signify material and moral obligations towards reparation.
- Fifth, in sum through these four, there is the ethical obligation to forge a new humanness of co-existence.

All these obligations emphasize human and planetary *flourishing* as the basis for the urgent goal of *sustainability*, which requires co-operation and *solidarity* for its achievement and, in its turn, depends upon the *equal worth* of all being enacted and embodied in *respectful and caring democratic dialogue* through *equity* and respect for *plurality and co-existence*.

The realization of these political ethics is severely constrained by current economic, social, political, cultural and geo-political forms of organization and ideology. For this reason, many of these perspectives demand and develop new economic models, democratic practices, knowledges and understandings of social and human rights and how to determine these. All speak to the end of *homo economicus*.

In the contemporary crises of human and planetary existence, these new approaches centre upon determining the conditions and capabilities for material and physical security, care, and interpersonal and community relationships, in which possibilities for local empowerment, creativity and democratic deliberation and their underpinning by principles of equality, equity and respect are essential. Differences and tensions exist across these visions: in how far the conceptualizations of the human in the exercise of rights and the setting of universal principles still depend on an abstract normative Western-centric liberal individualist model; in how far notions of equality cover both the range and intersections of social relations of power to include not only gender and class inequalities but those of race, ethnicity, migration, disability, sexuality, faith and age; and in how far situated knowledges and experiences have legitimacy alongside 'science'.

I now want to bring the ethical and the prefigurative together to explore those recent practices or experiments relevant to social welfare that seem to enact these ethics and principles. As I said at the beginning of the book, prefigurative welfare practices were part of the history of feminist, anti-racist, service-user, service-provider and other struggles from the 1960s. I also argued in chapter 2 that a critical perspective should extend to 'criticality' – looking at how resistance to domination and subordination prefigures a 'reparative' and transformative view of the world. This move is reflected in intersectionality approaches that make the connection between theory, method and praxis, in which the last is an important part of theory itself.

In moving to prefigurative praxis for social policies I look now at examples centred upon different facets of 'relationality' – first, in building relationships in services; second, on the relationality of scale – building solidarities from local to global; and, third, in the relationality of intersectional dialogues and alliances. These examples take me, in the third section of the chapter, to a discussion of the social commons for welfare.

Relationality 1: Care and connection

Hilary Cottam (2018) argues that a 'Good Life' is not just something we imagine; it is something we grow. She argues for a new 'relational welfare' based on care and connection to replace the target-driven and audit-obsessed system. Her experiments in what she calls 'Radical Help' use a capabilities approach drawn from Nussbaum (see previous section) in which she sets five overarching capabilities: learning, health, community, relationships and work. However, in her experiences of working with those most marginalized, it is the fourth – relationships – that matters most, not only for a person needing support but between team members, within families, networks and wider communities. Relationships are the biggest resource in that, when they flourish, they can expand their reach and create a virtuous circle. Developing them involves changing the social relations of welfare – blurring the boundaries between helper and helped: acknowledging the knowledge, experience and expertise that both bring. Cottam saw that people who co-produced the design and aims of a common project found the process of having something to contribute meaningful, reciprocal and incremental.

One example Cottam gives is a set of projects for older people called Circle. This started out by workers asking older people what a good life in old age looked like. Three things emerged as mattering: someone to take care of little things – moving heavy furniture or changing an inaccessible light bulb; good company with people with whom you feel at ease; a sense of purpose and support in adapting to the changes in older age. In the project, many of the formal offers of organizing practical help were taken on by the older people and their networks: Circle replaced 'a managed pretence of personal service to create something very different. . . . it blends resources in new ways, it takes pressure off expensive medical systems, which can enable investment in good care at the end of life. Most important of all, with the shift in power and emphasis on relationships, this model places humanity at its heart. It is a culture of genuine care' (Cottam 2018: 191–2).

A separate example of relationality in action comes from the organization of general medical practice in Frome, a market town in Somerset whose local council has revitalized local democracy in innovative ways (MacFadyen 2019). Called 'The Compassion Project' and led by a local GP with NHS support, it transformed medical practice from one-to-one medication-led encounters to a network set up with local community groups, identifying gaps in support for presented needs, and filling those gaps with new groups organized by volunteers acting as 'community connectors'. By treating patients holistically (on the principles of kindness and compassion) and providing them with community support, the practice reduced hospital emergency admissions in the local population by 17 per cent over three years when the county's rates were going up by 29 per cent (Abel and Clarke 2020).

These sorts of projects are very localized and, in discussions about the social care system before and during the pandemic that revealed its precarious state, ideas for a National Care Service along the line of the National Health Service were mooted (Himmelweit 2018; Baron 2020). Cottam opposes this (Cottam 2020), as do others. Jessica Studdert (2020) of the New Local Government Network argues that both care services and the NHS should be located, accountable and properly funded and co-ordinated at local level with a community-based system of care support. The hospitals would be the safety net of last resort.[9] For Cottam, the role of the state would be concerned less with state or market as providers than with developing a new relationship between people, business and communities, promoting a new framework to 'create the conditions for investment in social capability' (Cottam 2018: 265), guiding the behaviour, funding and activities of others. This would be a relational-tending welfare state: 'setting out the design, planting, tending, nurturing and, where necessary, weeding' (ibid.: 266).

Cottam's is a positive and reassuring vision of what is possible. In common with similar approaches (Rustin 2013; Goss 2020), and in line with some of the ethics outlined above, it concentrates on the flourishing and tending aspects of the relational state within national and local scales. There is less of a steer on other compelling issues that face these national and local scales, such as racism, gender violence, the racialization of violent borders, or what John Clarke (2020) calls the 'dark side' of the state and the difficult question of how we reimagine the coercive state. The Care Collective (2020) offers a more stout view of the relationship between caring communities, caring states and caring economies. The caring state's central responsibility would be to create and maintain a sustainable infrastructure of care. The principle of care would not only underpin the support for communities and services across the life course and the cultivation of democratic deliberation for how these were run, it would also underpin belonging, citizenship and rights and revoke birthplace, identity or national territorial claims. A 'commitment to care will be the only pledge of allegiance necessary to live in the caring state's domain' (ibid.: 68). This would be a state that would rethink criminal justice, the legacies of racialized policies, and racial and sexual divisions of labour. In relation to the economic organization of services, the state would have to address the expansion of the market principle into everyday life. This would involve resocializing and insourcing (as opposed to outsourcing) care services, re-regulating eco-socialist markets (especially against offshore tax havens),[10] defetishizing consumption, and developing new co-operative forms of ownership. In fact, on a small scale, many of these activities are already happening, as the next section discusses.

Relationality 2: Scales of possibility

The emphasis on the local as the relational place of community, belonging and experiment is evidenced by recent developments around new co-operative schemes, social enterprises, models of co-production and service delivery, new democratic modes such as citizens' assemblies, and transition towns. Many of these are associated with new forms of municipalism, community organizing, and moves to demand greater power for self-determining regions and cities (Chakrabortty 2018; Hartnell and Knight 2019; Miller 2020; Shenker 2019; Featherstone et al. 2020; Newman 2020). This has been a contradictory development. On the one hand, some of these evolved as a response to government initiatives, such as New Labour's social entrepreneurship and David Cameron's 'Big Society', which sought to responsibilize localities into providing services. Through subsequent austerity, funding was cut back to those services, to local authority funding and voluntary sector organizations, where many smaller ones went under. On the other hand, the period saw the revitalization of democracy on the ground and attempts to remunicipalize local services (Featherstone et al. 2020; Newman 2020). This contradiction also emerges in policies to deal with health inequalities. The recommendations over the past decade from Michael Marmot's work with the Institute of Health Equality have been ignored by successive governments. These include giving children the best start in life, enabling all children to maximize their capabilities and exercise control over their lives, creating decent work and a healthy standard of living for all, developing healthy and sustainable places and communities, and strengthening the role of health prevention (IHE 2020). Yet they have become vital principles to enable and activate cities such as Coventry and Stoke (so-called Marmot Cities) to focus holistically on their health inequalities.

Preston is an example of new municipalism. A town that suffered badly from deindustrialization, it became the first living wage employer in the North of England in 2012. It developed a strategy that persuaded its public services to contract local suppliers and organizers ('insourcing') rather than contracting out to the cheapest. It organized a credit union to keep loan sharks at bay. These and its creation of workers' co-operatives helped local regeneration (Chakrabortty 2018). In 2020 it joined forces with Wirral and Liverpool councils to create a co-operative bank. Further stories of local empowerment exist for councils in other deindustrialized areas, such as Barking and Dagenham, whose new municipal model has been built through coalitions by civil society organizations and faith networks on three pillars: a new local economy, empowering public service, and citizenship and participation. Empowering public services aims to transform bureaucratic, paternalistic and siloed delivery by means of integrating them via a co-production and consultation model with parents and carers, children and young people, youth groups, teachers and social workers through which needs are articulated (Miller 2020). In their different ways, these projects all contest the hegemony of highly centralized neoliberal governance.[11]

However, capitalism is global, and, in the discussion of political ethics, the point was made that care, climate and decolonial justice were global issues invoking transnational and global solidarities. How far does the focus on the local permit these forms of solidarity to grow? Where interdependence and community are fostered through local belonging, can that also extend to people's diasporic belonging or to migrants and refugees, or does it reinforce parochialism?

The global municipalist movement provides a good example of the ongoing attempt to make global and local connections by developing solidarities across different groups *within* the city and translocally *across* cities of different countries (#Fearless Cities).[12] This development has involved 'taking back control' at city level of the commons of water supply and energy, creating a right to housing, clean air, and access to public space, fighting corruption, restraining the private sector, and insisting on transparency. The radicalization of democracy in such 'Fearless Cities' is committed to and builds on feminist and anti-racist politics, both of which are enacted interpersonally as well as locally (Pérez 2019; Taleb 2019).[13] Social empowerment, the expansion of neighbourhood democracy, especially in poorer parts of cities, and reconnecting institutions to the common good have created a trust in local governance and a sense of independence from national neoliberal politics. Indeed, the movement aims to address what national governments do not/will not address, namely the environment and migration (Agustin 2020). Probably the movement's most successful example is Barcelona en Comu, which has been run by a left progressive coalition headed by the mayor, Ada Colau, since 2015. As national governments equivocated about the movement of refugees in 2017, 160,000 people in Barcelona demonstrated, under the slogan *Casa Nostra, Casa Vostra* (Our Home, Your Home), to demand that more refugees were taken in. Barcelona became part of the global network of 'Sanctuary Cities' (started in the US) that speak to a new humanism:

> If we want to support newcomers becoming active co-producers of the right to the city we must find ways of providing refuge and a sanctuary that do not turn newcomers into clients or leave them internally excluded. And if we want to go beyond the idea of 'assimilation into the nation', the process of inviting people into our neighbourhoods, movements and institutions must be one that transforms us all. (Barcelona en Comu et al. 2019: 138)

In 2017, Barcelona hosted the 'Fearless Cities' summit, which attracted over seven hundred participants from every continent (Pisarello 2019), creating a new transformative politics of global translocal solidarity. While substantial economic and political power still reside in international corporations and governance at national and global scales, the power these cities generate is of possibility and hope in new forms of solidarity that challenge patriarchal, racist and xenophobic populist nationalisms. At the same time, there is a tension as to where the national state is positioned in these global–local relationships and whether the aims are to override the power of the state or to convert it (see Featherstone et al. 2020).

Relationality 3: Intersectional dialogues and alliances

The engendering of intersectional solidarity is rhetorically uplifting, but it is hard work. It may be urgent, but it takes time and committed effort. So far, English new municipalism has been less radical than the Fearless Cities – less sure, especially in the light of Brexit, of how to challenge a sense of belonging that is English/British and more constrained by the most centralized national government in Europe. Nonetheless, changes are happening.

Abigail Gilbert analyses how this is happening in Barking and Dagenham. On London's outskirts, this is one of the most deprived boroughs in the country. Its ethnicity has changed from 80 per cent white British in 2001 to 37.5 per cent in 2019 (Gilbert 2020: 69–70). In 2006 almost all its councillors were British National Party members. Its shift to new municipalism came after the Labour Party and community organizations spent dedicated time in anti-racist work, engaging and conversing with the community. While the borough has constantly voted Labour in parliamentary elections, it also voted for Brexit. Wary of divisions undermining the solidarity existing in its community interventions, the local authority works on projects which aim 'to curate alternative, more collectivist subjectivities' – away from fatalistic individualism towards hopeful reciprocity (ibid.: 80–1). The borough initiated conversations between residents based on their different values – what matters to them – and the opportunity to be able to speak, listen and learn from others, however central or marginal.[14] This is similar to the notion of pluriversality mentioned earlier and essential to address the rise of polarizing social 'bubbles' (around Brexit or anti-vaccination movements, for example). Away from Barking and Dagenham, some have argued that devolving power to the regions in England would provide a better basis from which to develop identities that do not rest on the imperialist history of the nation (Niven 2019). Of course, it could also work the other way and encourage nativist regionalism, but, as Gilbert comments, such a project is less about scale and more about those 'social institutions of encounter that shape inclusivity', and at present municipalities seem to offer opportunities for such reshaping (Gilbert 2020: 82).

Other forms of deliberative democracy that have become more institutionalized in councils, campaign groups and governments are citizens' (or people's) assemblies. These seek to develop structured deliberations on topics where there are different views and experiences with the aim of reaching consensus. This is especially important where social media generate conspiracy theories. In Ireland they were held on abortion and same-gender marriage. In the UK, the Citizens Climate Assembly reported in September 2020. This brought together 108 individuals to learn about the climate crisis, to deliberate and to make recommendations for change in the UK (Climate Assembly UK 2020). The participants were recruited to reflect the population in terms of age, gender, ethnicity, education, geography and attitude towards climate change. The report is an exemplar of the practice of deliberative democracy in how people weighed up their own and others' experiences and views and how they balanced competing values of freedom of choice and fairness to different social groups. Their overall recommendations were collective-oriented and stressed urgency. They focus on education and information and the accessibility and affordability of green products, as well as the responsibility of the state to take a strong lead and, among other things, to support the development of green public transport and public services and to have strong regulations on business and taxation measures for reducing carbon.[15]

It is in those groups most committed to intersectionality in which these processes of dialogic deliberation over different views are most honed. As Ishkanian and Peña Saavedra (2019) explain in their participatory action research on Sisters Uncut, a women's anti-austerity organization, social movements that are committed to inclusivity as a principle of intersectionality aim to develop such practices both within the organization of the group *and* in their demands for societal change. The researchers argue that this is a form of radical democratic politics which they call 'intersectional prefiguration' – enacting in the here and now the solidarities necessary for a transformed future. In this case, the focus is on making visible how the social relations of power and inequality operate within the group/movement and working to ensure that these are not reproduced formally or informally. Its intersectional approach reflects a commitment to participation, to listening and learning, and to ensuring that no one is marginalized because of their gender, race, class, disability, sexuality, trans status or immigration status. Its website says: 'Sisters Uncut aims to create a respectful, understanding and kind space where people feel able to express themselves and ask questions without fear of reprisal or humiliation' (Sisters Uncut 2020). This aim requires reflexivity on the part of activists to acknowledge how inequalities surface and to be prepared for the 'uncomfortable conversations' that follow (Ishkanian and Peña Saavedra 2019: 986). While such conversations involve time, passion and conflict, they also create a clearer sense of collective values of care and commitment. These attempt to develop a caring democracy and to ensure that marginalized voices are heard and respected, which can further solidarities. This means, for example, that they prefigure the necessary conversations to be had from the Black Lives Matter protests about the embodiment and enactment of white privilege.

At the time of writing, as the UK is reeling from both austerity and the ongoing Covid-19 pandemic, the possibility of a new future being forged through progressive alliances increasingly surfaces both within and outside formal party politics (Lawson 2019; Mason 2019; Ostrowski 2020). Ishkanian and Ali's (2018) research on the possibilities for alliances between voluntary organizations and anti-austerity activist groups carried out between 2013 and 2015 was doubtful. Not only had the contractual relations between government and larger voluntary organizations reined in the latter's capacity for campaigning, but the clash between activists' focus on system change and that of voluntary organizations on reform was too great for anything other than brief liaisons. However, my account above of the recent rise of new municipalism, localized innovations, the combination of successful diverse mobilizations since 2017 of the global municipal movement and its commoning of resources, along with global movements since Occupy around feminism, XR and Black Lives Matter, as well as the realities of the pandemic, have all made progressive alliances more real.[16] One part of a programme for both transitional and transformative change in social policy would be a social or welfare commons.

Towards the eco-welfare commons

In many ways, the activities of prefigurative politics in the previous section represent different enactments and embodiments of the key political ethics that were discussed earlier – relationality, multiple forms of interdependence, flourishing and sustainability, equality, justice and plurality, new humanisms of co-existence, and new knowledge reflected in transformative economic models. These have found expression in:

- transforming local economies;
- workers' co-operatives;
- new forms of social services based on the value of care and relationships, on blurring the historical social relations of welfare, on co-production of design and delivery, and on collective articulation of needs;
- the forging of solidarities across local and global scales and across the

intersections of the social relations of power – most commonly, class, gender and race, ethnicity and migration, as well as disability, sexuality and age;
- localized planning for environmental sustainability and the re-embedding of energy and technology sources in local control;
- participatory budgeting;[17]
- commitments to deeper interpersonal, local and national democratic deliberation to facilitate empowerment and participation based on listening, trust, respect and learning, and addressing uncomfortable, divisive and contentious issues with care;
- the role of a caring state: instating the principle of care and relationality into relationships, communities, services, education (including early education and child care), citizenship, rights and economies to engender deeper democracy and solidarities;
- shorter working week to provide time to care, buttressed by some form of basic income (discussed below).

This begins to set out some features of a welfare commons. The concept of 'the commons' is important because it links together in a holistic way those resources that we all need, in terms of both natural resources of air, water, energy and land and our needs for physical and emotional security and wellbeing: healthy food, clean water, close and social relationships of care, health care, decent housing, decent work, sufficient income, education and creativity, transport, and protection from violence. Second, the commons enable a focus on the processes through which common rights to these resources have been taken away or limited – for example, by privatization, extractivism, exploitation, commodification and colonialism (as discussed in chapter 3). Third, the concept originates from a notion of interdependence among humans as well as between humans and nature (Ostrom 1990). Fourth, the dimensions of the commons depend upon us, as 'commoners', having the collective means to define our needs and claim our rights. The commons is a site for disagreement and deliberation as well as signifying a vision of something non-capitalistic in its form, and thus is a way of imagining and living out possibilities for transformation. As Francine Mestrum says: 'Social commons constitute a conceptual framework that allows us to think about the future of a better and broader social justice system. It is not a blueprint. It can only offer ideas civil society can work with and can reflect on' (2015: 432).[18]

There are already some important initiatives in applying the concept of the commons to those areas we historically think of as the welfare state but adding in issues to do with environmental resources and the climate crisis. Thus Mestrum's *The Social Commons: Rethinking Global Justice in Post-Neoliberal Societies* (2015) develops the notion of social protection globally. The ideas come out of two years of discussions in the organization Global Social Justice on alternatives to neoliberalism. Mestrum argues that proposals such as the ILO's for a global social protection floor represented a significant buffer against neoliberalism. This was the proposal that all countries across the globe should establish basic social security guarantees to ensure that, over the life cycle, all in need have access to essential health care and income security (Deacon 2013). But, she argues, it did not go far enough. The proposals are based on rights and guarantees for individuals, but they do not address the collective dimension of the commons – interdependence and solidarity – which also require support and protection. In contrast, her proposals for the social commons include universal contributions and benefits which are multi-levelled from local to global, involving national and international redistributive policies – not only contributory and non-contributory systems for education, health and social services but also protection for the environment ('We should care for nature as we should care for people' – Mestrum 2015: 26). She emphasizes the need for alliances of collective struggles and democratic participation to articulate the commons. In reviewing alternatives to the capitalist economy, she concludes that they would not necessarily work outside of markets or states but in between and with them, focusing on the enhancement of welfare, social integration and sustainability. The social commons would not be subsumed under the economy but would shape it by, for example, regulating agricultural prices, land affordability and accessibility, sanitation and communication.

A set of arguments along similar lines comes from Ian Gough (2017), who sets out an agenda for a more ecologically sustainable future. This links the threat of climate change, capitalist accumulation and economic growth with the decline in social wellbeing and equality.[19] All three need to be tackled together. Gough proposes a three-stage transition, from green economic growth, through to recomposing people's consumption and, finally, to a post-growth economy. This post-growth society would combine redistribution with meeting the needs for wellbeing, requiring state intervention to cap excessive incomes and spread the dividend from ownership of wealth and capital to all citizens. It would, along with technology and reduced work hours, create more time to be involved in the social economy – time for learning, caring, community, creativity. This would be supported by social services that are co-produced in that people are directly involved in the development and delivery of social and care provision. Between the state and the local social economy is the deliberative sphere, through which debate takes place on how to meet human needs, to resource sustainability and to develop the social commons.

These ideas on the social commons are developed further by Anna Coote (2017), who spells out the principles and actions that would foster and be fostered by the commons: solidarity and collective action; social justice and [action against] inequality; sustainability and security. It would change the relationship between citizens (defined as citizens and residents) and the state. Local initiatives and conversations would feed into people's assemblies and the regional level. These would shape parliamentary action to enable building the social commons country-wide. It would support local decision-making and control realized through different forms of dialogic deliberation and conversations at this level. Legislation and public institutions would set resource levels and rights of equal access. 'The state works with and for the people to enable us all to work together, share risks and pool resources, in order to claim, build and secure access to life's necessities' (ibid.: 14).

These ideas of an imagined transformation of the relations between the state and citizens are also developed by Newman and Clarke, who propose 'an approach to the state that enhances notions of the commons, that reasserts collective (public) interests and enables collective (public) action' (2014: 7–8). Here they address a tension I raised earlier in notions of the relational state: between a state that is both 'widely dispersed and porous', in order to enable local initiatives and participation, and sufficiently centralized to guarantee rights, to enforce equality and to regulate against corruption, tax fraud, environmental standards, and so on. For this reason, a 'dialogic state' is needed in which such tensions are part of democratic debate between multiple publics and multiple parts of the state.

Neal Lawson has conceptualized these spaces for dialogue as '45° change' along an axis of 45 degrees running between differently positioned institutions with government, media, political parties and NGOs, on the one side, and civil society networks of community organizations, new media, pressure groups, social enterprises, and more, on the other (Lawson 2019). In a set of proposals based on 45° change that rest not on the commons but on the concept of 'The Good Society' (Rutherford and Shah 2006), Ruth Lister spells out, in the context of the pandemic, what the 'building blocks' are for moving towards a good society: 'material, ethical/emotional, political and cultural'. The arguments combine human rights and the ethics of care, interdependence and compassion. The 'material' addresses the growing insecurity felt by many through the threat to both income and access to housing. This also has to address both human dignity and equality of opportunity which poverty can take away – being treated as 'less than human' is exacerbated by intersecting inequalities of class, ethnicity, race, gender, sexuality and disability (Lister 2020: 5; and see chapters 4 and 5). It requires decent and dignified work and, for those who cannot work, decent benefits as of right funded by a fair taxation of income and wealth. It would include policies to redistribute the balance of unpaid care work between men and women, which would be supported by a shorter working week and a revaluation of those jobs which were identified as performed by 'key workers' during the pandemic and are the lowest paid and most precarious, especially health and social care (see chapter 4). This is expanded in the building blocks of ethics, emotions and democracy, which are underpinned by the ethics of care, kindness and love essential to the social organization of paid care and of time for care. Such ethics are equated with a culture of human rights which asserts the rights to dignity and respect of individuals and extend to rights to culture and creativity. Democracy too requires kindness, openness and compassion in which all are enabled to participate. These proposals are supplemented by two principles which recall the earlier discussion on ethics. First, that of *flourishing* from cradle to grave, which highlights the need to see children and older people as citizens with rights to happiness and wellbeing. Second, solidarity is extended to the *international sphere*, which includes an end to the hostile environment, an inclusive approach to asylum seekers and refugees, and a commitment to environmental sustainability.

It is clear there are many commonalities in these different approaches. In their widening of the social to the environmental, all offer ways of moving away from GDP to wellbeing as a measure for the economy. All focus on deeper forms of democracy. Mestrum is focused more on the global geo-political implications for the commons, and her and Lister's ideas are shaped more by the interconnection of human rights, environmental rights and care ethics (with different emphases). There are differences too: one area is around a universal basic income. While Mestrum, Gough and Coote are adamantly opposed to a universal basic income, Lister proposes a 'partial basic income'. In recent years the demand for some form of basic income has gained in popularity (and some application – see BIEN 2020). The discussions around this have been intense, but I will be brief and address the question only as it relates to the commons concept.

A basic income, or universal basic income (UBI), is 'a modest regular payment to every legal resident in the community, paid unconditionally as a right, regardless of income, employment or relationship status' (Standing 2019: 339; see also Reed and Lansley 2016; Torry 2018). In his book *Plunder of the Commons* (2019), Guy Standing develops a charter addressing six sets of commons: natural, social, civil, cultural, knowledge, and funds and commons dividends. It is this last one which proposes a social dividend – a common fund based on levies on commercial use or exploitation of the commons, creating ecologically sustainable common wealth (for example, through a carbon emissions levy) out of which dividends should be paid to all as a basic income (ibid.: 349–56). (It would be clawed back in taxes from those above a certain income.) Although initially, while funds were being built up, this would not be enough to live on, it would give everyone basic security as of right. At this moment in time this is seen as crucial, enabling the rent to be paid or allowing people to work part-time and have time to care. It is proposed that it would undermine the poverty trap and give people a stronger bargaining position in relation to an oppressive employer or a violent partner. Standing argues that it would contribute to slaying eight giants: inequality, insecurity, debt, stress, precarity, automation of jobs, planetary crisis, and rising right-wing populism.

The case against a basic income by Mestrum, Gough and Coote focuses on three things. First, that it would be very expensive, and even to provide a small amount would still leave those unable to work dependent on the current system of selective benefits. Second, that it is an individualistic and monetary approach to meeting people's needs which reinforces them as atomized consumers rather than participating collectively in shaping a social commons. It does not fundamentally change the relationship between the state and people or aim to increase solidarities and reciprocity. Third, it detracts from the need for funding and provision of universal basic services and improving *their* quality. The preferred case for reforming the system is a guaranteed minimum income for people not in employment with a more generous universal and taxable child benefit and a time credit system for carers (Coote 2017; see also Davis et al. 2018). Nonetheless, arguments in the time of Covid-19 have focused on a UBI as a transitional way of moving out of the probability of high unemployment, especially if accompanied by the development of green jobs. However, any such move would have to be underpinned by fundamental commitments to equality or it could reinforce inequalities. In the hands of a neoliberal government it might provide the legitimacy to introduce universal charging for services. Also, given that women experienced greater unemployment during the pandemic and, with schools closed, there was a significant re-traditionalizing of the gendered division of labour in the home (WBG

2020a, 2020b), introducing a basic income could freeze these gender inequalities. On the other hand, domestic violence increased during the pandemic with a scarcity of housing to help women and families, and in this situation having independent access to some income would help. It is in the deliberation around such tensions, such as through a people's assembly, that resolution could be productive.

In comparison to the scenario of ethics and prefigurative politics that I present in this chapter, there are areas which, while not ignored in these proposals, are the least developed. The first is the important place of antiracism, the generating of solidarities across race, ethnicity and migration and their intersection with class and gender, as part of a reparative discussion on white privilege and the relevance of the history of imperialism. Earlier I noted a difference between some environmentalists in their understanding of universalism and its relation to difference. This referred to Ian Gough's argument that, while they are important for local communities, such politics are, first, practically not replicable at the global level and, second, theoretically rooted in the cultural relativism of 'post-modernism, postcolonialism and post-structuralism' (Gough 2017: 40), which runs counter to the pursuit of universalist measures. This, in my view, not only lumps together three very different perspectives but misunderstands the quest, which Hollo (2019) refers to in relation to climate change justice, and which is the basis of an intersectional approach: one that can pursue commonalities that do not lose sight of specificities of difference and specificities which do not lose sight of commonalities (see chapter 2). Unless that is seen as part of the political project in the spaces for possibility at the local, national or international scale, then the danger is that the specifics (of gender, race, disability or other equalities) get tagged on to universal claims rather than reconstructing universalism through a new humanist understanding.

Second is the question of the international implications of geo-political inequalities for these inequalities. These are reflected in many organizations fighting for racial justice. Take, for example, the demands presented by the open letter of the Wretched of the Earth coalition written in May 2019 and discussed earlier. This was signed by an alliance of forty-eight grassroots activist groups, some international, organizing around intersecting environmental, gender, racism, migration, refugee and LBTQI issues and identities. Its main focus is on systemic change for climate justice, but it provides a good example of bringing together climate, decolonial and social justices and thinking about an eco-welfare commons. Two of these demands attend specifically to social welfare:[20]

- *guarantee flourishing communities both in the global north and the global south* in which everyone has *the right* to free education, an adequate income whether in or out of work, universal healthcare including support for mental wellbeing, affordable transportation, affordable healthy food, dignified employment and housing, meaningful political participation, a transformative justice system, gender and sexuality freedoms, and, for disabled and older people, to live independently in the community.
- *end the hostile environment* of walls and fences, detention centers and prisons that are used against racialised, migrant, and refugee communities. Instead, the UK should acknowledge its historic and current responsibilities for driving the displacement of peoples and communities and honour its obligation to them. (Wretched of the Earth 2019)

What is different here is a framing of hostile environment issues in terms of historic and current geo-political inequalities and border management. I would add more immediate issues to this: making refugee routes safe, stopping the 'no recourse to public funds' rule, and creating rights to work for asylum seekers. Also, from my perspective, the flourishing communities guarantee should include a right to child care and reference to the policies that now are being developed worldwide to support gender equality and care work (Esquivel and Kaufmann 2017). Nonetheless, this provides a good 'border-thinking' basis for thinking creatively about the eco-welfare and relating it to the above proposals. For example, Mestrum's suggestions for multi-levelled national and international redistributive policies could be one way of creating a framework for considering issues of reparation for both climate justice and historic claims. Wretched of the Earth also raise one important aspect which this book has referred to but not developed[21] – the criminal justice system. This is central to the institutionalization of racism and, as I mentioned earlier, how the commons would deal with the 'dark' sides of the state (Clarke 2020). The issue of 'defunding the police' is about both accountability of state and local authority budgets and finding 'non-police solutions to the problems poor people face' such as improved housing, income, health and mental health care, issues best approached through those people themselves (Levin 2020; www.leedspovertytruth.org.uk/humanifesto/).

Decolonizing the commons would also include, as the quotation from Rebecca Solnit at the beginning of the chapter indicated, the need to develop other stories about who we are, what we want and what is possible. This involves dialogues and new knowledges about national stories – critically examining in the UK the different national stories of England,

Scotland, Wales and Northern Ireland and their different histories of colonialism. Some of that has started with the Black Lives Matter protests about the history of empire told in statues to those who profited from slavery. Decolonizing school and university curricula is an important part of this.[22] But it also needs to address the role of national borders which have been integral to the subordination of different racialized groups. This involves supporting the demands made, for example, by Kanlungan (2020) representing Filipino workers, many of them health workers, for 'Status Now' for undocumented residents. It means challenging the use of health and welfare workers in bordering practices. Organizations such as Global Justice Now and No Borders envision the future as a world without borders. While this seems unimaginable to many, it should be noted that national borders controlling movement are historically recent. They were part of the nineteenth-century development of nation-states. Since then, there has been an increase in capital's freedom of movement and the restriction of people's freedom of movement. 'No borders' is not an immediate demand, for, as Pettifor (2020) points out, it could give way to the power of financial capital, which dislikes borders. Nevertheless, the argument for more 'open' or 'porous' borders is an important one. It enables us to think about and discuss further what borders are for as well as the transformations that are needed in the power relations between the Global North and the Global South. It would still be possible to have national administrative entities for the setting of contributions, obligations and social rights, but this would focus attention on a different meaning, role and interdependence of nations. Gary Younge's challenge is an important one for anyone who wants to develop a new humanism:

> Make no mistake, a world with open borders would demand a radical transformation of much of what we have now. It would demand a rethinking not only of immigration, but our policies on trade and war, the environment, health and welfare, which would in turn necessitate a reevaluation of our history, of our understanding of ourselves as a species and as a nation. (Younge 2018b)

Conclusion

The focus in this chapter has been, first, on those political ethics with concerns most proximate to the unfolding crises of the last decade as I described them in chapter 3 – financialized capitalism, care and social reproduction, environment and climate change, and internal and external racialized borders. The chapter elaborated the points of commonality and difference in the ethics of care, of environmentalism and of decoloniality. Together these expanded the universe of moral obligations beyond the interdependence of national citizenry, which is how it is most commonly understood in welfare states. This interdependence is pluriversally global and planetary, including human and non-human beings and living organisms; it commits to future generations, and it reckons with the injustices done to past generations. They also generated an important set of both ethical guidelines and social, political and economic frameworks to address major crises in the world today. I then looked at existing possibilities for change in the grounded, transformative and prefigurative politics of civil society actors, noting how these were attempting in new ways to apply the principles of multiple interdependencies, relationality, democratic deliberation, and interpersonal, local and translocal solidarities. Recent writing that develops ideas of the social commons has been an important and inspiring way of connecting these local innovations to a transformation in the relationship between states and citizens locally, nationally and internationally. Within these new developments there are tensions (around basic income) and areas that need much more development (around race and decoloniality, borders and criminal justice) that I highlighted. This is less with the aim of correction than with pointing up the extent to which the understanding and dialogue between multiple publics is an urgent and complex one. Yet it is here that hope resides for a new humanism that can reconstruct an eco-welfare society for future generations with a commitment to learn from the dehumanizations of the past. Within this there are implications for learners, teachers and researchers in social policy, the subject of my next and final chapter.

Conclusion: Multidimensional Thinking for Social Policy

Introduction

In providing a critical and intersectional analysis of social policy, this book responds to a number of connected concerns and challenges about social policy as a field of study. In this concluding chapter I explain how the analysis I have developed tries to meet some of these concerns. I then suggest three ways of thinking about the implications for social policy teaching, learning and research through reconstituting knowledge, relational knowledge and practices, knowledge for post-Covid reconstruction and reimagining for the future.

One major challenge was expressed by the UK Social Policy Association's commission into *The Missing Dimension: Where Is 'Race' in Social Policy Teaching And Learning?* (Craig et al. 2019), which noted the lack of attention to issues of race and racism in the teaching curricula and research publications of the discipline, low proportions of BAME students and staff, especially at higher levels, and a sense that BAME students found the social policy courses they were studying to be irrelevant. While recognizing it as a priority with important specific dynamics, I identify this as part of a general trend within the mainstream of the discipline. This is the tendency to divest issues of their radical implications, not only race and racism but also others emerging from struggles and campaigns over inequalities, such as gender, care, climate change, disability, migration, age and childhood. This happens in a number of ways and for a range of reasons both within the discipline and external to it, discussed in chapter 2. Within the discipline these can be summarized as (i) the separate chapter / lecture / module syndrome which fails to address the overall approach to social policy; (ii) the associated view that these critiques represent specialisms; (iii) the reduction of complex intersecting social relations of power to multiple 'variables'; and (iv) the treatment of these issues as 'new social risks' – which they are, but they are also much more than that. They are old / new social relations of inequality and power reconstituted in neoliberal ways in a social, cultural and political economy of welfare (Phillips and Williams 2021).

I combined an intersectional analysis with critical approaches to social policy in order to grasp the multiple and complex social relations of inequality and of welfare. In other words, this combination provides the possibility of framing different socio-economic inequalities in a way that recognizes their multiplicity as well as the ways in which they interlock. Following this, I suggested an understanding of these social relations as intersecting in ways that are contingent upon time and place so that some may become more salient than others at particular conjunctures. For example, in chapter 4 I showed how the construction of a 'post-racial' society and support for Brexit in ethno-nationalist terms had direct and harmful effects on black, Asian, minority ethnic and migrant groups, as well as shaping the subjugation of other groups impoverished by welfare reforms and austerity cuts. At the same time, policies that compelled parents to be 'hard-working' in the exercise of their responsibilities intersected with the depletion of care services through privatization and financialization, resulting in poverty and stress for particular groups of mothers in terms of race and ethnicity, migrant status, single status, and having a disabled child. The Covid-19 pandemic superimposed on these another set of conjunctural and intersecting forces, which cast an unforgiving spotlight on the complex formations of inequalities that then began to spread to more groups.

Such analysis was made possible by applying an intersectional approach to the political economy of welfare, which was conceptualized through two frames. First, the four connected crises and areas of contestation to have shaped welfare states in this century: not only the global financial crisis but also the global crises of care and social reproduction, the environment and climate change, and the racialization and racism of and within national borders. For analysis at the national scale I nested within this a second frame of four intersecting institutional, discursive and relational domains: family, nation, work and nature. I argued that, in relation to the policies and politics of welfare states, these represent central challenges to the making of contemporary neoliberal welfare settlements as well as to their unsettling. To some, this extension of intersectionality beyond group categories to institutionalized domains might be seen to misconstrue or even devalue the concept. However, my representation of these domains is underpinned by the social relations of inequality inherent in their embodiment and enactment. As such, I aim for this to provide greater explanatory power to the understanding of categorical intersectionality.

The book developed and applied this analysis further to highlight the radical implications of political and intellectual critiques of inequality and power as integral to social policy thinking. In doing this, my intention is not to displace or detract from the specific intellectual developments of the critiques of, say, gender or disability or race. The pursuit of these as separate fields of social relations is crucial. Rather, the intention is, first, to strengthen their combined significance in thinking through concepts intrinsic to social policy as a field of study, such as the meaning and practice of universalism and equality, the understanding of agency in formations of solidarity, and the constitution of a matrix of socio-ethical obligations.

Furthermore, the importance of an intersectional approach is that it links theory to political praxis in the dialogic forging of solidarities across different social positionings and identities. In critical approaches to social policy, this is expressed as the importance of prefigurative welfare practices in providing transformative possibilities. These thread through my analysis of agency in chapter 5 and the meaning of global social justice to emerge from an intersectional analysis of migrant care work in chapter 6. Both highlighted the significance of an ethics of care for solidarity and justice. Chapter 7 extended this by returning to the challenges posed by the crises of care, the environment and racialized borders to examine and compare the key political ethics associated with struggles around these crises. The ethics of care, environmentalist ethics, and ethics of decoloniality all share in one way or another, and to a greater or lesser degree, a critique of Western-centric abstracted notions both of the autonomous, rational white male able-bodied heterosexual subject and of the neoliberal understanding of individualism and competition as the basis for action. Instead they favour a relational understanding of interdependence as the basis of human action with human flourishing as its central principle: care for others and care for the world. The environmentalists add planetary flourishing to this principle, while decolonial ethics excavate these issues further to challenge how far colonized and racialized peoples have ever, since the beginning of colonialism and the development of slavery, been included in the normative understanding of 'human'. Here the struggle is for a new form of planetary humanism in which all are recognized as equal in their differences.

Together these three approaches represent a powerful challenge to global capitalism and neoliberal ideology. They provide key ethical values and consequent obligations that a welfare society needs to recognize and nurture: the practices of care, the needs of the planet and the pluriversality of being human. These expand an understanding of interdependencies from those between close and distant others in one's own society to, first, people across the globe; second, to humans and non-human and living organisms of the planet; third, to future generations to ensure they inherit a living planet; and, fourth, to past generations in terms of the need to repair former racial injustices which continue to structure institutional and everyday racism, inequality, and white privilege. These ethics are also expressed in deeper forms of deliberative, dialogic democracy, intersectional solidarity-building and alliances, and new economic models based on human and planetary wellbeing. They find reflection in many prefigurative welfare practices and in local, translocal, regional, devolved and transnational mobilization, which in turn inform different creative expressions of an eco-welfare commons. Given the existence of social and political forces that constrain such practices, such as the rise of authoritarian political leaders, the ongoing pursuit of racist, sexist and ethno-nationalist policies, and the post-Covid-19 possibility of increasing impoverishment, exhaustion and conflict, the importance at this moment in time of such reimagining, grounded in political practices and supported by political alliances, cannot be overstated.

At the same time, it is important to look critically at such proposals. My assessment in terms of the political priorities and ethical obligations raised by the discussion of care, the environment and decolonial ethics suggested that there was a need to explore such ideas further. These included the tensions between universalism and pluriversalism; the balance between financial support (such as basic income) and the development of public services and how far this balance affects existing inequalities; and between the state's relational role (creating opportunities for deliberation and dialogue and supporting the local co-production of services) and its regulatory role in addressing justice (for example, racial and gender violence, or tax evasion). What would be the place of national borders in a situation of the inequities of climate change? How can societies still saturated in different forms of colonial and settler relations develop different stories of who they are, and what forms of reparation does that imply?

Finally, I outline briefly what the implications of this analysis are for teaching, learning and researching the field of social policy in terms of reconstituting knowledge; relational knowledge and analysis; and post-Covid-19 reconstruction and reimagination.

Reconstituting the knowledge base of social policy

When Testament, the hip-hop MC, beatboxer and playwright, read the first sentence in Peter Fryer's wonderful book *Staying Power: The History of Black People in Britain* (Fryer 1984), he said he felt immense relief that he belonged to the country where he had been born and brought up (BBC 2020b). That sentence reads: 'There were Africans in Britain before the English came here.'

Fryer's book is an excellent example of transforming and reconstituting knowledge that is important for social policy (see also Virdee 2014; Shilliam 2018). He demonstrates that the history of black people in Britain is not a separate history, a specialism, but integral to British history. That history, especially through empire, is integral to the early forms of collectivism and the development of what was the post-war welfare state. It is a history that still needs to be mined. For example, we know that the profits and taxes from the colonies financed welfare state expenditure, but how far was the fiscal crisis that hit the UK in the early 1970s, which is usually explained as the result of the oil crisis, also the consequence of these sources drying up after colonial independence?[1] In addition, how far was this connected to imperialist extractivism which fuelled the economic growth on which welfare state development depended? The details require research. The different postcolonial processes in different welfare states, along with the struggles of racialized minorities in relation to those of class and gender, serve to provide a much more politically dynamic history than that told in welfare regime analysis.

The Social Policy Association report on the teaching of race and racism in higher education institutions, mentioned above, begins to answer the question 'Why is my curriculum white?', a movement that began in 2015 to challenge the relevance of curricula that were Eurocentric and did not represent colonial or settler histories from the perspective of colonized and/or dispossessed peoples. While part of this is about making teaching and research in social policy more relevant to and inspiring for BAME students, it is also about demonstrating the relevance of these histories and struggles to white teachers' and learners' understanding of our/their own social positionings and identities. In other words, it is as much the whiteness of the subject matter and its key theories and theorists that need to be the focus for developing a critical understanding.[2]

I have argued for the specifics of race and racism to become integral both in themselves but also in their relation to three other sets of relations: family, care and intimacy; paid and unpaid work; the construction of nation and nationality; and the environment (family–nation–work–nature). Appendix I details the concepts and indicators attached to these intersecting sets of social relations which I have employed to reassemble a social policy analysis. They can stand as an aide-mémoire of the sorts of issues to explore in developing knowledge. Simplifying them – and just putting intersectionality on hold for a moment while sticking with the example of race and racism – the implications suggest six processes. First, as referred to above, is the importance of historical reconstruction.[3] Second is empirical detail about institutionalized racism in key services such as the criminal justice system, the benefits system, housing allocation, health and education. A third process involves a critical interpretation of the practices of institutional racism. Here I found Mbembe's concept of necropolitics particularly illuminating. Fourth is the analysis of how everyday racism enters the delivery of services and the social relations between users and providers and the knock-on impact on dehumanizing other service-users. In relation to this I have referred to 'bordering practices' and the ways in which these affect different groups. Fifth, powerful and contradictory politico-cultural discourses frame provision to BAME groups, such as the idea of being post-racial – a form of institutionalized gaslighting which denies the very processes of subjugation it creates and sustains white privilege. In addition, competing ideologies that reference a particular understanding of the nation – from multicultural to ethno-national and punitively assimilationalist – serve to shape or fragment everyday solidarities between groups. Sixth, and related, is the question of contestation. I pointed to the multiple forms in which people exercise their agency to contest from campaigns and mobilizations to the quieter forms of commitments and reciprocity with others. Because I provide an intersectional analysis, each of these processes requires an understanding of how they dovetail with the effects of and mitigation strategies for climatic instability, with processes of sexism, ablism, classism, ageism, restrictions attached to heteronormativity and migrant or any other excluded status, and how salient those intersections are for different groups. I also suggest that such an analysis, even as it emphasizes multiplicity and fluidity, requires a strong framing mechanism to hold it in place (see appendix I and figure 3.1 in chapter 3). This may seem paradoxical, but these frameworks are heuristic devices which are underpinned by an analysis of power dynamics and forces for change rather than by simple causal mechanisms.

Relational knowledge and practices

Three of the issues I discussed in chapters 5 and 7 in relation to welfare politics – co-production, deliberative democracy and alliances – can be applied to the production of social policy knowledge.

One important re-emergence in this century has been that of *scholar activism* and its focus on the co-production, or co-creation, of knowledge in research.[4] Here students and researchers interrupt the conventional social relations of investigation where research subjects provide information and the researcher as expert develops this into knowledge. In the co-production model, the expert is the person with the experience and the researcher is a facilitator and co-worker. In their publication on scholar activism in research on sex work, Laura Connelly and Teela Sanders (2020) provide a thoughtful account of the different relationships involved in this process.[5] First the researchers saw themselves as 'in service' to the sex workers' rights movement, whose demands include the decriminalization of sex work and human rights to enable safety and dignity at work. As a result, they didn't set the research agenda but responded to the movement's concerns.[6] As academic activists, they used their skills to lobby for change and appear publicly without fear of stigma that a sex worker might face. Second, the relationships with the sex workers in the project were guided by the principles of democracy and emancipation in participatory action research. This meant that the sex workers became peer paid researchers and shared ownership of the research process, as well as opportunities to develop their skills. Third, there were collaborative partnerships with statutory and third-sector projects and practitioners, including the police, who were informed by the priorities of sex-worker-led research and impact. The fourth set of relationships, with universities and funding bodies, contained more tensions in carrying out these principles. For example, administrative rules on payments and contracts made for difficulties in being sensitive to sex workers' circumstances and needs for anonymity. Similarly, the requirements of funding bodies to have cut-and-dried research questions and parameters can hinder the possibility of these moving when co-researchers are involved. While the Research Excellence Framework has placed a premium on 'impact', Connelly and Sanders make the important point that the hierarchies of impact (with, say, government departments or business as most valued) need to be resisted in order to respect scholar activism, especially that with marginalized groups.[7]

Co-production can also apply to developing the curriculum. It is in the context of facilitating deliberations around not only curriculum planning, design and assessment but also knowledge content that students and teachers can enter into a different set of relations and explore the question of diversity of experience and perspective (Bovill et al. 2011).

Forging political alliances and working alongside others, developing dialogue and deliberation across groups, sometimes called 'transversal politics' (Yuval-Davis 1999), is an important part of intersectionality praxis.

So, too, I would argue that building *conceptual alliances* is important to keep multiple dimensions of power, policies, and/or politics in the picture. The concept of 'welfare bricolage' (Phillimore et al. 2021), discussed in chapter 5, is one example. The idea of an eco-welfare commons, as discussed in chapter 7, also represents an important alliance node that can bring together different areas of both critique and resistance and enable their arguments to be deliberated.

If conceptual alliances are about the relations between ideas, then relationality of disciplines is also important. While social policy is an eclectic discipline with porous boundaries, inflected by different disciplines in different countries (usually sociology, economic and political science, management studies and social history), there is a mainstream of core theories through which the relevance of other approaches is directly and indirectly appraised. Yet creative developments in the discipline are often marked by cross-disciplinary and cross-national collaboration, especially in Global North and Global South collaboration. An intersectional approach by its very nature emerged out of interdisciplinary thinking and practices.[8]

Reconstruction and reimagination in post-Covid-19 futures

Chapter 7 focused on prefigurative practices and reimagining for an eco-welfare commons. However, in the immediate context there is the aftermath of the Covid-19 crisis to face. The pandemic was in part the consequence of nature's destruction and represented the sort of global environmental shocks that climate change can bring (Pettifor 2020: 173–80). Reconstruction following the social and political impoverishment of the austerity decade is urgent, requiring significant research collaboration to investigate the social and economic impact of both the pandemic and the mitigation strategies within, for the UK, the context of Brexit. This urgency does not diminish the need for reimagining; it is important to see both reconstruction and reimagination as connected – a map with multiple points where the landscape and paths are uncertain and contingent. It is not that one is pragmatic and the other idealist, for I argued in chapter 7 that imagining the commons needs to be based in prefigurative and actually existing practices of the present. What reimagining does is provide some frames, emerging guidelines and links from the present need for reconstruction – building back better – to future possibilities for transforming societies. Ruth Lister's (2020) 'good society' approach and the Care Collective's *Care Manifesto* discussed in chapter 7 are good examples of how to combine immediate needs to combat physical and material insecurity with a more transitional agenda which articulates together the material, ethical, emotional, political, cultural and international dimensions.

The reconstruction work has already begun in many quarters. For example, in the summer of 2020, academics from social sciences, humanities and the arts met through the British Academy to discuss 'a positive post-pandemic future for peoples, economies and environments' (Morgan Jones et al. 2020). The report provides a basis to consider what knowledge and which areas are needed to attend to the socio-economic, political and cultural needs of the immediate future. The urgent and linked imperatives for renewal are reported as inequalities and inclusivity, sustainability and the environment, and education and skills. In addition, there should be strong and robust governance, the voice of different communities, and responsiveness to the local and historical contexts of people's lives. It also recommends interdisciplinary collaboration across the different social sciences, humanities and arts, as well as medical, biological and physical sciences. This is a report, in the main, from academics and therefore not carrying the sort of democratic knowledge co-production that a citizens' assembly or scholar activist research might produce. The pressures for a public inquiry or a people's inquiry (White 2020) might eventually fulfil that (but see also the Covid Realities project, https://covidrealities.org)

Drilling down into social policy reconstruction for the immediate future, given the likelihood of increased unemployment, impoverishment and homelessness, it needs urgently to address the immediate issue of material and physical insecurities resulting from the overlaying of the pandemic upon existing socio-economic inequalities. This highlights the need to rethink the tax and benefit system through more focused taxation of wealth and broadening national insurance, as well as creating new sources from tax/insurance to fund health and social care. Increases in benefit rates, especially for child benefit, and a social protection floor through a guaranteed minimum income or a form of basic income are necessary. Equally urgent is the need for accessible, affordable homes, better skills training and education, a humane migration, refugee and asylum system, the strengthening of anti-discrimination measures, protection from violence, an employment and employment protection strategy, expanded child care and social care services, the restoration of legal aid, and a major review of the criminal justice system.

These represent key areas, but two connected arguments in this book have been to provide a way of understanding inequalities as multiple and intersecting social relations and to contextualize these inequalities within a broader understanding of the destructive and dehumanizing effects of capitalism and neoliberalism. Over the last decade the drive to restore both power and profits to financialized capital has resulted not only in substantial parts of labour being disempowered and impoverished by precarity but also, centrally, the devaluation and depletion of care, the destruction of the planet, and racially structured dynamics of expropriation and dehumanization. This means that strategies for reconstruction need to take account of these – that is, to have a more complex understanding of the social relations of power and inequality and to ensure that strategies for reconstruction are aligned with the valuing and ethics of care, with climate change justice, with racial justice and with a new humanism which recognizes equality in difference. Such strategies need also to enhance the state's capacity to re-regulate markets and the offshore accumulation of wealth as well as to enable and facilitate dialogic deliberation and democratic co-production of public services at community, regional, national and transnational scales. More localized and inclusive forms of democracy would enable and be enabled by solidarities forged through alliances of labour, climate change activism, feminism, anti-racism, migration rights, disability and sexual rights movements, and other progressives at all these levels. Thus we would need to ask how far reconstruction policies align with the valuing of paid and unpaid care. Do education, employment and training strategies include a revaluation of rewards for person-centred care work?. Do they conform to net zero and associated strategies for environmental sustainability? Do climate change mitigation policies address both the protected characteristics of the Equality Act and also intersecting inequalities? Do local and national housing/health-care/education policies institutionalize sustainability in their buildings and work practices? Do reconstruction policies give not only space to implement stronger anti-discriminatory strategies but also opportunities to engage democratically (through, say, local and national assemblies and all levels of education) with historical and current forms of racial injustice and reparative measures to combat these?

There is also the complexity of inequalities to address. This was discussed in chapter 4, but it is worth repeating the point, for it implies a much more dynamic and fluid approach to explaining and researching inequalities. The Covid-19 pandemic has had different types of impact – medical/physical, mental/emotional, socio-economic and environmental. These intersect in different ways with inequalities emerging from age (old people, young people, children), race and ethnicity, gender, disability, citizenship status, employment status, caring responsibilities, income, wealth and housing, and regional and local geography. Some of these impacts are felt as immediate, some will be felt over a longer period as income support is reduced, and some will endure into the future. Some relate to long-standing inequalities and the effects for BAME groups of institutionalized racism in housing, employment and access to health care; or, in the case of women, inequalities at home and at work and lack of access to adequate care and financial support for children. Again, it would be expected that these two effects would intersect in particular ways, especially given the relatively higher number of women and of BAME and migrants as key workers with a proximity to the virus. These groups, along with younger people, will be most hit by unemployment, while older people have been most vulnerable to the virus yet not as an overall group affected financially. In addition, children's educational opportunities have been differentially affected, especially socio-economically, by school closures, cancelled examinations, stress and anxiety.

How far and in which ways mitigation strategies reinforce or moderate these inequalities is one important question. Overall, however, it is the capacity to explain the multiplicity of such effects in order to develop policies, practices and ways of thinking that is an essential task for social policy. It requires an intersectional analysis, for which this book argues, but also a multidimensional approach that can connect the present with both the past and the future, one that can dynamically connect different scales and sites of intervention and draw on different political ethics to guide priorities. This can provide us with the tools to envision ways of reconciling universalism with difference. It is an approach which sees the aim of social polices not only to meet needs but also to enable and sustain solidarities and alliances that permit differently positioned groups to articulate those needs. It is through the cracks and contradictions of a racial, patriarchal and extractivist capitalism that such solidarities emerge and in which hope resides.

Appendix I:
Elaborating Family–Nation–
Work–Nature and Welfare

Welfare states are central to the ways in which states attempt to consolidate and resettle the organization, conditions and social relations of family, nation, work and, more recently, nature, especially when they have been subject to challenge or change. However, such settlements are rarely 'settled' as such but represent 'fragile equilibria' as past catches up with present (Newman and Clarke 2009). The following spells out what the four domains reference and how they intersect in mutually constitutive ways with welfare policies, provision and practice.

Family, care and intimacy: while recognizing that not all households are families and that care and intimacy involve familial and non-familial relationships, this domain refers to the multiple social relations inherent in dependent and interdependent familial and non-familial care and intimate sites and practices. These involve, among others, gender, class, ethnicity, religion, sexuality, disability and generation. They take place within historically and culturally specific conditions and forms of organization, such as heteronormative, queer, extended, nuclear, diverse and non-traditional, which may or may not be based on coupledom or gendered divisions of sexuality, housework or care. These conditions and dynamics are signified through meanings and discourses (of what is seen as 'natural', of parenting and partnering, of masculinity and femininity, of sexuality, of unrespectable/respectable families, etc.). Associatedly, social, legal, cultural, professional and institutional practices manifest their own forms of inclusion and exclusion to rights and recognitions. For example, which relationships have legal or social recognition? How are disabled people or sexual minorities positioned in relation to family life? Who is eligible for motherhood? Who are 'good' and 'bad' mothers/fathers/citizens? Who has access to benefits – mothers, carers, people who require support? All these dimensions give rise to forms of contestation and mobilization, such as for or against reproductive rights, for LGBTQI+ recognition and rights for care support, or for independent living.

Nation refers to the social relations which are inscribed in the formation, organization and conditions not only of the nation-state but also of those systems which help to define or build nationhood, such as colonialism and imperialism, migration and settlement, wars and internal conflicts. It involves both internal and external dynamics that affect national sovereignty, such as devolution, regionalization, globalization and associated geo-political inequalities. The social relations of power caught up in these processes are not only between nationals and non-nationals but imply forms of domination and subordination between indigenous and settler peoples, between colonizers and colonized, between differently constituted ethnic, religious or racialized groups. These may be generated either by specific systems, such as colonialism, migration systems and bordering practices, or indentured labour, or by legacies of subordination or conflict, for example, anti-Semitism, anti-Catholicism or slavery. Again, these relations generate forms of mobilization and resistance – pro- / anti-nationalism or internationalism, anti-racism, extending the rights of settlement, human rights. These influence and are influenced by the discourses, meanings and discursive institutional and interpersonal practices attached to the narratives of nation articulating with gender, class, race, ethnicity, culture, religion, disabilities and sexualities. These are evident in the promotion of eugenics, assimilation, segregation, multiculturalism, forms of nativism, hate crime, racism (structural, institutional, everyday), ablism, ageism, etc. Processes of exclusion, marginalization and inclusion are closely linked to formal and informal conceptions of the boundaries of citizenship, which can also determine rights of movement and access to social rights.

Work constitutes the third domain of significance in this analytical triad and refers to those conditions and forms of organization of production and the social relations these generate (for example, capital accumulation, labour conditions and social protection – hours, care and sick leave, etc. – commodification, distinctions between paid and unpaid labour, between core and casual labour, education, training and skilling processes, indentured and bonded labour, slavery, migrant labour and the interaction of these with gender, class, racialization, disability, age, etc.). The key social relations of power and forms of mobilization and resistance are those based on the organizations of workers and employers. These are shaped by class and its legacies, but not exclusively, for the processes of inclusion and exclusion involve other social groups – women, older people, disabled people, racialized groups, sexual minorities, and so on. Mobilizing groups may resist not only forms of exclusion from paid work but also exclusion from the benefits which may be attached to wage-earning. Forms of contestation from workers are also embedded within certain contradictory historical legacies (such as a tradition of corporatism, racism, internationalism/nationalism, the devaluation of care work), as well as affecting and being affected by discourses and meanings of work which may be nationally, historically and/or culturally specific (work as the basis of citizenship or moral virtue).

. **Nature:** in terms of social policy and the environment, nature can be narrowly understood as clean air and transport policy, but here it is intended to refer to those policies mitigating the effects of climate change and damage to the ecosystem, including floods, fires and earthquakes, toxification and planetary extractivism, as well as epidemics such as HIV-AIDS, the 2003 SARS-CoV and the global pandemic of Covid-19. Welfare states in Western developed countries are only at the start of making the environment and sustainability an organizing principle, pushed particularly by the 2016 Paris Accord, the 2018 report of the UN Intergovernmental Panel on Climate Change, policies such as the Green New Deal and, of course, significant protest and mobilization. However, Covid-19 was to shape social policies such as health and public health, social care, education, income maintenance and homelessness. Nature engages with a new set of social relations of power – those between the human and the non-human living world and living organisms. These are exercised historically and today through forms of domination, exploitation, extractivism and extinction-generation. These processes are closely aligned with forms of capitalism, colonialism (both settler and exploitation), imperialism and patriarchy, involving the domination of people's land and resources and their elimination as custodians of the planet. Over time these have been justified by discourses of a hierarchy of 'races', with the racialized women and men, poor women, and disabled people being perceived as 'closer' to the non-human living world. Contemporary justificatory discourses privilege 'progress', 'profit', 'production' and 'growth' over the planet's resources. For example, in 2019, as wildfires raged across Australia, the Australian government continued to justify the mining of coal as its contribution to economic growth based on its being the world's largest exporter of coal. Different approaches to sustainability range from market environmentalism, which looks to innovative solutions from the market, and sustainable capitalism, which introduces greater regulation and tax incentives. On the other side, a 'systems change' strategy seeks to develop a post-growth approach to the economy and democracy (see chapter 7). Mobilization has been significant in this century in line with this second set of strategies.

Welfare states are always more than 'the state' or 'welfare': the meanings and conditions attached to 'the state' and 'welfare' change over time.

In addition, in order to meet their needs, people may draw on national or local public, private or voluntary provision as well as community associations, neighbours, families, friends, workplaces, the internet, and self-help and mutual aid groups as sources of welfare. These may be local, national or transnational. Welfare states exist in a dynamic relationship to the work–family–nation triad in that they reconstitute family, nation and work and are reconstituted by them. Increasingly, too, policies and relations of nature shape and are shaped by welfare state concerns.

However, welfare states are also complex actors in their own right creating, juggling, and assembling policies, narrative and practices in relation to all four domains. This is manifest through different areas of intervention (health, education, social security, housing, social services, environment), cultural legacies (forms of inclusive/exclusive eligibilities and entitlement; shame; stigma, meanings of 'public'), modes of organization and delivery, technologies of governance (professional, bureaucratic, managerial, consumerist, biopolitical, individualizing, responsibilizing), commitments to expenditure and sources of funding (fiscal, contributory), sites of operation and power (central, federal, local) and sectors of provision (state, voluntary not-for-profit, community, family, faith institutions, and private-for-profit). Each of these is subject to political and economic conditions and the social and moral relations that these engender (e.g. between providers and users, between professional and ancillary workers, deserving and undeserving, taxpayers and claimants, providers and consumers), with their forms of inclusion, marginalization and exclusion (access enhanced or limited by class, gender, age, race, religion, respectability, normativity, postcode, residential and migrant status) and their associated competing discourses (e.g. market efficiency, welfare dependency, welfare consumerism/citizenship, public service, equity, justice, fairness). All of these dimensions have been and continue to be the basis of mobilization and contestation.

As a simple exercise in applying this framework, take any political party leader's speech to their annual conference over the past five years and analyse the meanings they give to these four domains and their articulation with each other and with social policy (or 'the welfare state'). You could start with Keir Starmer's 2020 address to the Labour Party conference (Starmer 2020).

Appendix II:
Situating the Author in Social Policy

Social policy has been part of my life for a long time. I've been a provider, a student, an activist, a teacher and a researcher, and like most people I'm a service-user. It started in December 1964, when I was interviewed by two professors at the University of London's Bedford College and accepted on to the Branch III of the university's sociology degree. Branch III combined sociology with 'social administration', as the discipline of social policy was then called, and the course was taught across Bedford College and the LSE. The two professors were Oliver McGregor and Lady Gertrude Williams. Oliver McGregor was an energetic social progressive who had written the definitive history of divorce in England (McGregor 1957) and went on to serve on the Finer Committee on one-parent families. Gertrude Williams was what was then called a social economist, and her statistical research, including that on working women, shaped the post-war welfare state (Williams 1945). They were intellectuals and social reformers in the line of Charles Booth and Seebohm Rowntree. At the LSE the lecturers included Richard Titmuss, David Donnison and Roy Parker, enduring influences in the discipline.

In common with many of that post-war generation, I was the first in my close and extended family to go to university. I arrived in London from a small mixed grammar school in a Yorkshire town, eager for new ideas to change the world. I was disappointed. Much social administration was, quite literally, about the administration and implementation of social policies. It's not that it wasn't interesting, it's just that it seemed to have little personal or political reference to the world of 1965–8, which, outside the lecture room doors, was a world of student rebellion, anti-imperialism (against the Vietnam War) and even the faint stirrings of a women's movement. One week in May 1968, I listened to a lecture by David Donnison on council house allocation, the next week to a talk in the same lecture theatre by Daniel Cohn-Bendit, one of the student leaders from Paris (later a Green MEP). One was turning me into a progressive administrator for the state, the other an activist against the state. The strategy Cohn-Bendit

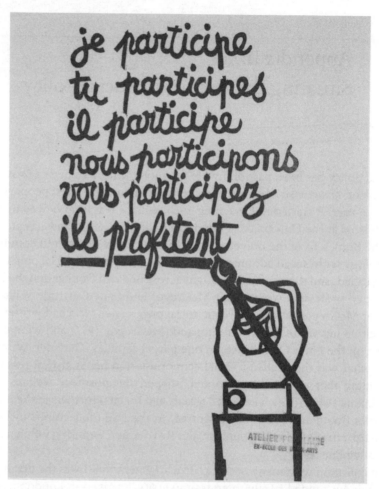

Figure A.1 Poster used in the May '68 student-worker rebellions, produced by Atelier Populaire, ex-Ecole des Beaux-Arts, Paris

presented was of students forming alliances with the working class and rural workers in order to defeat the capitalist system, as the poster from the French worker-student demonstrations of May '68 argues (figure A.1). It conjugates the verb 'to participate': I, you, he (*sic*), we participate, but *they* profit. This was more exciting than the prospect of social work or the civil service.

My interests also lay in anti-colonial struggles. My early years in the late 1940s and early 1950s were spent in Cairo, where my father, a working-class socialist, was an engineer contracted to troubleshoot problems on the Egyptian railways. He was sympathetic to President Nasser, and my first political memories, in 1956, were of the outrage in our household (now back in England) at the British bombardment of the Suez Canal – an act of imperialist aggression in a newly postcolonial world. In the same month, the Soviet army invaded Hungary to quell the uprising there, an event that was also to influence my politics later. A number of friendships and relationships I had at university were with people who had had direct experience of these and similar events, and from them I learned a lot. In 1968, by the good fortune of a Commonwealth scholarship, I went to Ibadan University in Nigeria to start a PhD on the impact of colonialism on West African women's autonomy. It combined my interests in imperialism with women's emancipation. It was a big idea for which I found little (well, no) support. The academics interested in women were anthropologists doing micro-scale research on the spatial relationships of women's market trade work. Those interested in emancipation were researching the development of African working-class trade union movements. I fell between many stools: good theme, wrong person, wrong time. I returned to London in the early 1970s, placed my thesis notes in two black and gold 'Biba' bags,[1] and went into teaching welfare professionals.

In 1972 I applied for a job at the then North-Western Polytechnic, later to become the University of North London, in the Applied Social Studies Department. I collected an application form, sat in the students' common room, and filled in my personal statement with a page-long critique of the social administration I had been taught as an undergraduate. To my surprise it was warmly received, and I got the job. They were heady days of socialist and feminist activism in that department, where teaching and community, trade union and political activism were all rolled into one. Influenced mainly by the new left of Marxism and Trotskyism to begin with, our commitments forced us to provide our students with on-the-hoof critiques of the mainstream approaches to housing, social security, health care, education and personal social services. It felt as though we and the (mainly mature) students were all piecing knowledge and ideas together. As well as the mainstream Fabian social policy writers, our key texts included Jim Kincaid's analysis *Poverty and Equality in Britain* (973), Ken Coates and Richard Silburn's *Poverty: The Forgotten Englishmen* (1970), two radical analyses of the welfare state, by Dorothy Wedderburn (1965) and John Saville (1957–8) and Sivanandan's writing in *Race & Class*, plus some of the *Fabian Society* pamphlets. Out of the ferment came *Case-Con: The Revolutionary Magazine for Social Workers*, which Bob Deacon, Crescy Cannon and Celia Burgess set up with others and ran from 1971 to 1975.

Elizabeth Wilson was also a colleague and was one of the authors of another influential set of pamphlets organized by a feminist group, *Red Rag*. The one entitled *Women and the Welfare State* was the basis for her ground-breaking eponymous book (Wilson 1977).

The politics of the time shaped a new analysis of the welfare state as an uneasy truce between the interests of capitalism for a healthy, disciplined workforce and the interests of the working class for protection from poverty, unemployment and ill health. This analysis fed into a political strategy for us as the new public-sector professionals which relieved the tension of being both agents of the state *and* committed to defend working-class interests. We became active public-sector trade unionists, developing radical rank-and-file movements. Trade union identities allowed us both to critique and to distance ourselves from the authority that our professionalism represented *and* be part of a working-class movement as a sort of new white-collar proletariat.

By 1973, the impact of the oil crisis led to public expenditure cuts, and this fuelled the militancy of blue-collar ancillary workers, nurses, even doctors, and white-collar unions. It also created opportunities for alliances to defend the welfare state. The politics of '68 thus conjugated itself into a new public-sector politics, as the poster of a mass rally for public-sector trade unionists shows (see figure A.2 and compare with figure A.1). The rally filled a very large conference room in the Friends Meeting House on Euston Road in March 1973. This strategy of alliances against the cuts, important as it was in defending the jobs and conditions, especially of the increasingly black, Asian and female low-paid ancillary workers, faced new tensions and contradictions which we were only beginning to appreciate. In particular, defending against cuts in the welfare state had to go beyond the defence of 'more of the same'. In 1973, I was secretary of the Camden and Islington Public Sector Alliance when local social security counter staff, not noted for their radicalism, threatened strike action for the first time over pay (see figure A.3). On the eve of the strike, the Alliance faced a deputation from the local Claimants' Union[2] – also Alliance members – urging suspension of the strike because it would hit families on benefit who were due to draw their payments the next day. This had a knock-on effect for social workers, who were supporting the strike but would be pressed to make emergency payments for the claimants. For the Claimants' Union, social security counter staff were Public Enemy no. 1. For the trade union-organized counter staff, the Claimants Union was considered anarchist and undisciplined. The situation exposed deep fissures of distrust between users and providers of welfare which we had hardly begun to make sense of.

Figure A.2 Poster for public-sector workers' rally, 1973

What exposed these tensions even more was the unlocking of women's experiences of welfare through the activities of the women's movement. More importantly, however, it was their practices and strategies which began to resolve such tensions. Feminist politics was practical: if the housing department refused to provide a refuge for women to escape domestic violence, then create one; if no one in authority would listen to women who had been raped or abused, then set up a rape crisis line; if women felt that doctors didn't listen to them, then push the health authority to provide a well-women centre.

By the second half of the 1970s, I was living in Plymouth with two small children, and our Plymouth Women's Group did all these things and more. Practically, personally and politically, feminism reached those parts that other theories and practices couldn't. The radical theories of the welfare state up until then talked of welfare as a truce between capital and labour, for which read: it was a man-thing. What we experienced was that welfare was very much a woman-thing. Women were as

Figure A.3 Demonstrating against the cuts: Islington High Street, March 1973 (I have the megaphone on the right)

central to welfare as welfare was important to them. They were more likely to be users of welfare services, and they made up the majority of providers as nurses, cleaners, clerks and teachers, or in an unpaid capacity as carers in the home. The welfare state was the focus of women's claims for greater autonomy. The original demands of the Women's Liberation Movement – for nurseries; a fair deal for part-time staff; contraception and abortion; equality in pensions and social security – were mainly claims upon the welfare state. These activities in all parts of the country had a major influence on the subsequent provision of services. In setting up voluntary or part-subsidized women's services we attempted to prefigure a new kind of relationship between provider and user – one which was more equal and respectful. At the same time, women working within the welfare services also began to formulate new ways of working with clients, patients and tenants, as well as challenging the structures of public services which found women and minority ethnic groups on the lower rungs. Defending against cuts in the welfare state had begun to go beyond the defence for 'more of the same'.

This idea was part of the remit of a new journal set up in 1981 – *Critical Social Policy (CSP)* – by Bob Deacon and Gordon Peters, the latter then director of Hackney Social Services. Its founding conference, an inspiring occasion whose speakers included Mary McIntosh and the young and – then – left-wing leader of 'red' Sheffield City Council, David Blunkett (later to become home secretary in Tony Blair's New Labour government), was held in Queen Mary College in London and drew an audience of almost one thousand people. For almost a decade *CSP*'s annual conferences were among the most exciting and popular on the British social science scene – mainly, I think, because they combined with ease debates between activists, intellectuals and practitioners. In 1985 I joined the editorial collective, and in 1986, with Avtar Brah, Suzy Croft, Jen Dale, Lesley Day, Miriam David, Eva Eberhardt and Ruth Madigan, co-edited a special feminist issue (*CSP* 16, 1986).

At the same time, within the women's movement there were intense debates about sisterhood: women were not a homogeneous, uniform group; there were differences between us of race, class, sexuality, age and disability which gave rise to different experiences and different ways of seeing the world. This particularly affected how women experienced the welfare state, and minority ethnic women had different stories to tell and different battles to fight about the racism they and their families experienced at the hands of the police or schools (Bryan et al. 1985).

Many black and white activists got involved with anti-racist politics through the Anti-Nazi League, set up in 1977 to oppose the rise of the National Front, a racist and fascist organization which often paraded through multicultural localities. More influential was when the Anti-Nazi League worked with 'Rock against Racism' to mobilize 100,000 people in April 1978 to march from Trafalgar Square to a huge concert in Victoria Park, Hackney. The Clash, X-Ray Spex, Steel Pulse and Misty in Roots all played. So did the Tom Robinson Band, whose song about homophobia, 'Glad to Be Gay', was banned from being played on BBC Radio's Top 40 charts show. Counter-cultural mobilization was extensive at this time, with important alliances across social and trade union movements. The national abortion campaign, set up in 1975 to oppose a government bill to restrict access to abortion, was supported by a large number of trade unions. The Women's Peace Camp at Greenham Common, started in 1981 (it eventually closed in 2000), against the government's consent for the site to be used as a base for nuclear cruise missiles drew coachloads every weekend. That same year Ken Livingstone took over leadership of the Greater London Council, which established policies meeting the rights and representation of working-class groups, women, minority ethnic groups, disabled and gay men, and lesbians. In 1984 the miners' strike found support from many of these organizations. Margaret Thatcher saw this activism as 'insurrection' against democracy and began to weaken their powers.

Back in the discipline of social policy, these experiences, campaigns and policies drove a search for deeper ways of understanding the welfare state. From the mid-1970s, higher education contracted. I found, after having two children, I could not get back into permanent or full-time employment. For many years I taught and researched social policy in part-time jobs in Plymouth and Bristol. By the 1980s, feminist critiques of welfare had gained a foothold in the discipline, positioning 'the family' and gender relations as central to understanding the welfare state. But this was still not sufficient to explain the experiences that had been thrown up by grassroots campaigns, especially those around anti-racism. *Social Policy: A Critical Introduction: Issues of Race, Gender and Class* (Williams 1989) was my attempt to take that on.[3]

In the mid-1980s Bob Deacon and I worked together on an ESRC-funded comparative research project on the British and Hungarian welfare states. Bob's book, *Social Policy and Socialism: The Struggle for the Socialist Relations of Welfare* (1983), had explored social policy in 'actually existing' socialist countries (including communist countries) in terms of equality and redistribution, and found many wanting. The denigration of socialist and democratic values in communist countries was a central issue facing Marxists and socialists in the post-1960s world for whom social democracy had also fallen short. If not that way, and if not neoliberalism, then which way? In the course of this research we visited Hungary and became firm friends with Juli Szalai, an outstanding political intellectual and sociologist then working at the Academy of Social Sciences. If ever we had harboured even the remotest romantic idea about the forms of state socialism that emerged out of Soviet communism (which, as former Trotskyists, we rarely had), they were dispelled. On one visit we went to a town outside Pécs to talk to the local doctor, who was from the Roma community and acted as their spokesperson. He was not available. We eventually found that he was remonstrating with the local authorities, who, on finding that one of the Roma children in school had fleas, had collected all the Roma children, stripped them and hosed them down publicly in a field. It was chilling. Some twenty years later I assisted Juli in setting up an EU-funded research programme (EDUMIGROM) investigating the experiences of minority ethnic and Roma youth in education across seven Western, Central and Eastern European countries.

Feminist orthodoxy in the 1980s held patriarchy to be the regime of women's oppression and the family one of its main sites (Barrett and

McIntosh 1982). However, as mentioned, this did not fully account for racialized experiences. The research we did in Hungary had to confront a different complexity, best illustrated by a moment at an international conference that Bob, Juli and I organized in Leeds in 1988 intended to generate debate between US, Western, Central and Eastern European researchers. To the US and Western European women at the conference, feminism had become an indispensable lens through which to re-evaluate policy and practice. It was something about which many of our male colleagues felt ambivalent. They weren't opposed to it – many were supportive – but they were content for women academics to develop and discuss the lens separately. To many of the women delegates from Central and Eastern Europe (still communist countries), feminism was understood as part of the official discourse of communism and far from emancipatory. The obligation for women to work was not viewed as a freedom but, rather, as an imposition. A Polish woman delegate gave an impassioned intervention against our discussions of the gendered divisions of labour: she had only solidarity with her husband in their struggle against the state, their oppressor. For her, family life was their fiercely protected site of freedom from state interference. For us, this was an important lesson about how time and place configure relations and solidarities differently.[4]

In 1988 I was offered my first full-time job since 1974 (not for want of trying). The Department of Health and Social Welfare at the Open University invited me to join their team developing a course on learning disability. In particular, they asked me to apply the sort of analysis I had used for race, gender and class to this disability. It was daunting but became one of the most thought-provoking projects I had been involved with. One of its outcomes was an anthology which Dorothy Atkinson and I put together, called *'Know Me as I Am': An Anthology of Prose, Poetry and Art by People with Learning Difficulties* (1990), one of the earliest of books to give voice and agency to people with learning difficulties. It was at the Open University that I also got to know and work with John Clarke, Gail Lewis and John's partner, Janet Newman, and their ideas have sustained me since.

The 1990s saw the internationalization of both activism and academic research. With the development of the social dimension of the European Commission of the EU, this became a focus for feminist activity. I had been involved with the European Forum of Socialist Feminists, which by 1990 had changed its name to the European Forum of Left Feminists (ELF). After the Berlin Wall fell in 1989, there was an anxiety among progressives that the label 'socialist' was in danger of being too narrowly associated with the socialism of the former communist countries. The Saturday in 1990 that the forum met in a room in the University of London Union building, there were many meetings in different rooms of similar social-ist groups worrying over the same issue. ELF went on to do important work, particularly around the experiences and representation of migrant and minority ethnic women in EU bodies (European Women's Lobby 1995; Williams 2003).

Developing networks of international feminist activist academics was one of the most important and supportive experiences in my academic life. In 1993, Barbara Hobson, an American academic working at the Department of Sociology at Stockholm University, invited me to a confer-ence on an island in the archipelago off Stockholm. Barbara has always had an impressive aptitude for extracting huge amounts of money to support imaginative and risky projects (but always eventually productive) from sedate bodies not noted for their radicalism. This time it was the Swedish Central Bank. My first memory of that conference was of arriving on an island late at night and stumbling along a track through silver birches (it was like a Bergmann film set) to come upon an old mansion, in which I was introduced, in turn, to many of the feminist writers who had been – or were to become – frequent inhabitants of my bibliographies: Linda Gordon, Nancy Fraser, Jane Lewis, Ann Orloff, Mary Daly, Sonya Michel, Rianne Mahon, Chiara Saraceno, Ilona Ostner, Jane Jenson, Trudie Knijn and, of course, Barbara herself. Ann, Barbara and Sonya were planning a new journal, *Social Politics: An International Journal of Gender, State and Society*, to which they invited me to contribute an article (Williams 1995) and later in 1999 to join them and Rianne Mahon as a co-editor. At that conference and in that journal we were concerned with the new welfare regime analysis spearheaded by Esping-Andersen (1990), which had very little gender analysis in it. Indeed, that was becoming the case for much of the new internationalist focus, whether on globalization, migration or citizenship. It seemed the bigger the canvas, the greater the recourse to unreconstructed analysis. In the pursuit of this developing critique of com-parative social policy I found myself working in different international research collaborations: Barbara's *Recognition Struggles* group (Hobson 2003) and Ruth Lister's *Gendering Citizenship in Western Europe* (Lister et al. 2007).[5]

In 1996 I was appointed professor of social policy at the University of Leeds and later became director of a five-year ESRC-funded research pro-gramme on Care, Values and the Future of Welfare, or CAVA as it became known. The research proposal that a group of us put together – Carol

Smart, Sasha Roseneil, Simon Duncan, Alan Deacon and myself – sought to engage with social changes in family lives and personal relationships (especially the increasingly diverse family forms of cohabitation, same-gender relationships, working mothers and post-divorce families) in the context of the new political developments (New Labour) and concepts (especially individualization) in social theory. It was a big interdisciplinary research team that included Wendy Hollway, Bren Neale, Sarah Irwin and Jennifer Mason. Our research set out to investigate people's 'moral agency' in relation to changes in family lives. In this we were pursuing the new focus on understanding 'agency', voice and experience (Williams et al. 1999) as well as getting away from a deficit approach to family change. The CAVA research introduced me to feminist philosophy of the ethics of care, which has stayed with me. It also gave me a better understanding of the processes of change in what Raymond Williams called 'structures of feeling' (see chapter 5).

After 2000 I combined my interest in care and a political ethic of care with the racialization of geo-political inequalities in a series of international collaborations in research on migrant care workers (Williams and Gavanas 2008; Williams 2011, 2012, 2018; Williams and Brennan 2012).[6] In some ways this topic brought me full circle, both to my research in Nigeria in the late 1960s and to the work I did for my first book on race, gender and class in social policy in the 1980s. Except that an invitation from the Heinrich Böll Foundation, via Paul Stubbs at the Institute of Economics in Zagreb, to teach at the Green Academy Summer School held on the beautiful eco-island of Vis off the Dalmatian coast, forced me to think again about the relationship of social policy to the environment and climate change. Especially important were the discussions there with Paul, Francine Mestrum, Anna Coote and Ian Gough, who produced ground-breaking work over subsequent years (discussed in chapter 7).

So it's in the accumulation of these experiences that I write this book as an older, queer-identifying, white, cis-woman with past experience of an invisible impairment (epilepsy). I am occasionally asked in a hesitant way (by white colleagues) what I feel as a white woman writing about race and racism. On the whole, I feel that it's my responsibility as a white feminist and anti-racist academic to do so. Also, 'border-thinking', whether from scholars, novelists or poets who are queer, disabled or people of colour, often provides a better lens to understand the world. That said, I am well aware of the limitations of my understanding in the privilege I carry, but I listen, try to learn, and offer this contribution.

Notes

Chapter 1 Introduction

1 'Prefigurative' politics means practising in the here and now that which is demanded for the future: for example, setting up alternative services which meet the needs of women in which policies and practices are deliberated by women service-users.
2 They are here described differently from Williams (2016).

Chapter 2 A Critical and Intersectional Approach to Social Policy

1 This is a summary of the analysis in Williams (1989) and was shaped by the different feminist and anti-racist writings of the time referenced in that book.
2 This is not the case in *Capital and Ideology* (Piketty 2020), where the history of slavery is seen as central to capitalism's development.
3 For a more developed discussion see Nash (2019).
4 This podcast and video explain this more fully: www.kingsfund.org.uk/audio-video/podcast/covid-19-racism-health-inequality; www.thebritishacademy.ac.uk/events/british-academy-10-minute-talks-covid-19-and-inequalities/.

Chapter 3 Intersecting Global Crises and Dynamics of Family, Nation, Work and Nature

1 See Clarke (2019b) on the problem with scales.
2 For more discussion on this distinction, see Bhattacharya (2017); Williams (2018); Mezzadri (2019).
3 For a critique of this normative model, see Daly (2011).
4 The concept 'nature' is not without problems. First, feminist theory has done much to challenge the resort to naturalism as an explanation for male domination. So it should be emphasized that nature as I use the term refers to the material conditions and social relations of the human and non-human living world. Second, Bruno Latour rejects 'nature' as too large a concept, encompassing as it does not just the planet but the stratosphere and beyond (Suzuki 2018). Instead he suggests we should stick to 'critical zone' – that which we experience and know is in crisis. My thanks to Wendy Hollway for this reference.

Chapter 4 Unsettling/Settling Family–Nation–Work–Nature

1 By 'hollowed-out' I am referring in particular to the outsourcing of government functions and constituents of public services. For a fuller analysis of the term, see Jessop (2013).
2 At the time of writing, the proposal in the new Immigration and Social Security (EU

withdrawal) Bill to disallow family reunion of refugees, which would put children into extreme vulnerability, was defeated in the House of Lords.

3 My thanks to Celia Burgess-Macey for giving me permission to publish her letter.

4 The response of the British government to the UN special rapporteur's report on racism can be found at www.gov.uk/government/news/un-human-rights-council-41-uk-response-to-the-special-rapporteurs-report-on-racism.

5 The research of Professor David Williams at Harvard University looks at the correlation of racist experiences and health morbidities: https://scholar.harvard.edu/davidrwilliams/home.

6 For detailed analysis of SERCO and other companies used for outsourcing, see White (2016).

Chapter 5 The Social Relations of Welfare

1 Unlike orthodox Marxism, which identifies resistance in the collective organized forces of the working class, Foucault differentiated many different forms of resisting agency from the marginalized: those who work through the cracks of power; those who develop their own subjugated knowledges; those who defy normativity; and those who speak a different truth to power.

2 'Minority women' is a term used by the authors for women who experience subordination through racialization, class, gender and legal status (Bassel and Emejulu 2018: 6).

Chapter 6 Intersections in the Transnational, Social and Political Economy of Care

1 There is an ongoing discussion as to whether 'care work' is better discussed as care or reproductive labour (see Kofman 2012; Williams 2018: 548–50).

2 I use the word 'arguably' because there is a case for also considering the *equality regime* as a specific policy area rather than its cutting through all these other three, as my analysis implies (Halvorsen et al. 2017). By 'equality regime', I mean the framework of anti-discrimination policies, which have significance for both workers and service-users in relation to disability, gender, racial, ethnic and religious discrimination, LGBTQI+, and age. These can also influence the local provision and practices for accessible housing; transport; education; safe and accessible public space and neighbourhood terrains; where relevant, accessible and affordable public amenities (technologies, places of worship, cinemas, etc.); supportive attitudes to older and disabled people; and action to deal with violence and abuse.

3 Migrant workers are hired under the 'Kafala' sponsorship system which ties their legal right of residency to their contract with an employer. This makes changing jobs impossible and protesting against employer abuse highly risky (Amnesty International 2020).

4 The UK was one of just eight countries that abstained from voting in favour of the Convention, together with Sudan, Malaysia, El Salvador, Panama, Singapore, the Czech Republic and Thailand.

5 See the ILO report *Care Work and Care Jobs for the Future of Decent Work* (Addati et al. 2018) as marking a shift in this direction.

Chapter 7 Towards an Eco-Welfare Commons

1 This capacity for self-determination is also the basis for a set of important arguments about 'capabilities' (Sen 2009; Nussbaum 2001, 2006).

2 The first woman to win a Nobel Prize for economics.

3 My thanks to Gail Lewis for introducing me to the work of Sylvia Wynter in a seminar she gave at Leeds University in December 2019. The interpretation is mine, faults and all.

4 As a contemporary example, see Naila Kabeer's observations that the Sustainable Development Goals, while admirable in promoting equality for all ('none left behind'), still need to grasp how some are left behind because they fall into the intersecting axes of different forms of gendered, racial, ethnic, caste and spatial inequalities (Kabeer 2016).

5 In sub-Saharan Africa, the moral personhood of Ubuntu is: I am what I am because of who we all are (Tutu 2008).

6 Arundhati Roy (2019) recounts the local struggles against the building of the Sardar Sarovar Dam in western Gujarat.

7 See the website of the World Social Forum for discussions of pluriversality in action, https://fsm2016.org/en/sinformer/a-propos-du-forum-social-mondial/, and Conway and Singh (2011).

8 Lister bears this out in relation to people in poverty, for whom human rights have in this century become a mobilizing tool because they enable both material claims and claims for dignity and respect as the right of all human beings (Lister 2013). See also the Leeds Poverty Truth Commission's 'HuManifesto', www.leedspovertytruth.org.uk/humanifesto/.

9 See also Alex Fox's proposals for a 'Health and Wellbeing Service' for long-term adult social care, which strikes more of a balance between state-funded preventative and empowering services that are integrated and built round investment in communities (Fox 2018: chap. 8).

10 See Pettifor's (2020) arguments for a new global financial system.

11 Such initiatives have also developed in smaller localities. The example of 'flatpack democracy' in Frome in Somerset is one where a group of local people ran for office as non-partisan independents based on how they wanted to change how local democracy was done (see https://iffrome.org.uk). So far they have been successful in both aims.

12 Fearless Cities: http://fearlesscities.com/en.

13 The impact of feminist mobilization in Spain has been impressive. On international women's day in 2018, 5 million women joined the 'feminist strike' against gender violence, the gender wage gap, sexism and the burden of unremunerated work.

14 The project, called 'Deep Democracy', is from BRAP, at www.brap.org.uk.

15 See a proposal for a people's inquiry into the pandemic by Stuart White, at www.compassonline.org.uk/wp-content/uploads/2020/06/PeoplesInquiry_SW_FINAL-1.pdf.

16 See, for example, *A Guide to Progressive Alliances*, at www.compassonline.org.uk/wp-content/uploads/2019/11/Progressive-Alliances-in-2019-a-guide-by-Compass.pdf.

17 Not discussed here, but see Miller (2020).

18 Reflecting this process, Peter Linebaugh's *Magna Carta Manifesto: Liberty and Commons for All* cautions: 'To speak of the commons as if it were a natural resource is misleading at best and dangerous at worst – the commons is an activity and, if anything, it expresses relationships in society that are inseparable from relations to nature. It might be better to keep the word as a verb, an activity, rather than as a noun, a substantive' (2008: 279). My thanks to John Clarke for this point.

19 Gough (2017) includes the application of *A Theory of Human Need* (Doyal and Gough 1991) to a universal measure of basic human needs which a post-growth society should aspire to meet.

20 Its climate justice demands centre on implementing a transition with justice at its core; a global Green New Deal; holding transnational corporations accountable; and taking the planet off the stock market; see www.redpepper.org.uk/an-open-letter-to-extinction-rebellion/.

21 A case of falling foul of the siloing of social policy fields.
22 See, for example, the Centre for the Legacies of British Slave-Ownership at UCL: www. ucl.ac.uk/lbs/project/lbspp1.

Chapter 8 Conclusion

1 This was referred to by Gurminder Bhambra in her plenary lecture to the Social Policy Association on 17 July 2020. She also suggested that international aid might be the mechanism to deliver redistributive reparations.
2 By whiteness here I mean primarily the economic, social and cultural privileges and opportunities that accrue to being white (Bhopal 2018). This can carry with it certain other subjective characteristics: the assumption that white experience is generic; that it relates only to economics and that racial disadvantage can be erased with money; that privilege affects others (racists/rich people) but not oneself.
3 While I have mentioned all these processes in this book, the discussion of them has not been comprehensive to all services. I have instead referred to particular examples as part of a particular case (e.g. Grenfell Tower and institutionalized racism in housing allocation). In addition, I have been necessarily selective in demonstrating the aspects of family, nation, work and nature that I have brought into connection.
4 Action research has long been part of poverty research in British social policy and emancipatory research as part of feminist, anti-racist and disability research (Beresford 2016; Priestley et al. 2010; Leavy and Harris 2018; Lister 2021). An example of such a project is organized by the University of Leeds and Leeds Poverty Truth Commission: https:// static1.squarespace.com/static/5a8e6605d74cff1010c58689/t/5ce5522605a4ed00019c a2e9/1558532825440/Summary+of+Workshop+1+-+Final.pdf.
5 The publication was co-produced with sex workers whose requested anonymity in authorship was respected.
6 There are similarities with Raworth's principles for economists (chapter 7), which, as well as being 'in service', included respecting the autonomy of communities by ensuring their engagement and consent and recognizing their differences, exercising prudential policy-making which minimizes harm, and working with humility by being transparent, accepting one's limitations and being open to alternatives (Raworth 2017: 161).
7 Another example of the development of democratic knowledge-building is the role of citizens' (or people's) assemblies. The report published in September 2020 by Climate Assembly UK surprised commentators in how far it went beyond the current parliamentary plans for action, discussed in chapter 7.
8 A similar approach is the 'Ontologies Project', which focuses on the multiplicity of institutional sites, temporalities and actors and how they coalesce in different ways. This moves away from fixed, linear and boundaried categories, policies and social relations. See www.policyontologies.org/about.html and Dobson (2020). Also see the social policy, cultural studies and anthropology collaboration to investigate and resituate the concept of citizenship in Clarke et al. (2014).

Appendix II

1 Biba was a clothes shop in the mid-1960s in Kensington Church Street, London, which sold modish but affordable clothes.
2 The Claimants' Union was a grassroots organization established by and for people on supplementary benefits which started in Birmingham in 1969. It was part of a development in the late 1960s of extending the principles of participatory democracy to groups of people who used services – as benefit claimants, as mental health users, as disabled

people, as lone parents, and so on. It contrasted with the Child Poverty Action Group, which, while progressive, was organized *for* poor families.

3 The naming of 'race' and 'nation' as neglected but important points of inquiry in academic social policy was not straightforward. When I submitted an article, 'Racism and the discipline of social policy: a critique of welfare theory' (Williams 1987), to *Critical Social Policy* in 1986, there were deep splits on the editorial collective as to whether it should be published, as some felt it was too critical of existing Marxist and feminist perspectives.

4 This was not the case across all of Eastern Europe: the former Yugoslavia had a different history. The situation changed after liberalization of the communist countries, when grassroots feminist organizations began to develop. In 2018 Victor Orbán in Hungary tried to close down all gender studies departments – unsuccessfully so far.

5 Ruth Lister and I later worked together on the Compass project on *The Good Society* (Rutherford and Shah 2006). Invitations from international and often younger academics educated me more than my own research ever could – Majda Hrženjak at the Peace Institute in Ljubljiana in 2008; Kaori Katada from the Saitama Prefectural University in Japan in 2011; Helen Meekosha, Deb Brennan and Jen Skatterbol at UNSW in Sydney between 2000 and 2014; and Greg Marston in Queensland. I was also fortunate to enjoy visiting professorships at Queens University in Belfast during the 'Troubles' in the early 1990s, at Stockholm University in 2009, and at the Social Policy Research Unit at the University of New South Wales from 2012.

6 Among my longstanding international collaborators in this work, I should mention Helma Lutz, Rianne Mahon, Sonya Michel and Ito Peng.

References

Abel, J., and Clarke, L. (2020) *The Compassion Project*. London: Aster.

Abrahams, A. (2019) *Queer Intentions: A (Personal) Journey through LGBTQ+ Culture*. London: Picador.

Action Aid (2019) 'Climate change and gender', www.actionaid.org.uk/about-us/what-we-do/womens-economic-empowerment/food-hunger-and-sustainable-livelihoods/climate-change/climate-change-and-gender.

Addati, L., Catteneo, U., Esquivel, V., and Valarino, I. (2018) *Care Work and Care Jobs for the Future of Decent Work*. Geneva: ILO; www.ilo.org/wcmsp5/groups/public/---dgreports/---dcomm/---publ/documents/publication/wcms_633166.pdf.

Age UK (2019) *Care Deserts: The Impact of a Dysfunctional Market in Adult Social Care Provision*, www.ageuk.org.uk/globalassets/age-uk/documents/reports-and-publications/reports-and-briefings/care--support/care-deserts---age-uk-report.pdf.

Agustin, O. G. (2020) 'New municipalism as a space for solidarity', in D. Featherstone, J. Littler and S. Davison (eds), *Soundings, 74: New Municipal Alternatives*: 54–67.

Akilade, E. (2020) 'Is support growing for a radical, anti-racist independent Scotland?', *gal–dem*, 18 August, https://gal-dem.com/is-support-growing-for-a-radical-anti-racist-independent-scotland/.

Alesina, A., and Glaeser, E. L. (2004) *Fighting Poverty in the US and Europe: A World of Difference*. Oxford: Oxford University Press.

Amnesty International (2020) *COVID-19 Makes Gulf Countries' Abuse of Migrant Workers Impossible to Ignore*, 30 April, www.amnesty.org/en/latest/campaigns/2020/04/covid19-makes-gulf-countries-abuse-of-migrant-workers-impossible-to-ignore/.

Amos, V., Lewis, G., Mama, A., and Parmar, P. (eds) (1984) *Many Voices, One Chant: Black Feminist Perspectives*, *Feminist Review*, no. 17 [special issue].

Andersen, K. (2019) 'Universal Credit, gender and unpaid care: mothers' accounts of the new welfare conditionality regime', *Critical Social Policy*, 40(3): 430–49.

Anderson, B. (2000) *Doing the Dirty Work*. London: Zed Press.

Anderson, B. (2010) 'Migration, immigration controls and the fashioning of precarious workers', *Work Employment and Society*, 24(2): 300–17.

Anderson, B. (2013) *Us and Them? The Dangerous Politics of Immigration Controls.* Oxford: Oxford University Press.

Andreouli, E., Kaposi, D., and Stenner, P. (2019) 'Brexit and emergent politics: in search of a social psychology', *Journal of Community and Applied Social Psychology*, 29(1): 6–17.

Andrews, K. (2015) 'The black studies movement in Britain: addressing the crisis in British academia and social life', in C. Alexander and J. Arday (eds), *Aiming Higher: Race, Inequality and Diversity in the Academy.* London: Runnymede Trust.

Anghel, R. G. (2020) 'When diaspora meets pandemic', *Northern Notes*, 20 March, University of Leeds, https://northernnotes.leeds.ac.uk/when-diaspora-meets-pandemic/.

Anning, A., and Ball, M. (eds) (2008) *Learning from Sure Start: Improving Services for Children and Families.* London: Sage.

Anthias, F, and Yuval-Davis, N. (1992) *Racialised Boundaries: Race, Nation, Gender, Colour and Class and the Anti-Racist Struggle.* London: Routledge.

Anthony, C. (2017) *The Earth, the City, and the Hidden Narrative of Race.* New York: New Village Press.

Atkinson, D., and Williams, F. (1990) *'Know Me as I Am': An Anthology of Prose, Poetry and Art by People with Learning Difficulties.* London: Hodder & Stoughton in association with the Open University.

Atkinson, H., Bardgett, S., Budd, A., Finn, M., Kissane, C., Qureshi, S., Saha, J., Siblon, J., and Sivasundaram, S. (2018) *Race, Ethnicity and Equality in UK History: A Report and Resource for Change.* London: Royal Historical Society.

AVID (Association of Visitors to Immigration Detainees) (2020) 'What is immigration detention?', www.aviddetention.org.uk/immigration-detention/what-immigration-detention.

Bachmann, C. L., and Gooch, B. (2017) *LGBT in Britain: Hate Crime and Discrimination.* London: Stonewall; www.stonewall.org.uk/system/files/lgbt_in_britain_hate_crime.pdf.

Barcelona en Comú with Bookchin, D., and Coalu, A. (eds) (2019) *Fearless Cities: A Guide to the Global Municipal Movement.* Oxford: New Internationalist.

Barnes, M. (2001) 'From private carer to public actor: The Carers' Movement in England', in M. Daly (ed.), *Care Work: The Quest for Security.* Geneva: International Labour Office.

Barnes, M. (2006) *Caring and Social Justice.* Basingstoke: Palgrave Macmillan.

Barnes, M. (2012) *Care in Everyday Life: An Ethic of Care in Practice.* Bristol: Policy Press.

Barnes, M., and Prior, D. (2009) *Subversive Citizens: Power, Agency and Resistance in Public Services.* Bristol: Policy Press.

Barnett, A. (2020) *Out of the Belly of Hell: COVID-19 and the Humanisation of*

Globalisation. London: Open Democracy; www.opendemocracy.net/en/opendemocracyuk/out-belly-hell-shutdown-and-humanisation-globalisation/.

Baron, S. (2020) 'Covid-19 has exposed UK's battered social care system. But there is a solution', *The Guardian*, 1 May, www.theguardian.com/society/2020/may/01/covid-19-uk-social-care-solution.

Barreto, J.-M. (2018) 'Decolonial thinking and the quest for decolonising human rights', *Asian Journal of Social Science*, 46(4–5): 484–502.

Barrett, M., and McIntosh, M. (1982) *The Anti-Social Family*. London: Verso.

Bassel, L., and Emejulu, A. (2018) *Minority Women and Austerity: Survival and Resistance in France and Britain*. Bristol: Policy Press.

Bates, L. (2014) *Everyday Sexism*. London: Simon & Schuster.

BBC (2011) *In Full: David Cameron's Immigration Speech*, 14 April, www.bbc.co.uk/news/uk-politics-13083781.

BBC (2017) *At Lunch with . . . Angela Rayner*, Radio 4, 17 October, www.bbc.co.uk/sounds/play/p05k6qns.

BBC (2019a) *Europe and Right-Wing Nationalism: A Country-by-Country Guide*, 13 November, www.bbc.co.uk/news/world-europe-36130006.

BBC (2019b) 'Whorlton Hall: hospital "abused" vulnerable adults', 22 May, www.bbc.co.uk/news/health-48367071.

BBC (2020a) *Earlier lockdown would have halved death toll*, 10 June, www.bbc.co.uk/news/health-52995064.

BBC (2020b) *Pick of the Week*, Radio 4, 2 August.

Béland, D. (2009) 'Ideas, institutions, and policy change', *Journal of European Public Policy*, 16(5): 701–18.

Béland, D., and Mahon, R. (2016) *Advanced Introduction to Social Policy*. Cheltenham: Edward Elgar.

Bennett, F. (2012) 'Universal Credit: overview and gender implications', in M. Kilkey, G. Ramia and K. Farnsworth (eds), *Social Policy Review 24*. Bristol: Policy Press.

Bennett, F. (2019) 'UK: changing politics of crisis management', in S. Ólafsson et al. (eds), *Welfare and the Great Recession: A Comparative Study*. Oxford: Oxford University Press.

Beresford, P. (2016) *All Our Welfare: Towards Participatory Social Policy*. Bristol: Policy Press.

Beresford, P., and Croft, S. (1986) *Whose Welfare? Private Care or Public Services*. Brighton: Lewis Cohen Urban Studies Centre.

Bettio, F., Simonazzi, A., and Villa. P. (2006) 'Change in care regimes and female migration: the care drain in the Mediterranean', *Journal of European Social Policy*, 16(3): 271–85.

Bhambra, G. K. (2014) 'Postcolonial and decolonial dialogues', *Postcolonial Studies*, 17(2): 115–21.

Bhambra, G. K. (2017) 'Brexit, Trump and "methodological whiteness": on the misrecognition of race and class', *British Journal of Sociology*, 68(S1): 214–32.

Bhambra, G. K., and Holmwood, J. (2018) 'Colonialism, postcolonialism and the liberal welfare state', *New Political Economy*, 23(5): 574–87.

Bhambra, G. K., Gebrial, D., and Nişancioğlu, K. (2018) *Decolonising the University*. London: Pluto Press.

Bhattacharya, T. (ed.) (2017) *Social Reproduction Theory: Remapping Class, Recentering Oppression*. London: Pluto Press.

Bhattacharyya, G. (2018) *Rethinking Racial Capitalism*. London: Rowman & Littlefield.

Bhavnani, K.-K., and Coulson, M. (1986) 'Transforming socialist-feminism: the challenge of racism', *Feminist Review* 23(1): 82–91.

Bhopal, K. (2018) *White Privilege: The Myth of a Post-Racial Society*. Bristol: Policy Press.

BIEN (Basic Income Earth Network) (2020) 'About basic income', https://basicincome.org/about-basic-income/.

Blythe, M. (2013) *Austerity: The History of a Dangerous Idea*. Cambridge: Cambridge University Press.

Boddy, J., Phoenix, A., Walker, C., Venman, U., Austerberry, H., and Latha, M. (2016) 'Telling "moral tales"? Family narratives of responsible privilege and environmental concern in India and the UK', *Families, Relationships and Societies*, 5(3): 357–74.

Bogues A. (2010) *Empire and Liberty: Power, Desire and Freedom*. Hanover, NH: Dartmouth College Press.

Bogues, A. (2020) 'Black Lives Matter and the moment of the now', *b2o: an online journal*, 28 July, www.boundary2.org/2020/07/anthony-bogues-black-lives-matter-and-the-moment-of-the-now/.

Bone, K. M. (2017) 'Trapped behind the glass: crip theory and disability identity', *Disability & Society*, 32(9): 1297–314.

Bonoli, G. (2007) 'Time matters: postindustrialization, new social risks, and welfare state adaptation in advanced industrial democracies', *Comparative Political Studies*, 40(5): 495–520.

Boris, E. (1995) 'The racialized gendered state: constructions of citizenship in the United States', *Social Politics*, 2(2): 160–80.

Boris, E., and Undén, M. (2017) 'From the local to the global: circuits of domestic worker organizing', in S. Michel and I. Peng (eds), *Gender, Migration, and the Work of Care: A Multi-Scalar Approach to the Pacific Rim*. Basingstoke: Palgrave.

Bovenkerk, F., Miles, R., and Verbunt, G. (1990) 'Racism, migration and the state in Western Europe: a case for comparative analysis', *International Sociology*, 5(4): 475–90.

Bovill, C., Cook-Sather, A., and Felten, P. (2011) 'Students as co-creators of teaching approaches, course design, and curricula: implications for academic developers', *International Journal for Academic Development*, 16(2): 133–45.

Boyd, M. (2017) 'Assessing Canada's changing policy for migrant caregivers', in S. Michel and I. Peng (eds), *Gender, Migration, and the Work of Care: A Multi-Scalar Approach to the Pacific Rim*. Basingstoke: Palgrave.

Boyson, R. (1971) *Down with the Poor: An Analysis of the Failure of the 'Welfare State' and a Plan to End Poverty*. London: Churchill Press.

Bradby, H., Lindenmeyer, A., Phillimore, J., Padilla, B., and Brand, T. (2020) '"If there were doctors who could understand our problems, I would already be better": dissatisfactory health care and marginalisation in superdiverse neighbourhoods', *Sociology of Health & Illness*, 42(4): 739–57.

Brah, A. (1996) *Cartographies of Diaspora: Contesting Identities*. London: Routledge.

Braidotti, R. (2013) *The Posthuman*. Cambridge: Polity.

Brennan, D., and Oloman, M. (2009) 'Child care in Australia: a market failure and spectacular public policy disaster', Canadian Centre for Policy Alternatives; www.policyalternatives.ca/sites/default/files/uploads/publications/National%20Office/2009/04/Child%20Care%20in%20Australia.pdf.

Brennan, D., Charlesworth, S., Adamson, E., and Cortis, N. (2017) 'Changing patterns of care, migration and employment regulation in Australia: assessing Canada's changing policy for migrant caregivers', in S. Michel and I. Peng (eds), *Gender, Migration, and the Work of Care: A Multi-Scalar Approach to the Pacific Rim*. Basingstoke: Palgrave.

Brown, J. (2020) *Police Powers: Stop and Search*, House of Commons briefing paper no. 3878, 4 November, https://researchbriefings.files.parliament.uk/documents/SN03878/SN03878.pdf.

Brown, W. (2015) *Undoing the Demos: Neoliberalism's Stealth Revolution*. New York: Zone Books.

Brubaker, W. R. (1990) 'Immigration, citizenship and the nation-state in France and Germany: a comparative historical analysis', *International Sociology*, 5(4): 379–407.

Bruzelius, C., and Shutes, I. (2019) 'Mobility and the making of migrants in welfare states research', Paper presented at the ESPAnet Conference, University of Stockholm, September.

Bryan, B., Dadzie, S., and Scafe, S. (1985) *The Heart of the Race: Black Women's Lives in Britain*. London: Virago.

Bulkely, H., Edwards, G. A. S., and Fuller, S. (2014) 'Contesting climate justice in the city: examining politics and practice in urban climate change experiments', *Global Environmental Change*, 25: 31–40.

Bunting, M. (2020) *Labours of Love: The Crisis of Care*. London: Granta.

Burch, L. (2018) '"You are a parasite on the productive classes": online disablist hate speech in austere times', *Disability & Society*, 33(3): 391–415.

Burgen, S., and Jones, S. (2020) 'Poor and vulnerable hardest hit by pandemic in Spain', *The Guardian*, 1 April, www.theguardian.com/world/2020/apr/01/poor-and-vulnerable-hardest-hit-by-pandemic-in-spain.

Burgess-Macy, C., Kelly, C., and Ouvry, M. (2021) 'Rethinking early years: how the neoliberal agenda fails children', in D. Featherstone (ed.), *Soundings 76: Goodbye 2020*; www.lwbooks.co.uk/soundings/76.

Butler, J. (1990) *Gender Trouble: Feminism and the Subversion of Identity*. London: Routledge.

Byrne, B., Alexander, C., Khan, O., Nazroo, J., and Shankley, W. (eds) (2020) *Ethnicity, Race and Inequality in the UK: State of the Nation*. Bristol: Policy Press.

Cabinet Office (2018) *Race Disparity Audit Summary Findings from the Ethnicity Facts and Figures Website*. London: Cabinet Office; https://assets.publishing.service.gov.uk/government/uploads/system/uploads/attachment_data/file/686071/Revised_RDA_report_March_2018.pdf.

Cahill, M. (2002) *The Environment and Social Policy*. London: Routledge.

Calhoun, C. (2009) 'Cosmopolitan Europe and European studies', in C. Rumford (ed.), *The Sage Handbook of European Studies*. London: Sage, pp. 637–54.

Calhoun, C. (2016) 'Brexit is a mutiny against the cosmopolitan elite', *New Perspectives Quarterly*, 33(3): 50–8; https://onlinelibrary.wiley.com/doi/10.1111/npqu.12048.

Cameron, D. (2010) 'We must tackle Britain's massive deficit and growing debt', 7 June, https://conservative-speeches.sayit.mysociety.org/speech/601466.

Cameron, D. (2011) 'PM statement on violence in England', speech delivered in the House of Commons, 11 August, www.gov.uk/government/speeches/pm-statement-on-violence-in-england.

Campbell, B. (2013) *End of Equality: The Only Way is Women's Liberation*. London: Seagull Books.

Campbell, J., and Oliver, M. (1996) *Disability Politics: Understanding Our Past, Changing Our Future*. London: Routledge.

Cangiano, A., Shutes, I., Spenser, S., and Leeson, G. (2009) *Migrant Care Workers in Ageing Societies: Research Findings in the UK*. Oxford: COMPAS.

Cantat, C., and Rajaram, P. K. (2019) 'The politics of the refugee crisis in Hungary: bordering and ordering the nation and its others', in C. Menjívar, M. Ruiz and I. Ness (eds), *The Oxford Handbook of Migration Crises*. Oxford: Oxford University Press.

Cantle, T. (2001) *Community Cohesion: A Report of the Independent Review Team*. London: Home Office.

Carastathis, A. (2016) *Intersectionality: Origins, Contestations, Horizons*. Lincoln: University of Nebraska Press.

Carbonnier, C., and Morel, N. (2015) *The Political Economy of Household Services in Europe*. Basingstoke: Palgrave Macmillan.

Care Collective (2020) *The Care Manifesto*. London: Verso.

CarersUK (2011) *Half a Million Voices: Improving Support for BAME Carers*, www.carersuk.org/for-professionals/policy/policy-library/half-a-million-voices-improving-support-for-bame-carers#:~:text=Half%20a%20Million%20Voices%3A%20improving%20support%20for%20BAME%20carers,-28%20March%202011&text=This%20report%20shows%20that%20BAME,and%20with%20stereotyping%20around%20caring.

CarersUK (2019) 'Value my care', www.carersuk.org/news-and-campaigns/previous-campaigns/we-care-don-t-you/value-my-care.

CarersUK (2020) 'Our campaigns', www.carersuk.org/news-and-campaigns/campaigns.

Castles, S., and Miller, M. (1993) *The Age of Migration*. London: Macmillan.

Chakrabortty, A. (2018) 'Yes, there is an alternative. These people have shown how to "take back control"', *The Guardian*, 26 September, www.theguardian.com/commentisfree/2018/sep/26/alternatives-take-back-control-local-projects-austerity.

Chandola, T., and Zhang, N. (2018) 'Re-employment, job quality, health and allostatic load biomarkers: prospective evidence from the UK Household Longitudinal Study', *International Journal of Epidemiology*, 47(1): 47–57.

Children's Society (2012) *Into the Unknown: Children's Journeys through the Asylum Process*, https://resourcecentre.savethechildren.net/node/6755/pdf/6755.pdf.

Cho, S., Crenshaw, K. W., and McCall, L. (2013) 'Toward a field of intersectionality studies: theory, application and praxis', *Signs*, 38(4): 785–810.

Chouha, K., and Nazroo, J. (2020) 'Health inequalities', in B. Byrne et al. (eds), *Ethnicity, Race and Inequality in the UK: State of the Nation*. Bristol: Policy Press.

CHPI (Centre for Health and the Public Interest) (2017) *PFI Profits from Infirmaries*, https://chpi.org.uk/papers/reports/pfi-profiting-from-infirmaries/.

Clark, K. (2006) 'Childhood, parenting and early intervention: a critical examination of the Sure Start National Programme', *Critical Social Policy*, 26(4): 699–721.

Clark, K., and Shankley, W. (2020) 'Ethnic minorities in the labour market in Britain', in B. Byrne et al. (eds), *Ethnicity, Race and Inequality in the UK: State of the Nation*. Bristol: Policy Press.

Clark Miller, S. (2010) 'Cosmopolitan care', *Ethics and Social Welfare*, 4(2): 145–57.

Clarke, J. (2004) *Changing Welfare, Changing States: New Directions in Social Policy*. London: Sage.

Clarke, J. (2019a) 'A sense of loss? Unsettled attachments in the current conjuncture', *New Formations*, 96–7: 132–46.

Clarke, J. (2019b) 'Foreword', in N. Papanastasiou, *The Politics of Scale in Policy*. Bristol: Policy Press.

Clarke, J. (2020) 'Harmful thoughts: reimagining the coercive state?', in D. Cooper, N. Dhawan and J. Newman (eds), *Reimagining the State*. London: Routledge, pp. 213–30.

Clarke, J., and Newman, J. (1997) *The Managerial State: Power, Politics and Ideology in the Making of Social Welfare*. London: Sage.

Clarke, J., and Newman, J. (2012) 'The alchemy of austerity', *Critical Social Policy*, 32(3): 299–319.

Clarke, J., and Newman, J. (2017) '"People in this country have had enough of experts": Brexit and the paradoxes of populism', *Critical Policy Studies*, 11(1): 101–16.

Clarke, J., and Newman, J. (2019) 'What's the subject? Brexit and politics as articulation', *Journal of Community and Applied Social Psychology*, 20(1): 67–77.

Clarke, J., Collins, K., Dagnino, E., and Neveu, C. (2014) *Disputing Citizenship*. Bristol: Policy Press.

Clarke, J., Bainton, D., Lendvai, N., and Stubbs, P. (2015) *Making Policy Move: Towards a Politics of Translation and Assemblage*. Bristol: Policy Press.

Climate Assembly UK (2020) *The Path to Net Zero: Climate Assembly Full Report*, www.climateassembly.uk/report/read/index.html.

Coates, K., and Silburn, R. (1970) *Poverty: The Forgotten Englishmen*. London: Penguin.

Cochrane, A. (2019) 'From Brexit to the break-up of . . . England? Thinking in and beyond the nation', in M. Gunderjan, H. Mackay and G. Stedman (eds), *Contested Britain: Brexit, Austerity and Agency*. Bristol: Bristol University Press.

Cohen, B., and Tufail, W. (2017) 'Prevent and the normalization of Islamophobia', in F. Elahi and O. Khan (eds), *Islamophobia: Still a Challenge for Us All*. London: Runnymede Trust.

Cole, B., Craig, G., and Ali, N. (2020) '"Race": the missing dimension in social policy higher education?', in J. Rees, M. Pomati and E. Heins, *Social Policy Review 32*. Bristol: Policy Press.

Comaroff, J., and Comaroff, J. L. (2015) *Theory from the South: Or, How Euro-America is Evolving Toward Africa*. London: Routledge.

Combahee River Collective ([1977] 1995) *The CRC Statement*, http://circuitous.org/scraps/combahee.html.

Connell, J., and Buchan, J. (2011) 'The impossible dream? Codes of practice and international migration of skilled health workers', *World Medical and Health Policy*, 3(3): 1–17.

Connelly, L., and Sanders, T. (2020) 'Disrupting the boundaries of the academe: co-creating knowledge and sex work "academic-activism"', in S. Walklate,

K. Fitz-Gibbon and J. McCulloch (eds), *The Emerald Handbook of Feminism, Criminology and Social Change*. Bingley: Emerald.

Conway, J., and Singh, J. (2011) 'Radical democracy in global perspective: notes from the pluriverse', *Third World Quarterly*, 32(4): 689–706.

Cook, T., Kursumovic, E., and Lennane, S. (2020) 'Deaths of NHS staff from Covid-19 analysed', *Health Service Journal*, 22 April, www.hsj.co.uk/exclusive-deaths-of-nhs-staff-from-covid-19-analysed/7027471.article.

Coole, D., and Frost, S. (2010) *New Materialisms: Ontology, Agency and Politics*. London: Duke University Press.

Cooper, D., Dhawan, N., and Newman, J. (eds) (2020) *Reimagining the State*. London: Routledge.

Cooper, K., and Lacey, N. (2019) *Physical Safety and Security: Policies, Spending and Outcomes 2015–2020*, SPDO Research paper, Centre for Analysis of Social Exclusion, LSE; https://sticerd.lse.ac.uk/dps/case/spdo/spdorp05.pdf.

Coote, A. (2017) 'Building a new social commons: the people, the commons and the public realm', New Economics Foundation, 2 May, https://neweconomics.org/2017/05/building-new-social-commons.

Coote, A., and Franklin, J. (eds) (2013) *Time on our Side: Why we All Need a Shorter Working Week*. London: New Economics Foundation.

CoP (Commission on Poverty) (2002) *Participation and Power: An Evaluation*. York: Joseph Rowntree Foundation.

Coram Children's Legal Centre (2013) *Growing up in a Hostile Environment: The Rights of Undocumented Migrant Childen in the UK*, www.childrenslegal-centre.com/wp-content/uploads/2017/04/Hostile_Environment_Exec_summary_Final.pdf.

Cottam, H. (2018) *Radical Help: How We Can Remake the Relationships between Us and Revolutionise the Welfare State*. London: Virago.

Cottam, H. (2020) 'It's bloody complicated – with Hilary Cottam', *Compass*, 28 April, www.compassonline.org.uk/events/its-bloody-complicated-with-hilary-cottam-episode-6/ [podcast].

Cowburn, A. (2020) '"Who is in charge?" Leading UK scientist launches scathing attack on government's coronavirus response', *The Independent*, 22 May, www.independent.co.uk/news/uk/politics/coronavirus-government-science-response-criticism-nurse-nobel-a9527746.html.

Craig, G. (2007) '"Cunning, unprincipled, loathsome": the racist tail wags the welfare dog', *Journal of Social Policy*, 36(4): 605–23.

Craig, G., Cole, B., Ali, N., and Qureshi, I. (2019) *The Missing Dimension: Where Is 'Race' in Social Policy Teaching and Learning?* London: Social Policy Association.

Cranford, C., and Chun, J. J. (2017) 'Immigrant women and home-based elder care in Oakland, California's Chinatown', in S. Michel and I. Peng (eds), *Gender, Migration, and the Work of Care: A Multi-Scalar Approach to the Pacific Rim*. Basingstoke: Palgrave.

Crenshaw, K. (1989) 'Demarginalizing the intersection of race and sex: a black feminist critique of antidiscrimination doctrine, feminist theory and antiracist politics', *University of Chicago Legal Forum*: 139–67.

Crossley, S. (2016) '"Realising the (troubled) family", "crafting the neoliberal state"', *Families, Relationships and Societies*, 5(2): 263–79.

Crouch, C. (2011) *The Strange Non-Death of Neo-Liberalism*. Cambridge: Polity.

CRPD (Committee on the Rights of Persons with Disabilities) (2017) *Concluding Observations on United Kingdom*, CRPD/C/GBR/CO/1. Geneva: United Nations.

Cruz, K., Davidson, J. O., and Taylor, J. S. (2019) 'Tourism and sexual violence and exploitation in Jamaica: contesting the "trafficking and modern slavery" frame', *Journal of the British Academy*, 7(1): 189–214.

CSI (Centre for Social Investigation) (2019) 'Did hate crime double after Brexit?', Briefing no. 34, Nuffield College, Oxford University; http://csi.nuff.ox.ac.uk/wp-content/uploads/2019/06/CSI34_hate-crime.pdf.

Dagnino, E. (2007) 'Participation, democracy and citizenship: perverse consequences and displacements of meanings', in C. Neveu (ed.), *Cultures et pratiques participatives: perspectives comparatives*. Paris: L'Harmattan.

Daly, M. (2002) *Care Work: The Quest for Security*. Geneva: International Labour Office.

Daly, M. (2011) 'What adult worker model? A critical look at recent social policy reform in Europe from a gender and family perspective', *Social Politics: International Studies in Gender, State & Society*, 18(1): 1–23.

Daly, M., and Ferragina, E. (2018) 'Family policy in high-income countries: five decades of development', *Journal of European Social Policy*, 28(3): 255–70.

Daly, M., and Kelly, G. (2015) *Families and Poverty: Everyday Life on a Low Income*. Bristol: Policy Press.

Davis, A., Hirsch, D., Pedley, M., and Shepherd, C. (2018) *A Minimum Income Standard for the UK 2008–2018: Continuity and Change*. York: Joseph Rowntree Foundation.

Davis, K. (2008) 'Intersectionality as buzzword: a sociology of science perspective on what makes a feminist theory', *Successful Feminist Theory*, 9(1): 67–85.

Dawson, M. (2016) 'Hidden in plain sight: a note on legitimation crises and the racial order', *Critical Historical Studies*, 3(1): 143–61.

DBEIS (Department for Business, Energy & Industrial Strategy) (2018) *The Characteristics of Those in the Gig Economy: Final Report*, https://assets.publishing.service.gov.uk/government/uploads/system/uploads/attachment_data/file/687553/The_characteristics_of_those_in_the_gig_economy.pdf.

DBEIS (Department for Business, Energy & Industrial Strategy) (2020) *The Ten Point Plan for a Green Industrial Revolution: Policy Paper*, www.gov.uk/government/publications/the-ten-point-plan-for-a-green-industrial-revolution/title.

DCLG (Department of Communities and Local Government) (2014) 'Troubled families programme turning 117,000 lives around', www.gov.uk/govern ment/news/troubled-families-programme-turning-117000-lives-around.

DCLG (Department for Communities and Local Government) (2015) *English Indices of Deprivation, 2015*, www.gov.uk/government/statistics/english-indices-of-deprivation-2015.

DCLG (Department for Communities and Local Government) (2016) *National Evaluation of the Troubled Families Programme*, www.basw.co.uk/system/files/resources/basw_52344-7_0.pdf.

Deacon, A., and Mann, K. (1999) 'Agency, modernity, and social policy', *Journal of Social Policy*, 28(3): 413–35.

Deacon, B. (1983) *Social Policy and Socialism: The Struggle for Socialist Relations of Welfare*. London: Pluto Press.

Deacon, B. (ed.) (1992) *The New Eastern Europe: Social Policy Past, Present and Future*. London: Sage.

Deacon, B. (2007) *Global Social Policy and Governance*. London: Sage.

Deacon, B. (2013) *Global Social Policy in the Making: The Foundations of the Social Protection Floor*. Bristol: Policy Press.

Deacon, B., and Castle-Kanerova, M. (1992) *The New Eastern Europe: Social Policy Past, Present and Future*. London: Sage.

de Genova, N. (2018) 'The "migrant crisis" as racial crisis: do Black Lives Matter in Europe?', *Ethnic and Racial Studies*, 41(10): 1765–82.

de Haas, H. (2010) 'Migration and development: a theoretical perspective', *International Migration Review*, 44(1): 227–64.

Dean, J., and Maiguashca, B. (2018) 'Gender, power, and left politics: from feminization to "feministization"', *Politics & Gender*, 14(3): 376–406.

Deleuze, G., and Guattari, F. ([1972] 1984) *Anti-Oedipus: Capitalism and Schizophrenia*. London: Athlone Press.

Dennis, N., and Erdos, G. (1992) *Families without Fatherhood*. London: IEA Health and Welfare Unit.

di Martino, A., Biondo Dal Monte, F., Boiasno, I., and Raffaelli, R. (2013) *The Criminalization of Irregular Immigration: Law and Practice in Italy*. Pisa: University of Pisa Press.

Diana, P. (2018) *Saving the World*. London: Quartet Books.

Dobson, R. (2020) 'Local government and practice ontologies: agency, resistance and sector speaks in homelessness services', *Local Government Studies*, 46(4): 583–603.

Dorling, D. (2011) 'Unique Britain', Open Democracy, 15 May, www.opendemocracy.net/en/shine-a-light/unique-britain/.

Dorling, D. (2016) 'Brexit: the decision of a divided country', *BMJ*, 6 July, www.bmj.com/content/354/bmj.i3697.

Dorling, D. (2020) 'Want to understand the Covid map? Look at where we live and how we work', *The Observer*, 29 November, www.theguardian.com/

commentisfree/2020/nov/29/want-to-understand-the-covid-map-look-at-where-we-live-and-how-we-work.

Dowling, E. (2017) 'In the wake of austerity: social impact bonds and the financialisation of the welfare state in Britain', *New Political Economy*, 22(3): 294–310.

Doyal, L., and Gough, I. (1991) *A Theory of Human Need*. London: Macmillan.

Duffy, N. (2019) 'Cabinet shifts against LGBT rights as Therese Coffey replaces Amber Rudd', www.pinknews.co.uk/2019/09/08/cabinet-shifts-against-lgbt-rights-as-therese-coffey-replaces-amber-rudd/.

Duncan, S., and Edwards, R. (1999) *Lone Mothers, Paid Work and Gendered Moral Responsibilities*. London: Palgrave Macmillan.

Duncan, S., and Smith, D. (2002) 'Geographies of family formations: spatial differences and gender cultures in Britain', *Transactions of the Institute of British Geographers*, 27: 471–93.

Duncan, S., Edwards, R., Reynolds, T., and Alldred, P. (2003) 'Motherhood, paid work and partnering: values and theories', *Work, Employment and Society*, 17(2): 309–30.

Duncan Smith, I. (2006) *Breakdown Britain*. London. Social Justice Policy Group.

Dunford, R. (2017) 'Toward a decolonial global ethics', *Journal of Global Ethics*, 13(3): 380–97.

Dussel, E. (2013) *Ethics of Liberation in an age of Globalization and Exclusion*. Durham, NC: Duke University Press.

Dwyer, P. J. (2016) 'Citizenship, conduct and conditionality: sanction and support in the 21st century UK welfare state', in M. Fenger, J. Hudson and C. Needham (eds), *Social Policy Review 28*. Bristol: Policy Press

Dwyer, P. J. (2018) 'Punitive and ineffective: benefit sanctions within social security', *Journal of Social Security Law*, 25(3): 142–57.

Eddo-Lodge, R. (2017) *Why I'm No Longer Talking to White People about Race*. London: Bloomsbury.

Edmiston, D. (2018) *Welfare Inequality and Social Citizenship: Deprivation and Affluence in Austerity Britain*. Bristol: Policy Press.

Edmiston, D. (forthcoming) 'Plumbing the depths: the changing (socio-demographic) profile of poverty', *Journal of Social Policy*.

Edmiston, D., and Humpage, L. (2018) 'Resistance or resignation to welfare reform? The activist politics for and against social citizenship', *Policy & Politics*, 46(3): 467–84.

Ehrenreich, B., and Hochschild, A. (eds) (2003) *Global Woman: Nannies, Maids and Sex Workers in the New Economy*. London: Granta.

Elliott, L., Carrell, S., and Stewart, H. (2019) 'McCluskey sparks Labour backlash over tough line on free movement', *The Guardian*, 13 November, www.theguardian.com/politics/2019/nov/13/mccluskey-tells-corbyn-defy-calls-extend-freedom-of-movement.

Ellison, N. (2017) 'The whys and wherefores of Brexit', in J. Hudson, C. Needham and E. Heins (eds), *Social Policy Review 29*. Bristol: Policy Press, pp. 3–22.

Emejulu, A., and Bassel, L. (2018) 'Austerity and the politics of becoming', *Journal of Common Market Studies*, 56(S1): 109–19.

ENDS Report (2009) 'UK notification to the European Commission to extend the compliance deadline in meeting PM10 limit values in ambient air to 2011', https://web.archive.org/web/20110710192634/http://www.ends report.com/docs/20090820a.pdf.

Engster, D. (2007) *The Heart of Justice: Care Ethics and Political Theory*. Oxford: Oxford University Press.

Escobar, A. (2004) 'Beyond the Third World: imperial globality, global coloniality and anti-globalisation social movements', *Third World Quarterly*, 25(1): 207–30.

Escobar, A. (2007) 'Worlds and knowledges otherwise', *Cultural Studies*, 21(2–3): 179–210.

Esping-Andersen, G. (1990) *The Three Worlds of Welfare Capitalism*. Cambridge: Polity.

Esping-Andersen, G. (1999) *Social Foundations of Postindustrial Economies*. Oxford: Oxford University Press.

Esping-Andersen, G. (2009) *The Incomplete Revolution: Adapting to Women's New Roles*. Cambridge: Polity.

Esquivel, V., and Kaufmann, A. (2017) *Innovations in Care: New Concepts, New Actors, New Policies*. Berlin: Friedrich Ebert.

European Women's Lobby (1995) *Confronting the Fortress: Black and Migrant Women in the European Union*. Brussels: European Parliament.

Faist, T. (1995) 'Ethnicization and racialization of welfare-state politics in Germany and the USA', *Ethnic and Racial Studies*, 18(20): 219–50.

Faist, T. (2018) *The Transnationalized Social Question: Migration and the Question of Social Inequalities in the Twenty-First Century*. Oxford: Oxford University Press.

Fanon, F. ([1952] 2008) *Black Skin, White Masks*. London: Pluto Press.

Farnsworth, K., and Irving, Z. (eds) (2015) *Social Policy in Times of Austerity: Global Economic Crisis and the New Politics of Welfare*. Bristol: Policy Press.

Fawcett Society (2012) *The Impact of Austerity on Women*, www.fawcettsociety.org.uk/the-impact-of-austerity-on-women.

Fawcett Society (2015) *Where's the Benefit? An Independent Inquiry into Women and Jobseeker's Allowance*, www.fawcettsociety.org.uk/wheres-the-benefit.

Featherstone, B., White, S., and Morris, K. (2014) *Re-Imagining Child Protection: Towards Humane Social Work with Families*. Bristol: Policy Press.

Featherstone, D., Littler, J., and Davison, S. (eds) (2020) *Soundings, 74: New Municipal Alternatives*, www.lwbooks.co.uk/soundings/74.

Federici, S. (2012) *Revolution at Point Zero: Housework, Reproduction, and Feminist Struggle*. Oakland: PM Press.

Finch, J., and Groves, D. (1983) *A Labour of Love: Women, Work, and Caring*. London: Routledge & Kegan Paul.

Fish, J. N. (2017) *Domestic Workers of the World Unite! A Global Movement for Dignity and Human Rights*. New York: New York University Press.

Fitzpatrick, T. (2011) *Understanding the Environment and Social Policy*. Bristol: Policy Press.

Fitzpatrick, T. (2014) *Climate Change and Poverty: A New Agenda for Developed Nations*. Bristol: Policy Press.

Fitzpatrick, T., and Cahill, M. (eds) (2002) *Environment and Welfare: Towards a Green Social Policy*. Basingstoke: Palgrave Macmillan.

Floro, M. S. (2012) *The Crises of Environment and Social Reproduction: Understanding Their Linkages*, Working Papers 2012-04, American University, Department of Economics, https://ideas.repec.org/p/amu/wpaper/2012-04.html.

Flynn, R., and Craig, G. (2019) 'Policy, politics and practice: a historic review and its relevance to current debates', in G. Craig et al. (eds), *Understanding 'Race' and Ethnicity*. Bristol: Policy Press.

Food Foundation (2020) 'Vulnerable groups: who is at risk and how are they being helped?', https://foodfoundation.org.uk/vulnerable-groups/.

Fox, A. (2018) *A New Health and Care System: Escaping the Invisible Asylum*. Bristol: Policy Press.

Franklin, B., and Brancati, C. U. (2015) *Moved to Care: The Impact of Migration on the Adult Social Care Workforce*. London: Independent Age; https://independent-age-assets.s3.eu-west-1.amazonaws.com/s3fs-public/2016-05/IA%20Moved%20to%20care%20report_12%2011%2015.pdf.

Franzoni, J. (2008) 'Welfare regimes in Latin America: capturing constellations of markets, families, and policies', *Latin American Politics and Society*, 50(2): 67–100.

Fraser, N. (1995) 'From redistribution to recognition? Dilemmas of justice in a "post-socialist" age', *New Left Review*, I/212: 68–92.

Fraser, N. (2009) 'Feminism, capitalism and the cunning of history', *New Left Review*, 56: 97–117.

Fraser, N. (2013) 'A triple movement? Parsing the politics of crisis after Polanyi', *New Left Review*, 81: 119–32.

Fraser, N. (2016a) 'Expropriation and exploitation in racialized capitalism: a reply to Michael Dawson', *Critical Historical Studies*, 3(1): 163–78.

Fraser, N. (2016b) 'Contradictions of capital and care', *New Left Review*, 100: 99–117.

Froggett, L. (2002) *Love, Hate and Welfare*. Bristol: Policy Press.

Fryer, P. (1984) *Staying Power: The History of Black People in Britain*. London: Pluto Press.

Geiger, M., and Pécoud, A. (eds) (2010) *The Politics of International Migration Management*. Basingstoke: Palgrave Macmillan.

Gentleman, A. (2019) *The Windrush Betrayal: Exposing the Hostile Environment*. London: Guardian Books.

GEO (Gender Equalities Office) (2018) *LGBT Action Plan 2018: Improving the Lives of Lesbian, Gay, Bisexual and Transgender People*, www.gov.uk/government/publications/lgbt-action-plan-2018-improving-the-lives-of-lesbian-gay-bisexual-and-transgender-people.

Gewirtz, S. (2001) 'Cloning the Blairs: New Labour's programme for the re-socialization of working-class parents', *Journal of Education Policy*, 16(4): 365–78.

GHSI (2019) *Global Health Security Index: Building Collective Action and Accountability*, www.ghsindex.org/wp-content/uploads/2020/04/2019-Global-Health-Security-Index.pdf.

Gilbert, A. (2020) '"Take back control": English new municipalism and the question of belonging', in D. Featherstone, J. Littler and S. Davison (eds), *Soundings, 74: New Municipal Alternatives*, www.lwbooks.co.uk/soundings/74/%E2%80%98take-back-control%E2%80%99-english-new-municipalism-and-the-question-of-belonging.

Gill, S. (2019) 'Towards planetary governance?', *Global Affairs*, 5(2): 131–7.

Gilligan, C. (1982) *In a Different Voice*. Cambridge, MA: Harvard University Press.

Gilroy, P. (2000) *Against Race: Imagining Political Culture beyond the Color Line*. Cambridge, MA: Harvard University Press.

Gilroy, P. (2005) *Postcolonial Melancholia*. New York: Columbia University Press.

Gilroy, P. (2014) *The Tanner Lectures on Human Values*, delivered at Yale University, 21 February, https://tannerlectures.utah.edu/Gilroy%20manuscript%20PDF.pdf.

Ginsburg, N. (1979) *Class, Capital and Social Policy*. London: Macmillan.

Ginsburg, N. (1992) *Divisions of Welfare: A Critical Introduction to Comparative Social Policy*. London: Sage.

Gitlin, T. (1995) *The Twilight of Common Dreams: Why America is Wracked by Culture Wars*. New York: Metropolitan Books.

Glenn, E. N. (1992) 'From servitude to service work: historical continuities in the racial division of women's paid reproductive labour', *Signs*, 18(1): 1–44.

Glenn, E. N. (2002) *Unequal Freedom: How Race and Gender Shaped American Freedom and Labor*. Cambridge, MA: Harvard University Press.

Goldberg, D. T. (2015) *Are We All Postracial Yet?* (Cambridge: Polity).

Goodfellow, M. (2018) '"Race" and racism in the UK', in L. Macfarlane (ed.), *New Thinking for the British Economy*. London: Open Democracy; www.opendemocracy.net/en/opendemocracyuk/new-thinking-for-the-british-economy/.

Goodhart, D. (2004) 'Too diverse?' *Prospect*, 20 February, www.prospectmaga zine.co.uk/magazine/too-diverse-david-goodhart-multiculturalism-brit ain-immigration-globalisation.

Goodhart, D. (2017) *The Road to Somewhere: The Populist Revolt and the Future of Politics*. Oxford: Oxford University Press.

Goodley, D., Lawthom, R., and Runswick-Cole, K. (2014) 'Posthuman disability studies', *Subjectivity*, 7: 342–61.

Gordon, L. (1988) *Heroes of Their Own Lives: The Politics and History of Family Violence – Boston, 1880–1960*. New York: Viking.

Goss, S. (2020) *Garden Mind: An Eco-System View of Change and a Different Role for the State*. London: Compass.

Gough, I. (1979) *The Political Economy of the Welfare State*. London: Macmillan.

Gough, I. (2017) *Heat, Greed and Human Needs*. Cheltenham: Edward Elgar.

Gough, I., Wood, G., Barrientos, A., Bevan, P., Davis, P., and Room, G. (2004) *Insecurity and Welfare Regimes in Asia, Africa and Latin America: Social Policy in Development Contexts*. Cambridge: Cambridge University Press.

Gramsci, A. (1971) *Selections from the Prison Notebooks*. London: Lawrence & Wishart.

Gray, H., and Franck, A. K. (2019) 'Refugees as/at risk: the gendered and racialized underpinnings of securitization in British media narratives', *Security Dialogue*, 50(3): 275–91.

Gregson, N., and Lowe, M. (1994) *Servicing the Middle Classes: Class, Gender and Waged Domestic Labour in Contemporary Britain*. London: Routledge.

Grierson, J. (2020) '"I live in fear of the unknown": life in a refuge under lockdown', *The Guardian*, 21 May, www.theguardian.com/society/2020/may/21/i-live-in-fear-of-the-unknown-life-in-a-refuge-under-lockdown.

Griffin, M. (2018) 'Brexit adverts used by Leave campaign in Facebook revealed', *The Independent*, 26 July, www.independent.co.uk/life-style/gadgets-and-tech/news/brexit-facebook-ads-leave-campaign-nhs-immigrat ion-boris-johnson-a8465516.html.

Grosfoguel, R. (2011) 'Decolonizing post-colonial studies and paradigms of political-economy: transmodernity, decolonial thinking, and global coloniality', *Transmodernity: Journal of Peripheral Cultural Production of the Luso-Hispanic World*, 1(1), https://escholarship.org/content/qt21k6t3fq/qt21k6 t3fq.pdf.

The Guardian (2020) 'How coronavirus advice from Boris Johnson has changed', 23 March, www.theguardian.com/world/2020/mar/23/how-coronavirus-advice-from-boris-johnson-has-changed.

Guentner, S., Lukes, S., Stanton, R., Vollmer, B. A., and Wilding, J. (2016) 'Bordering practices in the UK welfare system', *Critical Social Policy*, 36(3): 391–411.

Guevarra, A. R. (2010) *Marketing Dreams, Manufacturing Heroes: The*

Transnational Labour Brokering of Filipino Workers. New Brunswick, NJ: Rutgers University Press.

Gustafsson, M. (2020) *Young Workers in the Corona Virus Crisis*, www.resolution foundation.org/publications/young-workers-in-the-coronavirus-crisis/.

Gutiérrez Rodríguez, E. (2014) 'Domestic work – affective labor: on feminizat ion and the coloniality of labor', *Women's Studies International Forum*, 46: 45–53.

Gyimah, S. (2015) Speech to Nursery World Business Summit, London, 11 November.

Hagan, A. (2018) 'The Tower', *London Review of Books*, 7 June.

Hall, P. (1993) 'Policy paradigms, social learning and the state: the case of economic policy-making in Britain', *Comparative Politics*, 25(3): 225–96.

Hall, P., and Soskice, D. (eds) (2001) *Varieties of Capitalism*. Oxford: Oxford University Press.

Hall, S. (1996) 'Introduction: who needs identity?', in S. Hall and P. Du Gay (eds), *Questions of Cultural Identity*. London: Sage.

Hall, S. (2011) 'The neo-liberal revolution', *Cultural Studies*, 25(6): 705–28.

Hall, S., Critcher, C., Jefferson, T., Clarke, J., and Roberts, B. (1978) *Policing the Crisis: Mugging, the State and Law and Order*. London: Macmillan.

Hall, S. M. (2020) 'The personal is political: feminist geographies of/in auster ity', *Geoforum*, 110(20): 242–51.

Halliday, J. (2020) 'Covid-19 strategy too nationally driven, warn regional mayors', *The Guardian*, 19 May, www.theguardian.com/world/2020/may/18/covid-19-strategy-too-nationally-driven-warn-uks-regional-mayors.

Halvorsen, R., Hvinden, B., Bickenbach, J., Ferri, D., and Guillén Rodriguez, A. M. (eds) (2017) *The Changing Disability Policy System: Active Citizenship and Disability in Europe*, Vol. 1. London: Routledge.

Hammar, T. (1990) *Democracy and the Nation State*. Aldershot: Avebury.

Hancock, A.-M. (2016) *Intersectionality: An Intellectual History*. New York: Oxford University Press.

Hankivsky, O. (2014) 'Rethinking care ethics: on the promise and potential of an intersectional analysis', *American Political Science Review*, 108(2): 252–64.

Hankivsky, O., and Jordan-Zachery, J. (eds) (2019) *The Palgrave Handbook of Intersectionality in Public Policy*. London: Palgrave Macmillan.

Harper, A., and Martin, A. (2018) *Achieving a Shorter Working Week in the UK*. London: New Economics Foundation.

Hartnell, C., and Knight, B. (2019) 'Supporting local initiatives: the state we need', Rethinking Poverty, 23 January, www.rethinkingpoverty.org.uk/45-degree-change/the-state-we-want/.

Hayden, C., and Jenkins, C. (2014) '"Troubled Families" Programme in England: "wicked problems" and policy-based evidence', *Policy Studies*, 35(6): 631–49.

Held, D. (2002) 'Law of states: law of peoples', *Legal Theory*, 8(1): 1–44.

Held, V. (2006) *The Ethics of Care: Personal, Political and Global*. 2nd edn, Oxford: Oxford University Press.

Hellesund, T., Roseneil, S., Crowhurst, I., Santos, A. C.,and Stoilova, M. (2019) 'Narrating and relating to ordinariness: experiences of unconventional intimacies in contemporary Europe', *Ethnologia Scandinavica: A Journal for Nordic Ethnology*, 49: 92–113.

Hellgren, Z., and Serrano, I. (2017) 'Transnationalism and financial crisis: the hampered migration projects of female domestic workers in Spain', *Social Sciences*, 6(8): 2–18.

Hesse, B. (2011) 'Self-fulfilling prophecy: the postracial horizon', *South Atlantic Quarterly*, 110(1): 155–78.

Hesse, B. (2014) 'Racism's alterity: the after-life of black sociology', in W. D. Hund and A. Lentin (eds), *Racism and Sociology*. Zurich: LIT, pp. 141–74.

Heyzer, N., a'Nijeholt, G. L., and Weerakoon, N. (1994) *The Trade in Domestic Workers*, Vol.1. London: Zed Press.

Hill, K., and Hirsch, D. (2019) *Family Sharing – a Minimum Income Standard for People in their 20s Living with Parents*. Loughborough: Centre for Research in Social Policy Loughborough University.

Hill Collins, P. (1990) *Black Feminist Thought: Consciousness and the Politics of Empowerment*. Boston: Unwin Hyman.

Hill Collins, P., and Bilge, S. (2016) *Intersectionality*. Cambridge: Polity.

Hills, J. (2017) *Good Times, Bad Times: The Welfare Myth of Them and Us*. Bristol: Policy Press.

Himmelweit, S. (2018) 'Transforming care', in L. Macfarlane (ed.), *New Thinking for the British Economy*. London: Open Democracy; www.opendemocracy. net/en/opendemocracyuk/new-thinking-for-the-british-economy/.

Hines, S. (2013) *Gender Diversity, Recognition and Citizenship: Towards a Politics of Difference*. Basingstoke: Palgrave Macmillan.

Hines, S., Davy, Z., Monro, S., Motmans, J., Santos, A. C., and Van Der Ros, J. (2018) 'Introduction to the themed issue: Trans* policy, practice and lived experience within a European context', *Critical Social Policy*, 38(1): 5–12.

Hirano, H. (2020) 'Social citizenship guarantee for minorities in Japan: present and future', *International Journal of Japanese Sociology*, 29(1): 8–21.

HM Revenue & Customs and DWP (Department for Work & Pensions) (2019) *Child Tax Credit and Universal Credit claimants, 2 April 2019* https://assets.publishing.service.gov.uk/government/uploads/system/uploads/attachment_data/file/821773/Two_children_and_exceptions_in_tax_credits_and_Universal_Credit_April_2019.pdf.

Hobolt, S. B. (2016) 'The Brexit vote: a divided nation, a divided continent', *Journal of European Public Policy*, 23(9): 1259–77.

Hobson, B. (ed.) (2003) *Recognition Struggles and Social Movements: Contested Identities, Power and Agency*. Cambridge: Cambridge University Press.

Hochschild, A. R. (2016) *Strangers in Their Own Land: Anger and Mourning on the American Right*. New York: New Press.

Hodkinson, S. (2018) 'Grenfell foretold: a very neoliberal tragedy', in C. Needham, E. Heins and J. Rees (eds), *Social Policy Review 30*: 5–26.

Hoggett, P. (2000) *Emotional Life and the Politics of Welfare*. London: Palgrave MacMillan.

Hoggett, P. (2001) 'Agency, rationality and social policy', *Journal of Social Policy*, 30(1): 37–56.

Hoggett, P. (ed.) (2019) *Climate Psychology: On Indifference to Disaster*. New York: Springer.

Hollo, T. (2019) 'Towards ecological democracy – a political theory for the 21st century', Presentation given to the Fenner School of Environment and Society, Australian National University, 20 August, https://fennerschool.anu.edu.au/news-events/events/seminar-towards-ecological-democracy-political-theory-21st-century.

Hollway, W. (2006) *The Capacity to Care: Gender and Ethical Subjectivity*. London: Routledge.

Home Office (2018) *Hate Crime, England and Wales, 2017/18*, https://assets.publishing.service.gov.uk/government/uploads/system/uploads/attachment_data/file/748598/hate-crime-1718-hosb2018.pdf.

Home Office (2019) 'Fact sheet: right-wing terrorism', https://homeofficemedia.blog.gov.uk/2019/03/19/factsheet-right-wing-terrorism/.

Hondagneu-Sotelo, P. (2001) *Domestica: Immigrant Workers Cleaning and Caring in the Shadows of Affluence*. Berkeley: University of California Press.

Hong, L. (2017) 'Fractured elder care in China: rural–urban dualism among workers in Shanghai', in S. Michel and I. Peng (eds), *Gender, Migration, and the Work of Care: A Multi-Scalar Approach to the Pacific Rim*. Basingstoke: Palgrave.

Honneth, A. (1995) *The Struggle for Recognition: The Moral Grammar of Social Conflict*. Cambridge: Polity.

hooks, b. (1981) *Ain't I a Woman? Black Women and Feminism*. Boston: South End Press.

Hope, C. (2016) 'Boris Johnson hails Brexit victory', *The Telegraph*, 24 June, https://www.telegraph.co.uk/news/2016/06/24/boris-johnson-hails-brexit-victory---full-statement/.

Hopkins, N. (2019) 'Grenfell: toxic contamination found in nearby homes and soil', *The Guardian*, 28 March, www.theguardian.com/uk-news/2019/mar/28/grenfell-toxic-contamination-found-in-nearby-homes-and-soil.

Hoskyns, C. (1996) *Integrating Gender: Women, Law and Politics in the European Union*. London: Verso.

House of Commons (2009) *The Nationalisation of Northern Rock: Report by the Public Accounts Committee*, HC 394, https://publications.parliament.uk/pa/cm200809/cmselect/cmpubacc/394/394.pdf.

House of Commons (2019) 'Committee questions Amber Rudd on benefit levels "driving destitution and poverty"', 4 March 2019, https://old.parlia ment.uk/business/committees/committees-a-z/commons-select/work-and-pensions-committee/news-parliament-2017/benefit-freeze-evidence-session-17-19/.

House of Commons (2020) *Work and Pensions Committee on DWP Preparations for the World of Work: Written Evidence from Baroness/Professor Ruth Lister,* PCW0017, https://committees.parliament.uk/work/302/dwps-preparations-for-changes-in-the-world-of-work/publications/written-evidence/?page=2.

House of Lords Library (2020) 'Domestic abuse in the UK: government support', 21 October, https://lordslibrary.parliament.uk/domestic-abuse-in-the-uk-government-support/.

Hudson, B. (2016) *The Failure of Socialised Private Care in England: What Is to Be Done?,* Centre for Health and the Public Interest, https://chpi.org.uk/wp-content/uploads/2016/11/CHPI-SocialCare-Oct16-Proof01a.pdf.

Hull, G. T., Bell Scott, P., and Smith, B. (1982) *All the Women Are White, All the Blacks Are Men: But Some of Us Are Brave.* New York: Feminist Press.

Humphris, R. (2019) *Home-Land: Romanian Roma, Domestic Spaces and the State.* Bristol: Bristol University Press.

Hunter, S. (2003) 'A critical analysis of approaches to the concept of social identity in social policy', *Critical Social Policy,* 23(3): 322–44.

Hunter, S. (2015) *Power, Politics and the Emotions: Impossible Governance.* London: Routledge.

Hutton, C., and Lukes, S. (2015) *Models of Accommodation and Support for Migrants with No Recourse to Public Funds (NRPF): A Resource for Practitioners and Groups Who Want to Get Involved,* www.homeless.org.uk/sites/default/files/site-attachments/Models-of-accommodation-and-support-for-migrants-with-NRPF.pdf.

IFS (Institute for Fiscal Studies) (2019) 'English council funding: what's happened and what's next?', Briefing Note, 29 May.

IFS (Institute for Fiscal Studies) (2020) 'The economic response to coronavirus will substantially increase government borrowing', 26 March, www.ifs.org.uk/publications/14771.

IHE (Institute of Health Equity) (2020) *Health Equity in England: The Marmot Review 10 Years On.* London: IHR.

ILO (International Labour Office) (2009) *Global Employment Trends for Women.* Geneva: ILO.

ILO (International Labour Office) (2015) *Global Estimates on Migrant Workers: Special Focus on Domestic Workers.* Geneva: ILO.

ILO (International Labour Office) (2016) *Non-Standard Employment around the World.* Geneva: ILO.

Inglehart, R. F., and Norris, P. (2016) *Trump, Brexit, and the Rise of Populism:*

Economic Have-Nots and Cultural Backlash, HKS Working Paper no. RWP16-026, https://papers.ssrn.com/sol3/papers.cfm?abstract_id=2818659.

Institute for Government (2020) 'Netzero: how government can meet its climate change target', www.instituteforgovernment.org.uk/explainers/net-zero-target.

Inter-Parliamentary Union (2016) 'Sexism, harassment and violence against women parliamentarians', Issues Brief, http://archive.ipu.org/pdf/publica tions/issuesbrief-e.pdf.

IOM (International Organization for Migration) (2016) 'Migrant, refugee deaths at sea pass 3,000 as arrivals near 250,000', 26 July, www.iom.int/ne ws/migrant-refugee-deaths-sea-pass-3000-arrivals-near-250000.

Ionesco, D. (2019) 'Let's talk about climate migrants, not climate refugees', www.un.org/sustainabledevelopment/blog/2019/06/lets-talk-about-climate-migrants-not-climate-refugees/.

Irvine, J., Lang, S., and Montoya, C. (2019) *Gendered Mobilizations and Intersectional Challenges*. London: Rowman & Littlefield.

Ishkanian, A., and Ali, I. S. (2018) 'From consensus to dissensus: the politics of anti-austerity activism in London and its relationship to voluntary organiza-tions', *Journal of Civil Society*, 14: 1–19.

Ishkanian, A., and Peña Saavedra, A. (2019) 'The politics and practices of intersectional prefiguration in social movements: the case of Sisters Uncut', *Sociological Review*, 67(5): 985–1001.

Isin, E. (2007) 'City state: critique of scalar thought', *Citizenship Studies*, 11(2): 211–28.

Jackson, T. (2009) *Prosperity without Growth? Steps to a Sustainable Economy*. London: Sustainable Development Commission.

Jackson, T. (2016) *Prosperity without Growth: Foundations for the Economy of Tomorrow*. London: Routledge.

Jacobs, B. (2018) 'Trump defends Mexican rapists claim during conspiracy-laden speech', *The Guardian*, 5 April, www.theguardian.com/us-news/2018/apr/05/trump-mexico-caravan-voter-claims-speech-west-virginia.

Jamieson, L. (2016) 'Families, relationships and "environment": (un)sustain-ability, climate change and biodiversity loss', *Families, Relationships and Society*, 5(30): 335–55.

Jensen, T. (2018) *Parenting the Crisis: The Cultural Politics of Parent-Blame*. Bristol: Policy Press.

Jensen, T., and Tyler, I. (2015) 'Benefits broods: the cultural and political craft-ing of anti-welfare commonsense', *Critical Social Policy*, 35(4): 470–91.

Jessop, B. (2013) 'Hollowing out the nation state and multi-level governance', in P. Kennett (ed.), *A Handbook of Comparative Social Policy*. Cheltenham: Edward Elgar, pp. 11–26.

Jessop, B. (2015) 'Neoliberalism, finance-dominated accumulation and endur-ing austerity: a cultural political economy perspective', in K. Farnsworth and Z. Irving (eds), *Social Policy in Times of Austerity: Global Economic Crisis and the New Politics of Welfare*. Bristol: Policy Press, pp. 87–112.

Johns Hopkins University (2020) *Covid-19 Dashboard*, https://gisanddata.maps.arcgis.com/apps/opsdashboard/index.html#/bda7594740fd40299423467b48e9ecf6.

Jones, K. (2020) 'How we can win', Commentary on Black Lives Matter, 9 June, www.youtube.com/watch?v=llci8MVh8J4.

Jones, O. (2011) *Chavs: The Demonization of the Working Class*. London: Verso.

JRF (Joseph Rowntree Foundation) (2017) *UK Poverty 2017*, www.jrf.org.uk/sites/default/files/jrf/files-research/uk_poverty_2017.pdf

JRF (Joseph Rowntree Foundation) (2020) *UK Poverty 2019/20*, www.jrf.org.uk/report/uk-poverty-2019-20.

Jupp, E. (2017a) 'Home space, gender and activism: the visible and the invisible in austere times', *Critical Social Policy*, 37(3): 348–66.

Jupp, E. (2017b) 'Families, policy and place in times of austerity', *Area*, 49(3): 266–72.

Kaasch, A., and Stubbs, P. (eds) (2014) *Transformations in Global and Regional Social Policies*. Basingstoke: Palgrave.

Kabeer, N. (2016) '"Leaving no one behind": the challenge of intersecting inequalities', in UNESCO, *World Social Science Report: Challenging Inequalities. Pathways to a Just World*. Paris: UNESCO.

Kanlungan (2020) *A Chance to Feel Safe: Precarious Filipino Migrants amid the UK's Coronavirus Outbreak*, www.kanlungan.org.uk/?page_id=118.

Kaufmann, E. (2017) 'Can narratives of white identity reduce opposition to immigration and support for hard Brexit? A survey experiment', *Political Studies*, 67(1): 31–46.

Keskinen, S., Norocel, O. C., and Jorgensen, M. B. (2016) 'The politics and policies of welfare chauvinism', *Critical Social Policy*, 36(3): 1–9.

Kettunen, P., Michel, S., and Pedersen, K. (eds) (2015) *Race, Ethnicity and Welfare States: An American Dilemma?* Cheltenham: Edward Elgar.

Kincaid, J. C. (1973) *Poverty and Equality in Britain*. Harmondsworth: Penguin.

King, A. D., and Harrington, L. J. (2018) 'The inequality of climate change from 1.5 to 2°C of global warming', *Geophysical Research Letters*, 45(10): 5030–3, https://agupubs.onlinelibrary.wiley.com/doi/full/10.1029/2018GL078430.

King's Fund (2019) *Brexit: The Implications for Health and Social Care*, www.kingsfund.org.uk/publications/articles/brexit-implications-health-social-care.

King's Fund (2020a) *NHS Hospital Bed Numbers: Past, Present, Future*, www.kingsfund.org.uk/publications/nhs-hospital-bed-numbers.

King's Fund (2020b) *Workforce Race Inequalities and Inclusion in NHS Providers*, www.kingsfund.org.uk/publications/workforce-race-inequalities-inclusion-nhs.

Kittay, E. (1999) *Love's Labor: Women, Dependence and Equality.* New York: Routledge.

Kittay, E. (2015) 'A theory of justice based on an ethics of care as fair terms of social life given our inevitable dependency and our inextricable interdependency', in D. Engster and M. Hamington (eds), *Ethics of Care and Political Theory.* Oxford: Oxford University Press.

Klein, N. (2020) 'We must not return to the pre-covid-19 status quo, only worse', *The Guardian*, 13 July, www.theguardian.com/books/2020/jul/13/naomi-klein-we-must-not-return-to-the-pre-covid-status-quo-only-worse.

Knight, B. (2020) '#Buildbackbetter', Rethinking Poverty, 7 April, www.rethinkingpoverty.org.uk/rethinking-poverty/building-back-better/.

Kofman, E. (2012) 'Rethinking care through social reproduction: articulating circuits of migration', *Social Politics*, 19(1): 142–57.

Krefis, A. C., Augustin, M., Heinke Schlünzen, K., Oßenbrügge, J., and Augustin, J. (2018) 'How does the urban environment affect health and well-being? A systematic review', *Urban Science*, 2(1): 21.

Laliberté, A. (2017) 'A multi-scalar comparison of responses to abuse against domestic migrant workers in Taiwan, Hong Kong, and Shanghai', in S. Michel and I. Peng (eds), *Gender, Migration, and the Work of Care: A Multi-Scalar Approach to the Pacific Rim.* Basingstoke: Palgrave.

Lawrence, D. (2020) *An Avoidable Crisis: The Disproportionate Impact of Covid-19 on Black, Asian and Minority Ethnic Communities*, www.lawrencereview.co.uk/?utm_source=bsd&utm_medium=email&utm_campaign=LawrenceReview&source=20201027_LawrenceReview&subsource=bsd_email.

Lawrence, M., and Taylor, Y. (2019) 'The UK government LGBT action plan: discourses of progress, enduring stasis, and LGBTQI+ lives "getting better"', *Critical Social Policy*, 40(4): 586–607.

Lawson, N. (2019) *45° Change: Transforming Society from Below and Above.* London: Compass.

Leavy, P., and Harris, A. (2018) *Contemporary Feminist Research from Theory to Practice.* New York: Guilford Press.

Le Grand, J. (1997) 'Knights, knaves or pawns? Human behaviour and social policy', *Journal of Social Policy*, 26: 149–69.

Leon, M. (2010) 'Migration and care work in Spain: the domestic sector revisited', *Social Policy and Society*, 9(3): 409–18.

Leslie, J. (2021) *The Missing Billions.* London: Resolution Foundation; www.resolutionfoundation.org/publications/the-missing-billions.

Levin, I. (2004) 'Living apart together: a new family form', *Current Sociology*, 52): 223–40.

Levin, S. T. (2020) 'What does "defund the police" mean? The rallying cry sweeping the US – explained', *The Guardian*, 6 June, www.theguardian.com/us-news/2020/jun/05/defunding-the-police-us-what-does-it-mean.

Levitas, R. (2013) *Utopia as Method: The Imaginary Reconstitution of Society*. Basingstoke: Palgrave Macmillan.

Lewis, G. (1996) 'Situated voices: "black women's experience" and social work', *Feminist Review*, 53: 24–56.

Lewis, G. (2000) *'Race', Gender, Social Welfare: Encounters in a Postcolonial Society*. Cambridge: Polity.

Lewis, G., and Parmar, P. (1983) 'Review essay of American black feminist literature', *Race and Class*, 25(2): 86–91.

Lewis, J. (1992) 'Gender and the development of welfare regimes', *Journal of European Social Policy*, 2(3): 159–73.

Lewis, J. (2011) 'Parenting programmes in England: policy development and implementation issues, 2005–2010', *Journal of Social Welfare and Family Law*, 33(2): 107–21.

Lewis, J., and West, A. (2016) 'Early childhood education and care in England under austerity: continuity or change in political ideas, policy goals, availability, affordability and quality in a childcare market?', *Journal of Social Policy*, 46(2): 331—48.

Lewis, J., Knjin, T., Martin, C., and Ostner, I. (2008) 'Patterns of development in work/family reconciliation policies for parents in France, Germany, the Netherlands, and the UK in the 2000s', *Social Politics*, 15(3): 261–86.

Lewis, P., Roberts, D., and Newburn, T. (2011) *Reading the Riots: Investigating England's Summer of Disorder*. London: Guardian Shorts.

Lewis, S. L., and Maslin, M. A. (2015) 'Defining the Anthropocene', *Nature*, 519: 171–80.

Leys, C. (2016) 'The English NHS: from market failure to trust, professionalism and democracy', in S. Davison and D. Featherstone (eds), *Soundings, 64: Critical Times*: 11–40; www.lwbooks.co.uk/soundings/64/the-english-nhs.

Linebaugh, P. (2008) *The Magna Carta Manifesto: Liberties and Commons for All*. Berkeley: University of California Press.

Lister, R. ([1997] 2003) *Citizenship: Feminist Perspectives*. Basingstoke: Palgrave Macmillan.

Lister, R. (2003) 'Investing in the citizen-workers of the future: transformation of citizen and state under New Labour', *Social Policy and Administration*, 37(5): 437–43.

Lister, R. (2004) *Poverty: Key Concepts*. Cambridge: Polity.

Lister, R. (2010) *Understanding Theories and Concepts on Social Policy*. Bristol: Policy Press.

Lister, R. (2011) 'The age of responsibility: social policy and citizenship in the early 21st century', in C. Holden, M. Kilkey and G. Ramia (eds), *Social Policy Review 23*. Bristol: Policy Press.

Lister, R. (2013) '"Power, not pity": poverty and human rights', *Ethics and Social Welfare*, 7(2): 109–23.

Lister, R. (2015) '"To count for nothing": poverty beyond the statistics', *Journal of the British Academy*, 3: 139–65.

Lister, R. (2018) *From Windrush to Universal Credit – the art of 'institutional indifference'*, London: Open Democracy; www.opendemocracy.net/en/opendemocracyuk/from-windrush-to-universal-credit-art-of-institutional-indifference/.

Lister, R. (2020) *Towards a Good Society*. London: Compass.

Lister, R. (2021) *Poverty*. Cambridge: Polity.

Lister, R., Williams, F., Antonnen, A., Bussemaker, J., Gerhardt, U., Heinen, J., Johansson, S., Leira, A., Siim, B., and Tobio, C. (2007) *Gendering Citizenship in Western Europe*. Bristol: Policy Press.

Local Government Association (2019) 'Children's care cash crisis: nine in 10 councils pushed into the red', www.local.gov.uk/about/news/childrens-care-cash-crisis-nine-10-councils-pushed-red.

Lockley, F. (2019) 'A powerful protest highlights the ongoing tragedy of DWP deaths', *The Canary*, 22 July, https://www.thecanary.co/uk/news/2019/07/22/a-powerful-protest-highlights-the-ongoing-tragedy-of-dwp-deaths/.

Lugones, M. (2011) 'Toward a decolonial feminism', *Hypatia*, 25(4): 742–59.

Lutz, H., Herrera Vivar, M. T., and Supik, L. (2011) *Framing Intersectionality*. Farnham: Ashgate.

McCall, L. (2001) *Complex Inequality: Gender, Race and Class in the New Economy*. New York: Routledge.

McCall, L. (2005) 'The complexity of intersectionality', *Signs: Journal of Women in Culture and Society*, 30(3):1771–800.

McCoy, D. (2020) 'Coronavirus has exposed the dangerous failings of NHS marketisation', *The Guardian*, 5 May, www.theguardian.com/commentisfree/2020/may/05/coronavirus-nhs-marketisation-pandemic.

McEnhill, L., and Taylor-Gooby, P. (2018) 'Beyond continuity? Understanding change in the UK welfare state since 2010', *Social Policy & Administration*, 52(1): 252–70.

MacFadyen, P. (2019) *Flatpack Democracy 2.0: Power Tools for Reclaiming Local Democracy*. Bath: Ecologic Books.

McGregor, O. R. (1957) *Divorce in England: A Centenary Study*. London: Heinemann.

Mckenzie, L. (2017) 'The class politics of prejudice: Brexit and the land of no-hope and glory', *British Journal of Sociology*, 68(S1): 265–80.

McKittrick, K. (ed.) (2015) *Sylvia Wynter: On Being Human as Praxis*. Durham, NC: Duke University Press.

McNicoll, L. (2016) 'Virgin Care set to run social work service in unprecedented deal', *Community Care*, 9 November, www.communitycare.co.uk/2016/11/09/virgin-care-set-run-social-work-service-unprecedented-deal/.

Macpherson, W. (1999) *Macpherson Inquiry into Matters Arising from the Death of Stephen Lawrence*. London: HMSO.

McRobbie, A. (2004) 'Postfeminism and popular culture', *Feminist Media Studies*, 4(3): 255–64.

McRuer, R. (2006) *Crip Theory: Cultural Signs of Queerness and Disability*. New York: New York University Press.

Mahon, R. (2018) 'Through a fractured gaze: the OECD, the World Bank and transnational care chains', *Current Sociology*, 66(4): 562–76.

Mahon, R. (2021) 'Gendering the global governance of migration', in C. Mora and N. Piper (eds), *The Palgrave Handbook of Gender and Migration*. Basingstoke: Palgrave.

Mahon, R., and Robinson, F. (eds) (2011) *Feminist Ethics and Social Politics: Toward a New Global Political Economy of Care*. Vancouver: UBC Press.

Malik, K. (2020) 'The Grenfell Inquiry exposes market forces at their deadliest', *The Guardian*, 13 December, www.theguardian.com/commentisfree/2020/dec/13/the-grenfell-inquiry-exposes-market-forces-at-their-deadliest.

Manchanda, N. (2019) 'Whither race in planetary governance? A response to Stephen Gill', *Global Affairs*, 5(2): 145–8.

Mandel, H., and Shalev, M. (2009) 'Gender, class, and varieties of capitalism', *Social Politics: International Studies in Gender, State & Society*, 16(2): 161–81.

Marx, K., and Engels, F. (1886) *The Manifesto of the Communist Party*. London: International.

Mason, P. (2019) *Clear Bright Future: A Radical Defence of the Human Being*. London: Penguin.

Massey, D. (ed.) (1999) *Soundings, 12: Transversal Politics*. London: Lawrence & Wishart.

Mathers, S. J., and Smees, R. (2014) *Quality and Inequality: Do Three- and Four-Year-Olds in Deprived Areas Experience Lower Quality Early Years Provision*. London: Nuffield Foundation.

May, T. (2016) Statement from the new Prime Minister, 13 July, www.gov.uk/government/speeches/statement-from-the-new-prime-minister-theresa-may.

May, V. (2015) *Pursuing Intersectionality, Unsettling Dominant Imaginaries*. New York: Routledge.

Mayblin, L., Wake, M., and Kazemi, M. (2019) 'Necropolitics and the slow violence of the everyday: asylum seeker welfare in the postcolonial present', *Sociology*, 54(1): 107–23.

Mazzucato, M. (2020) 'The Covid-19 crisis is a chance to do capitalism differently', *The Guardian*, 18 March, www.theguardian.com/commentisfree/2020/mar/18/the-covid-19-crisis-is-a-chance-to-do-capitalism-differently.

Mbembe, A. (2003) 'Necropolitics', *Public Culture*, 15(1): 11–40.

Mbembe, A. (2019) *Necropolitics*. Durham, NC: Duke University Press.

Mbembe, A. (2020) 'The universal right to breathe', *Critical Inquiry*, 13 April, https://critinq.wordpress.com/2020/04/13/the-universal-right-to-breathe/.

Meer, N. (2017) 'Modelling equality policy in the "Brexit Archipelago" – what will race equality look like in Brexit Britain?', *Journal of Social Policy*, 46(4): 657–74.

Meer, N. (2020) 'Race equality policy making in a devolved context: assessing the opportunities and obstacles for a "Scottish Approach"' *Journal of Social Policy*, 49(2): 233–50.

Mestrum, F. (2015) *The Social Commons: Rethinking Social Justice in Post-Neoliberal Societies*. Brussels: Global Social Justice.

Mezzadri, A. (2019) 'On the value of social reproduction: informal labour, the majority world and the need for inclusive theories and politics', *Radical Philosophy*, 2(4): 33–41.

Michel, S., and Peng, I. (2012) 'All in the family? Migrants, nationhood, and care regimes in Asia and North America', *Journal of European Social Policy*, 22(4): 406–18.

Michel, S., and Peng, I. (eds) (2017) *Gender, Migration and the Work of Care: A Multi-Scalar Approach to the Pacific Rim*. Basingstoke: Palgrave.

Midgley, J., and Piachaud, D. (eds) (2011) *Colonialism and Welfare: Social Policy and the British Imperial Legacy*. Cheltenham: Edward Elgar.

Mies, M., and Shiva, V. (1993) *Ecofeminism*. Halifax, NS: Fernwood.

Mignolo, W. (2011) *The Darker Side of Western Modernity*. Durham, NC: Duke University Press.

Migrant Advisory Committee (2020) 'Migration Advisory Committee reviews shortage occupation lists', 29 September, www.gov.uk/government/news/migration-advisory-committee-reviews-shortage-occupation-lists.

Migration Observatory (2019) *Immigration Detention in the UK*, https://migrationobservatory.ox.ac.uk/resources/briefings/immigration-detention-in-the-uk/.

Millar, J., and Bennett, F. (2017) 'Universal Credit: assumptions, contradictions and virtual reality', *Social Policy and Society*, 16(2): 169–82.

Millar, J., and Ridge, T. (2017) *Work and Relationships Over Time in Lone-Mother Families*. York: Joseph Rowntree Foundation; www.jrf.org.uk/report/work-relationships-lone-mother-families.

Miller, C. (ed.) (2020) *Participation at 45°: Techniques for Citizen-Led Change*. London: Compass.

Ministry of Justice (2017) *The Lammy Review: An Independent Review into the Treatment of, and Outcomes for, Black, Asian and Minority Ethnic Individuals in the Criminal Justice System*, www.gov.uk/government/publications/lammy-review-final-report.

Mink, G. (1990) 'The lady and the tramp: gender, race, and the origins of the American welfare state', in L. Gordon (ed.), *Women, the State, and Welfare*. Madison: University of Wisconsin Press, pp. 92–117.

Miyashita, Y., Akaleephan, C., Asgari-Jirhandeh, N., and Sungyuth, C. (2017) 'Cross-border movement of older patients: a descriptive study on health service use of Japanese retirees in Thailand', *Globalization and Health*, 13(14), https://globalizationandhealth.biomedcentral.com/articles/10.1186/s12992-017-0241-9.

Modood, T. ([2007] 2013) *Multiculturalism*. Cambridge: Polity.

Modood, T. (2020) 'Islamophobia and normative sociology', *Journal of the British Academy*, 8, www.thebritishacademy.ac.uk/publishing/journal-british-academy/8/islamophobia-and-normative-sociology/.

Monbiot, G. (2020) 'The UK government was ready for this pandemic. Until it sabotaged its own system', *The Guardian*, 19 May, www.theguardian.com/commentisfree/2020/may/19/uk-government-pandemic.

Moore, S., Antunes, B., White, G., Tailby, S., and Newsome, K. (2017) *Non-Standard Contracts and the National Living Wage: A Report for the Low Pay Commission*, https://assets.publishing.service.gov.uk/government/uploads/system/uploads/attachment_data/file/660561/MooreAntunesTailbyNewsomeWhiteGreenwich_NonStandardContractsandtheNLW_FINAL_2017_Report.pdf.

Moore-Bick, M. (2019) *Grenfell Tower Inquiry: Phase 1 Report Overview*, https://assets.grenfelltowerinquiry.org.uk/GTI%20-%20Phase%201%20report%20Executive%20Summary.pdf.

Mora, A. G., and Rutkowski, M. (2020) *Remittances in Times of the Coronavirus – Keep them Flowing*, https://blogs.worldbank.org/psd/remittances-times-coronavirus-keep-them-flowing.

Moraga, C., and Anzaldúa, G. (eds) (1983) *This Bridge Called My Back: Writings by Radical Women of Color*. Watertown, MA: Persephone Press.

Morgan Jones, M., Abrams, D., and Lahiri, A. (2020) 'Shape the future: how the social sciences, humanities and the arts can SHAPE a positive, post-pandemic future for peoples, economies and environments', *Journal of the British Academy*, 8: 167–266.

Morris, J. (1991) *Pride against Prejudice: Transforming Attitudes to Disability*. London: Women's Press.

Morris, L. (2019) 'Reconfiguring rights in austerity Britain: boundaries, behaviours and contestable margins', *Journal of Social Policy*, 48(2): 1–21.

Morris, L. (2020) 'Activating the welfare subject: the problem of agency', *Sociology*, 54(2): 275–91.

Murji, K. (2017) *Racism, Policy and Politics*. Bristol: Policy Press.

Murray, C. (1990) *The Emerging British Underclass*. London: Institute for Economic Affairs.

Nash, J. (2019) *Black Feminism Reimagined after Intersectionality*. Durham, NC: Duke University Press.

Ndhlovu, F. (2016) 'A decolonial critique of diaspora identity theories and the notion of superdiversity', *Diaspora Studies*, 9(1): 28–40.

NEF (New Economics Foundation) (2020) 'Unemployment set to be above 2 million by Christmas 2021 without further government action', Press release, 6 July, https://neweconomics.org/2020/07/unemployment-set-to-be-above-2-million-by-christmas-2021-without-further-government-action.

Newman, J. (2012a) *Working the Spaces of Power: Activism, Neoliberalism and Gendered Labour*. London: Bloomsbury Academic.

Newman, J. (2012b) 'Beyond the deliberative subject? Problems of theory, method and critique in the turn to emotion and affect', *Critical Policy Studies*, 6(4): 465–79.

Newman, J. (2014) 'Governing the present: activism, neoliberalism, and the problem of power and consent', *Critical Policy Studies*, 8(2): 133–47.

Newman, J. (2020) 'The political work of reimagination', in D. Cooper, N. Dhawan, and J. Newman (eds), *Reimagining the State*. London: Routledge, pp. 19–36.

Newman, J., and Clarke, J. (2009) *Publics, Politics and Power*. London: Sage.

Newman, J., and Clarke, J. (2014) 'States of imagination', in J. Newman and J. Clarke (eds), *Soundings, 57: Spaces of Debate*: 153–69.

Newsom, R. (2020) 'The green plan looks good but the government must live up to its promises', *The Guardian*, 18 November, www.theguardian.com/commentisfree/2020/nov/18/green-politics-10-point-green-plan-looks-good-but-boris-johnson-government-must-live-up-to-promises.

Niven, A. (2019) *New Model Island: How to Build a Radical Culture beyond the Idea of England*. London: Repeater.

Noddings, N. (1984) *Caring: A Feminist Approach to Ethics and Moral Education*. Berkeley: University of California Press.

Nussbaum, M. (2001) *Women and Human Development: The Capabilities Approach*. Cambridge: Cambridge University Press.

Nussbaum, M. (2006) *Frontiers of Justice: Disability, Nationality, Species Membership*. Cambridge, MA: Belknap Press.

Obolenskaya, P., and Hills. J. (2019) *Flat-Lining or Seething beneath the Surface? Two Decades of Changing Economic Inequality in the UK*, Centre for Analysis of Social Exclusion, https://sticerd.lse.ac.uk/CASE/_NEW/PUBLICATIONS/abstract/?index=6301.

OBR (Office for Budget Responsibility) (2020) 'Coronavirus analysis', July 2020. https://obr.uk/coronavirus-analysis/.

O'Brien, M., and Penna, S. (1998) *Theorising Welfare: Enlightenment and Modern Society*. London: Sage.

O'Connor, J. (1973) *The Fiscal Crisis of the State*. London: Routledge.

O'Connor, J. S., Orloff, A. S., and Shaver, S. (1999) *States, Markets, Families: Gender, Liberalism and Social Policy in Australia, Canada, Great Britain and the United States*. Cambridge: Cambridge University Press.

Odysseos, L. (2017) 'Prolegomena to any future decolonial ethics: coloniality, poetics and "being human as praxis"', *Millennium*, 45 3): 447–72.

OECD (2015) *Labor Force Survey 2015*, https://stats.oecd.org/Index.aspx?DataSetCode=LFS_SEXAGE_I_R.

OECD (2019) *OECD Employment Outlook 2020*, https://read.oecd-ilibrary.org/view/?ref=134_134947-lyixdpsqh2&title=Employment-Outlook-UnitedKingdom-EN.

OECD and UN-DESA (2013) *World Migration in Figures*, www.oecd.org/els/mig/World-Migration-in-Figures.pdf.

Offe, C. (1984) *Contradictions of the Welfare State*. Cambridge, MA: MIT Press.

Olafsson, S., Daly, M., and Palme, J. (2019) *Welfare and the Great Recession: A Comparative Study*. Oxford: Oxford University Press.

Oliveira, G. (2017) 'Caring for your children: how Mexican immigrant mothers experience care and the ideals of motherhood', in S. Michel and I. Peng (eds), *Gender, Migration, and the Work of Care: A Multi-Scalar Approach to the Pacific Rim*. Basingstoke: Palgrave.

Olufemi, L. (2020) *Feminism Interrupted: Disrupting Power*. London: Pluto Press.

O'Neill, D. W., Fanning, A. L., Lamb, W. F., and Steinberger, J. (2018) 'A good life for all within planetary boundaries', *Nature Sustainability*, 1: 88–95.

ONS (Office for National Statistics) (2018a) *Domestic Abuse in England and Wales, Year Ending March 2018*, www.ons.gov.uk/peoplepopulationandcommunity/crimeandjustice/bulletins/domesticabuseinenglandandwales/yearendingmarch2018.

ONS (Office for National Statistics) (2018b) *Gender Pay Gap in the UK*, www.ons.gov.uk/employmentandlabourmarket/peopleinwork/earningsandworkinghours/bulletins/genderpaygapintheuk/2018.

ONS (Office for National Statistics) (2019) *The UK Contribution to the EU Budget*, www.ons.gov.uk/economy/governmentpublicsectorandtaxes/publicsectorfinance/articles/theukcontributiontotheeubudget/2017-10-31.

ONS (Office for National Statistics) (2020a) *Coronavirus (Covid-19) Related Deaths by Ethnic Group, England and Wales: 2 March 2020 to 15 May 2020*, www.ons.gov.uk/peoplepopulationandcommunity/birthsdeathsandmarriages/deaths/articles/coronaviruscovid19relateddeathsbyethnicgroupenglandandwales/2march2020to15may2020.

ONS (Office for National Statistics) (2020b) *Deaths involving COVID-19 in the Care Sector, England and Wales*, www.ons.gov.uk/peoplepopulationandcommunity/birthsdeathsandmarriages/deaths/articles/deathsinvolvingcovid19inthecaresectorenglandandwales/latest.

ONS (Office for National Statistics) (2020c) *Covid-19 Roundup*, www.ons.gov.uk/peoplepopulationandcommunity/healthandsocialcare/conditionsanddiseases/articles/coronaviruscovid19roundup/2020-03-26#deaths.

O'Reilly, J., Smith, M., Deakin, S., and Burchell, B. (2015) 'Equal pay as a moving target: international perspectives on forty years of addressing the gender pay gap', *Cambridge Journal of Economics*, 39(2): 299–317.

Orloff, A. S. (1993) 'Gender and the social rights of citizenship: the comparative analysis of gender relations and welfare states', *American Sociological Review*, 58(3): 303–28.

Orloff, A. S. (2009) 'Gendering the comparative analysis of welfare states: an unfinished agenda', *Sociological Theory*, 27(3): 317–43.

Osborne, D., and Gaebler, T. (1992) *Reinventing Government*. Reading, MA: Addison-Wesley.

Ostrom, E. (1990) *Governing the Commons: The Evolution of Institutions for Collective Action*. Cambridge: Cambridge University Press.

Ostrowski, M. S. (2020) *Left Unity: Manifesto for a Progressive Alliance*. London: Policy Network.

O'Toole, T., Meer, N., Nilsson DeHanas, D., Jones, S. H., and Modood, T. (2016) 'Governing through Prevent? Regulation and contested practice in state–Muslim engagement', *Sociology*, 50(1): 160–77.

Parekh, B. (2000) *The Future of Multi-Ethnic Britain: The Parekh Report*. London: Runnymede Trust.

Parreñas, R. (2001) *Servants of Globalization*. Stanford, CA: Stanford University Press.

Parreñas, R. (2005) *Children of Global Migration: Transnational Families and Gendered Woes*. Stanford, CA: Stanford University Press.

Parveen, N. (2019) 'Boris Johnson's burqa comments "led to surge in anti-Muslim attacks"', *The Guardian*, 2 September, www.theguardian.com/politics/2019/sep/02/boris-johnsons-burqa-comments-led-to-surge-in-anti-muslim-attacks.

Patel, P., Kapoor, A., and Treloar, N. (2020) *Ethnic Inequalities in Covid-19 Are Playing Out Again – How Can We Stop Them?*, 19 October, www.ippr.org/blog/ethnic-inequalities-in-covid-19-are-playing-out-again-how-can-we-stop-them.

Pateman, C. (1989) *The Disorder of Women: Democracy, Feminism, and Political Theory*. Stanford, CA: Stanford University Press.

Patrick, R. (2016) 'Living with and responding to the "scrounger" narrative in the UK: exploring everyday strategies of acceptance, resistance and deflection', *Journal of Poverty and Social Justice*, 24(3): 245–59.

Patrick, R. (2018) 'What we can learn from Scotland's approach to social security', Social Policy Association blog, 15 October 15, www.social-policy.org.uk/50-for-50/scotland-social-security/.

Pearson, R. (2019) 'A feminist analysis of neoliberalism and austerity policies in the UK', in S. Davison (ed.), *Soundings, 71: Neoliberalism, Feminism and Transnationalism*: 28–39.

Pegg, G. (2020) 'Covid-19: did the UK government prepare for the wrong kind of pandemic?' *The Guardian*, 21 May, www.theguardian.com/world/2020/may/21/did-the-uk-government-prepare-for-the-wrong-kind-of-pandemic.

Pemberton, S., Phillimore, J., Bradby, H., Padilla, B., Lopes, J., Samerski, S., and Humphris, R. (2019) 'Access to healthcare in superdiverse neighbourhoods', *Health & Place*, 55: 128–35.

Peng, I. (2017) 'Explaining exceptionality: care and migration policies in Japan and South Korea', in S. Michel and I. Peng (eds), *Gender, Migration and the Work of Care: A Multi-Scalar Approach to the Pacific Rim.* Basingstoke: Palgrave.

Peng, I., and Wong, J. (2008) 'Institutions and institutional purpose: continuity and change in East Asian social policy', *Politics and Society,* 36(1): 61–88.

Penn, H. (2018) 'Why parents should fear childcare going the way of Carillion', *The Guardian,* 14 May, www.theguardian.com/commentisfree/2018/may/14/parents-carillion-childcare-collapse-nursery-provider.

Pérez, L. (2019) 'Feminizing politics through municipalism', in Barcelona en Comú with D. Bookchin and A. Coalu (eds), *Fearless Cities: A Guide to the Global Municipal Movement.* Oxford: New Internationalist, pp. 21–5.

Pettifor, A. (2020) *The Case for the Green New Deal.* London: Verso.

Phillimore, J., Bradby, H., Knecht, M., Padilla, B., Brand, T., Cheung, S. Y., Pemberton, S., and Zeeb, H. (2015) 'Understanding healthcare practices in superdiverse neighbourhoods and developing the concept of welfare bricolage: protocol of a cross-national mixed-methods study', *BMC International Health and Human Rights,* 15(1): 16.

Phillimore, J., Bradby, H., Doos, L., Padilla, B., and Samerski, S. (2019a) 'Health providers as bricoleurs: an examination of the adaption of health ecosystems to superdiversity in Europe', *Journal of European Social Policy,* 29(3): 361–75.

Phillimore, J., Bradby, H., Knecht, M., Padilla, B., and Pemberton, S. (2019b) 'Bricolage as conceptual tool for understanding access to healthcare in superdiverse populations', *Social Theory & Health,* 17: 1–22.

Phillimore, J., Brand, T., Bradby, H., and Padilla, B. (2019c) 'Healthcare bricolage in Europe's superdiverse neighbourhoods: a mixed-methods study', *BMC Public Health,* 19(1): 1325.

Phillimore, J., Bradby, H., Brand, T., Padilla, B., and Pemberton, S. (2021) *Exploring Welfare Bricolage in Europe's Superdiverse Neighbourhoods.* Abingdon: Routledge.

Phillips, C. (2019) 'Utilising "modern slave" narratives in social policy research', *Critical Social Policy,* 40(1): 30–49.

Phillips, C., and Williams, F. (2021) 'Sleepwalking into the "post-racial": social policy and research-led teaching', *Social Policy and Society.*

Phillips, C., Earle, R., Parmar, A., and Smith, D. (2020) 'Dear British criminology: where has all the race and racism gone?', *Theoretical Criminology,* 24(3): 427–46.

Phoenix, A. (1987) 'Theories of gender and black families', in G. Weinger and M. Arnot (eds), *Gender under Scrutiny: New Inquiries in Education.* London: Hutchinson.

Pierson, P. (1996) 'The new politics of the welfare state', *World Politics,* 48(2): 143–79.

Pierson, P., and Skocpol, T. (2002) 'Historical institutionalism in contemporary political science', in I. Katznelson and H. V. Milner (eds), *Political Science: The State of the Discipline*. New York: W. W. Norton.

Piketty, T. (2014) *Capital in the Twenty-First Century*. Cambridge, MA: Belknap Press.

Piketty, T. (2020) *Capital and Ideology*. Cambridge, MA: Harvard University Press.

Pillinger, J. (2011) *Quality Health Care and Workers on the Move: International Migration and Women Health and Social Care Workers Programme*. Ferney Voltaire: Public Services International.

Piper, N., and Rother, S. (2012) 'Let's argue about migration: advancing a right(s) discourse via communicative opportunities', *Third World Quarterly*, 33(9): 1735–50.

Pisarello, G. (2019) 'Introduction', in Barcelona en Comú with D. Bookchin and A. Coalu (eds), *Fearless Cities: A Guide to the Global Municipal Movement*. Oxford: New Internationalist: pp. 7–11.

Platenga, J., and Remery, C. (2005) *Reconciliation of Work and Private Life: A Comparative Review of Thirty European Countries*. Brussels: European Commission.

Platt, E. (2017) 'Grenfell Tower: chronicle of a tragedy foretold', *New Statesman*, 9 October.

Plumwood, V. (1993) *Feminism and the Mastery of Nature*. London: Routledge.

Pogge, T. W. (1992) 'Cosmopolitanism and sovereignty', *Ethics*, 103(1): 48–75.

Pogge, T. (2002) *World Poverty and Human Rights: Cosmopolitan Responsibilities and Reforms*. Cambridge: Polity.

Polanyi, K. ([1944] 1957) *The Great Transformation: The Political and Economic Origins of Our Time*. Boston: Beacon Press.

Ponzanesi, S., and Blaagaard, B. (2012) *Deconstructing Europe: Postcolonial Perspectives*. London: Routledge.

Porter, T., Shakespeare, T., and Stockel, A. (2019) 'Performance management: a qualitative study of relational boundaries in personal assistance', *Sociology of Health & Illness*, 42(1): 191–206.

Powell, M. (2006) 'Social Policy and Administration: journal and discipline', *Social Policy and Administration*, 40(3): 233–49.

Priestley, M., Waddington, L., and Bessozi, C. (2010) 'Towards an agenda for disability research in Europe: learning from disabled people's organisations', *Disability and Society*, 25(6): 731–46.

Pring, J. (2020) 'WCA death doctor: DWP put 'immense pressure' on Atos to find claimants fit for work', Disability News Service, 5 December, www.disabilitynewsservice.com/wca-death-doctor-dwp-put-immense-pressure-on-atos-to-find-claimants-fit-for-work/.

Public Accounts Committee (2020) *Immigration Enforcement*, 16 September, https://publications.parliament.uk/pa/cm5801/cmselect/cmpubacc/407/40703.htm.

Public Health England (2020a) *Beyond the Data: Understanding the Impact of COVID-19 on BAME Groups*, https://assets.publishing.service.gov.uk/government/uploads/system/uploads/attachment_data/file/892376/COVID_stakeholder_engagement_synthesis_beyond_the_data.pdf.

Public Health England (2020b) *Covid-19: Deaths of People with Learning Disabilities*, www.gov.uk/government/publications/covid-19-deaths-of-people-with-learning-disabilities.

Public Health England (2020c) *Disparities in the Risks and Outcomes of Covid-19*, https://assets.publishing.service.gov.uk/government/uploads/system/uploads/attachment_data/file/908434/Disparities_in_the_risk_and_out comes_of_COVID_August_2020_update.pdf.

Puig de la Bellacasa, M. (2017) *Matters of Care: Speculative Ethics in More than Human Worlds*. Minneapolis: University of Minnesota Press.

Pulido, L. (2016) 'Flint, environmental racism, and racial capitalism', *Capitalism Nature Socialism*, 27(3): 1–16.

Qureshi, K., Hill, S., Meer, N. and Kasstan, B. (2020a) 'COVID-19 and BAME inequalities – the problem of institutional racism', Centre for Health and the Public Interest blog, https://chpi.org.uk/blog/covid-19-and-bame-inequalities-the-problem-of-institutional-racism/.

Qureshi, K., Kasstan, B., Meer, N., and Hill, S. (2020b) *Submission of Evidence on the Disproportionate Impact of Covid-19, and the UK Government Response, on Ethnic Minorities in the UK*, https://ghpu.sps.ed.ac.uk/wp-content/uploads/2020/04/Qureshi-Kasstan-Meer-Hill_working-paper_COVID19-ethnic-minorities_240420.pdf

Rai, S., Hoskyns, C., and Thomas, D. (2014) 'Depletion: the social cost of reproduction', *International Feminist Journal of Politics*, 16(1): 86–105.

Ramose, M. B. (2003) 'The philosophy of ubuntu and ubuntu as a philosophy', in Coetzee and Roux (eds), *The African Philosophy Reader*. 2nd edn, London: Routledge, pp. 230–8.

Rancière, J. (2004) *The Philosopher and His Poor*. Durham, NC: Duke University Press.

Rankine, C. (2014) *Citizen: An American Lyric*. London: Penguin Random House.

Rankine, C. (2020) *Just Us: An American Conversation*. London: Penguin Random House.

Rashid, N. (2017) '"Everyone is a feminist when it comes to Muslim women": gender and Islamophobia', in F. Elahi and O. Khan (eds), *Islamophobia: Still a Challenge for Us All*. London: Runnymede Trust.

Raworth, K. (2017) *Doughnut Economics. Seven Ways to Think Like a 21st-Century Economist*. London: Random House Business Books.

Razavi, S., and Staab, S. (2012) *Global Variations in the Political and Social Economy of Care: Worlds Apart*. London: Routledge.

Rebughini, P. (2017) 'Critical agency and the future of critique', *Current Sociology*, 66(1): 3–19.

Red Pepper (2020) *Climate Revolutions, Red Pepper* no. 228.

Reed, H., and Lansley, S. (2016) *Universal Basic Income: An Idea whose Time Has Come?* London: Compass.

Refugee and Migrant Children's Consortium (2018) *Evidence for 'Windrush: Lessons Learned Review'*, Coram Children's Legal Centre. www.childrenslegalcentre.com/wp-content/uploads/2019/04/RMCC_WindrushLessonsLearned_Oct2018_FINAL.pdf.

Refugee Council (2020) *The Truth about Asylum*, www.refugeecouncil.org.uk/information/refugee-asylum-facts/the-truth-about-asylum/.

Rhodes Must Fall (2018) *Rhodes Must Fall: The Struggle to Decolonise the Racist Heart of Empire*. London: Zed Books.

Ridge, T. (2009) '"It didn't always work": low-income children's experiences of changes in mothers' working patterns in the UK', *Social Policy and Society*, 8(4): 503–13.

Ridge, T., and Wright, S. (eds) (2008) *Understanding Inequality, Poverty and Wealth: Policies and Prospects*. Bristol: Policy Press.

Robinson, F. (1999) *Globalizing Care: Ethics, Feminist Theory, and International Relations*. Boulder, CO: Westview Press.

Robinson, F. (2013) 'Global care ethics: beyond distribution, beyond justice', *Journal of Global Ethics*, 9(2): 131–42.

Robinson, M. (2018) *Climate Justice: A Man-Made Problem with a Feminist Solution*. London: Bloomsbury.

Romero, M. (1992) *Maid in the USA*. New York: Routledge.

Romero, M. (2018) *Introducing Intersectionality*. Cambridge: Polity.

Rose, N. (1999) *Powers of Freedom: Reframing Political Thought*. Cambridge: Cambridge University Press.

Roseneil, S. (2011) 'Criticality, not paranoia: a generative register for feminist social research', *NORA – Nordic Journal of Feminist and Gender Research*, 19(2): 124–31.

Roseneil, S., Crowhurst, I., Hellesund, T., Santos, A. C., and Stoilova, M. (2020) *The Tenacity of the Couple-Norm: Intimate Citizenship Regimes in a Changing Europe*. London: UCL Press.

Ross, A. (2013) *Theresa May, Citizenship and the Power to Make People Stateless*. London: Open Democracy; www.opendemocracy.net/en/opendemocracyuk/theresa-may-citizenship-and-power-to-make-people-stateless/.

Rother, S. (2018) 'Angry birds of passage – migrant rights networks and counter-hegemonic resistance to global migration discourses', *Globalizations*, 15(6): 854–69.

Rottenburg, C. (2018) *The Rise of Neoliberal Feminism*. Oxford: Heretical Thought.

Rowland, D. (2019) 'Corporate care home collapse and "light touch" regulation: a repeating cycle of failure', LSE blog, 8 May, https://blogs.lse. ac.uk/politicsandpolicy/corporate-care-homes/.

Roy, A. (2019) *My Seditious Heart: Collected Non-Fiction*. London: Hamish Hamilton.

Roy, A. (2020) 'The pandemic is a portal', *Financial Times*, 3 April, www. ft.com/content/10d8f5e8-74eb-11ea-95fe-fcd274e920ca.

Ruane, S., and Byrne, D. (2014) 'The political economy of taxation in the 21st-century UK', in K. Farnsworth, Z. Irving and M. Fenger (eds), *Social Policy Review 26*. Bristol: Policy Press.

Rustin, M. (2013) 'A relational society', in S. Davison and B. Little (eds), *Soundings, 54: Hope and Experience*: 23–36.

Rutherford, J., and Shah, H. (2006) *The Good Society: Compass Programme for Renewal, Part 1*. London: Lawrence & Wishart.

Ryan, F. (2019) *Crippled: Austerity and the Demonization of Disabled People*. London: Verso.

Sager, A. (2020) 'The uses and abuses of "Migrant Crisis"', in T. Fouskas (ed.), *Immigrants and Refugees in Times of Crisis*. Athens: European Public Law Organization.

Sahraoui, N. (2019) *Racialised Workers and European Older-Age Care: From Care Labour to Care Ethics*. Basingstoke: Palgrave Macmillan.

Sainsbury, D. (1994) *Gendering Welfare States*. London: Sage.

Sainsbury, D. (2012) *Welfare States and Immigrant Rights: The Politics of Inclusion and Exclusion*. Oxford: Oxford University Press.

Samuel, M. (2020) 'Covid-19 deaths among social care staff far outstripping those in healthcare', *Community Care*, 11 May, www.communitycare.co.uk/ 2020/05/11/covid-19-deaths-among-social-care-staff-far-outstripping-healthcare/.

Sandberg, S. (2013) *Lean In: Women, Work, and the Will to Lead*. New York: Alfred A. Knopf.

Sassen–Koob, S. (1984) 'Notes on the incorporation of Third World women into wage-labor through immigration and off-shore production', *International Migration Review*, 18(4): 1144–67.

Saville, J. (1957–8) 'The welfare state: an historical approach', *New Reasoner*, 3: 5–25.

Scope (2017) 'Why we need to see changes in support for disabled people in work', Scope blog, 14 February, https://blog.scope.org.uk/2017/02/14/ why-we-need-to-see-changes-in-support-for-disabled-people-in-work/.

Scullion, L. C. (2018) 'Sanctuary to sanction: asylum seekers, refugees and welfare conditionality in the UK', *Journal of Social Security Law*, 25(3): 158–72.

Sedgwick, E. K. (2003) 'Paranoid reading and reparative reading, or, you're so paranoid, you probably think this essay is about you', in E. K. Sedgwick, *Touching Feeling: Affect, Pedagogy, Performativity*. Durham, NC: Duke University Press.

Sen, A. (2009) *The Idea of Justice*. Cambridge, MA: Belknap Press.

Sevenhuijsen, S. (1998) *Citizenship and the Ethics of Care*. London: Routledge.

Seymour, R. (2014) *Against Austerity*. London: Pluto Press.

Shakespeare, T. (2000) *Help*. Birmingham: Venture Press.

Shakespeare, T. (2014) *Disability Rights and Wrongs Revisited*. Abingdon: Routledge.

Shakespeare, T., and Williams, F. (2019) 'Care and assistance: issues for persons with disabilities, women and care workers', Report for the International Labour Organization (unpublished).

Shamsie, K. (2018) 'Exiled: the disturbing story of a citizen made unBritish', *The Guardian*, 17 November, www.theguardian.com/books/2018/nov/17/unbecoming-british-kamila-shamsie-citizens-exile.

Shankley, W., and Finney, N. (2020) 'Ethnic minorities and housing in Britain', in B. Byrne et al. (eds), *Ethnicity, Race and Inequality in the UK: State of the Nation*. Bristol: Policy Press.

Shaver, S. (1990) *Gender, Social Policy Regimes and the Welfare State*, Discussion paper no. 26, University of New South Wales, Social Policy Research Centre.

Shelter (2019) *The Story of Social Housing*, https://england.shelter.org.uk/support_us/campaigns/story_of_social_housing.

Shenker, J. (2019) *Now We Have Your Attention: The New Politics of the People*. London: Penguin.

Shildrick, T., MacDonald, R., Furlong, A., Roden, J., and Crow, R. (2012) *Are 'Cultures of Worklessness' Passed Down the Generations?* York: Joseph Rowntree Foundation.

Shilliam, R. (2018) *Race and the Undeserving Poor*. Newcastle-upon-Tyne: Agenda.

Shutes, I. (2016) 'Work-related conditionality and the access to social benefits of national citizens, EU and non-EU citizens', *Journal of Social Policy*, 45(4): 691–707.

Shutes, I. (2017) 'Controlling migration: the gender implications of work-related conditions in restricting rights to residence and social benefits', in J. Hudson, C. Needham and E. Heins (eds), *Social Policy Review 29*. Bristol: Policy Press.

Shutes, I., and Chiatti, C. (2012) 'Migrant labour and the marketisation of care for older people: the employment of migrant care workers by families and service providers', *Journal of European Social Policy*, 22(4): 392–405.

Sian, K. P., Law, I., and Sayyid S. (2013) *Racism, Governance, and Public Policy: Beyond Human Rights*. New York: Routledge.

Silvers, A. (1995) 'Reconciling equality to difference: caring (f)or justice for people with Disabilities', *Hypatia*, 10(1): 30–5.

Simic, A., and Blitz, B. K. (2019) 'The modern slavery regime: a critical evaluation', *Journal of the British Academy*, 7(S1): 1–34; www.thebritishacademy.

ac.uk/publishing/journal-british-academy/7s1/modern-slavery-regime-critical-evaluation/.

Simonazzi, A. (2009) 'Care regimes and national employment models', *Cambridge Journal of Economics*, 33: 211–32.

Sisters Uncut (2020) 'Safer spaces policy', www.sistersuncut.org/saferspaces/.

Skills for Care (2017) *Individual Employers and Personal Assistants*, www.skillsforcare.org.uk/Documents/NMDS-SC-and-intelligence/NMDS-SC/Analysis-pages/Individual-employers-and-personal-assistants-2017.pdf.

Skills for Care (2020) *The State of the Adult Social Care Sector and Workforce in England*, www.skillsforcare.org.uk/adult-social-care-workforce-data/Workforce-intelligence/publications/national-information/The-state-of-the-adult-social-care-sector-and-workforce-in-England.aspx.

Smith, G., Sylva, K., Smith, T., Sammons, P., and Omonigho, A. (2018) *Stop Start*. London: Sutton Trust.

Snell, C., and Haq, G. (2014) *A Short Guide to Environmental Policy*. Bristol: Policy Press.

Social Platform (2012) *Recommendations for Care that Respects the Rights of Individuals, Guarantees Access to Services and Promotes Social Inclusion*, www.socialplatform.org/wp-content/uploads/2013/03/20121217_SocialPlatform_Recommendations_on_CARE_EN1.pdf.

Solnit, R. (2020) '"The way we get through this is together": the rise of mutual aid under the corona virus pandemic', *The Guardian*, 14 May, www.theguardian.com/world/2020/may/14/mutual-aid-coronavirus-pandemic-rebecca-solnit.

Solón, P. (2018) *Vivir bien: Old Cosmovisions and New Paradigms*, Great Transitions Initiative, https://greattransition.org/publication/vivir-bien.

Standing, G. (2019) *Plunder of the Commons: A Manifesto for Sharing Public Wealth*. London: Penguin.

Starke, P. (2006) 'The politics of welfare state retrenchment: a literature review', *Social Policy and Administration*, 40(1): 104–20.

Starmer, K. (2020) Full Text of Keir Starmer's Speech at Labour Connected, 22 September, https://labour.org.uk/press/full-text-of-keir-starmers-speech-at-labour-connected/.

Step Up Migrant Women (2020) 'Domestic Abuse Bill must protect migrant survivors, say campaigners', press release, https://stepupmigrantwomen.org/2020/03/03/domestic-abuse-bill-must-protect-migrant-survivors-say-campaigners-press-release/.

Stephens, M., and Fitzpatrick, S. (2018) *Country Level Devolution: Scotland*, SPDO Research Paper, http://sticerd.lse.ac.uk/dps/case/spdo/spdorp01.pdf.

Straw, J. (2006) 'I felt uneasy talking to someone I couldn't see', *The Guardian*, 6 October, www.theguardian.com/commentisfree/2006/oct/06/politics.uk.

Streeck, W. (2014) 'How will capitalism end?', *New Left Review*, 87.

Streeck, W. (2017) 'The Return of the repressed', *New Left Review*, 104.

Stubbs, P. (1984) 'The employment of black social workers: from ethnic sensitivity to anti-racism', *Critical Social Policy*, 12(4): 6–27.

Studdert, J. (2020) 'The NHS taking over social care would be a disaster: make services truly local instead', *The Guardian*, 20 July, www.theguardian.com/society/2020/jul/20/nhs-taking-over-social-care-disaster-make-services-local.

Suzuki, Y. (2018) *Booting up the Critical Zone: An Interview with Bruno Latour*, Tokyo University of the Arts, Graduate School of Global Arts, http://ga.geidai.ac.jp/en/indepth/bruno2018en/.

Syal, R., Weaver, M., and Walker, P. (2020) 'Johnson's defence of Dominic Cummings sparks anger from allies and opponents alike', *The Guardian*, 24 May, www.theguardian.com/politics/2020/may/24/boris-johnson-defence-dominic-cummings-anger-from-allies-and-opponents-alike.

Taleb, F. (2019) 'Standing up to the far right', in Barcelona en Comú with D. Bookchin and A. Coalu (eds), *Fearless Cities: A Guide to the Global Municipal Movement*. Oxford: New Internationalist, pp. 26–30

Taylor, B. (2020) 'Solitary citizens: the politics of loneliness', *The Guardian*, 27 June, www.theguardian.com/books/2020/jun/27/solitary-citizens-the-politics-of-loneliness.

Taylor-Gooby, P. (2013) *The Double Crisis of the Welfare State and What to Do about It*. Basingstoke: Palgrave Macmillan.

Taylor-Gooby, P., and Dale, J. (1981) *Social Theory and Social Welfare*. London: Edward Arnold.

Titmuss, R. (1970) *The Gift Relationship: From Human Blood to Social Policy*. London: Allen & Unwin.

Titterton, M. (1992) 'Managing threats to welfare: the search for a new paradigm of welfare', *Journal of Social Policy*, 21(1):1–23.

Todd, M. J., and Taylor, G. (eds) (2004) *Democracy and Participation: Popular Protest and New Social Movements*. London: Merlin Press.

Torry, M. (2018) *Why We Need a Citizen's Basic Income*. Bristol: Policy Press.

Townsend, P. B. (1979) *Poverty in the United Kingdom: A Survey of Household Resources and Standards of Living*. Harmondsworth: Penguin.

Toynbee, P., and Walker, D. (2020) *The Lost Decade*. London: Guardian Books.

Tronto, J. (1993) *Moral Boundaries: A Political Argument for an Ethic of Care*. London: Routledge.

Tronto, J. (2013) *Caring Democracy: Markets, Equality, and Justice*. New York: New York University Press.

TUC (Trades Union Congress) (2018) *Disability Employment and Pay Gaps 2018*, www.tuc.org.uk/sites/default/files/Disabilityemploymentandpaygaps.pdf.

Tutu, D. (2008) 'Who we are: human uniqueness and the African spirit of Ubuntu', www.youtube.com/watch?v=ftjdDOfTzbk.

Tyler, I. (2013) *Revolting Subjects: Social Abjection and Resistance in Neoliberal Britain*. London: Zed Press.

Tyler, I. (2015) 'Classificatory struggles: class, culture and inequality in neoliberal times', *Sociological Review*, 63(2): 493–511.

UKHCA (United Kingdom Home Care Association) (2020) *Migration Policy*, https://ukhcablog.com/2020/02/.

UN (2015) *The 17 Sustainable Development Goals*, https://sdgs.un.org/goals.

UN (2017) *International Migration Report*, www.un.org/en/development/desa/population/migration/publications/migrationreport/docs/MigrationReport2017.pdf.

UN (2019) *Report of the Special Rapporteur on Extreme Poverty and Human Rights*, https://undocs.org/A/HRC/41/39/Add.1.

UN Human Rights Office (2019) 'United Kingdom: UN expert condemns entrenched racial discrimination and inequality', www.ohchr.org/EN/NewsEvents/Pages/DisplayNews.aspx?NewsID=24698&LangID=E.

UN Women (2017) 'UN Women and the World Bank unveil new data analysis on women and poverty', www.unwomen.org/en/news/stories/2017/11/news-un-women-and-the-world-bank-unveil-new-data-analysis-on-women-and-poverty.

UNHCR (2013) *War's Human Costs*, UNHCR Global Trends 2013. Geneva: UNHCR; www.unhcr.org/5399a14f9.html.

UNICEF (2020) *Children in Lockdown: What Coronavirus Means for UK Children*. www.unicef.org.uk/coronavirus-children-in-lockdown/.

UNRISD (United Nations Research Institute for Social Development) (2016) 'Care policies: realizing their transformative potential', in *Policy Innovations for Transformative Change*. Geneva: UNRISD; www.unrisd.org/flagship2016-chapter3.

van Hooren, F. (2008) 'Welfare provision beyond national boundaries: the politics of migration and elderly care in Italy', *Rivista Italiana di Politiche Pubbliche*, 3: 87–113.

Vertovec, S. (2007) 'Super-diversity and its implications', *Ethnic and Racial Studies*, 30(6): 1024–54.

Vincze, E. (2013) 'Urban landfill, economic restructuring and environmental racism', *Philobiblon: Transylvanian Journal of Multidisciplinary Research in Humanities*, 18(2): 389–405.

Virdee, S. (2014) *Racism, Class and the Racialized Outsider*. Basingstoke: Palgrave Macmillan.

Walcott, R. (2015) 'Genres of human: multiculturalism, cosmo-politics, and the Caribbean Basin', in K. McKittrick (ed.), *Sylvia Wynter: On Being Human as Praxis*. Durham, NC: Duke University Press, pp. 183–202.

Walker, A. (ed.) (2005) *Understanding Quality of Life in Old Age*. Buckingham: Open University Press.

Walker, R. (2014) *The Shame of Poverty*. Oxford: Oxford University Press.

Wallerstein, I. (2004) *World-Systems Analysis: An Introduction*. Durham, NC: Duke University Press.

Ward, H. (2019) 'More than 8,000 SEND children have no access to education', 25 June, www.tes.com/news/more-8000-send-have-no-access-education.

Watkins, S. (2018) 'Which feminisms?', *New Left Review*, 109: 5–76.

WBG (Women's Budget Group) (2018a) *Disabled Women and Austerity*, https://wbg.org.uk/analysis/2018-wbg-briefing-disabled-women-and-austerity/.

WBG (Women's Budget Group) (2018b) *Briefing: Violence against Women and Girls*, https://wbg.org.uk/analysis/2018-wbg-briefing-violence-against-women-and-girls/

WBG (Women's Budget Group) (2019) *Benefits or Barriers: Making Social Security Work for Survivors of Domestic Violence across the UK's Four Nations*, https://wbg.org.uk/wp-content/uploads/2019/06/Benefits-or-barriers-4-nations-report.pdf.

WBG (Women's Budget Group) (2020a) *Crises Collide: Women and Covid-19*, https://wbg.org.uk/wp-content/uploads/2020/04/FINAL.pdf.

WBG (Women's Budget Group) (2020b) *The Covid-19 Report: The Impact on Women in Coventry*, https://wbg.org.uk/wp-content/uploads/2020/07/Covid-19-report-The-impact-on-women-in-Coventry.pdf

WBG (Women's Budget Group) (2020c) *Disabled Women and Covid-19 – Research Evidence*, https://wbg.org.uk/wp-content/uploads/2020/06/Disabled-Women-and-Covid-19.pdf.

WBG (Women's Budget Group) (2020d) *Migrant Women and the Economy*, https://wbg.org.uk/wp-content/uploads/2020/05/WBG-28-Migrant-Women-Report-v3-Digital.pdf.

WBG (Women's Budget Group) (2020e) *Creating a Caring Economy: A Call to Action*, https://wbg.org.uk/wp-content/uploads/2020/10/WBG-Report-v10.pdf.

WBG (Women's Budget Group) and Runnymede Trust, with RECLAIM and Coventry Women's Voices (2017) *Intersecting Inequalities: The Impact of Austerity on Black and Minority Ethnic Women in the UK*, http://wbg.org.uk/wp-content/uploads/2018/08/Intersecting-Inequalities-October-2017-Full-Report.pdf.

Wedderburn, D. (1965) 'Facts and theories of the welfare state', *Socialist Register*, 2: 127–46.

Weeks, J. (1977) *Coming Out: Homosexual Politics in Britain from the Nineteenth Century to the Present*. London: Quartet Books.

Weeks, J. (2007) *The World We Have Won: The Remaking of Erotic and Intimate Life*. London: Routledge.

WEF (World Economic Forum) (2020a) 'Coronavirus isn't an outlier, it's part of our interconnected viral age', 4 March, www.weforum.org/agenda/2020/03/coronavirus-global-epidemics-health-pandemic-covid-19/.

WEF (World Economic Forum) (2020b) 'Do we need a new Marshall Plan to rebuild Europe after Covid-19?', www.weforum.org/agenda/2020/04/marshall-plan-spain-europe-coronavirus/.

WelCond (2018) *Final Findings Report: Welfare Conditionality Project, 2013–2018*. Swindon: ESRC; http://www.welfareconditionality.ac.uk/wp-content/uploads/2018/06/40475_Welfare-Conditionality_Report_complete-v3.pdf.

Welshman, J. (2013) *Underclass: A History of the Excluded since 1880*. London: Bloomsbury Academic.

White, A. (2016) *Shadow State: Inside the Secret Companies Who Run Britain*. London: One World.

White, S. (2020) *A People's Inquiry? Deliberative Democracy and the Pandemic*. London: Compass and European Cultural Foundation.

WHO (World Health Organization) (2010) *World Health Report*. Geneva: WHO.

WHO (World Health Organization) (2016) *Global Strategy on Human Resources for Health: Workforce 2030*, www.who.int/hrh/resources/global_strategy_workforce2030_14_print.pdf.

Williams, F. (1987) 'Racism and the discipline of social policy: a critique of welfare theory', *Critical Social Policy*, 7(20): 4–29.

Williams, F. (1989) *Social Policy: A Critical Introduction: Issues of Race, Gender and Class*. Cambridge: Polity.

Williams, F. (1992) 'Somewhere over the rainbow: universality and diversity in social policy', in N. Manning and R. Page (eds), *Social Policy Review* 4: 200–19.

Williams, F. (1995) 'Race, ethnicity, gender and class in welfare states: a framework for comparative analysis', *Social Politics: International Studies in Gender, State and Society*, 2(1): 127–59.

Williams, F. (1996) 'Postmodernism, feminism and the question of difference', in N. Parton (ed.), *Social Theory, Social Change and Social Work*. London: Routledge.

Williams, F. (1999) 'Good-enough principles for welfare', *Journal of Social Policy*, 28(4): 667–87.

Williams, F. (2001) 'In and beyond New Labour: towards a new political ethics of care', *Critical Social Policy* 21(4): 467–93.

Williams, F. (2003) 'Contesting "race" and gender in the European Union: a multi-layered recognition struggle', in B. Hobson (ed.), *Recognition Struggles and Social Movements: Contested Identities, Power and Agency*. Cambridge: Cambridge University Press, pp. 121–44.

Williams, F. (2004) *Rethinking Families*. London: Calouste Gulbenkian Foundation.

Williams, F. (2010) *Claiming and Framing in the Making of Care Policies: The Recognition and the Redistribution of Care*. Geneva: UNRISD.

Williams, F. (2011) 'The transnational political economy of care', in R. Mahon and F. Robinson (eds), *The Global Political Economy of Care: Integrating Ethical and Social Politics*. Vancouver: UBC Press, pp. 21–38.

Williams, F. (2012) 'Converging variations in migrant care work in Europe', *Journal of European Social Policy*, 22(4): 363–76.

Williams, F. (2014) 'Making connections across the transnational political economy of care', in B. Anderson and I. Shutes (eds), *Care and Migrant Labour: Theory, Policy and Politics*. Basingstoke: Palgrave.

Williams, F. (2015) 'Towards the welfare commons: contestation, critique and criticality in social policy', in Irving, Fenger and Hudson (eds), *Social Policy Review 27*: 93–111. Bristol: Policy Press.

Williams, F. (2016) 'Critical thinking in social policy: the challenges of past, present and future', *Social Policy and Administration* 50(6): 628–47.

Williams, F. (2018) 'Care: intersections of scales, inequalities, and crises', *Current Sociology*, 66(4): 547–61.

Williams, F., and Brennan D. (2012) 'Care, markets and migration in a globalizing world: introduction to the special issue', *Journal of European Social Policy*, 22(4): 355–62.

Williams, F., and Churchill, H. (2006) *Empowering Parents in Sure Start Local Programmes: Report 018*: Nottingham: DfES.

Williams, F., and Gavanas, A. (2008) 'The intersection of child care regimes and migration regimes: a three-country study', in H. Lutz (ed.), *Migration and Domestic Work: A European Perspective on a Global Theme*. London: Routledge.

Williams, F., and Roseneil, S. (2004) 'Public values of parenting and partnering: voluntary organizations and welfare politics in New Labour's Britain', *Social Politics*, 11(2): 181–216.

Williams, F., Popay, J., and Oakley, A. (1999) *Welfare Research: A Critical Review*. London: UCL Press.

Williams, G. (1945) *Women and Work*. London: Nicholson & Watson.

Williams, R. (1977) *Marxism and Literature*. Oxford: Oxford University Press.

Wilson, A. R. (ed.) (2013) *Situating Intersectionality: Politics, Policy and Power*. London: Palgrave Macmillan.

Wilson, E. (1977) *Women and the Welfare State*. London: Tavistock.

Winant, H. (2006) 'Race and racism: towards a global future', *Ethnic and Racial Studies*, 29(5): 986–1003.

Windebank, J. (2017) 'Change in work–family reconciliation policy in France and the UK since 2008: the influence of economic crisis and austerity', *Journal of International and Comparative Social Policy*, 33(1): 55–72.

Withers, M. (2019a) 'Decent care for migrant households: policy alternatives to Sri Lanka's family background report', *Social Politics: International Studies in Gender, State & Society*, 26(3): 325–47.

Withers, M. (2019b) 'Temporary labour migration and underdevelopment in Sri Lanka: the limits of remittance capital', *Migration and Development*, 8(3): 418–36.

Withers, M., and Piper, N. (2018) 'Uneven development and displaced care in Sri Lanka', *Current Sociology*, 66(4): 590–601.

Women's Environmental Network (2019) 'Why women and climate change', www.wen.org.uk/wp-content/uploads/Why-women-and-climate-change-briefing-1.pdf.

Women's Resource Centre (2016) *Challenging Austerity: The Impact of Austerity Measures on Women's Voluntary Community Organisations and the Response of the Women's Sector*. London: WRC.

Wood, R. (1991) 'Care of disabled people', in G. Dalley (ed.), *Disability and Social Policy*. London: Policy Studies Institute, pp. 199–202.

World Bank (2018) 'Expanded Pacific labor schemes could fill looming aged care gap', www.worldbank.org/en/news/press-release/2018/09/06/expanded-pacific-labor-schemes-could-fill-looming-aged-care-gap.

World Meteorological Organization (2019) *United in Science 2020*, https://public.wmo.int/en/resources/united_in_science.

Wretched of the Earth (2019) 'An Open Letter to Extinction Rebellion', 3 May, www.redpepper.org.uk/an-open-letter-to-extinction-rebellion/.

Wright, S. (2016) 'Conceptualising the active welfare subject: welfare reform in discourse, policy and lived experience', *Policy & Politics*, 44(2): 235–52.

Wynter, S. (2003) 'Unsettling the coloniality of being/power/truth/freedom: towards the human, after man, its overrepresentation – an argument', *New Centennial Review*, 3(3): 257–337.

Yeandle, S., and Buckner, L. (2007) *Carers, Employment and Services: Time for a New Social Contract?* London: CarersUK.

Yeandle, S., and Starr, M. (2007) *Action for Carers and Employment: Impact of the ACE partnership 2002–7*. London: Carers UK.

Yeates, N. (2001) *Globalization and Social Policy*. London: Sage.

Yeates, N. (2009) *Globalizing Care Economies and Migrant Workers*. Basingstoke: Palgrave.

Yeates, N. (ed.) (2014) *Understanding Global Social Policy*. Bristol: Policy Press.

Yeates, N., and Pillinger, J. (2019) *International Health Worker Migration and Recruitment: Global Governance, Politics and Policy*. London: Routledge.

Yeatman, A., Dowsett, G., Fine, M., and Gursansky, D. (2009) *Individualization and the Delivery of Welfare Services: Contestation and Complexity*. Basingstoke: Palgrave Macmillan.

Younge, G. (2018a) 'Hounding Commonwealth citizens is no accident. It's cruelty by design', *The Guardian*, 13 April, www.theguardian.com/commentisfree/2018/apr/13/commonwealth-citizens-harassment-british-immigration-policy.

Younge, G. (2018b) 'Dare to dream of a world without borders', *Red Pepper*, 30 July, www.redpepper.org.uk/dare-to-dream-of-a-world-without-borders/.

Yuval-Davis, N. (1999) 'What is transversal politics?', in D. Massey (ed.), *Soundings, 12: Transversal Politics*. London: Lawrence & Wishart, pp. 94–8.

Yuval-Davis, N., Weymiss, G., and Cassidy, K. (2019) *Bordering*. Cambridge: Polity.

Index